Endtimes Essentials

Book #1

Christ's Endtimes Teaching
The Biblical Sequence of Endtime Events

Kurt Jurgensmeier

Copyright 2023 by Kurt Jurgensmeier

All parts of this publication may be used in any form. No part of this publication may be sold for profit.

Author may be contacted at: info@trainingtimothys.com

An electronic version of *Christ's Endtimes Teaching* is available at: www.trainingtimothys.com

Part I
Introduction to Understanding the Endtimes
The importance & challenges of understanding the most complex & shocking topic in Scripture

1: Understanding the Endtimes   p. **1**
2: Introduction to the Endtimes   p. **23**
3: Introduction to Christ's Endtimes Sermon   p. **35**

Part II
Christ's Endtimes Teaching
The biblical sequence of Endtime events

4: The Sequence of Endtime Events According to Jesus Christ   p. **61**
5: The Sequence of Endtime Events According to the Apostle Paul   p. **81**
6: The Sequence of Endtime Events According to Revelation 6-7   p. **98**
7: The Sequence of Endtime Events According to the Prophet Daniel   p. **112**
8: Conclusions on Christ's Endtimes Teaching   p. **128**
9: The Nature of Christ's Return & the Church's Rescue   p. **145**
10: Commands in Christ's Endtimes Teaching   p. **171**

Part III
Biblically Evaluating Endtime Views
Including 13 myths taught by Pre-tribulationism

11: A Biblical Evaluation of Various Views of the Endtimes   p. **184**
12: A Biblical Evaluation of Amillennialism & Preterism   p. **198**
13: A Biblical Evaluation of Pre-tribulationism   p. **234**
14: When Does Christ's Endtime Wrath Begin?   p. **258**
15: Refuting More Myths in Pre-tribulationism   p. **279**
16 The Practical & Spiritual Harm of Popular Teaching on the Endtimes   p. **303**

Appendices

A: Detailed Table of Contents for *Christ's Endtimes Teaching* p. **330**
B: Glossary for the *Endtimes Essentials* series p. **337**
C: Graphic: Sequence of Endtime Events According to Jesus, Paul, & Daniel p. **342**
D: Summary of *Christ's Endtimes Teaching* p. **344**

Index of Figures

Table: Endtime Events According Christ's Endtimes Teaching p. 73

Graphic: Endtime Events According to Jesus p. 74

Table: Endtime Events According to the Apostle Paul p. 90

Graphic: Endtime Events According to the Apostle Paul p. 92

Table: Sequence of Endtime Events in Matthew 24 & Revelation 6-7 p. 106

Graphic: Sequence of Endtime Events in Matthew 24 & Revelation 6-7 p. 107

Table: The Sequence of Endtime events according to Daniel p. 124

Graphic: Endtime Events According to Daniel p. 124

Table: 7 Primary Endtime Events According to Scripture p. 129

Table: Contrasting Christ's Two Appearances During His 2nd Coming p. 152

Graphic: Contrasting Christ's Two Appearances During His 2nd Coming p. 152

Part I

Introduction to Understanding the Endtimes
The most complex & shocking topic in Scripture

Chapter 1 [1]

Understanding the Endtimes [2]

Enduring this doctrine to be approved

Contents

A) Christ's clarity on the Endtimes
B) Popular approaches that hinder our understanding of Christ's Endtimes sermon *Being afraid, academic, and apathetic*
C) Being approved on the doctrine of the Endtimes *2 Tim 2:15*

Primary points

- 21% of the NT is devoted to the doctrine of the Endtimes. Salvation is the only topic in Scripture mentioned more than the Endtimes.
- Unfortunately, there is a lot of confusion in the Church today about the Endtimes.
- Christ's sermon on the Endtimes is perhaps the most ignored, diminished, distorted, and misunderstood teaching in all of the Gospels. But this sermon is also the clearest, most detailed, most important teaching we have in all of Scripture on the doctrine of the Endtimes.
- If your view of what Scripture teaches about the Endtimes does <u>not</u> shock and deeply sadden you, because of what YOU and the Christians you love may experience, then you need to re-evaluate your view.
- Another reason for the widespread error, neglect, and confusion on this topic is that what God says about the Endtimes is painful.
- Being academic is the tendency to study systems instead of Scripture.
- Bible scholars teach at least 14 different views on the interpretation of prophetic Scripture and understanding the Endtimes.
- Most of the academic views on the Endtimes have one thing in common: they are rather painless.

- Most of the academic systems on the Endtimes will <u>not</u> help you <u>at all</u> to better understand Christ's Endtimes sermon. Instead, they distort its meaning and diminish its value.
- Almost 600 biblical prophecies have already been fulfilled in history. Contrary to the popular metaphorical approach, every single one of them was fulfilled in a physical way by a person, place, or event.
- How can we hope to understand the Endtimes accurately, clearly, and confidently? By studying Scripture instead of the systems.
- Many Christians suggest that understanding the details of the Endtimes is not important. This apathetic view greatly dishonors our Lord and completely ignores His clear intention to teach some specific details about the Endtimes.
- Popular approaches to the Endtimes have left the Church unprepared to face it in a God-glorifying way.
- Instead of being afraid, academic, or apathetic about the doctrine of the Endtimes, let us be approved by God by enduring it with a focused mind and a brave and humble heart.

A) Christ's clarity on the Endtimes

This chapter is an introduction to a series of books I wrote called the *Endtimes Essentials*. The Endtimes is a very big topic in the Bible. There are about 100 references to Christ's <u>First</u> Coming in Scripture. But there are over 2,000 references to Christ's <u>Second</u> Coming! [3] 70% of the chapters in the NT refer to the Endtimes. [4] The Apostle Paul alone mentions it 50 times. [5] One scholar has calculated that 21% of the NT is devoted to the doctrine of the Endtimes. [6] Salvation is the only topic in Scripture mentioned more than the Endtimes. It is clear that God wants His people to understand the doctrine of the Endtimes in Scripture!

But it seems to be the part of God's Word that Christians understand the least, and differ on the most. This confusion in the Church on the doctrine of the Endtimes is confirmed by a recent study conducted by the respected Pew Research Center. In it, 45% of American Evangelical Christians claimed: "It is impossible to know the circumstances that will precede Jesus' return." [7] Really?

Do these good Christians know that Jesus Christ gave a sermon that clearly explained exactly what events will precede His Return? Let us read a few parts of this sermon from Christ. As we do, notice something. Contrary to 45% of American Evangelical Christians, does Jesus clearly explain the circumstances that will precede His Return?

In Matthew 24, starting in verse 3 we read:

> **Later, Jesus sat on the Mount of Olives. His disciples came to him privately and said, "Tell us, when will all this happen? What sign will signal your return and the end of the world?"**
>
> **Jesus told them, "Don't let anyone mislead you, for many will come in my name, claiming, 'I am the Messiah.' They will deceive many. And you will hear of wars and threats of wars, but don't panic. Yes, these things must take place, but the end won't follow immediately."**
>
> **"Nation will go to war against nation, and kingdom against kingdom. There will be famines and earthquakes in many parts of the world. But all this is only the first of the birth pains, with more to come. Then you will be arrested, persecuted, and killed..."**
>
> **"And many false prophets will appear and will deceive many people. Sin will be rampant everywhere, and the love of many will grow cold. But the one who endures to the end will be saved..."**
>
> **"The day is coming when you will see what Daniel the prophet spoke about—[the abomination that causes desolation, NIV] standing in the Holy Place." (Reader, pay attention!)**
>
> **"Then those in Judea must flee to the hills... How terrible it will be for pregnant women and for nursing mothers in those days...** (Matt 24:3-9, 11-13, 15-16, 19 NLT)
>
> **"For then there will be great [*thlipsis*- persecution], unequaled from the beginning of the world until now— and never to be equaled again. If those days had not been cut short, no one would survive, but for the sake**

of the elect those days will be shortened." (Matt 24:21-22 NIV)

"But immediately after the [*thlipsis*- persecution] of those days THE SUN WILL BE DARKENED, AND THE MOON WILL NOT GIVE ITS LIGHT, AND THE STARS WILL FALL from the sky, and the powers of the heavens will be shaken."

"And then the sign of the Son of Man will appear in the sky, and then all the tribes of the earth will mourn, and they will see the SON OF MAN COMING ON THE CLOUDS OF THE SKY with power and great glory."

"And He will send forth His angels with A GREAT TRUMPET and THEY WILL GATHER TOGETHER His elect from the four winds, from one end of the sky to the other." (Matt 24:29-31 NASB)

Again, we are answering the question, is it <u>impossible</u> to know the circumstances that will precede Jesus' return, as 45% of Evangelical Christians claim. We have just read Christ saying many circumstances that will immediately precede His Return.

Jesus clearly taught there will be unprecedented wars and famines, then the Antichrist will desecrate a temple in Jerusalem which will begin The Greatest Persecution. When the persecution is completed, there will be Cosmic Signs in the sky and then everyone in the world ... **will see the SON OF MAN COMING** with **glory**. And then **He will send forth His angels ... and THEY WILL GATHER TOGETHER His elect ... from one end of the sky to the other**. So, it would seem at least 45% of American Evangelical Christians are wrong about a relatively basic teaching of Christ on the Endtimes. That is a serious error.

Before continuing let me say a few things. First, I may write something in this chapter that you strongly disagree with. In response, I would say this. First, please know that I respect Christians who would believe or teach differently on these things. They are the chosen and dearly loved children of Almighty God, regardless of their view on the doctrine of the Endtimes. Please hear me on that.

Secondly, let me state something now so that I will not have to unnecessarily repeat it in this chapter. Virtually everything I write in this first chapter is more fully supported with biblical arguments in this book. Again, I understand you might disagree with something you read. I would only ask you <u>not</u> to immediately dismiss it, but instead humbly evaluate the biblical arguments I offer in all three of the books in the *Endtimes Essentials* series.

So, it would seem there is a lot of confusion and controversy in the Church on the doctrine of the Endtimes. [8] Why is this? I believe one reason is that Christ's sermon on the Endtimes is perhaps the most ignored, diminished, distorted, and misunderstood teaching in all of the Gospels. That's unfortunate. Because this sermon is also the clearest, most detailed, most important teaching we have in all of Scripture on the doctrine of the Endtimes. And even so, many Christians do not understand it, and the Church is greatly divided about its meaning.

B) Popular approaches that hinder our understanding of Christ's Endtimes Sermon

Why is there so much controversy and confusion even about Christ's Endtimes sermon? I believe there are three popular approaches to the doctrine of the Endtimes that contribute to this. These are: 1) being AFRAID about the Endtimes; 2) being ACADEMIC about the Endtimes; and 3) being APATHETIC about the Endtimes. Let me explain each of these and how Jesus confronts all of them.

B.1) Being afraid of the doctrine of the Endtimes

First, I think there are a significant number of Christians who are AFRAID of the Endtimes. We must admit that Jesus predicted a lot of pain and suffering for His people. He said after the catastrophic wars and famines, **Then you will be arrested, persecuted, and killed** (Matt 24:8-9 NLT). Later in the sermon He said after the Antichrist comes to power, **there will be great** [*thlipsis-* **persecution**], **unequaled from the beginning of the world until now—and never to be equaled again** (v. 21).

I will demonstrate in chapter 3 that the Greek word often translated **tribulation** means persecution. Also, three times in this sermon Jesus said these events will be experienced by **the elect**. It will also be demonstrated in chapter 3 that **the elect** refers to Christians in the Church in the NT. Therefore, Jesus clearly taught the Last Generation Church will experience the unprecedented wars, famines, and plagues of The Beginning of Birth Pains and The Greatest Persecution of the Antichrist. Again, I will demonstrate this in later chapters.

The Prophet Daniel saw visions of some of the things Jesus talked about. Daniel said, **As I watched, this horn** [the Antichrist] **was waging war against the saints and defeating them** (Dan 7:21 NIV [9]). He added, the Antichrist will **oppress his saints** and **He will cause astounding devastation and ... He will destroy ... the saints** (Dan 7:25; 8:24 NIV).

Let us remember, Daniel was a very courageous man. Even so, what was Daniel's response to these visions of what the Antichrist will do to **the saints**? After seeing them the Prophet said, **I, Daniel, was deeply troubled by my thoughts, and my face turned pale ... I fainted and was sick for many days** (Dan 7:28; 8:27 [10]).

Therefore, if your view of what Scripture teaches about the Endtimes does <u>not</u> shock and deeply sadden you, because of what YOU and the Christians you love may experience, then may I humbly suggest that you need to re-evaluate your view.

Having said all of that, I understand the temptation to be afraid of the Endtimes. I have a wife I have loved for over 30 years. I have five children, all married to wonderful Christian spouses. They are all active members in the local church I help to pastor. All of my 12 precious grandchildren live within 15 minutes of my house. My church is full of people, families, and little children that I love. I don't want to see any of these dear people go through what Jesus predicted about the Endtimes.

So I have no problem telling you and God, that there is a part of me that does <u>not</u> want the Endtimes to happen in my lifetime. I struggle with this. I love the ministry I have been doing for several years now in countries I should not name. God has given me the tremendous privilege of teaching hundreds of Pastors through conferences and my books, in the places on Earth where Christianity may be growing the fastest of anywhere in the world. I want to keep doing that and see the kingdom of God grow there. I want to see all my grandchildren grow up. I do not want to see any of them suffer, <u>at all</u>.

So if you understand the biblical truth for the Church about the Endtimes, it is tempting to be afraid. But even in the midst of the catastrophic events Jesus predicted in His Endtimes sermon, did you notice His command: **don't panic... these things must take place** (Matt 24:6 NLT). Therefore, when it comes to the Endtimes, we all must imitate Jesus in the Garden of Gethsemane. We must say, **"Father, if you are willing, please take this cup of suffering away from me. Yet I want your will to be done, not mine"** (Luke 22:42 NLT). And we must face whatever future God gives us with the Spirit's courage instead of sinful fear.

Granted, the doctrine of the Endtimes is by far the most complex topic in all of Scripture. [11] But the difficulty of grasping what the Bible truly teaches on this topic is <u>not</u> just because it is complex. Another reason for the widespread error, neglect, and confusion on this topic is that what God says about the Endtimes is painful.

Therefore, we must also endure this doctrine with a brave heart. Do you desire God's truth about the Endtimes no matter what it may mean for you and your loved ones? We cannot underestimate the great bias that especially American Christians have against suffering, and how much this bias may distort how we interpret Scripture. Fear will keep you from properly understanding God on this biblical topic. You will never understand the Endtimes if you are afraid to do so.

The failure of God's people to endure the challenging truth of God's Word has been a repeated problem. For example, God's Prophets often warned God's people of impending disasters. But because the people did not want to hear such things, they rejected the truth and believed false prophets and teaching. God described such people when He said: **"They tell the prophets, "Don't tell us what is right. Tell us nice things. Tell us lies. Forget all this gloom""** (Isa 30:10-11 NLT).

Unfortunately, this is a common response to anyone who is trying to teach the biblical truth about what the Endtimes will mean for the Church. But, **this is the reply of the Holy One of Israel: "Because you despise what I tell you and trust instead in ... lies, calamity will come upon you suddenly"** (vs. 12-13 NLT).

And this will be true of Christians who enter the Endtimes without a biblical understanding of them. The Endtimes will come upon them suddenly and unexpectedly, which is not what God wanted. Such misinformed Christians will experience paralyzing shock and confusion, and be very unprepared to endure the challenges of the Endtimes in a God-glorifying way.

B.2) Being academic about the doctrine of the Endtimes

I think being afraid of the Endtimes is one attitude that has hindered the Church in understanding this doctrine in Scripture. I think a second approach has done the same. This is what I call being ACADEMIC. What do I mean by that? Being academic is the tendency to study <u>systems</u> instead of <u>Scripture</u>.

Did you know that Bible scholars teach at least 14 different views and systems on the interpretation of prophetic Scripture and understanding the Endtimes? 14! These include: Pre-millennialism, Post-millennialism, Amillennialism, Pre-tribulationism, Mid-tribulationism, Post-tribulationism, Pre-wrath Rapture, Preterism, Futurism, Historicism, Idealism, and Classic, Revised, and Progressive Dispensationalism. [12]

It is perfectly O.K. if you do not even know what some of those labels mean. But these are all distinct approaches to interpreting prophetic Scripture and understanding the Endtimes. [13]

In my opinion, it is being academic that has led to all these different and conflicting systems of understanding the Endtimes. Unfortunately, a focus on these systems is how many Christians and teachers approach their study and teaching on the Endtimes. For example, it is common for a Pastor to explain various systems on the Endtimes and then say it's up to his listeners to decide which one is best. Unfortunately, that approach often causes more confusion on the topic.

I started studying these systems and reading books on eschatology 36 years ago. I have studied many scholarly books and commentaries that support these systems. May I suggest a few things about my own experience with them?

First, I believe there is some truth in some of them. That's why really smart Christians teach them. And I understand the value of having a system of doctrine. If we are going to teach a topic as large as eschatology, we need to reconcile all the Scriptures on that topic into a comprehensive whole, and then simplify all of this by putting a label on it. I do the same in my books.

But there are some problems with the academic approach to the doctrine of the Endtimes. First, most of these systems are rather painless. That should get our attention. I believe Jesus clearly taught the Endtimes will be painful for His people. So when a popular academic system diminishes the pain of the Endtimes for the Church, it does <u>not</u> seem to be in agreement with Jesus on this topic.

Second, some of the most popular academic systems on the Endtimes have very little truth in them. I realize that is a strong statement, and again I mean no unnecessary offense to anyone who would teach or believe those views. But I believe I clearly and biblically support this statement in this book. Some of the most popular academic systems on the Endtimes being taught in the Church today have very little truth in them.

Let me illustrate this by saying something else. I believe I have a good understanding of these academic systems on the doctrine of the Endtimes. But the great majority of them have <u>not</u> helped me <u>at all</u> to have a better understanding of Christ's Endtimes sermon. In my opinion, most of the academic systems of Endtimes doctrine do two things to Christ's Endtimes sermon: 1) distort its meaning, and 2) diminish its value.

That is a very significant statement considering the fact that Christ's Endtimes sermon is the clearest and most important text in all of Scripture on the doctrine of the Endtimes. If most of the academic systems distort or devalue this sermon, then it is evidence of a rather intense spiritual battle surrounding Christ's Endtimes sermon.

Let me offer some examples. First, there is the very popular academic system that teaches the Church will be "raptured" or rescued from the Earth <u>before</u> <u>any</u> of the events described by Jesus even occur. First, we notice such a view is rather completely painless. I am concerned this is one reason it is so popular. But it also seems to distort the meaning of Christ's Endtimes sermon, and it certainly diminishes the value of this sermon for the Church.

Notice that this very popular view rather completely depends on one thing. Proving that the first 28 verses of Christ's Endtimes sermon has nothing to do with the Church. Even those who teach this view admit the last 66 verses of the sermon do apply to the Church. So did Jesus completely change His intended audience in the middle of His Sermon? No, He did not.

Friends, if your view of the Endtimes depends on proving that the first 28 verses of Christ's Endtimes sermon has nothing to do with the Church, then I suggest again that you need to re-evaluate your view.

Other surprisingly popular academic views claim that Christ's predictions have been essentially fulfilled in the past, and promote great doubts about their value for the future. Again, these are rather painless views of Christ's sermon. And in my opinion they distort His meaning and diminish the value of Christ's sermon for the Church.

There is another popular academic system that seems to do the same thing. This view denies we should interpret the fulfillment of Christ's predictions literally. The claim of this approach is that we should expect Christ's predictions to be fulfilled in spiritual metaphors.

For example, a recent survey claimed that 50% of Protestant Pastors deny or are not sure that Scripture predicts there will be a literal and physical Antichrist in the future. [14] This is another indication of how much confusion there is in the Church on the Endtimes and Christ's Endtimes sermon. Instead, many of these metaphorical interpreters believe the prophecies about the Antichrist simply refer to the spiritual reality of growing evil in the Endtimes.

I would suggest again, this popular metaphorical view seeks to diminish the pain of the Endtimes for the Church. It does little to warn the Church that it will face the Antichrist in the Endtimes. And in my opinion, the metaphorical approach certainly distorts the meaning of Christ's Endtimes sermon.

What did Jesus say about the Antichrist? He said to His elect people who will encounter the Endtimes: **when you see the ABOMINATION OF DESOLATION** [the Antichrist] **which was spoken of through Daniel the prophet, <u>standing</u> in the holy place (let the reader understand), then those who are in Judea must flee to the mountains...** (Matt 24:15-16 NASB).

Why will those in Judea need to flee at that time? Because when the Antichrist desecrates a rebuilt temple in Jerusalem, He will begin the Greatest Persecution. Both Daniel and Jesus taught that a literal Antichrist will be **standing** in a rebuilt Jewish temple in the Endtimes.

Contrary to 50% of Protestant Pastors who cannot confidently claim the Antichrist will be a real person, the Apostle Paul did this very thing when he wrote of the Antichrist: **the man of lawlessness ... will oppose and will exalt himself over everything that is called God or is worshiped, so that he sets himself up in God's temple, proclaiming himself to be God** (2 Thess 2:3-4 NIV). Clearly, Paul believed the Antichrist would be a real person in the future. Scripture could not be more clear on this, and those who reject a literal interpretation of the fulfillment of biblical prophecy could not be more wrong on this.

Unfortunately, in many academic systems on the Endtimes there is a clear agenda to eliminate or diminish a priority of interpreting biblical prophecies literally. It has become popular to claim biblical prophecy will merely be fulfilled in spiritual realities, rather than physical people, places, and events. But this metaphorical approach completely ignores how God has fulfilled prophecy in the past.

For example, when the Prophet Micah predicted that Christ would be born in Bethlehem, Jesus was born in the literal and physical village of **Bethlehem** (cf. Micah 5:2). It wasn't just a spiritual metaphor.

In fact, did you know that almost 600 biblical prophecies have already been fulfilled in history. And every single one of these 592 prophecies were fulfilled in a physical way by a person, place, or event. [15] None of them were fulfilled in merely a spiritual or metaphorical way. And this is a great problem for the many Christian teachers claiming this is the primary or only way God will fulfill prophecy in the future.

I can confidently tell you that God has not changed the way He is going to fulfill biblical prophecy. So again, with all due respect, if your primary approach to interpreting biblical prophecy is to ignore or diminish its literal and physical fulfillment, then you need to re-evaluate your approach.

I realize my brief comments here may not persuade someone who is committed to one of these academic systems. I understand the issues are more complex than I have made them here. I devote several chapters in this book to biblically evaluate many of these views.

So, what is the solution to all the confusion and controversy caused by these academic systems? How can we hope to understand the Endtimes accurately, clearly, and confidently? By studying Scripture instead of the systems. More specifically, understanding just the first 28 verses of Christ's Endtimes sermon.

Christian, I have some really good news for you. If you correctly understand just the first 28 verses of Christ's Endtimes sermon, then it will help you understand the Endtimes better than <u>all</u> of the most popular academic systems. I'm not exaggerating.

Second, understanding the first 28 verses of Christ's Endtimes sermon will give you a foundation to understand the more obscure prophetic Scriptures in the OT Prophets and the Revelation. Fortunately, Christ's Endtimes sermon is <u>not</u> communicated through a vision with multi-layered symbols like Daniel and Revelation. That type of Scripture is the most difficult of any to interpret. Therefore, we should be grateful that Jesus gave us a <u>literal teaching</u> on the essentials of the Endtimes without complex symbolic visions.

Finally, if you understand just the first 28 verses of Christ's Endtimes sermon, you will be sufficiently equipped to biblically evaluate <u>all</u> of the 14 academic systems on the Endtimes mentioned above. Fortunately, these 28 verses are much more clear and simple than those academic systems. This is one more reason we must begin our study of the Endtimes with Scripture, instead of the systems.

Our approach is similar to how bank tellers are trained to identify the many different types of fake money. They <u>do not</u> study all of the various versions of counterfeit bills. Instead, they study the look and feel of real money, so it is crystal clear in their mind. Then when they encounter even a slight variation from real money, they can detect it. The same will be true for discerning the truth and error in all of the various academic views of the Endtimes, if you correctly understand just the first 28 verses of Christ's Endtimes sermon.

B.3) Being apathetic about the doctrine of the Endtimes

So, I believe being AFRAID and being ACADEMIC, studying and teaching systems, instead of Scripture, have both contributed to the confusion and controversy in the Church today about the doctrine of the Endtimes. And these two approaches have led to perhaps the most common approach to this doctrine: APATHY.

Many Christians suggest that understanding the details of the Endtimes is not important. The claim is that these things are too obscure in Scripture, or controversial in the Church, to be dogmatic about them. It is common to hear Christians and Pastors say that we simply need to put our hope in Christ's Return and not worry about the details surrounding it. In fact, such a view practically denies that it is God's will for us to understand what hundreds of verses of Scripture teach on the Endtimes.

I understand some of the reasons for this apathy. In part, it is a response to the two popular approaches to the Endtimes that we have been discussing: being AFRAID and being ACADEMIC. For example, those apathetic about the Endtimes are often the first ones to tell us, "Hey, we just need to trust God with these things no matter what happens." Those who are apathetic about the Endtimes tend to also be less afraid about the Endtimes.

This apathy also comes from the frustration and doubts caused by having 14 different and often contradictory academic systems being taught in the Church on this doctrine. It seems that many of the people teaching these 14 different views on the Endtimes are equally smart and godly Christians. Therefore, it is easy to assume it must be impossible to clearly understand this doctrine in Scripture. So I sympathize with those who are apathetic about the doctrine of the Endtimes because of their concerns about being afraid, or their frustration and doubts about the popular academic systems.

Finally, the apathetic view is often based on a wrong interpretation of something Christ said in His Endtimes sermon. Speaking of the timing of His Return, Jesus said:

> **"But about that day or hour no one knows** [*oiden*, present tense]**, not even the angels in heaven, nor the Son, but only the Father"** (Matt 24:36 NIV).

This is wrongly interpreted in many ways. Some think this means Christ's Return could happen at any time without any clear warning. Others misuse this statement to criticize those who would point to current events indicating the Endtimes are near. Wrongly interpreting Matthew 24:36 is probably why 45% of Evangelical Christians claim "It is impossible to know the circumstances that will precede Jesus' return." In many ways, the apathetic view of the Endtimes is based on wrongly interpreting Christ's statement that no one knows the timing of His Return.

The first mistake is a failure to notice that **knows** is in the present tense. This is missed by almost everyone who interprets this verse. Jesus did not say "no one will ever know the **day or hour**" of His Return. He said, when He was speaking with His disciples over 2,000 years ago, **"no one now knows about that day or hour."** Jesus gave us several signs of His Return that we are supposed to be looking for. Before those happen, no one can know the timing of His Return. But in a verse just before verse 36, Jesus said: **When you see all these things** [the signs of His Return], **you know that it is near, right at the door.** (Matt 24:33 NIV). So at some point in time, we are supposed to know Christ's Return is very near.

The apathetic interpretation of Matthew 24:36 also ignores Christ's repeated commands to be watching for signs of His Return. Remember, the Apostles asked Him: **"What sign will signal your return and the end of the world?"** (Matt 24:3 NLT). In response Jesus very carefully and intentionally described many signs and events that will **signal** His **Return**.

This is why throughout Christ's sermon on the Endtimes He commanded: **"Be on guard! Be alert!"** ... **"keep watch"** ... **"What I say to you, I say to everyone: 'Watch!'"** (Mark 13:33, 34, 37 NIV). **Watch!** for what? Current events in our world that would signal the beginning of the Endtimes, and that Christ's Return is near. There is no other way to practically obey Christ's command. And those with an apathetic view of the Endtimes consistently disobey Christ's commands to **Watch!** and are critical of those who are trying to obey His commands to **Watch!**

This leads us to another serious problem with this apathy about the biblical doctrine of the Endtimes. It greatly dishonors our Lord

Jesus Christ. The apathetic view completely ignores Christ's clear intention to teach some specific details about the Endtimes. Again, what prompted this sermon of Christ? The disciples asked Jesus, **"What sign will signal your return and the end of the world?"** (Matt 24:3 NLT).

Listening to many Christians today, you would think that Jesus simply answered: "Guys, the details don't matter. All I want you to know is that I'm coming back." But that is not what our Savior said! And to talk and act as if He did, dishonors our Lord. So does the 45% of Evangelical Christians who claim "It is impossible to know the circumstances that will precede Jesus' return."

Unfortunately, the popular metaphorical view usually leads to the apathetic view. And contrary to both of these views, Jesus taught a very intentional and specific sequence of Endtime events that He expects His followers to carefully study, correctly understand, and confidently teach. This is why throughout the first 28 verses of His sermon Jesus repeatedly used words like **then**, **when**, **immediately after** and, **at that time**.

One of my favorite Bible teachers is John MacArthur. He said something recently that is important, especially for those who have a metaphorical or apathetic approach to the doctrine of the Endtimes. Dr. MacArthur said:

> [The doctrine of the Endtimes] is strangely treated with an attitude of indifference [apathy]... It is a continual burden to me, a continual discouragement, that the Reformed movement, so popular in being precise about sound doctrine, has been indifferent toward that doctrine [of the Endtimes]."
>
> "How can you do that? How can you think that God spoke clearly about everything but the end? That it doesn't matter. It's almost a badge of academic nobility not to have a view [on the Endtimes]... For some it seems to be a defect to take the Bible literally on this topic." [16]

I could not have said it better. I know many people think the apathetic approach is a humble approach to this doctrine. But we must be careful that our supposed humility about the Endtimes is not simply a cover for our apathy, confusion, or laziness about this doctrine.

To my brothers and sisters who may be rather apathetic about the doctrine of the Endtimes, let me say this. Stop letting all the contradictory academic systems on the Endtimes give you an excuse for <u>not</u> understanding Christ's Endtimes sermon. At the very least, you can confidently believe and teach what the first 28 verses of Christ's Endtimes sermon teaches. [17] Can we at least agree on that?

B.4) Being unprepared for the Endtimes

There is always a cost when God's people do not correctly or confidently understand God's Word. This is true of the doctrine of the Endtimes. This is <u>not</u> simply an academic debate. The current confusion and controversy in the Church on this doctrine would greatly hurt Christians if the Endtimes begin any time soon. For example, because many of the popular views on the Endtimes are rather <u>painless</u>, they are also rather <u>useless</u> to prepare the Church to glorify God if the Endtimes begin in our generation.

All of these views ignore the fact that Jesus wanted to warn His Church about the unprecedented catastrophes and persecutions of the Endtimes. Why was Jesus so concerned about warning His Church of these things? To help them be prepared to face them in a God-glorifying way.

If the Endtimes began today, I believe many Christians would be greatly confused, and that confusion would greatly hinder their ability to enter the Endtimes with courage, clarity, and confidence. That is not what God wanted. Which is why Jesus gave us a rather simple, clear, although painful sermon about what the Endtimes will mean for the Church. This was so His people could be spiritually prepared for the Endtimes if they occurred in their lifetime.

But what do popular views of the Endtimes teach us? Either we will not even be here for these things, or the details of the Endtimes don't matter. Saying the details don't matter, means that Christ's warnings don't matter either.

Not to be too harsh, but there seems to be an arrogance in the apathetic and metaphorical views on this doctrine. It seems foolish to believe that Christians will be quickly equipped to respond to the Endtimes in a God-glorifying manner when they are confused about what Scripture teaches on this doctrine. This danger might explain why our **enemy the devil** (1 Pet 5:8) has fought so hard to cause so much confusion and controversy in the Church on the Endtimes.

Unfortunately, it is widely assumed that God's people <u>can</u> be prepared to face the Endtimes in a God-glorifying manner even if they don't understand what Christ was warning His Church of. Do you know better than Jesus? He believed the Church needed to know the substance and sequence of Endtime events. Do you? Jesus intentionally and faithfully warned His Church about these things because He knew the Church needs to know more than what many are teaching on this topic today.

C) Being approved on the doctrine of the Endtimes

Accordingly, Paul wrote especially to those with the God-given responsibility of teaching His Word:

> **Work hard so you can present yourself to God and receive his <u>approval</u>. Be a good worker, one who does not need to be ashamed and who <u>correctly explains the word of truth</u>** (2 Tim 2:15 NLT).

Do you see the goal? Instead of being AFRAID, ACADEMIC, or APATHETIC about the doctrine of the Endtimes, let us be APPROVED by God. Do you see God's expectation especially for Pastors and Teachers in the Church? To **correctly explain the word of truth**, including the word of truth about the Endtimes.

God gave us hundreds of verses of Scripture about the Endtimes. Let us <u>not</u> dishonor God by putting these Scriptures into virtual trash cans labeled "too obscure," "too controversial," or "too scary," or "just symbolic." This does not please the Author of these Scriptures.

My friends, could I suggest we can all do more to **present ourselves to God and receive his approval** on the doctrine of the Endtimes. What will that require? Paul said He expects us to **Work hard so** we can **correctly explain the word of truth** about the Endtimes.

Another way to say this is that the doctrine of the Endtimes must be ENDURED. The Apostle Paul wrote:

> **The time will come when they will <u>not</u> endure sound doctrine; but wanting to have their ears tickled, they**

will accumulate for themselves teachers in accordance to their own desires, and will turn away their ears from the truth and will turn aside to myths. (2 Tim 4:3-4 NASB)

Did you notice the prophecy here? Paul said **the time will come when** Christians **will not endure sound doctrine**.[18] I believe this biblical prophecy has certainly been fulfilled today in relation to the doctrine of the Endtimes. Many Christians have not endured this doctrine and either ignore it, fail to understand it, or believe many **myths** about it.

Why must the doctrine of the Endtimes be endured? Because, as I've already said, this is one of the most emotionally challenging topics in the Bible. Jesus is predicting a lot of suffering for His people who encounter the Endtimes. Again, we should not underestimate the bias that especially American Christians have against suffering. And such a bias can distort how we interpret Scripture. Which is why we must **endure** these Endtimes Scriptures with a brave heart.

Otherwise, we too will fulfill the Apostle's prophecy and **accumulate for** ourselves **teachers in accordance to** our **own desires, and will turn away** our **ears from the truth** about the Endtimes **and will turn aside to myths** because they are easier to accept and believe.

Why else must the doctrine of the Endtimes be **endure**d? Because as I've also said, the Endtimes is by far the most complex doctrine in Scripture. Therefore, it will require a focused time of study to sufficiently understand even its essentials. This is why Paul said we must **Work hard so** we **can present** ourselves **to God and receive his approval** because we can **correctly explain the word of truth** about the Endtimes. Being able to accurately understand and explain this doctrine will require hard work. Which is one reason many in the Church have not **endure**d this doctrine.

People have said to me, "Kurt, Christians are not going to devote the time and energy to read your three books on this topic." Or, "Kurt, you have to make the videos no more than 15 minutes or people will not watch them." But Christian, you cannot sufficiently understand this doctrine in mere sound bites. Anyone who has been **approved by God** because they can **correctly explain** this doctrine, had to **work hard**. I hope that the *Endtimes Essentials* materials can help your study be as simple and effective as possible.

I believe the Author of these prophetic Scriptures is asking you to emotionally and mentally ENDURE the doctrine of the Endtimes, so that instead of being merely AFRAID, ACADEMIC, or APATHETIC, you can be APPROVED by God, because you can correctly explain this doctrine.

I am not expecting anyone to be convinced of everything I have said in one chapter. I am asking all of us to set aside our fears and systems and apathy and go back to Scripture and seek to understand what God has revealed about the Endtimes. Let us be noble like the Bereans. In Acts 17:11 these people were commended for biblically evaluating the teaching of an Apostle. I am not an Apostle, so you can be sure God will be pleased if you biblically evaluate my teaching before accepting it.

And that is all that I am asking. Let us study the prophetic Scriptures together. Let me dialogue with you, and humbly challenge you about your beliefs on the Endtimes. Let us endure the study of the Endtimes together with a focused mind, a brave heart, and an attitude of humility.

You are invited to start your study with the *Endtimes Essentials Summary Series* videos. This chapter is the text of the first of those. There are five more videos that explain the highlights of all three books in the series. They give you an opportunity to decide if you want to study this material further.

If you think this material is helpful, please encourage your Pastor to evaluate this material as well. I have no desire to bypass his God-given spiritual authority in your life.

All of the *Endtimes Essentials* materials are available free of charge at my website: www.trainingtimothys.com. The books are available free of charge in html and PDF formats. They are also available in print and Kindle versions at Amazon.com for a small fee. The advantage of the printed editions is the many endnotes. These contain valuable information on the Greek text of the passages being discussed, and quotes and interaction with the best Evangelical commentaries on these Scriptures. There are also video and audio versions of the material available at the website. [19]

May God our Father, through His Spirit, grant you the grace to interpret the prophetic Scriptures correctly and courageously, and to evaluate and recognize whatever sound doctrine there may be in the *Endtimes Essentials* materials.

[1] The primary Bible versions used in the *Endtimes Essentials* are the NIV, NLT, and NASB. Sometimes a suggested translation is offered that is often a combination of these. The goal is to help you understand the Scriptures in modern, everyday English.

For more information on the reference works and abbreviations used throughout *Endtimes Essentials* see the bibliography in the introduction section of the website at www.trainingtimothys.com.

[2] This chapter is essentially the same as video message #1 in the *Endtimes Essentials Summary Series*, but with the endnotes added.

[3] Prophecy author Ed Knoor writes:

There are 1,845 references to Christ's Second Coming in the Old Testament, and 318 such references in the New Testament [that equals 2,163 total references]. Compare that to the 109 declarations in the Bible about His first coming [LaHaye, 2012].

In the Bible, the doctrine of salvation is mentioned the most in Scripture; then, Christ's Second Coming; and in third place, we have the tribulation, which is mentioned in more than 60 Scripture passages [LaHaye, 2011a; Hindson, 2021].

The Apostle Paul mentioned the Second Coming 50 times, baptism 13 times, and communion twice. (8) Ed Knorr, "Revelation and Bible Prophecy"; available online at https://www.cs.ubc.ca/~knorr/public/comparison_of_eschat_models.pdf.

[4] These statistics on biblical references to Christ's Return can be found online at https://davidjeremiah.blog/the-second-coming-of-christ/.

[5] Knoor, 9.

[6] Hitchcock, *The End*, 4.

[7] https://www.pewresearch.org/fact-tank/2022/12/08/about-four-in-ten-u-s-adults-believe-humanity-is-living-in-the-end-times/

[8] The confusion of American Evangelical Christians is further illustrated by another result of the survey. 65% of American Evangelical Christians claimed to "believe we are already living in the endtimes." Biblically speaking, it is doubtful the Endtimes have actually begun. So how can 65% of American Evangelical Christians claim to believe "we are already living in the endtimes"? Especially when in the same study, only about 21% of American Evangelical Protestants "say they believe Jesus will definitely or probably return during their lifetime."

https://www.pewresearch.org/fact-tank/2022/12/08/about-four-in-ten-u-s-adults-believe-humanity-is-living-in-the-end-times/

This means that about 44% of American Evangelical Christians believe they are already living in the Endtimes, but they do not believe Christ will Return in their lifetime. Again, this seems to reflect the lack of biblical teaching in the American Church on the doctrine of the Endtimes.

9 Here and throughout the *Endtimes Essentials* the NIV 1984 version will be used to preserve the word **saints** whenever the original Hebrew reflects this. It is believed that this Bible version was correct to translate the Hebrew word *qaddish* and Greek word *hagiōn* as **saints** instead of the more general term **God's holy people**. This is demonstrated in the NASB translation of all of these texts. Christians have traditionally understood that the **saints** refers to members of the Church. This more accurately reflects what the biblical authors are communicating. This will be demonstrated in *Christ's Endtimes Teaching*, chs. 4-7.

10 A suggested translation of Dan 8:27 would be, **Then I, Daniel, fainted and was sick for many days** (Dan 8:27). **Fainted** translates the Hebrew word *hayah* which can mean "to fall" (*NASEC*). NASB has **exhausted**, NLT has **overcome**, and NIV has **worn out**.

11 The influential Bible prophecy scholar Dwight Pentecost, long-time Professor of NT at Dallas Theological Seminary, and author of the classic textbook, *Things to Come,* wrote in its introduction:
> Biblical Eschatology is the capstone of systematic theology. It is not only climactic, the terminus and consummation of theological study, but the presentation of eschatology is also the supreme demonstration of theological skill. (ix)

Likewise, John Piper has recently written: "To the best of my knowledge, I've never spoken to any Christian—scholar or layman—who is not perplexed about some biblical text on the second coming" (180).

12 For some reference to these versions of Dispensationalism see online at https://www.monergism.com/dispensationalism-defined. There it is referred to variously as: "Historic or classic Dispensationalism ... neo or revised Dispensationalism ... and progressive Dispensationalism."

13 Millard Erickson's *A Basic Guide to Eschatology* (Baker, 1998), is a helpful introduction to many of these Endtimes views. In this author's opinion, the ones that have little if any truth to them are Post-millennialism, Amillennialism, Pre-tribulationism, Historicism, and Idealism. The views that are most helpful in understanding Christ's Endtimes sermon and the biblical doctrine of the Endtimes include Futurism, Pre-millennialism, Post-tribulationism, and especially the Pre-wrath Rapture view. The author's own Pre-wrath Rescue position differs slightly from the more well known Pre-wrath Rapture view. That difference is described in ch. 8, endnote #1.

[14] The survey of Protestant Pastors on the Endtimes can be found online at https://news.lifeway.com/2016/04/26/pastors-the-end-of-the-world-is-complicated/.

It is stated in this section that: "a recent survey claimed that 50% of Protestant Pastors <u>deny</u> or are <u>not sure</u> that Scripture predicts there will be a literal and physical Antichrist in the future." This is based on the following result from the study.

49% of Protestant Pastors claimed the Antichrist will be a "Figure who will arise sometime in the future." The remaining respondents claimed various things including the Antichrist will be a "Personification of evil" (14%), "No individual Antichrist" (12%), "Not a person but an institution" (7%), "Figure who already arose sometime in the past" (6%), "None of these" (7%), "Not sure" (4%). These equal 50%.

[15] For the biblical data on these prophecies see ch. 12, sec. A.4 and endnotes there.

[16] MacArthur, "Hope for the Remnant" online at https://youtu.be/pqJRmnzQC1l.

[17] For more on the apathetic view of the Endtimes see the further discussion of Pan-tribulationism, ch. 11, sec. A.

[18] Unfortunately, Wiersbe (*loc.* 2 Tim 4:1) and Knight (454) believe Timothy's ministry being described in 2 Tim 4:1-4 was to be focused on unbelievers or false Christians and teachers. But Timothy's ministry to **Patiently correct, rebuke, and encourage your people with good teaching** (2 Tim 4:2) was certainly primarily directed toward Christians. And of course, we know from personal experience that real Christians can fail to **endure sound doctrine**. Accordingly, Fee writes:

> Timothy is to carry on Paul's ministry in a world in which there is no promise of eager response—even on the part of God's people... In this case it focuses on the believers themselves, rather than the false teachers, and it clearly lays some of the blame at their feet—despite the emphasis heretofore on their being deceived. (*Pastorals,* 285)

[19] In addition to the three currently completed books in the *Endtimes Essentials* series, a fourth volume will be added entitled, *The Greatest Persecution.* In addition, a supplemental online resource entitled *Additional Studies of the Endtimes* (*ASE*) at www.trainingtimothys.com is available in the "Endtimes Essentials Studies" section. This addresses several more minor points and questions that may be prompted by the *Endtimes Essentials* material.

Chapter 2

Introduction to the Endtimes

Their purpose & pain

Contents

A) The purpose & pain of the Endtimes

B) The importance of understanding the Endtimes

C) The 7 Primary Endtime Events

D) A preview of Christ's Endtimes Teaching

Primary Points

- The Endtimes consist of certain events predicted in Scripture surrounding Christ's Second Coming.
- God's purpose for Endtime events is to take control over this Earth.
- There will be a surprisingly long, painful, shocking, and even bloody road to get to the perfect and eternal New Earth.
- There are many reasons that understanding what the Bible teaches on the Endtimes is very important for our Christian life.
- There are seven primary Endtime events taught in Scripture.
- This book will give you an understanding of the sequence of Endtime events as Jesus taught in His Endtimes Teaching.

A) The purpose & pain of the Endtimes

Jesus Christ IS COMING BACK! His Return will change the world more than any other event in human history. In fact, it will end this world. This is why this topic is called the Endtimes. The Endtimes consist of certain events predicted in Scripture surrounding Christ's Second Coming. [1]

Therefore, what is God's purpose for Endtime events? To take control over this Earth. Ever since Lucifer rebelled, there has been a Cosmic War for Glory between God and Satan. The battlefield has been the people of this Earth ever since Satan's great victory in the Garden of Eden. Since then, in God's sovereign plan, **the whole world is under the control of the evil one** (1 John 5:19 NIV).

Satan, sin, demons, and death reign on this Earth and rule most of the people in the world. There are many, many more people obeying and glorifying the Devil, than those obeying and glorifying God.

But we are to pray every day: **Our Father in Heaven, may your name be honored, may your kingdom come, and your will be done, on Earth as it is in Heaven** (Matt 6:9-10 [2]). Christian, the Day is coming when this prayer will be granted in full!

Now, God's name is <u>not</u> **honored**, but rather, used as a curse word all over the world. But the Bible says of God, **All the nations you have made will come and worship before you, Lord; they will bring glory to your name** (Ps 86:9 NIV). That is a promise that will be fulfilled in the Endtimes.

Today, God's **will <u>is not</u> done on earth as it is in Heaven**. The world is full of His rebellious enemies. However:

> **The end will come, when [Christ] hands over the kingdom to God the Father after he has destroyed all dominion, authority, and power. For he must reign until he has put all his enemies under his feet.** (1 Cor 15:25 NIV)

The book of Revelation predicts and describes Christ's defeat of **all his enemies**, and God's ultimate victory in the Cosmic War for Glory. His victory is so certain that it is described in Revelation in the <u>past</u> tense. For example, John heard **loud voices in heaven** proclaiming, **"The world <u>has now become</u> the Kingdom of our Lord and of his Christ, and he will reign forever and ever"** (Rev 11:15 NLT).

Eventually, all the Endtime events will bring about God's ultimate purpose and will for this Earth. This is to create a New Earth where:

> **God's dwelling place is now among the people, and he will dwell with them. They will be his people, and God himself will be with them and be their God. He will wipe every tear from their eyes. There will be no more death or mourning or crying or pain, for the old order of things has passed away.** (Rev 21:1, 3b-4 NIV)

Understand it will not just be God the Son Who is coming to Earth. Twice in Revelation, God the Father is described as the One **Who is coming** (Rev 1:8; 4:8). The Endtimes will include God the Son's

Second Coming. But it will also result in God the Father's Coming. And He will bring all the purity and perfection of Heaven with Him to a New Earth, and eternally remove all impurity and sin. Hallelujah, that is where the whole world is headed!!!...

But there will be a surprisingly long, painful, shocking, and even bloody road to get there. As the Apostles said, **we must suffer many hardships to enter the Kingdom of God** (Acts 14:22 NIV).

First of all, the road to get to God's reign on Earth is LONG. The promises above in Revelation were given over 2,000 years ago. The one from Psalms 3,000 years ago. In Genesis, God promised that one day Christ would defeat Satan (cf. Gen 3:15). That promise was given over 6,000 years ago! No one knows when the Endtimes will begin (cf. Matt 24:36). This world could endure under Satan's rule for many more thousands of years. Even at the end of Endtime events there will be another 1,000 years of Christ ruling a world that ends in a massive rebellion against God (cf. Rev 20:7-9). The road to the End is LONG.

Secondly, it will be PAINFUL. Jesus said the world will experience the worst **wars, famines, earthquakes**, and **plagues** in human history (cf. Matt 24:4-8; Luke 21:11 NIV). To **His elect** He said, **"Then you will be arrested, persecuted, and killed. You will be hated all over the world because you are my followers"** (Matt 24:31 NASB; v. 9 NLT). And after that, during Christ's Wrath, **locusts** will **descend on the earth** and **sting like scorpions** and **torture** God's enemies **for five months. In those days people will seek death but will not find it. They will long to die, but death will flee from them!** (Rev 9:3-6 NLT). The road to the End will be PAINFUL.

And SHOCKING. As noted in chapter 1, Daniel received Endtime visions of how the Antichrist will **oppress his** [God's] **saints** and **He will cause a shocking amount of destruction** (Dan 7:25 NIV [3]; 8:24 NLT). Daniel was obviously a very brave man. But seeing what the Antichrist will do to the **saints** shocked him to the point that his face turned pale, and he felt weak and sick for several days (cf. Dan 7:7, 15, 19, 21, 25, 28; 8:26-27 [4]).

Finally, the road to get to the End of this world will be BLOODY. Christ's blood first made a way to enter the Paradise we are traveling to. Along the way, a **great multitude** of Christian martyrs in the

Endtimes will be **beheaded** (Rev 7:9; 20:4; cf. 6:9). The Bowl Punishments will turn all the **seas, rivers, and springs of water** on the Earth **into blood** (Rev 16:3-4 NIV). Because the wicked world will **shed the blood of** God's **saints**, He will **give them blood to drink as they deserve** (Rev 16:6 NIV).

And when Christ finally destroys His enemies at the Battle of Armageddon, "**blood** [will flow] ... **in a stream about 180 miles long and as high as a horse's bridle** (Rev 14:20 NLT; cf. Rev 19:15-18; Joel 3:1, 9-13).

God's path and plan to get to the End of this wicked world will be long, painful, shocking, and bloody. But His plan will result in the end of Satan, sin, and suffering forever. That is one purpose of the Endtimes.

All of this is why Jesus described the Endtimes as **birth pains** (Matt 24:8). Only women who birth a child can fully appreciate the metaphor. In Jesus' day it was relatively common for women to die a painful death in childbirth. Modern hospitals have reduced the risk, and medications can diminish the pain. Still, giving birth is among the most painful of all human experiences. That is one reason Jesus used it to represent the suffering of the Endtimes.

But there is another reason He called this period **birth pains**. God has ordained that pain comes before blessing. Accordingly, **birth pains** are the necessary human anguish that produces the wonderful new life of a baby. Likewise, the painful destruction of this current world is a necessary step to the creation of a whole New World. Which is why Jesus commanded us in the context of the Endtimes: "**Do not be frightened. These things <u>must</u> happen first**" (Luke 21:9 NIV). [5]

There is a lot of very bad news revealed in Scripture about the Endtimes. But in all the bad news about the temporary pain experienced in this world, do not forget the even better Good News about where everything is headed: a new, perfect, sinless, and Satan-less Earth where God reigns and we live forever!

B) The importance of understanding the Endtimes

There are several important reasons to understand what the Bible teaches about the Endtimes. First, as noted in the previous chapter,

"Salvation is the only topic in Scripture mentioned more than the Endtimes. It is clear that God wants His people to understand the doctrine of the Endtimes in Scripture!" (sec. A).

Accordingly, God wants us to be those **who have <u>loved</u> His appearing** (2 Tim 4:8 NASB). The Greek word here (*ēgapēkosi*) means to highly value something and experience great pleasure in it. [6] Unfortunately, however, the doctrine of the Endtimes is perhaps the most ignored, confusing, controversial, and frightening topic for Christians today. And all of this greatly hinders their ability to "experience great pleasure" in this doctrine.

Which is another reason for this book. As John Piper has recently written: "Love for Christ's appearing is deepened not only by seeing reasons for what makes it wonderful, but also by overcoming obstacles and misunderstandings." [7] A more biblical and clear understanding of the doctrine of the Endtimes will help God's people **love** Christ's **appearing** more.

Second, there is a theological reason for studying this topic. Nothing in Scripture reveals God's glory more than prophetic Scripture. Just read through the book of Revelation. Even if you do not fully understand all of it, its display of God's greatness, power, holiness, and GLORY will make you feel inspired with awe and reverence. That's God's intended affect for all the prophetic Scriptures.

There are also several practical reasons God wants us to understand the Endtimes. First, He wants His Church to be watching and ready for it, when it begins. We read: **Later, Jesus sat on the Mount of Olives. His disciples came to him privately and said, "Tell us, when will all this happen? What sign will signal your return and the end of the world?"** (Matt 24:3 NLT). In response Jesus very carefully described many signs and events that will signal His Return.

As also noted in the previous chapter, this is why throughout Christ's sermon on the Endtimes He said: **"Be on guard! Be alert!"** ... **"keep watch"** ... **"What I say to you, I say to everyone: 'Watch!'"** (Mark 13:33, 34, 37 NIV). **Watch!** for what? Current events in our world that would signal the beginning of the Endtimes, and that Christ's Return is near.

This leads to a second practical purpose God wants you to understand the Endtimes in Scripture. If you are living when they begin, you will need to be prepared for experiencing them. As discussed in the next chapter, there are popular teachings that claim the Church will <u>not</u> be present for the events that Jesus described in His Endtimes Teaching (cf. Matt 24:1-31). But as we study Christ's Endtimes sermon, that view will be proven false.

This is one reason the Bible has so much to say to <u>the Church</u> about the suffering that will occur in the Endtimes. The Church will be there! Therefore, having a more biblical understanding of this topic will help you and your family be prepared to experience the Endtimes.

Third, understanding what Scripture teaches about the Endtimes will help you to live a holy life. This is the repeated testimony of Scripture. The Apostle Paul wrote:

We should live in this evil world with wisdom, righteousness, and devotion to God, <u>while we look forward</u> with hope to that wonderful day when the glory of our great God and Savior, Jesus Christ, will be revealed (Tit 2:12-13 NLT).

Likewise, the Apostle John wrote:

We know that when Christ appears, we will be like Him because we will see Him as He really is. And all who have this eager expectation <u>will purify themselves</u>, just as He is pure (1 John 3:2-3 [8]; cf. Rom 13:11-14; 1 Cor 7:29-32; 2 Pet 3:10-14).

Too many Christians claim that studying and understanding biblical prophecy has no practical relevance to the Christian life. But what is more practical and relevant than holiness? God's word tells us the better we understand Christ's Second Coming, and have an **eager expectation** of it, it **will purify** our lives.

Finally, understanding the doctrine of the Endtimes will greatly help you have an eternal perspective on your life. Studying and understanding the biblical promises that this Earth will be destroyed, and an eternal New Earth is coming, will help you properly evaluate everything in your life.

Studying the Endtimes confronts us with this important reminder: **The world and its desires pass away, but whoever does the will of God lives forever** (1 John 2:17 NIV). Understanding the Endtimes is perhaps the very best thing we can do to help us obey the challenging command to: **set your hearts on things above, where Christ is, seated at the right hand of God. Set your minds on things above, not on earthly things.** (Col 3:1-2 NIV).

But here is a hard truth: Endtime events could literally begin TODAY, or not for another 1,000 years. That is the biblical truth.

Scripture's teaching on the Endtimes presents it this way. This is because God has wanted every generation of Christians to believe they could be living in the Last Generation Church. God wants us to live with this challenging tension between expectant watching and patient waiting. On one hand, to plan on living a long life. But also not be surprised if the Endtimes begin TODAY. It is this latter expectation that gives us a purifying and eternal perspective on our life. Which is why Jesus repeatedly commanded us to **Watch!** (Mark 13:33, 34, 37).

C) The 7 Primary Endtime Events

[Please stop and take a moment to read just the first 31 verses of Matt 24 before reading the following]

It is believed that Scripture generally reveals 7 Primary Endtime Events. Most of them are clearly mentioned in Christ's Endtimes sermon. These are listed below in the biblical order of their occurrence.

1) The Beginning of Birth Pains

Jesus said that a False Christ(s), devastating **wars, famines, earthquakes**, and **plagues** will be **the beginning of birth pains** (Matt 24:4-8 NIV; Luke 21:9-10; cf. Rev 6:1-8). The purpose of these is to prepare the world for Antichrist's worship and dictatorship.

2) Antichrist's Claim to be God

After **the beginning of birth pains,** Jesus said His people will **"see standing in the holy place 'the abomination that causes desolation'"** (Matt 24:15 NIV). Paul described this event when he wrote: **The man of lawlessness ... will oppose and will exalt himself over everything that is called God or is worshiped, so that he sets himself up in God's temple** [in Jerusalem], **proclaiming himself to be God** (2 Thess 2:3-4 NIV). And the world will believe him so that **All the people who belong to this world** [will] **worship the beast** [Antichrist] (Rev 13:7-8 NLT).

3) The Greatest Persecution

Jesus said after Antichrist's Claim to be God, **"then there will be the greatest persecution of God's elect people. It will be greater than any persecution since the world began, and it will never be equaled again"** (Matt 24:21 [9]). This will be the Antichrist's Wrath against God's **elect** and **saints** because they refuse to worship him (cf. Matt 24:9, 21-22; cf. Rev 6:9-11; 13:7-10; 14:12; Dan 7:21, 25).

4) Christ's Return

Jesus said, **"Immediately <u>after</u> the completion of the greatest persecution, <u>then</u> 'the sun will be darkened, and the moon will not give its light; the stars will fall from the sky and the heavenly bodies will be shaken.'**

<u>Then</u> the sign that the Son of Man is coming will appear in the sky. And then <u>all the peoples of the Earth</u> will mourn when they <u>see the Son of Man coming</u> on the clouds of Heaven, with power and great glory. (Matt 24:29-30 [10]).

5) The Church's Rescue

Jesus said <u>after</u> **all the peoples of the Earth ... see the Son of Man coming** <u>then</u> **He will send out His angels with a loud trumpet sound, and they will lift up and gather together God's elect people from one end of the sky to the other, from everywhere on Earth** (Matt 24:30-31 [11]). This is the "rapture" of the Church described elsewhere (cf. 1 Thess 4:15-17; 2 Thess 2:1-4; Rev 7:9-14). It occurs **Immediately after the completion of the greatest persecution of God's elect people** (Matt 24:21, 29), but before the time of Christ's Wrath.

The word "rapture" is a common term used by Christians, but it does not occur in Scripture, and does not describe this event as clearly as the Church's Rescue. Therefore this latter term will be used throughout the *Endtimes Essentials*.

6) Christ's Wrath

Jesus revealed that immediately after the Cosmic Signs marking His Return and the Church's Rescue, then everyone remaining on the **earth** will cry out **"hide us from the face of him who sits on the throne and the wrath of the Lamb!"** (Rev 6:15-17 NIV). This period of Christ's Wrath will include the Trumpet and Bowl Punishments and is completed with the Battle of Armageddon (cf. Matt 24:37-39; Rev 6:15-17; chs. 8-9; 15-16; 1 Thess 5:1-10; Isa 13:9-13).

7) Christ's 1000-year Reign on Earth

This event is often referred to as the Millennium (cf. Rev 20:1-10). During this period, God will literally fulfill many of His OT promises to Israel. But the Christians who experience The Greatest Persecution, will also be rewarded with the unique privilege of experiencing the First Resurrection and reigning with Christ on the Earth during this time (Rev 20:4; cf. 13:11-18; 14:11-12).

These are the 7 Primary Endtime Events predicted in God's Word. Most of them will be discussed in more detail in the *Endtimes Essentials* series. The Bible's teaching on the Endtimes can be simplified into these 7 Primary Endtime Events. But there are a vast number of additional Endtime events and details revealed in Scripture.

After the completion of the 7 Primary Endtime Events, Eternity will begin. Initial events in Eternity will include The Great White Throne Evaluation of every person who has ever lived (cf. Rev 20:11-15; Matt 25:31-46), and the creation of a New Earth (cf. Rev 21:1) for God and His people to live on for eternity.

D) Preview of *Christ's Endtimes Teaching*

This book is the first volume in a series called the *Endtimes Essentials*. By Christ's Endtimes Teaching we are referring to Christ's Endtimes sermon, or "the Olivet Discourse." Understanding this passage of Scripture is the primary goal of this book.

In the next chapter (3), important principles for interpreting Christ's Endtimes Teaching will be discussed. In chapter 4, Christ's Endtimes Teaching in Matthew 24 will give us a clear understanding of major Endtime events and their sequence. Jesus' sermon on His Coming will challenge and correct many popular views on the Endtimes.

Chapter 5 will demonstrate that several passages in Paul's letters to the Thessalonians will confirm our interpretation of Jesus. Fortunately, Jesus and Paul are much more simple and clear on the outline and order of Endtime events than many believe.

Chapters 6 and 7 will demonstrate that Jesus' Revelation and Daniel agree with the outline of Endtime events in Christ's Endtimes Teaching. Chapter 8 will draw some important initial conclusions from our study.

Chapter 9 will discuss some things in Christ's Endtimes Teaching that have been confusing and difficult for many to understand. Chapter 10 will discuss the important commands in Christ's Endtimes Teaching.

Chapters 11-16 will evaluate popular views of the Endtimes based on Christ's Endtimes Teaching. Unfortunately, it will be demonstrated that there are many misleading and harmful myths in the Church today on this doctrine.

In addition there are valuable Appendices included in this book. Appendix A is a detailed table of contents for *Christ's Endtimes Teaching*. Appendix B is a glossary of terms used throughout the *Endtimes Essentials* series. Appendix C is a collection of the graphics in *Christ's Endtimes Teaching* illustrating the sequence of Endtime events as taught by Jesus, Paul, and Daniel.

God's great grace to you as you study the most important passage in all of Scripture on the Endtimes for the Church.

[1] There is a biblical sense in which the Endtimes began with Christ's First Coming (cf. 1 Cor 10:11; 1 John 2:18). Theologians call this "realized eschatology" or the "already not yet" aspect of God's Kingdom on Earth. Christ's First Coming and the indwelling of the Holy Spirit have initiated some things that will be consummated in Christ's Second Coming and even after the completion of His 1,000 year Reign on Earth.

Unfortunately, some focus so much on what can be included in "realized eschatology" that they neglect a biblical understanding of what is still to be fulfilled in biblical prophecy. Therefore, the "Endtimes" throughout the *Endtimes Essentials* will be defined as certain events predicted in Scripture surrounding Christ's Second Coming.

[2] The suggested translation of Matt 6:9-10 is: **Our Father in Heaven, may your name be honored, may your kingdom come, and your will be done, on earth as it is in Heaven**.

Honored translates the Greek word *hagiastheto* which means "treat as holy, *reverence*" (*BDAG*). This is superior as most English speakers do not use the traditional word **hallowed** (NIV, NASB), nor readily understand what it means. The suggested translation is very close to the NET which also uses **honored** here.

[3] Here the NIV 1984 version is used to preserve the word **saints** which helps us understand these prophecies involve all of God's people, including the Church.

[4] Fear is repeatedly described in Scripture as a sin. Unfortunately, some Bible versions of Daniel's reaction suggest he was afraid. On the contrary, the Hebrew in these texts can also mean to "inspire awe," be "unpleasant or shocking," "upset, unsettle." None of them have to mean feeling afraid or terrified. For more on this see *Additional Studies on the Endtimes*, ch. 5.

[5] Birth pains as a prerequisite to restore Israel was alluded to in the Prophets (cf. Isa 66:8; Jer 23:23; Hos 13:13; Micah 4:9-10). *W&S* note:

> From these verses there arose in Judaism the idea that the messianic Kingdom must emerge from a period of suffering that was called the messianic woes or "the birth pangs of the Messiah." This does not mean the woes that the Messiah must suffer, but the woes out of which the messianic age is to be born. (921)

[6] *BDAG*, #2. As quoted the NASB translates 2 Tim 4:8 as, **who have loved His appearing**. This seems superior to other versions. The NIV has **longed for** and the NLT has **eagerly look forward to**. But *BDAG* does not list any NT or ancient Greek examples of the Greek word *ēgapēkosi* being used in these ways. Unfortunately, commentaries basically ignore helping us to understand this remarkable phrase. Fee and Marshall actually say nothing about it. Knight only mentions the NIV translation is a possibility, but gives no justification for it.

[7] Piper, 180.

[8] The suggested translation of 1 John 3:2-3 is a combination of the NIV and NLT.

[9] For an explanation of the suggested translation of Matt 24:21 see ch. 3, sec. E.

[10] For an explanation of the suggested translation of Matt 24:29-30 see ch. 3, sec. E.

[11] For an explanation of the suggested translation of Matt 24:31 see ch. 4, sec. C.

Chapter 3
Introduction to Christ's Endtimes Sermon
The clearest, most important passage of Scripture on the Second Coming

Contents
A) The battle over Christ's Endtimes Teaching

B) Expect Christ's Endtimes Teaching to be fulfilled in the future

C) Start with Christ's Endtimes Teaching, not the OT

D) Understand who Christ's Endtimes Teaching is meant for   *The meaning of* eklektous

E) Understand what Christ's Endtimes Teaching is warning of   *The meaning of* thlipsis

Primary Points
- Just the first 28 verses of Christ's Endtimes sermon is the clearest, most detailed, and most important teaching in all of Scripture on the substance and sequence of Endtime events. Which is probably why there has been such an intense spiritual battle over its meaning.
- Jesus clearly intended to teach that all of the events He described in His Endtimes Teaching will occur in the future Endtimes.
- The most popular view of the Endtimes (Pre-tribulationism) completely depends on one thing: Proving that the first third of Christ's Endtimes Teaching has absolutely nothing to do with Christians in the Church. That simply is not true.
- Jesus referred to **the elect** three times in His sermon. This word is used 18 times in the NT to refer to people, and every time it includes the Church, including its use in Matthew 24.
- Contrary to popular modern views, the Church had better pay attention to Christ's Endtimes Teaching and its warnings to **God's elect people** (Matt 24:22, 24, 31). If you are a Christian and living when the Endtimes begin, then you will suffer the unprecedented wars, famines, and plagues of The Beginning of Birth Pains, and the Antichrist's Greatest Persecution.

- The Greek word *thlipsis* is better translated as "persecution" rather than the more obscure and misleading word "tribulation." Therefore, Christ was warning of The Greatest Persecution of the Church, not just a "great tribulation" for the world.
- Bible versions that do not translate *thlipsis* as **persecution** in Matthew 24:21 make Jesus say something false.

[Please stop and read Matthew 24:1-31]

A) The Battle over Christ's Endtimes Teaching

One day Jesus and His disciples visited the temple in Jerusalem. When the disciples commented on its beauty Jesus responded with a prediction about its destruction (cf. Matt 24:1-2). Then we read:

Later, Jesus sat on the Mount of Olives. His disciples came to him privately and said, "Tell us, when will all this happen? What sign will signal your return and the end of the world? (Matt 24:3 NLT)

The disciples interpreted Christ's prediction of the complete destruction of the temple, as a reference to **the end of the world**. Therefore, like us, they wanted to know more. **Jesus answered** (v. 4) with the clearest teaching in all of Scripture on the substance and sequence of Endtime events. Its contents are so complete, Bible scholars refer to it as "the little apocalypse," suggesting it is a condensed version of the book of Revelation.

Because Jesus gave this teaching while He **sat on the Mount of Olives** (Matt 24:3), it is referred to as the "Olivet Discourse." This teaching was not given to a crowd. Rather, Mark records that only **Peter, James, John and Andrew** were present for this teaching (Mark 13:3 NIV). Still, this was a very important teaching being given during the last week of Jesus' life on Earth.

While we have chosen Matthew 24 as our primary text, the Discourse is repeated essentially verbatim in Mark 13:1-37 and with some variations in Luke 21:1-36. [1] Because this sermon was focused on the Endtimes, we will refer to it as Christ's Endtimes Teaching or sermon throughout the *Endtimes Essentials*.

As noted in chapter 1, just the first 28 verses of Christ's Endtimes Teaching is the clearest and most important teaching in all of Scripture on the substance and sequence of Endtime events. Which is probably why there has been such an intense spiritual battle over its meaning. As NT scholar D. A. Carson writes of the Olivet Discourse:

> Few chapters of the Bible have called forth more disagreement among interpreters than Matthew 24 and its parallels in Mark 13 and Luke 21. The history of the interpretation of this chapter is immensely complex. [2]

But if you correctly understand these 28 verses, their meaning becomes rather simple, and you recognize that all of the confusion and controversy regarding Christ's Endtimes Teaching is unnecessary. Along these lines, John MacArthur writes specifically regarding Matthew 24:

> Its truths are absolutely essential for understanding [Christ's] return and the amazing events associated with it... Among the many passages in Scripture that describe the Lord's coming again, Matthew 24-25 is unequaled because it is the message from Jesus' own lips about His return...
>
> The teaching of the Olivet discourse is much debated and frequently misunderstood, <u>largely because it is viewed through the lens of a particular theological system or interpretive scheme that makes the message appear complex and enigmatic.</u>
>
> But the disciples were not learned men, and Jesus' purpose was to give them clarity and encouragement, not complexity and anxiety. The intricate interpretations that are sometimes proposed for this passage would have left the disciples utterly dumbfounded. It is preferable to take Jesus' words as simply and as straightforwardly as possible. [3]

Unfortunately, MacArthur's concern about a distorting bias is common in how many interpret Christ's Endtimes Teaching. In this chapter we will discuss some important principles that simplify and clarify Christ's intended meaning for the first 28 verses of His Endtimes sermon.

B) Expect Christ's Endtimes Teaching to be fulfilled in the future

Something that has greatly distorted and complicated the interpretation of Christ's Endtimes Teaching is the popular claim among NT scholars that Jesus was <u>not</u> primarily predicting the future. [4]

Unfortunately, it is very common in the Church today to merely focus on how **the beginning of birth pains** (Matt 24:8) and **persecution** (v. 9) have occurred in history and diminish their value for the future. This view can be labeled as "Historicism" [5] and is related to Preterism which is more thoroughly evaluated later in this book in chapter 12 (sec. B). But some obvious reasons for interpreting Christ's Endtimes Teaching as prophecy about the future can be shared here.

First, the "historical" view ignores what the disciples asked Jesus. The disciples did <u>not</u> ask Jesus, "What catastrophes will occur throughout Church history?" They asked Him, **"What sign will signal your return and the end of the world?"** (Matt 24:3 NLT). Contrary to the "historical" view, Christ answered their question with **sign**s of His **return and <u>the end of the world</u>**.

Second, supporters of a merely "historical" view ignore the meaning of Christ intentionally calling these events **birth pains** (Matt 24:8). If He was describing events that would occur over more than 2,000 years, then His metaphor would be misleading. No one in the first century or today would understand **birth pains** in the way the "historical" view of Christ's Endtimes Teaching depends on. It is doubtful that Jesus expected us to believe **birth pains** could last for hundreds of years. **Birth pains** begin rather immediately before the birth. Likewise, **the beginning of birth pains** will occur rather immediately before the birth of Christ reigning on this Earth.

Third, Historicism ignores that Jesus said the **generation** that will **see all these things** signaling Christ's Return, **will certainly not pass away until all these things have happened** (Matt 24:34). Therefore, the Endtime events that Jesus described were not intended to refer to things that would occur to some degree throughout history. On the contrary, the events that will occur to signal Christ's Return will be unprecedented in their effect, and occur in one **generation**, when the Last Generation Church is on Earth. [6]

Fourth, supporters of the merely "historical" view of Christ's Endtimes Teaching usually admit that at least later parts of it will only occur in the future. This would include Christ's Return (cf. Matt 24:29-30). So how would a merely "historical" approach determine what parts of Christ's predictions were to be fulfilled throughout Church history, and which ones only in the Endtimes? The view cannot do this, nor does it usually attempt to do so.

This "historical" approach to Christ's Endtimes Teaching is also supported by a misinterpretation of Jesus' statement:

"You will hear of wars and rumors of wars, but see to it that you are not alarmed. Such things must happen, but the end is still to come" (Matt 24:6 NIV).

Many claim that because Jesus said this last statement, that the events He described before this have nothing to do with **the end**. Again, their view is that False Christs and wars were intended to describe things that will happen throughout Church history, and not a sign that His Return is near. Therefore, these scholars claim Jesus was actually discouraging His followers from monitoring current events for a sign of the Endtimes.

This is false for many reasons. First, it ignores Christ's repeated command to **"Watch"** for signs of His Return (cf. Mark 13:33, 35, 37). Second, it ignores Jesus' intention to answer His disciples' question: **"What sign will signal Your return and the end of the world?"** (Matt 24:3 NLT). Again, contrary to Historicism, Jesus answered their question.

Third, this view misinterprets Matthew 24:6. Jesus was simply saying the time between the first signs of the Endtimes (False Christs, wars, famines, etc. vs. 4-8), and His Return, will be a few years. Therefore, even after witnessing unprecedented wars, He did not want His people to assume His Return would quickly follow. Accordingly, the NLT translates Matthew 24:6 as **"You will hear of wars and threats of wars, but don't panic. Yes, these things must take place, but the end won't follow immediately."**

Of course, **wars, famines and earthquakes** (Matt 24:7-8) have been occurring throughout human history. This is because Jesus wanted every generation of Christians to obey His commands to **"Watch!"** (Mark 13:37) for signs of His Return and believe they could be the last generation. This is discussed more in chapter 10 (sec. D).

But how then will we recognize The Beginning of Birth Pains as signs of Christ's Return? They will occur with unprecedented intensity in a relatively short period of time. Revelation 6:1-8 graphically portrays these same **"beginning of birth pains."** There it is explained that they will culminate in the Endtimes to have **power over <u>a fourth of the earth</u> to kill by sword, famine and plague, and by the wild beasts of the earth** (Rev 6:8 NIV). Today, that would be about 2 <u>billion</u> people dying in a relatively short period of time. That has <u>never</u> happened before. Not even close.

Can you imagine the death of 2 billion people in the world? Recently our world experienced the Covid-19 pandemic. Its death toll is estimated to be currently over 6 million people. Its effects on society and the economy were enormous. But the death of <u>2 billion</u> people will be over <u>300 times</u> the deaths that have occurred from Covid.

In fact, how many people have been killed <u>in all of human history</u> from wars, genocides, massacres, famines, and plagues? Some have carefully estimated the total to be about 700 million people. [7] This has occurred over thousands of years of human history. But in just a few short years during The Beginning of Birth Pains, perhaps three times as many people will die from war, famine, and disease, <u>than in all of the similar catastrophes in human history combined</u>. Indeed, these kinds of catastrophes have been occurring throughout human history. But when the Endtimes begin, **the beginning of birth pains** will occur with an unprecedented intensity.

So will persecution. Again, God's people have been persecuted throughout history. But Jesus was predicting **the greatest persecution of those days** (Matt 24:29; cf. v. 21), referring to the Endtimes. Therefore, MacArthur is correct to note against the "historical" view of The Beginning of Birth Pains in Revelation 6:

> The first four seals clearly describe awe-inspiring, frightening judgments without parallel in human history. There is nothing that has happened since John had this vision that could be the fulfillment of these judgments. [8]

Focusing on how mere shadows of The Beginning of Birth Pains have occurred in human history does little to help the Church prepare for the great darkness that is coming. And such a popular approach does nothing to help the Church recognize when the Endtimes have begun. In fact, supporters of Historicism intentionally discourage that very thing. In the process, as noted, they also ignore Christ's repeated command in His Endtimes Teaching to **Watch!** (Mark 13:37) current events for the signs of His Return.

C) Start with Christ's Endtimes Teaching, not the OT

Unfortunately, many are encouraged to begin their study of the Endtimes with the book of Daniel. A common claim is that just three verses in Daniel (cf. 9:24-27) provide the best framework for understanding this topic. But Jesus was a greater Prophet than Daniel. Christ was the greatest Prophet of all. No one provided more and clearer revelation on the Endtimes than Jesus. If we want to understand biblical prophecy, we should begin with Christ. Therefore, most people would readily recognize that the almost 100 verses of teaching in Christ's Endtimes sermon, are a better place to start than 3 verses of an obscure explanation of a vision in Daniel. As noted in chapter 1:

> Fortunately, Christ's Endtimes sermon is not communicated through a vision with multi-layered symbols like Daniel and Revelation. That type of Scripture is the most difficult of any to interpret. Therefore, we should be grateful that Jesus gave us a literal teaching on the essentials of the Endtimes without complex symbolic visions (sec. B2)

In fact, Christ's Endtimes Teaching provides commentary on **'the abomination that causes desolation,' spoken of through the prophet Daniel** (Matt 24:15 NIV; cf. Dan 9:27). Therefore, it would be wise to start with what Jesus said about Daniel's vision, rather than using Daniel's vision to understand Jesus' teaching.

This is also because all knowledgeable Bible scholars know it is best to use the NT to accurately interpret the OT, especially for OT prophecies. That was certainly demonstrated in understanding the OT predictions of Christ's First Coming. The same will be true of His Second Coming. Those who begin their study of the Endtimes in the OT (e.g. Daniel) are trying to interpret the NT through their lens of the OT. [9] However, if we interpret Christ's Endtimes Teaching in its plainest sense, just as we do His other teachings, it will provide what He intended: A clear outline of the substance and sequence of Endtime events for God's elect people in the Church.

Unfortunately, the reason that many want to begin their Endtimes teaching with Daniel 9:24-27 is to support the idea that neither this passage, nor the first part of Christ's Endtimes Teaching has anything to do with the Church. But as demonstrated in the next section, this is not biblical.

D) Understand <u>who</u> Christ's Endtimes Teaching is meant for *The meaning of eklektous*

One of the most popular views on the Endtimes among Christians is something called Pre-tribulationism. Pre-tribulationism claims that the Church is "raptured" from the Earth <u>before</u> any other Endtime events occur. In other words, it is claimed that the Church will <u>not</u> experience <u>any</u> of the events Jesus described in the first 28 verses of His Endtimes Teaching. Therefore, Pre-tribulationism claims no Christians in the Church today can experience or witness the **wars, famines,** and **plagues** of **the beginning of birth pains**, or Antichrist's **abomination of desolation**, or the **greatest persecution** (Matt 24:4-7, 15, 21, 24; Luke 21:11).

Obviously, this is a very attractive view. In a survey, 36% of Protestant Pastors claimed Pre-tribulationism best reflected their beliefs on the Endtimes. [10] That was significantly higher than the percentage for any other views. This view has been especially promoted by the *Left Behind* fictional novels which have sold over 65 million copies worldwide. [11] Again, these novels are fiction. Still, <u>they have probably had more impact on the Church's Endtimes beliefs than any other resource</u>.

Pre-tribulationism will be discussed more thoroughly in chapters 13-16. Admittedly, it is a very complicated view of Scripture. But one thing can be stated here that is a great problem for Pre-tribulationism.

In essence, this popular view completely depends on <u>one thing</u>: Proving the first third of Christ's Endtimes Teaching (Matt 24:4-31) has absolutely <u>nothing</u> to do with Christians in the Church. Pre-tribulationism teaches that Christ's sermon on the Endtimes applies primarily to Jews or to some kind of "post-rapture" Christians. But if

Christ's sermon about His Return <u>does</u> apply to the Church in any way, then one of the most common views on the Endtimes in the Church today is biblically proven to be false.

Christ's Endtimes Teaching gives such a clear sequence of Endtimes events, it is essential to establish the fact that Christ <u>never</u> intended to <u>exclude</u> the Church from its teaching. To most Christians, it would seem odd that this is even a debated issue among Evangelical scholars. What other NT teachings would we allow to be labeled as "Not for the Church"? It is odd that the burden of proof has fallen on those who would say that this passage <u>does</u> include the Church. But that is where the burden of proof lies today, and it must be addressed before this passage can be used concerning the sequence of Endtimes events.

Pre-tribulationism primarily bases its claim that the first 28 verses of Christ's Endtimes Teaching has nothing to do with the Church on their interpretation of Daniel 9:24-27.

[Please stop and read Daniel 9:24-27]

This is a very complex biblical prophecy. It will be discussed further in chapter 7 (sec. B). In verse 24 Daniel is told this prophecy **is for your people and your holy city**, referring to Israel and Jerusalem. Therefore, it is assumed in Pre-tribulationism that the prophecy in verse 27 regarding Antichrist's **abomination that causes desolation** in the Endtimes cannot apply to the Church in any way. Because Christ mentions this same event in His Endtimes Teaching (cf. Matt 24:15), it is concluded that Christ's intended audience was <u>not</u> the Church.

But Pre-tribulationism ignores something critical in Daniel's prophecy. In verse 26 the prophecy states: **the Anointed One** [Christ] **will be put to death**. Surely this prediction of Christ's crucifixion applies to the Church! Therefore, Pre-tribulationism ignores the fact that the NT provides additional revelation regarding who Daniel's prophecy applies to. As noted, in a later chapter, more reasons will be given for understanding that Daniel's prophecies, including 9:24-27 apply to the Church.

Nevertheless, there is overwhelming evidence within Christ's Endtimes Teaching that His intended audience for the entire sermon included Christians in the Church. First, even Pre-tribulationism teaches that after Matthew 24:31, the remaining 66 verses of Christ's Endtimes sermon applies to the Church. This includes warnings about watching for signs of His Return and parables about His Second Coming. Therefore, if the latter 66 verses of Christ's sermon clearly apply to the Church, how can it be claimed the first 28 verses do not? Did Jesus intend such a drastic change of audience in the middle of His sermon? Contrary to Pre-tribulationism, He did not. [12]

Second, remember Who gave this teaching: **Christ, who is the head of his body, <u>the church</u>** (Eph 4:15 NLT; cf. 1:22; 5:23; Col 1:18). Pre-tribulationism wants to claim that when the Head, Savior, and Founder of the <u>Church</u>, gave the longest and most detailed teaching about His Second Coming in the NT, that its first third had absolutely <u>nothing</u> to say to Christians in the Church.

Third, remember who privately heard Christ's Endtimes Teaching: The Apostles Peter, James, and John (cf. Mark 13:3). Jesus had previously called Peter the foundational **"rock [of] my church"** (Matt 16:18 NIV). The NT called Peter, James, and John the **pillars of the <u>church</u>** (Gal 2:9 NLT). Why would **the head of his <u>church</u>** give His longest and most detailed teaching about His Return, to the **pillars of the <u>church</u>,** and the <u>Church's</u> foundational leaders and teachers, if its first third had nothing at all to do with the <u>Church</u>? Contrary to Pre-tribulationism, He would not. [13]

These arguments would be sufficient to reject the view that Christ's Endtimes Teaching has nothing to do with Christians in the Church. But the most compelling reason is this: Jesus intentionally addressed this teaching to **the elect** (*eklektous*) three times. Jesus said:

> **"Unless those days** [of **the greatest persecution**, v. 21] **had been cut short, no life would have been saved; but for the sake of <u>the elect</u>** [*eklektous*] **those days will be cut short."** (Matt 24:22 NASB; cf. Mark 13:20)

> **"For false Christs and false prophets will arise and will show great signs and wonders, so as to mislead, if possible, even <u>the elect</u>** [*eklektous*]**."** (Matt 24:24 NASB; cf. Mark 13:22)

> **"And He will send forth His angels with A GREAT TRUMPET and THEY WILL GATHER TOGETHER His elect** [*eklektous*] **from the four winds, from one end of the sky to the other"** (Matt 24:31 NASB; cf. Mark 13:27)

As noted above, Pre-tribulationism claims **the elect** in the verses above refers to Israel and some kind of "post-rapture" Christians, but not the Church. For example, John MacArthur, a promoter of Pre-tribulationism, seems to define **the elect** as virtually every group of God's people except Christians in the Church. Writing about Christ's use of **the elect** (*eklektous*) in Matthew 24, he writes:

> The elect could represent the nation of Israel, which is often referred to in the Old Testament as God's elect, or chosen, people (see, e.g., Isa. 45:4). It could also include those who become Christians during the Tribulation [and after the "rapture"]... Jesus is warning those who will be living during the end times, which will not include believers of the church age (who will either have died or been raptured before the Tribulation). [14]

Unfortunately, this rightly respected Bible teacher seems to ignore the context of Matthew 24 and the clear meaning of *eklektous* in the NT.

Whoever **the elect** are, Christ said they will experience **the beginning of birth pains** (Matt 24:8), **the greatest persecution** (v. 21 [15]), they will **see the Son of Man coming on the clouds of Heaven** (v. 30), and experience being **lift**ed **up and gather**ed **together** by **angels** into **the sky ... from everywhere on Earth** (v. 31 [16]). It is understandable that Pre-tribulationism would want to claim these events will not include the Church. But Christ corrected their error.

Every Christian who has read the NT knows that **the elect** is virtually synonymous with the Church. The Greek word is used 18 times in the NT to refer to a person or group of people. Every time it refers to, or includes Christians in the Church. There are no exceptions. For example, the Apostles wrote the following to the Church:

> **Who will bring a charge against God's elect** [*eklektōn*]? (Rom 8:33 NASB).

> **I endure everything for the sake of the elect** [*eklektous*] (2 Tim 2:10 NIV).
>
> **Paul, a servant of God and an apostle of Jesus Christ to further the faith of God's elect** [*eklektōn*] (Tit 1:1 NIV).
>
> **Peter, an apostle of Jesus Christ, to God's elect** [*eklektois*] (1 Pet 1:1 NIV)

Often the word is translated "chosen" as in **God's chosen** [*eklektoi*] **people, holy and dearly loved** (Col 3:12 NIV) or **you are a chosen** [*eklektōn*] **people, a royal priesthood** (1 Pet 2:9 NIV). Also, when the Apostle John is addressing Christians in a church he writes, **To the lady chosen** [*eklektē*] **by God** (2 John 1:1 NIV; cf. v. 13; Rev 17:14 [17]). Notice that those Apostles who heard Christ's Endtime Teaching to the **elect** (e.g. Peter and John) also used this term to refer to the Church.

It was noted above that Pre-tribulationism (and MacArthur) would claim that *eklektous* in Matthew 24 "could represent the nation of Israel." But there is no example of this in the NT. On the contrary, Paul used a related term to specifically exclude the nation of Israel when he wrote: **What Israel sought so earnestly it did not obtain, but the elect** [*eklogē*, the Church] **did** (Rom 11:7 NIV). Here, contrary to Pre-tribulationism, **Israel** is not **the elect**.

Those who want to claim that Jesus' use of *eklektous* excluded the Church in Matthew 24, ignore the fact that Jesus used this same word just two chapters earlier in Matthew 22 to clearly include the Church. There He shared a parable about a **wedding banquet** to illustrate what entering into **the kingdom of heaven is like** (v. 1). In conclusion He said, **"many are invited, but few are chosen** [*eklektoi*]**"** (v. 14 NIV). Jesus' point in the parable is that those who will enter **the kingdom of heaven** will be the **chosen**, the elect. Will these elect in Matthew 22 include the Church? Of course. And so will **the elect** spoken of two chapters later in Matthew 24.

Jesus used the same word when He said in reference to prayer, **"will not God bring about justice for His elect** [*eklektōn*] **who cry to Him day and night"** (Luke 18:7 NASB). [18] Was this teaching for people in His Church? Of course it was. Jesus always included the Church in the word **elect**. Including His teaching in Matthew 24.

In the NT, **the elect** always referred to Christians in the Church. Nowhere is there a single instance in the NT where *eklektous* or its related terms are used to refer to a person or group of people in a way that excludes the Church. [19] Only those with a preconceived bias against seeing the Church in Christ's Endtimes Teaching would assume this. [20]

NT scholar D. A. Carson corrects both MacArthur and Pre-tribulationism on this critical point of biblical interpretation when he writes regarding Matthew 24:

> The term 'elect' most naturally refers to all true believers, chosen by God; thus is it reasonable to assume that it does so here." [21]

Accordingly, the suggested translation of Matthew 24 used throughout the *Endtimes Essentials* will render *eklektous* as **God's elect people**.

Many Bible Teachers have taken too much liberty in labeling Christ's Endtimes Teaching as "Jewish" simply because Jesus mentioned **Judea** and **the Sabbath** (Matt 24:16, 20 NIV). These references simply reflect the fact that the Antichrist's **abomination that causes desolation** (v. 15) will occur **in God's temple** (2 Thess 2:4) in Jerusalem. Therefore, The Greatest Persecution will begin there, but spread throughout the world and include the Church (cf. Rev 12:13-17; 13:5-10).

Did Jesus intend the first third of His longest and most detailed teaching about His Second Coming to have absolutely nothing to do with Christians in the Church? The clear answer is "No." We need to interpret Christ's Endtimes Teaching as applying to the Church.

Therefore, it is humbly and respectfully suggested that there are serious biblical problems with Pre-tribulationism. If the reader still doubts this, then please read on in this book.

Contrary to popular modern views, the Church had better pay attention to Christ's Endtimes Teaching and its warnings to **God's elect people** (Matt 24:22, 24, 31). If you are a Christian and living when the Endtimes begin, then you will suffer the unprecedented wars, famines, and plagues of The Beginning of Birth Pains, and the Antichrist's Greatest Persecution.

E) Understand <u>what</u> Christ's Endtimes Teaching is warning of *The meaning of thlipsis*

The second important Greek term in Christ's Endtimes Teaching is *thlipsis*. It is also used three times in Matthew 24, verses 9, 21, and 29. The NASB translates it as **tribulation**:

(v. 9) **"Then they will deliver you to tribulation** [*thlipsin*]**, and will kill you."**

(v. 21) **"For then there will be a great tribulation** [*thlipsis*]**, such as has not occurred since the beginning of the world until now, nor ever will."**

(v. 29) **"But immediately after the tribulation** [*thlipsin*] **of those days THE SUN WILL BE DARKENED…"**

There are several problems with translating *thlipsis* in Matthew 24 as **tribulation** as some versions do (cf. NASB, ESV, CSB, NKJV). First, the best Bible version accurately translate the original Greek text into common everyday English. Therefore, because the word **tribulation** is hardly ever used in normal modern English, it should be avoided if possible.

Second, many Christians interpret **tribulation** as "suffering" or "hardship" in general. But this is <u>not</u> what the English word means. *Webster's Dictionary* defines "tribulation" as "distress or suffering <u>resulting from oppression or persecution</u>."

Therefore, even in proper English, **tribulation** does <u>not mean</u> "distress and suffering" <u>in general</u>, but specifically that which results from "<u>persecution</u>." But most English speakers do not equate the word **tribulation** specifically with "persecution." Therefore, when they read **tribulation** in the versions listed above in Matthew 24, they are likely to misunderstand what Jesus meant.

Third, the most common use of the noun *thlipsis* and its verb *thlibō* in the NT refers specifically to the persecution of Christians (38 of its 56 uses [22]). For example, Luke wrote of **those who had been scattered by the <u>persecution</u>** [*thlipseōs*] **that broke out when Stephen was killed** (Acts 11:19 NIV). Therefore, when *thlipsis* is used in Matthew 24, it is likely that it also refers to **persecution**.

Fourth, this is precisely what the context of Matthew 24 confirms. In verse 9 Jesus said, **"Then you will be handed over to be persecuted** [*thlipsin*] **and put to death, and you will be hated by all nations because of me** (NIV, cf. NLT, NET, CSB). Christ's meaning in verse 9 is clearly **persecution**. In Luke's version of this statement, he confirms that Jesus meant **persecution** by using the Greek word *diōxousin* here which means: "to harass someone, especially because of beliefs, *persecute*." [23] Accordingly, the NLT translates Luke 21:12 as **there will be a time of great persecution**.

Likewise, the context of the verses following in Matthew 24 is **persecution**. For example, in verses 15-20, Jesus is clearly describing the **persecution** of God's people:

> **"So when you see** [the Antichrist] **standing in the holy place** [causing] **'the abomination that causes desolation,' spoken of through the prophet Daniel—let the reader understand—then let those who are in Judea flee to the mountains.**
>
> **Let no one on the housetop go down to take anything out of the house. Let no one in the field go back to get their cloak. How dreadful it will be in those days for pregnant women and nursing mothers! Pray that your flight will not take place in winter or on the Sabbath."** (Matt 24:15-20 NIV)

Why does Jesus say that after Antichrist's **abomination that causes desolation**, that His people need to **flee**, escape with only the clothes on their back, and take **flight**? Because after Antichrist's Claim to be God in a rebuilt Jewish temple, The Greatest Persecution will immediately begin. This will be discussed further in the next chapter (4). But the above arguments are why the suggested translation of the next verse (21) is:

> **"Because then** [as a result of the **abomination of desolation**] **there will be the greatest persecution** [*megalē thlipsis*] **of God's elect people. It will be greater than any persecution since the world began, and it will never be equaled again."**

As noted, in verse 9, *thlipsis* is correctly translated as **persecution** in almost all Bible versions. The context leading up to verse 21 is clearly **persecution**. Therefore, **the greatest persecution** in all of human history is clearly the context of verse 21. Therefore, *megalē thlipsis* here should be translated as **the greatest persecution**. This will be the case throughout the *Endtimes Essentials*.

Likewise, then, the context of verse 29 is clearly **the greatest persecution** described in verse 21. Therefore, the suggested translation of verse 29-30 used throughout the *Endtimes Essentials* will be:

(29) "**Immediately after the completion of the greatest persecution [*thlipsin*] of those days, then 'the sun will be darkened, and the moon will not give its light; the stars will fall from the sky and the heavenly bodies will be shaken.'**

(30) **Then the sign that the Son of Man is coming will appear in the sky. And then all the peoples of the Earth will mourn when they see the Son of Man coming on the clouds of Heaven, with power and great glory.**"

The literal Greek in verse 29a reads: "Immediately after the *thlipsin* of those days..." Again, *thlipsin* is translated here as **persecution** because this is its most common meaning in the NT, and the **persecution** described in verses 9 and 21 are the context of verse 29. The **completion of the greatest persecution** is implied because Christ's Return described in verse 30 will stop the **persecution**.

The suggested translation of verse 29b above follows the NIV and verse 30 generally reflects the NLT. However, *ouranō* (**heavens**, NLT) is translated as **sky** because here it probably means: "firmament or *sky* over the earth." [24] **Earth** and **Heaven** are capitalized because they are deemed "proper nouns, such as specific people, places, or things." [25]

Unfortunately, other versions translate *thlipsis* in Matthew 24 verses 21 and 29 with more general terms such as **distress** (NIV), **anguish** (NLT), **suffering** (NRSV, NET, CEV), **trouble** (NCV, GNT), or the more obscure **tribulation** (NASB, ESV, CSB, KJV,

NKJV). This is so even when these versions translate *thlipsis* as **persecution** in verse 9 (e.g. NIV, NLT, NET, CSB).

Again, these translations imply that this period will simply be a time of suffering for everyone in the world. For reasons stated in this section, it is suggested these versions should have consistently translated *thlipsis* throughout Matthew 24 as **persecution**.

When Bible versions fail to do this in Matthew 24:21 they tend to make Christ state something false. For example, the NIV translates Jesus as saying: **For then** [after Antichrist's Claim to be God, v. 15] **there will be great distress, unequaled from the beginning of the world until now—and never to be equaled again** (Matt 24:21).

Is that true? Will humanity in general suffer the greatest **distress** it will ever experience, immediately after Antichrist's Claim to be God? Of course not. Christ's Wrath after Christ's Return (cf. Rev chs. 8-9, 16), or even Hell after that, will be the greatest **distress** humanity in general will ever experience. Therefore, Bible versions that do not correctly translate *thlipsis* in Matthew 24:21 as **the greatest persecution of God's elect people** tend to make Jesus say something false. [26]

What did Jesus really mean to say?

"Because then there will be the greatest persecution of God's elect people. It will be greater than any persecution since the world began, and it will never be equaled again" (Matt 24:21).

That is a true statement and it correctly reflects the meaning and context of *thlipsis* in this passage. [27] Therefore, Christ was warning of The Greatest Persecution of the Church, not just a "great tribulation" for the world.

Understanding the above helps us recognize an error in Pre-tribulationism. This view is based on a distortion of the meaning of *thlipsis*. In Pre-tribulationism the more misleading word "tribulation" is used to translate *thlipsis*. The obscurity of what the word "tribulation" means allows Pre-tribulationism to promote several errors.

First, it has essentially redefined the term "tribulation" to mean Christ's Wrath on the Earth. But the Greek word *thlipsis* never meant "wrath." Likewise, *Webster's* never defines "tribulation" as "wrath."

Secondly, Pre-tribulationism uses the word "tribulation" to label the entire period of the Endtimes as "the tribulation." More specifically, it labels the beginning of the Endtimes "the tribulation" and the latter part "the great tribulation."

These two errors lead to the foundational error of claiming that the entire period of the Endtimes is Christ's Wrath. Why is this misleading? Because there are NT promises that the Church will not experience Christ's Wrath. The Church is **to wait for his Son from heaven ... Jesus, who rescues us from the coming wrath** (1 Thess 1:10 NIV; cf. 5:9; Rom 5:9; Col 3:6).

Therefore, Pre-tribulationism claims the Church must be Rescued before "the tribulation" or any Endtime events begin because it is Christ's Wrath. But again, these conclusions are based on the error of mistranslating *thlipsis* in Christ's Endtimes Teaching and wrongly equating "tribulation" with "wrath." This error and the biblical teaching about the nature and timing of Christ's Wrath will be discussed further in chapter 14.

Contrary to Pre-tribulationism, how did Jesus label the various periods of Endtime events? First He described the initial Endtime events, including **wars ... famines and earthquakes** (Matt 24:6-7). Then He said, **"All these are the beginning of birth pains"** (v. 8). Therefore, we should follow Christ and call the initial period of the Endtimes The Beginning of Birth Pains instead of "the tribulation." This will be the case throughout the *Endtimes Essentials*.

Christ then described the next stage of Endtime events (after the Antichrist's Claim to be God), and called it **the greatest persecution** (*megalē thlipsis*). Again, we should follow Christ and call the Endtime period that follows **the beginning of birth pains**, The Greatest Persecution, not the more obscure term "great tribulation." This will be the case throughout the *Endtimes Essentials*.

Therefore, it is also suggested that we discard the misleading use of the labels "tribulation" and "great tribulation" in our discussions of the Endtimes. Instead, let us use the labels Christ used: The Beginning of Birth Pains (cf. Matt 24:8), The Greatest Persecution (cf. Matt 24:21), and **the wrath of the Lamb** (Rev 6:16) or Christ's Wrath. Jesus clearly said His visible Return will occur **immediately after**

the completion of the greatest persecution [*thlipsin*]. Therefore, it is more clear to say that Christ's Return is "post-persecution," rather than "post-tribulational."

All of this will be made more clear in the next chapter.

---

[1] The Olivet Discourse is repeated almost verbatim in Mark 13. On other occasions, Jesus taught similar things that are recorded in Luke. We choose Matthew's version over Mark's because there is slightly more detail. The unique emphases of Christ's Endtimes Teaching recorded by Luke will be addressed in ch. 12, sec. B where Preterism is discussed.

[2] Carson, "Matthew" in *EBC*.

[3] *MNTC*, Matthew. Surprisingly and ironically, Dr. MacArthur adheres to Pre-tribulationism which is a prime example of the distorting "theological system or interpretive scheme" he is warning of. This should humble us all as a reminder that even the most godly, biblical, and influential Bible Teachers can be in error.

[4] For example, the Amillennialist Kim Riddlebarger writes in support of a typical diminishing of The Beginning of Birth Pains as a sign of Christ's Return:
> In order to answer their questions, Jesus set forth a series of signs of the end, which he described as the "beginning of birth pains" (v. 8)... The "things mentioned here have characterized the entire church age, the intervening period between the first coming of Jesus and his return" [Hagner, *Matt*, 692]... These signs are not given to us so that well-intentioned Bible prophecy experts can correlate current events to the immediate coming of Christ. (164)

However, Riddlebarger does admit in one small phrase with no further comment: "These signs ... will come in greater frequency and more intensity" (165). Of the end? The author does not care to say because he does not seem to care enough about Christ's intention in His Teaching.

[5] One resource relates regarding "Historicisim":
> In Christian eschatology, **historicism** is a method of interpretation of biblical prophecies which associates symbols with historical persons, nations or events... Almost all Protestant Reformers from the Reformation into the 19th century held historicist views... Historicists believe that prophetic interpretation reveals the entire course of history of the church from the writing of the Book of Daniel, some centuries before the close of the 1st century, to the end of time. https://en.wikipedia.org/wiki/Historicism_(Christianity)

[6] For more on **this generation** (Matt 24:34) see ch. 12, sec. B.2.

7 See the Wikipedia article: "List of Wars and Anthropogenic Disasters by Death Toll." The article documents the median estimate of 380 million killed in 115 wars, 50 million in "war crimes, massacres, and ancient war atrocities," 62 million in "genocides, ethnic cleansing, and religious persecutions," 10 million from "political purges and oppressions," and 180 million in "outbreaks of disease and famine." This equals about 700 million.

8 MacArthur, *MNTC*, Revelation, 185. For a biblical evaluation of Preterism, see *Christ's Endtimes Teaching*, ch. 12, sec. B.

9 Pre-tribulation scholars are most prone to beginning their study and explanation of Endtime events in Daniel instead of Christ's Endtimes Teaching.

For example, Alva J. McClain, founder of Grace Theological Seminary and an influential teacher of Pre-tribulationism wrote that the three verses in Daniel 9:24-27 are "the indispensable chronological key to all New Testament prophecy" (*Daniel's Prophecy of the 70 Weeks* [Zondervan, 1969], 10). This simply is not true.

Likewise, the Pre-tribulationist John Walvoord writes regarding Daniel chapter 9:

> Because of the comprehensive and structural nature of Daniel's prophecies, both for the Gentiles and for Israel, the study of Daniel, and especially this chapter, is the key to understanding the prophetic Scriptures (*Daniel*, 201).

Contrary to both of these Pre-tribulational authors, the "key" to understanding the substance and sequence of Endtime events is studying Christ's Endtimes Teaching.

10 The survey of Protestant Pastors on the Endtimes can be found online at https://news.lifeway.com/2016/04/26/pastors-the-end-of-the-world-is-complicated/

11 Data on Tim Lahaye's *Left Behind* series can be found online at https://www.washingtonpost.com/news/act-four/wp/2016/07/13/the-left-behind-series-was-just-the-latest-way-america-prepared-for-the-rapture/

12 The Pre-tribulationist Wiersbe attempts to argue that Jesus did change His audience in the middle of this sermon. Starting at Matt 24:45 he writes:

> We noted that the "atmosphere" of the first section of the Olivet Discourse [Matt 24:1-44] was definitely Jewish. A careful reading of this section indicates that the "atmosphere" has changed... It seems reasonable to assign Matthew 24:45–25:30 to our present age of the church, during which time it appears that the Lord is delaying His return (2 Peter 3)...

We must not be surprised that our Lord suddenly changed from discussing His return as it relates to Israel to His return as it relates to the church. It is not uncommon in Scripture for a speaker or writer to change emphasis [but not audience!] right in the middle of a sentence.

For example, the entire church age occurs in the time period between the words "given" and "and" in Isaiah 9:6. A similar "leap" is seen in Isaiah 61:2, where the church age takes place in the period between the "year of the Lord" and the "day of vengeance."

Wiersbe is claiming that Jesus' audience up to verse 45 was the Jews. After that, he claims Christ's audience was the Church. How convenient when the first part of the sermon predicted suffering! Wiersbe suggests the reason to believe there is such a break is that at v. 45ff Jesus talked about "delaying His return." But wasn't His Return delayed for restoring the nation of Israel as well? There simply is no justification for a change of audience in the text of the Sermon.

In the second paragraph Wiersbe's examples are not valid. The Isaiah passages are prophecies in which events are described that have large gaps of time between them. This is not biblical justification nor a biblical example of a biblical author changing the audience they are addressing in the middle of their address without any indication of doing so.

[13] Most scholars agree that Jesus' teaching about His Return in John 14:1-6 applies to the Church. Like the Olivet Discourse, Jesus gave this teaching at the same time (His final week on Earth), to the same people (the Apostles), about the same topic (His Return). If John 14:1-6 applies to the Church, then there is no reason to deny Christ's Endtimes Teaching does also.

Likewise, in that same teaching Jesus used Jewish terminology when He warned the Apostles of the Church that: **They will put you out of the synagogue; in fact, the time is coming when anyone who kills you will think they are offering a service to God** (John 16:2). But few scholars would claim that because of the Jewish terminology here, this extended teaching of Christ only applies to Endtime Jews. Therefore, the Jewish terminology in Matthew 24 (**Judea, sabbath,** vs. 16, 20) should be interpreted the same.

[14] MacArthur, *Matthew,* at Matt 24:22. Unfortunately, MacArthur uncharacteristically offers no arguments for this interpretation of **the elect** in his Matthew commentary.

[15] For an explanation of the suggested translation of Matt 24:21 as **the greatest persecution**, see sec. E below.

[16] For an explanation of the suggested translation of Matt 24:30-31 see ch. 4, sec. C.

17 Thomas remarks on Rev 17:14: "'Called,' 'elect,' and 'faithful' can apply only to saints, not to angels" (1345).

18 The KJV and NKJV have another instance of *eklektous* at Matthew 20:16. This is because the more recent and few manuscripts of the *Textus Receptus* had this reading. However, the older and much greater number of NT manuscripts making up the *Nestle-Aland* or *United Bible Society* apparatuses reveal that this was an addition added by later copyists.

19 It was stated: "Nowhere is there a single instance in the NT where *eklektous* or its related terms are used in a way that excludes the Church." However, one will notice in Matt 24:31 that there is some variation in Christ's meaning for *eklektous* in His Endtimes Teaching.

In vs. 22, 24 it includes Israel as they will be included in The Greatest Persecution. But in v. 31 *eklektous* does not include Israel because lifting the Israelites into the sky to meet the Lord will not be part of God's plan at this time. What the Angels do for the Jews at the time Christ appears is described in Rev 7:3-4 where a protective **seal** will be put **on the foreheads of ... 144,000 from all the tribes of Israel** because they will remain on the Earth during Christ's Wrath.

Therefore, *eklektous* in v. 31 refers only to the Church and its Rescue.

Likewise, it was pointed out that in Rom 11:7, *eklektous* is used to refer to only the Church and excludes Israel.

Still, there is no instance in the NT where *eklektous* refers to people that it does not refer to Christians in the Church, as Pre-tribulationism needs to claim to make their view valid.

20 The *NIDNTT*, a highly respected Greek reference work, comments on the use of *eklektous* in the Olivet Discourse and notes: "[I]n the 'little apocalypse' the church is spoken of as the elect" (I.541).

Likewise, NT scholar D. A. Carson warns about the "Rigid application of [a] doubtful disjunction between Jews and church" in Christ's Endtimes Teaching. He adds concerning Matthew 24:

> Much dispensationalism [which Pre-tribulationism is based on], especially the older kind, holds that the "Rapture" is not mentioned in this chapter and justifies this view on the ground that Jesus is not talking to the church but to Jews. Dispensationalists use this disjunction to justify a number of theological points, but they are insensitive to historical realities. Even after Pentecost the earliest church was entirely Jewish. Here, Jesus is addressing... his Jewish disciples who will constitute the church. (at Matt 24:1).

21 Carson, 564; cf. Osborne "the true believers," 1279; France, 916.

22 The Greek noun *thlipsis* is used 45 times in the NT. It's related verb *thlibō* is used 11 times (for a total of 56 times). Both words originally and literally mean "pressing, pressure" (*BDAG*). Accordingly, *thlibō* is used once to refer

to people **crowding** Jesus (Mark 3:9), and once to refer to a **narrow** road (Matt 7:14). Only once in the NT does *thlipsis* mean "an inward experience of distress" (*BDAG* #2; cf. 2 Cor 2:4).

However, *Vine's* explains: "Both the verb [*thlibō*] and the noun [*thlipsis*], when used of the present experience of believers, refer almost invariably to that which comes upon them from without" (17). This is the meaning of the remaining 53 uses of these words in the NT. Those uses can be divided into two meanings: 1) general suffering; 2) persecution from people.

Mounce explains the latter meaning regarding the related verb *thlibō*:
> Figuratively *thlibō* describes the pressure of worldly persecutions common to all people (1 Tim 5:10), but it is usually related to the persecutions specific to believers. In the middle of a list of physical afflictions, the author of Hebrews describes the OT saints as "persecuted" for their faith (Heb 11:37; [thereby using *thlibō* to distinguish persecution from other kinds of suffering]. (508).

Unfortunately, many Bible versions translate these Greek words with English words that, to many, mean something like "general suffering." However, in these texts the biblical author intended to mean specifically the persecution of God's people.

For example, the NASB translates *thlibō* and *thlipsis* as **afflict, afflicted**, or **affliction(s)** 27 times in the NT. *Webster's* defines "afflict" as "to cause pain or suffering." It gives the example of "people *afflicted* with arthritis." Likewise, modern English speakers understand "affliction" to mean suffering in general.

But in 20 of those 27 instances in the NASB, the context or meaning of *thlibō* or *thlipsis* is the **persecution** of God's people by wicked people, not "affliction" or suffering in general. For example, the NASB translates 1 Thess 3:4 as follows: **For indeed when we were with you, we kept telling you in advance that we were going to suffer affliction.** Likewise, the ESV and NET do that same. Other versions have **suffer** (NCV, CEV) or the obscure word **tribulation** (KJV, NKJV), or **troubles** (NLT).

But what is the context of 1 Thess 3:4? Paul wrote earlier: **You suffered the same things from your own compatriots as they did from the Jews, who killed both the Lord Jesus and the prophets, and drove us out** (2:14-15 NASB). This is describing the persecution of God's people. Therefore, in 3:4 when Paul says, **we kept telling you in advance that we were going to suffer *thlipsis*** he did not mean general affliction, suffering, or trouble as these Bible versions imply. Therefore, the NIV is more accurate which reads: **In fact, when we were with you, we kept telling you that we would be persecuted** [*thlipsis*] (1 Thess 3:4 NIV, see also CSB, NRSV, GNT).

Unfortunately, the NASB repeats this distortion throughout the NT.

Again, 20 out of 27 times the context or meaning of *thlibō* or *thlipsis* is the **persecution** of God's people by wicked people. But the NASB uses the more general term for suffering: "affliction." These verses include: (Acts 7:10; 20:23; 2 Cor 1:4 (2), 6, 8; 2:4; 4:8, 17; 6:4; 7:4, 5; 8:2; 1 Thess 3:3, 4, 7; 2 Thess 1:4, 6, 7; Heb 11:37).

Likewise, there are 20 instances in the NASB where *thlipsis* is translated **tribulation**. However, as pointed out in this chapter (sec. E), this word even in English means "persecution."

As noted, in all, the NT uses *thlipsis* and *thlibō* 56 times. It is suggested that 38 of those times, it should be translated as the **persecution** of God's people. The NASB does this only once in Acts 11:19.

Vine's demonstrates an incorrect translation of *thlipsis* when it states: "It is used of the calamities of war, Matt 24:21, 29" (17). On the contrary, the immediate context is clearly persecution (cf. 9, 16-20).

23 *BDAG*, #2.

24 *BDAG*, #1.b.

25   https://www.britannica.com/dictionary/eb/qa/When-to-Capitalize-Nouns.

26 For more on the sequence of Endtime events in Christ's Endtimes Teaching see *Additional Studies on the Endtimes* (*ASE*) ch. 5, "The Sequence of Events in Matthew 24 & its Use of *Tote*."

27 Mark's version reads: **"those will be days of persecution [*thlipsis*] unequaled from the beginning, when God created the world, until now—and never to be equaled again"** (Mark 13:19). In addition, Mark writes: **"But in those days, following that persecution** [*thlipsin*] (v. 24). Mark agrees with Matthew.

However, Luke uses different Greek words in his version. In 21:12 we read, **"But before all this, they will seize you and persecute** [*diōxousin*] **you**." The Greek word here means: "to harass someone, especially because of beliefs, *persecute*" (*BDAG* #2).

But then, when referring to the same period of time, Luke writes in verse 23: **"There will be great distress [*ananke*] in the land and wrath against this people.**" The basic meaning of this word is "pressure" (*BDAG* #1 & #2). Therefore, there may be some relationship to *thlipsis* which in ancient Greek was used literally to mean "pressing, pressure" (*BDAG*). Therefore, an underlying meaning of both *ananke* and *thlipsis* is "pressure." In addition, *ananke* can refer to "torture" (*BDAG* #3), reflecting Matthew's and Mark's use of *thlipsis* in the same sayings of Jesus.

This is supported by another fact. Matthew and Mark clearly mention persecution earlier in the teaching (cf. Matt 24:9; Mark 13:9) and then refer to the same persecution later in the teaching (cf. Matt 24:21, 29; Mark 13:19;24).

It would seem Luke is doing the same, clearly mentioning persecution earlier in the teaching (cf. 21:12) and referring to the same persecution later in the teaching (v. 23).

However, it must be admitted that Luke perhaps intended to emphasize something else in Christ's Endtimes Teaching. Scholars have recognized that Luke's version focuses more on the Endtime experience of the Jews than Matthew's and Mark's versions. His mention of the **wrath against this people** (21:23) points to the punishment of Israel that will occur in Endtime events. Luke's intention may be reflected in that he never uses the word *eklektous* (the elect) to describe the people experiencing the events in Christ's Endtimes Teaching.

It is understandable that both Preterism and Pre-tribulationism prioritize the use of Luke's version of Christ's Endtimes Teaching. The former uses it to claim these things were primarily fulfilled in the attack on Jerusalem in A.D. 70. The latter use Luke to support the view that Christ's Endtimes Teaching applies primarily to the Jews and not at all to the Church.

Of course some things in Christ's Endtimes Teaching were partially fulfilled in A.D. 70. But it was merely a foreshadowing of the complete and final fulfillment that is yet future. Of course the Jews will be involved in the events Christ predicted, and persecuted along with the Church. But if we allow Matthew and Mark to influence our interpretation of Luke, we should be very slow to label this teaching as merely "Jewish."

Part II

Christ's Endtimes Teaching
The biblical sequence of Endtime events

Chapter 4
The Sequence of Endtime Events According to Jesus Christ
Matthew 24

Contents

A) Section 1. Jesus' overview of Endtimes events (vs. 4-14)

B) Section 2: The Antichrist's Claim to be God resulting in The Greatest Persecution of the Church (vs. 15-28)

C) Section 3: Christ's Return & the Church's Rescue: (vs. 29-31)

D) A summary of the sequence of Endtime events in Christ's Endtimes Teaching

Primary Points

- Jesus clearly taught the following sequence of Endtime events, which the Church will experience: 1) First, The Beginning of Birth Pains, including wars, famines, and plagues; 2) Then Antichrist's Greatest Persecution; 3) Then, the very obvious and visible Return of Christ; and 4) Then the Church's Rescue ("rapture").

- Matthew 24:31 is describing the Church's Rescue ("rapture")

[Read Matthew 24:1-31. Understand it in light of the fact that God's elect people, including Christians in the Church, will experience all that Christ predicts. Also, notice and underline the references to time ("then," "when," "after," etc.) and the sequence in the text.]

The purpose of this chapter is to discover a particular sequence of Endtime events taught by Christ. Matthew 24:4-31 can be divided into three sections which reflect this sequence of Endtime events: [1]

Section 1 (vs. 4-14): Jesus' overview of Endtime events.

Section 2 (vs. 15-21): The Antichrist's abomination of desolation resulting in The Greatest Persecution of the Church.

Section 3 (vs. 29-31): Christ's Return and the Church's Rescue ("rapture").

A) Section 1: Jesus' overview of Endtime events: *(vs. 4-14)*

In the following broad overview of Endtime events in Matthew 24:4-14, Jesus will describe three main events:

1) The Beginning of Birth Pains (wars, famines, etc.; vs. 4-8).
2) Persecution of God's people (vs. 9-13).
3) **Then the end will come** (v. 14).

[Read Matthew 24:3-14. Notice the broad overview of the substance and sequence of Endtime events]

Jesus said before His Second Coming there will be disastrous events on the Earth. These will include **wars** and **famines** and **earthquakes** (vs. 5-7). [2] In Luke's version He mentions **plagues** (Luke 21:11 NLT). Jesus summarized these events by saying "**All these are the beginning of birth pains**" (Matt 24:8 NIV). Then Christ said, "**Then**" God's people "**will be handed over to be persecuted**" (v. 9 NIV; cf. vs. 10-13). And then Jesus said, "**Then the end will come**" (v. 14 NIV). [3]

Christ's reference to the **end** refers to the original question the disciples had asked in verse 3: "**What will be the sign of your coming and of the end of the age?**" (NIV). The **end of the age** will be His Second Coming. Accordingly, the sequence of these three main events described in verses 4-14 can be depicted in the following graphic.

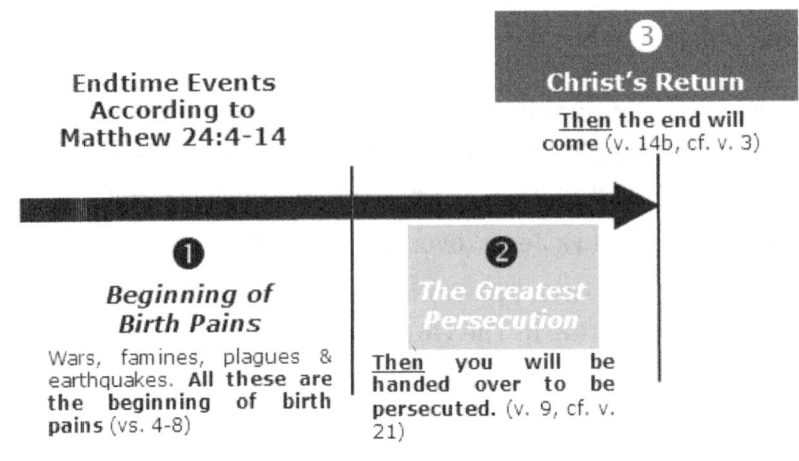

Endtime Events According to Matthew 24:4-14

❸ Christ's Return
Then the end will come (v. 14b, cf. v. 3)

❶ Beginning of Birth Pains
Wars, famines, plagues & earthquakes. **All these are the beginning of birth pains** (vs. 4-8)

❷ The Greatest Persecution
Then you will be handed over to be persecuted. (v. 9, cf. v. 21)

B) Section 2: The Antichrist's Claim to be God resulting in The Greatest Persecution of the Church *(vs. 15-28)*

We have seen that Christ gave an overview of Endtime events in Matthew 24:4-14. He began by describing **the beginning of birth pains** (v. 8 NIV), then said His people will be **persecuted** (vs. 9-14a), and then said, **then the end will come** (v. 14b NIV).

Often in prophetic Scripture, we are given a broad overview of events and then given more details about those events. Such is the case here. In vs. 9-13 Jesus referred to the persecution of His people as a part of Endtime events. As we read those verses, they prompt an important question. What will cause such an intense world-wide hatred and persecution of Christians?

It would not seem that **wars, famines, and earthquakes** (vs. 6-7 NIV) would lead to this. In fact, as demonstrated throughout Church history, Christians will be at the forefront of relief efforts during this time. Therefore, we are not surprised that Jesus went on in His Endtimes Teaching to explain more about the cause and nature of The Greatest Persecution. Starting at v. 15 He momentarily stopped explaining the remaining sequence of Endtime events to do this.

[Read Matthew 24:15-28 and note Christ's more detailed description of The Greatest Persecution. Notice what causes the persecution]

What will cause The Greatest Persecution? Jesus said when people in Jerusalem **"see standing in the holy place 'the abomination that causes desolation,' ... then let those who are in Judea flee to the mountains"** (vs. 15-16 NIV). This is because The Greatest Persecution led by the Antichrist will have begun.

The **abomination that causes desolation** (v. 15) refers to Daniel's description of the Antichrist entering a rebuilt Jerusalem temple and spiritually polluting it (cf. Dan 9:27). According Paul, this is when, **the man of lawlessness ... sets himself up in God's temple, proclaiming himself to be God** (2 Thess 2:3-4 NIV). Therefore, throughout the *Endtimes Essentials* the **abomination of desolation** is referred to as Antichrist's Claim to be God.

When the Antichrist does this, he will begin The Greatest Persecution of God's people because they will refuse to worship him. This is why Jesus went on to say:

"Pray that your flight will not take place in winter or on the Sabbath. Because then there will be the greatest persecution [*thlipsis*] **of God's elect people** [*eklektous*]. **It will be greater than any persecution since the world began, and it will never be equaled again"** (vs. 20-21).

For reasons given in the previous chapter (3, sec. E), the Greek word *thlipsis* is translated as **persecution** in the above suggested translation. The insertion of **God's elect people** reflects who will be persecuted. In the next verse Jesus said, **for the sake of God's elect people** [*eklektous*] **those days will be shortened** (v. 22 NIV). As also explained in the previous chapter (ch. 3, sec. D) the Greek word *eklektous* is used in the NT to refer to the Church.

Christ's use of **then** (*tote*, v. 21 NIV) clearly reflects His desire to teach a sequence of events. He shared the cause of the **persecution** noted in verse 9, as being **the abomination of desolation** in verse 15. Therefore, in verse 21, He was saying that The Greatest Persecution would follow Antichrist's Claim to be God. Accordingly, we can add Antichrist's Claim to be God to Christ's sequence of Endtime events as reflected in the following graphic.

Endtime Events According to Matthew 24:4-28

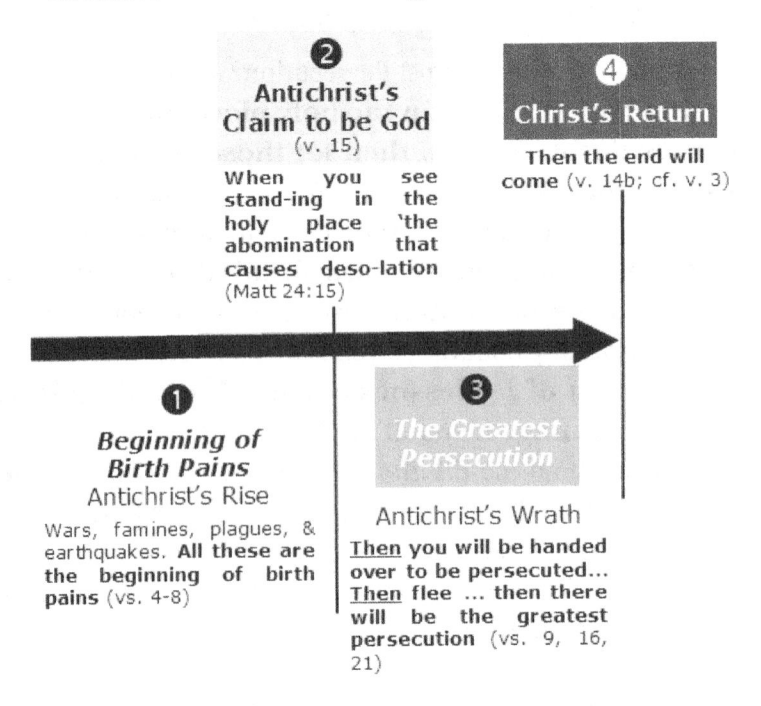

❷ Antichrist's Claim to be God (v. 15)

When you see stand-ing in the holy place 'the abomination that causes deso-lation (Matt 24:15)

❹ Christ's Return

Then the end will come (v. 14b; cf. v. 3)

❶ Beginning of Birth Pains
Antichrist's Rise

Wars, famines, plagues, & earthquakes. **All these are the beginning of birth pains** (vs. 4-8)

❸ The Greatest Persecution

Antichrist's Wrath

Then you will be handed over to be persecuted... **Then** flee ... then there will be the greatest persecution (vs. 9, 16, 21)

C) Section 3: Christ's Return & the Church's Rescue: *(vs. 29-31)*

[Read Matthew 24:29-31. Notice especially the description of the Church's Rescue ("rapture") in v. 31]

A suggested translation of this critical text would be:

²⁹ "Immediately <u>after</u> the completion of the greatest persecution, <u>then</u> 'the sun will be darkened, and the moon will not give its light; the stars will fall from the sky and the heavenly bodies will be shaken.'

³⁰ Then the sign that the Son of Man is coming will appear in the sky. And then all the peoples of the Earth will mourn when they see the Son of Man coming on the clouds of Heaven, with power and great glory. 4

³¹ And He will send out His angels with a loud trumpet sound, and they will lift up and gather together God's elect people from one end of the sky to the other, from everywhere on Earth."

The suggested translation of verses 29-30 was explained in the previous chapter (3, secs. D-E). Verse 31 is generally a combination of the NASB and NLT. **Sound** translates the Greek word *salpingos* meaning: "the sound made or signal given by a trumpet." 5 **Lift up** is implied by the fact that Christians are being lifted from the **Earth** into the **sky**.

Sky translates the Greek word *ouranōn* ("heavens") which here means: "as firmament or *sky* over the earth." 6 Accordingly, NASB translates it as **from one end of the sky to the other**. The **sky** will be the place of **gather**ing which is why Angels are being used. **Gather together** translates *episynaxousin* which is a "strengthened" form of "to gather," meaning: "to bring together, *gather (together)*." 7

From everywhere on Earth translates the literal Greek "from the four winds." This imagery is used elsewhere in the OT to refer to everywhere on earth (cf. Zech 2:6). Accordingly, Mark's version of Christ's teaching reads: **And he will send his angels and gather his elect from the four winds, <u>from the ends of the earth</u>** [*gēs*] **to the ends of the heavens** (Mark 13:27 NIV). The Greek word here (*gēs*) means: "surface of the earth as the habitation of humanity." 8

Thus, the suggested translation of Matthew 24:31 used is:
"And He will send out His angels with a loud trumpet sound, and they will lift up and gather together God's elect people from one end of the sky to the other, from everywhere on Earth." (Matt 24:31).

These verses clear up so much of the confusion about the sequence of Endtime events. We have said throughout our study of Christ's Endtimes Teaching that He was intentionally sharing a specific sequence of Endtime events. We have seen this in verses 4-28, and the next three verses are no exception. Clearly Christ is about to describe events that are **"Immediately after the completion of the greatest persecution"** (v. 29).

The sequence of events that Jesus taught is clear. In verse 21 Jesus said there will be The Greatest Persecution. Starting in verse 29 He taught what will happen **"Immediately after the completion of the greatest persecution."** This statement was made with remarkable precision. It implies that one stage of Endtime events will be completed, and another will follow. Now we can make several very valuable conclusions about the sequence of Endtime events.

C.1) Christ's Return will occur immediately after the completion of The Greatest Persecution & will be visible to the entire world (vs. 29-30)

There are several features of Christ's Return described here. First its timing: **"Immediately after the completion of the greatest persecution"** (v. 29). Therefore, Christ will not return for His Church until after Antichrist's Greatest Persecution.

Secondly, Christ's Return will be very obvious and visible. Christ said, **For as lightning that comes from the east is visible even in the west, so will be the coming of the Son of Man** (Matt 24:27 NIV). Likewise, at Christ's Return for **God's elect people** (v. 31), the Church, there will be Cosmic Signs in the **sun**, **moon**, and **stars** (v. 29). **Then the sign that the Son of Man is coming will appear in the sky. And then all the peoples of the Earth will mourn when they see the Son of Man coming on the clouds of Heaven, with power and great glory** (vs. 29-30). [9]

Cosmic Signs in the **sun, moon,** and **stars** (v. 29) will accompany Christ's Return. It might be assumed that these amazing and obvious events will be **the sign** of Christ's Return that the disciples had asked about (v. 3). However, Jesus went on to say after the Cosmic Signs, **Then the sign that the Son of Man is coming will appear in the sky** (v. 30). This **sign** is probably the Glory Cloud that is described throughout Scripture as indicating the presence of God. [10] Luke's version makes this more evident where Jesus says: **"At that time they will see the Son of Man coming in a cloud with power and great glory"** (Luke 21:27 NIV).

Earlier in the text Christ said The Greatest Persecution will be **cut short** (v. 22 NIV) or stopped. What event comes after The Greatest Persecution and stops it? Christ's Return. Therefore, verses 29-30 tell us that The Greatest Persecution of **God's elect people** in the Church will be stopped by Christ's Visible Return.

C.2) The Church's Rescue ("rapture") will occur at the time of Christ's Visible Return (v. 31)

What follows in Matthew 24 is one of the most important, astounding, overlooked, and misunderstood statements in Scripture. [11]

Contrary to what many believe in the Church today, Jesus Christ did teach about the "rapture" of the Church. But first, let us see how the Apostle Paul described this event:

> **For the Lord himself will come down from heaven, with a loud command, with the voice of the archangel and with the trumpet call of God, and the dead in Christ will rise first. After that, we who are still alive and are left will be caught up together with them in the clouds to meet the Lord in the air.** (1 Thess 4:16-17 NIV)

Virtually all Bible scholars agree that this text is describing what has been called the "rapture" of the Church. **Caught up** translates a Greek word (*harpagēsometha*) meaning "to grab or seize suddenly so as to remove or gain control, *snatch/take away*." [12] This is a common word in the NT. [13] So, how did we get the weird word "rapture" from this text?

In the late 4th century the Church used the popular Latin Vulgate version of the Bible. It translated the Greek word for "take away" into the Latin word *rapiemur* (pronounced rap'-ee-a-mer). Based on the Latin, some popular Bible commentaries in the 18th century, began using the invented word "rapture" to refer to this event. [14] Since its invention, this odd word has become popular in Christianity to refer to the Church's Rescue in the Endtimes.

However, weird and obscure words that are not in the Bible should not be used to explain Christian truth. Therefore, throughout the *Endtimes Essentials* the "rapture" will be referred to as the Church's Rescue because this is how the Bible describes it.

For example, Jesus said to the Church, **So when all these things begin to happen** [Cosmic Signs and Christ's Return], **stand and look up, because your rescue is drawing near** (Luke 21:28). **Rescue** translates a Greek word (*apolytrōsis*) which means "release from a captive condition, *release, redemption, deliverance.*" [15] Likewise, Paul wrote that the Church is **to wait for his Son from heaven … Jesus, who rescues** [*rhyomenon*, "to rescue from danger" [16]] **us from the coming wrath** (1 Thess 1:10 NIV). Therefore, **rescue** is a much more accurate, clear, and biblical word than "rapture" to describe this Endtime event.

Now, back to the text above from 1 Thessalonians. Read it again. Now, notice how Jesus described this same event in Matthew 24:31:

> **"And He will send out His angels with a loud trumpet sound, and they will lift up and gather together God's elect people from one end of the sky to the other, from everywhere on Earth."** (Matt 24:31).

First, did you notice that both Jesus and the Apostle described the **sound** of a **trumpet** occurring at the Church's Rescue? Secondly, both passages describe **God's elect people** being **caught up** or **lift**ed **up and gather**ed **together** into **the sky** to **meet the Lord in the air**. As discussed further in the next chapter, this is important evidence that Jesus and Paul were describing the same event.

As noted above, Christ clearly taught that His Visible Return will occur **"Immediately after the completion of the greatest persecution"** (v. 29). Then in verse 31 Jesus added that the Church's Rescue will also occur at the time of Christ's Visible Return. Therefore,

Christ's Visible Return occurs at the same time as the Church's Rescue (vs. 30-31). And both Christ's Return and the Church's Rescue occur **immediately** after **the completion of the greatest persecution of God's elect people** (vs. 29, 31).

Many Christians today would be surprised to know that Christ described the Church's Rescue ("rapture") in His Endtimes Teaching. But why would we be surprised by this? This is the longest and most detailed teaching in the NT on the Endtimes and Christ's Return. He described **the beginning of birth pains** (Matt 24:8), the **abomination that causes desolation** (v. 15), the **greatest persecution** (v. 21), the Cosmic Signs (v. 29), and His Second Coming (v. 30). Why would we expect Him to leave out a mention of the Church's Rescue that is described elsewhere in Scripture (cf. 1 Thess 4:13-18; Rev 7:9, 14)? We would not. [17]

Finally, for those who have wondered how Christians will be translated from the Earth to meet Jesus in the sky, Jesus explained it. **Angels** (24:31) will be appearing with Christ and physically (but gently, we're sure) grabbing believers, lifting them from the Earth, and carrying them to be with Jesus. [18] And as we are lifted up, our bodies will be transformed. The Apostle Paul explained:

> **Let me reveal to you a wonderful secret. We will not all die, but we will all be transformed! It will happen in a moment, in the blink of an eye, when the last trumpet is blown.**
>
> **For when the trumpet sounds** [the **loud trumpet sound** in Matt 24:31!], **those who have died will be raised to live forever. And we who are living will also be** [Rescued and] **transformed.** (1 Cor 15:51-52 NLT; cf. 1 Thess 4:15-17).

That will be a glorious thing! And did you notice that Paul again repeated the mention of a **trumpet sound** occurring at the time of the Church's Rescue and Resurrection, just like Jesus did. Therefore, we have three references to a **trumpet sound** accompanying Christ's Return and the Church's Rescue (cf. Matt 24:31; 1 Thess 4:16; 1 Cor 15:52).

All of the above corrects several popular errors about the Endtimes that will be discussed further in the following chapters. However, one of those errors can be mentioned here. Many Christians have been led to believe that the Church's Rescue will be some kind of "secret, silent, rapture" in which no one on Earth will know what has occurred.

In Matthew 24:29-31 Jesus clearly corrected that error. When **He will send out His angels** to **lift up and gather together God's elect people from one end of the sky to the other, from everywhere on Earth ... all the peoples of the Earth will ... see the Son of Man coming**, and there will be **a loud trumpet sound**. The idea of a "secret, silent, rapture" of the Church is <u>not</u> biblical.

C.3) Christ's Wrath comes after the Antichrist's Wrath (vs. 37-41)

The same sequence of events is confirmed in Luke's version of Christ's Endtimes Teaching. There, Jesus says:

> **There will be signs in the sun, moon, and stars. On the earth, nations will be in anguish and perplexity at the roaring and tossing of the sea. People will faint from terror, apprehensive of what is coming on the world, for the heavenly bodies will be shaken.**
>
> **At that time they will see the Son of Man coming in a cloud with power and great glory. So when all these things begin to happen, stand and look up, because <u>your rescue</u> is drawing near.** (Luke 21:25-28 [19])

Rescue from what? Wrath. Both the Antichrist's wrath and the real Christ's Wrath. First, Christ's Return will **rescue** Christ's Church from the Antichrist's Wrath in The Greatest Persecution. [20] Therefore, The Greatest Persecution will <u>not</u> be Christ's Wrath. It will be Antichrist's Wrath against **God's elect people** (Matt 24:21-22).

But these Cosmic Signs will <u>also</u> mark the Church's Rescue from <u>Christ's</u> Wrath. The Cosmic **signs in the sun, moon, and stars** (Luke 21:25) mark the beginning of Christ's Wrath throughout Scripture (cf. Matt 24:29; Joel 2:30-31; Rev 6:12-17). Therefore, none of the events Jesus described earlier in His Endtimes Teaching will be Christ's Wrath. This included The Beginning of Birth Pains and The Greatest Persecution. Only <u>after</u> **God's elect people** experience these things will the Church's Return and Christ's Wrath occur.

This important truth will be discussed further elsewhere in this book (ch. 14). As explained there, the NT promises that <u>before</u> Christ's Wrath begins, Christ will Return **from heaven** and **rescue us from the coming wrath** (1 Thess 1:10 NIV; cf. 5:9; Rom 5:9; Col 3:6). Therefore, when Jesus described the Cosmic Signs announcing His Wrath, what would we expect to happen next? The Church's Rescue. This is precisely what is described in Matthew 24:29-31, Mark 13:24-27, and Luke 21:25-28.

Accordingly, after describing the Cosmic Signs, Christ's Return, and the Church's Rescue (cf. Matt 24:29-31), Jesus next began to teach about His Wrath in His Endtimes Teaching. He illustrated its timing when He said it would be like the days of **Noah** and **Lot** (cf. Matt 24:37-41; Luke 17:26-36). He said on **the day Noah entered the ark** and was rescued, **then the flood** [God's wrath] **came and destroyed** the unbelievers (Luke 17:27 NIV; cf. Gen 7:11-13).

Likewise, He said, <u>the day</u> **Lot left Sodom, fire and sulfur** [God's wrath] **rained down from heaven and destroyed** the wicked (Luke 17:29 NIV). Here we see a biblical principle about the Endtimes: <u>The rescue of the righteous will immediately precede Christ's Wrath on the wicked</u>.

Jesus goes on in His Endtimes Teaching to describe the Church's Rescue from Christ's Wrath and leaving unbelievers on Earth to experience it when He says:

> **Two men will be in the field; one will be received** [and rescued by Christ at His Return], **and the other left** [on Earth to experience Christ's Wrath]. **Two women will be grinding with a hand mill; one will be received** [and rescued by Christ at His Return], **and the other left** [on Earth to experience Christ's Wrath]." (Matt 24:40-41 [21])

The Greek word translated **received** (*paralambanetai*) in the suggested translation often means in the NT to "take someone with oneself." [22] This is a good description of the Church's Rescue that Jesus had just described a few verses earlier (cf. v. 31). The same Greek word is used when Jesus described the same event in John 14:3. There He promised the Church, **"I will come again and receive** [*paralēmpsomai*] **you to Myself** (NASB).

Therefore, in Matthew 24:40-41 Jesus is describing the fact that Christians will be taken from the Earth when **His angels ... will lift up and gather together God's elect people in the sky, from everywhere on Earth** and **rescue** them from The Greatest Persecution (Antichrist's Wrath) and Christ's Wrath which is about to begin (cf. Matt 24:31, Luke 21:28). But unbelievers will be **left** on the Earth to experience the punishment of Christ's Wrath like the unbelievers in Noah's and Lot's day that Christ had just mentioned. [23]

There is one more parallel between **the days of Lot** (Luke 17:28) and Christ's Return and the Church's Rescue. Before God's punishment fell upon Sodom and Gomorrah, Angels rescued Lot and his family (cf. Gen 19:1). Likewise, at Christ's Return, Angels will again rescue God's people immediately before Christ's Wrath.

D) A summary of the sequence of Endtime events in Christ's Endtimes Teaching

Therefore, the sequence of Endtime events in Christ's Endtimes Teaching in Matthew 24 is as follows:

1) First, there will be **the beginning of birth pains** (v. 8) including **wars, famines,** and **plagues** (vs. 5-7, Luke 21:11).

2) Then, **you will see standing in the holy place 'the abomination that causes desolation'** (v. 15), or Antichrist's Claim to be God.

3) **Then there will be the greatest persecution of God's elect people.** (v. 21)

4) Then, **Immediately after the completion of the greatest persecution ... Then the sign that the Son of Man is coming will appear in the sky. And then all the peoples of the Earth will mourn when they see the Son of Man coming on the clouds of Heaven, with power and great glory.** (vs. 29-30). This is Christ's Return.

5) Then, **He will send out His angels with a loud trumpet sound, and they will lift up and gather together God's elect people from one end of the sky to the other, from everywhere on Earth"** (v. 31). This is the Church's Rescue.

6) Then, **Two men will be in the field; one will be received** and rescued by Christ at His Return, **and the other left** on Earth to experience Christ's Wrath. (v. 40)

Therefore, the biblical sequence of Endtime events can be displayed in the following table. Study it carefully, because it is a foundation for having a biblical understanding of the Endtimes. It summarizes the outline of Endtime events in Christ's Endtimes Teaching. It will also help you recognize unbiblical errors in other views. If you want, read through Matthew 24:4-31 again to be convinced of this sequence of Endtime events:

Endtime Events According to Christ's Endtimes Teaching

#	Endtime Event	Description
①	The Beginning of Birth Pains	Wars, famines, plagues, and earthquakes. (Matt 24:4-8; Luke 21:11)
②	Antichrist's Claim to be God	The "abomination of desolation" when Antichrist enters a rebuilt Jewish temple and proclaims himself to be God. (v. 15)
③	The Greatest Persecution	Antichrist's wrath against God's people. (vs 9, 16-21)
④	The Cosmic Signs	In the sun, moon, and stars signaling Christ's Return. (v. 29)
⑤	Christ's Return	His visible, glorious appearing. (v. 30)
⑥	The Church's Rescue	The "rapture" or lifting up of Christians who are still alive. (v. 31)
⑦	Christ's Wrath	God's wrath against His enemies on Earth. (vs. 37-41)

Finally, Christ's Endtime Teaching can be summarized in the following graphic:

Endtime Events According to Jesus

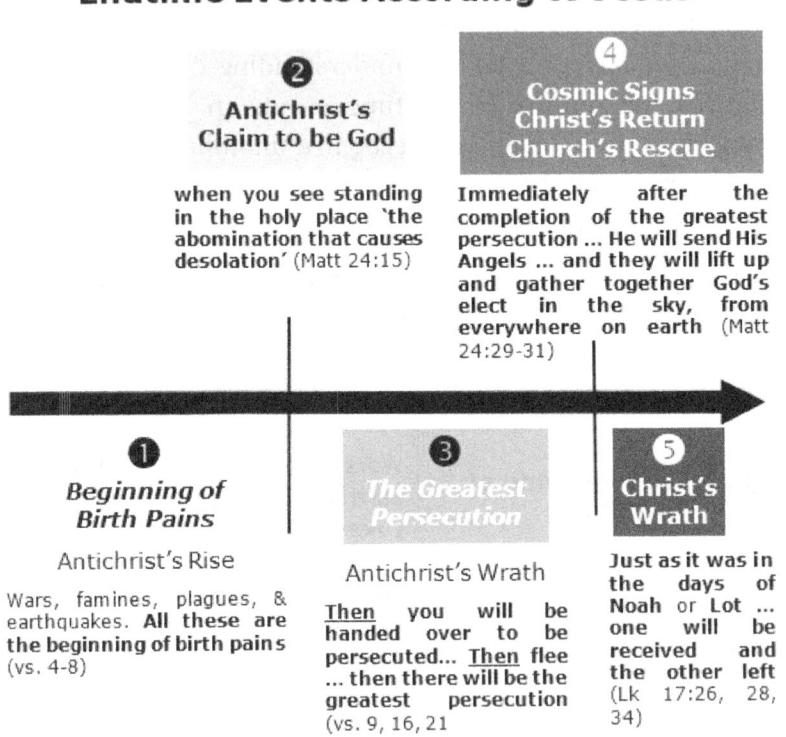

② Antichrist's Claim to be God

when you see standing in the holy place 'the abomination that causes desolation' (Matt 24:15)

④ Cosmic Signs Christ's Return Church's Rescue

Immediately after the completion of the greatest persecution ... He will send His Angels ... and they will lift up and gather together God's elect in the sky, from everywhere on earth (Matt 24:29-31)

① *Beginning of Birth Pains*

Antichrist's Rise

Wars, famines, plagues, & earthquakes. **All these are the beginning of birth pains** (vs. 4-8)

③ *The Greatest Persecution*

Antichrist's Wrath

Then you will be handed over to be persecuted... **Then** flee ... then there will be the greatest persecution (vs. 9, 16, 21

⑤ *Christ's Wrath*

Just as it was in the days of Noah or Lot ... one will be received and the other left (Lk 17:26, 28, 34)

---

[1] Unfortunately, Evangelical commentaries on Matthew 24 are often disappointing. The commentaries of France, Hagner, Nolland, and Osborne are marred by their emphasis on a Preterist interpretation that claims Christ's Endtimes Teaching was largely fulfilled in the first century. Preterism is discussed further in this book at ch. 12 (sec. B). The commentaries of France, Hagner, and Nolland also waste a lot of space discussing speculative and assumed textual critical issues between the Synoptic Gospels.

These commentaries are not helpful on correctly defining *thlipsis* in Matthew 24 either. Carson is right to correct Pre-tribulationism and say that the time of "great distress" should not be equated with Christ's Wrath, but he never even mentions persecution as a meaning for *thlipsis* (563).

² Jesus also mentioned **many will come in My name, saying, 'I am the Christ,' and will mislead many** as a part of **the beginning of birth pains** (vs. 5, 8 NASB).

In *Endtimes Essentials* Book #2, *The Beginning of Birth Pains*, it will be argued that the first and foremost False Christ will be the Antichrist who will emerge before the **many** False Christs. Therefore, Christ's reference to this will be labeled "False Christ(s)" throughout the *Endtimes Essentials*.

³ Luke's version of Christ's Endtimes Teaching shares the same sequence. He writes:

> Then he added, "Nation will go to war against nation, and kingdom against kingdom. There will be great earthquakes, and there will be famines and plagues in many lands, and there will be terrifying things and great miraculous signs from heaven. But before all this occurs, there will be a time of great persecution. (Luke 21:10-12 NLT)

In other words, **before** the **miraculous signs from heaven, there will be a time of great persecution.**

⁴ The suggested translation of Matt 24:29-30 is primarily based on the NLT and NASB and explained in ch. 3, secs. D & E.

⁵ *BDAG*, #2.

⁶ *BDAG* #1b.

⁷ *BDAG*.

⁸ *BDAG* #1.

⁹ This suggested translation of Matt 24:30 generally follows the NLT.

¹⁰ For more on the Glory Cloud, see *God's Miracles*, vol. 10, ch. 10.9, sec. B, in the "Scholar's Section" of the website at www.trainingtimothys.com.

¹¹ As stated, Matt 24:31 is one of the most important, astounding, overlooked, and misunderstood statements in Scripture. Unfortunately, Evangelical commentaries are again largely unhelpful. However, Osborne is willing to say:

> The combination of the coming of the Son of Man, and the trumpet blast, plus angels, and the resurrection of the saints, links this with 1 Cor 15:52 and 1 Thess 4:15–16 [the "rapture" passages]... The point is that every follower will be gathered from everywhere and will be caught up to be with the conquering King. (1292)

Oddly then, Osborne claims that Pre-tribulationism, Mid-tribulationism, and Post-tribulationism are all "viable" options. But this is not true if his interpretation of Matt 24:31 is correct, and it is. Eventually, Osborne writes: "I find the [Post-tribulation] position more in keeping with Matt 24 and the NT evidence (cf. 1 Thess 4:15-17; 5:1-12) (1293). Post-tribulationism will be discussed further in ch. 11, sec. D.

Like Osborne, Hagner somewhat agrees with the view argued in this chapter and writes on Matt 24:31:

> The gathering of the "elect" (see too 22:14; 24:22, 24), refers here not simply to the gathering of Israel but to the gathering of Christian disciples... In the NT a reference to the eschatological trumpet occurs in conjunction with the descent of the Lord from heaven in 1 Thess 4:16 [the classic "rapture" text] (714-15).

Likewise, *D&A* are willing to say of Matt 24:31, "The language ... probably denotes a rapture to heaven, as in 1 Thess 4.17... Commentators usually assume that the elect must be the Christian faithful" (III.364). It is unclear what "commentators" they are referring to.

As noted in the endnote above, France's and Nolland's commentaries are too focused on Preterism or textual criticism to be useful. Carson is simply not helpful, sharing only a few brief sentences on this important statement of Christ. Perhaps it is not surprising that MacArthur does the same in light of the fact that this verse is one of the most difficult in Scripture for the Pre-tribulationism he promotes.

[12] *BDAG* #2.

[13] See the use of *harpagēsometha* in Matt 11:12; 13:19; John 6:15; 10:28; Acts 8:39; 23:10, 25; 2 Cor 12:2, 4; 1 Thess 4:17; Jude 1:23; Rev 12:5.

[14] The fact that using "rapture" to refer to this event is an invented use of the word is supported by the fact that *Webster's* gives no definition of "rapture" to mean "take away," but does add: "to cause (a Christian believer) to be taken up into heaven during the end-time."

[15] *BDAG* #1 & #2.

[16] *BDAG*.

[17] Many of the errors being taught regarding Matt 24:31 come from Pre-tribulationism that will be biblically evaluated in chs. 13-16.

[18] The popular fiction series by Tim Lahaye and Jerry Jenkins entitled the *Left Behind Collection* (*LCS*), wrongly portrays Christians simply disappearing into thin air at the "rapture," with no mention of Christ appearing or the saints being visibly and physically lifted into the air by Angels as Jesus described. This is to support their belief in Pre-tribulationism and a "secret silent rapture" which is nowhere taught in Scripture.

[19] Luke 21:25-27 is from the NIV. Verse 28 is a combination of NLT and a suggested translation: **So when all these things begin to happen, stand and look up, because your <u>rescue</u> is drawing near. Rescue** translates the Greek word *apolytrōsis* which means "release from a painful interrogation" or "a captive condition, *release, redemption, deliverance*" (*BDAG* #1 & #2). It is most often used in the NT to refer to "redemption" from the effects of our sin. But here, it has the meaning of being rescued

from a painful situation. Likewise, *apolytrōsin* is used in Heb 11:35 to refer to being **released** from being **tortured**. Such a meaning would work well in the context here in Luke 21:28. It is clearly speaking of **rescue** from persecution that Jesus described earlier in the text (cf. Luke 21:11-12). It is probably also referring to a **rescue** from Christ's Wrath that will immediately occur after the Cosmic Signs (cf. Luke 21:25-27; Rev 6:12-17).

The NCV is similar to the suggested translation: **When these things begin to happen, look up and hold your heads high, because the time when God will free you is near!** (cf. CEV **set free**).

Unfortunately, **redemption** is the common rendering of the Greek word *apolytrōsis* in Luke 21:28 (cf. NIV, NASB, ESV, KJV, NKJV, CSB, NET). The NLT and GNT have **salvation**. Again, this is a possible meaning for *apolytrōsis*, but such a translation obscures Christ's meaning in Luke 21:28. "Redemption" normally means to "buy back" or to "release from blame or debt" (*Webster's*). That is not what Christ is talking about here, and it leads to wrong conclusions.

For example, the translation notes in NET state here, "With Jesus' return comes the manifestation of judgment and final salvation (redemption)." Bock says the meaning here is "deliverance from a fallen world" (1687). Morris says Jesus is referring to "the full implications" of the "redemption ... accomplished on the cross" (328). Nolland claims "*Apolytrōsis* is used here of ... the consummation of salvation" (777).

On the contrary, salvation from our sins is not what Christ is speaking of here. Nor is this event "the consummation of salvation." That does not occur until after the Millennium when Christ **has destroyed ... all of His enemies** including **death** (1 Cor 15:24-28). Contrary to these commentators, *apolytrōsis* in Luke 21:28 is referring to the Church's Rescue from The Greatest Persecution and Christ's Wrath.

Therefore, other commentators are more helpful. Osborne writes: "'Redemption' (*apolytrōsis*) is not meant in its Pauline sense of being liberated from sin but rather delivered from oppression and hard times" (472). Likewise, Fitzmyer writes: "As A. Plummer notes (*The Gospel*, 485), *apolytrōsis* is used [here] in the sense of "release, deliverance," without any connotation of "ransom" (*lytron*)... [Here] "deliverance/redemption" is not associated with Christ's death or resurrection, but with his coming again" (1350).

[20] The fact that this **rescue** is referring to the Church's Rescue from The Greatest Persecution is demonstrated earlier in Luke 21. In verses 11-12 Jesus had warned His people that **before** the **great signs from heaven ... they will seize you and persecute you** (Luke 21:11-12). Therefore, the Cosmic **signs** marking Christ's Return will also mark the Church's Rescue from The Greatest Persecution and Antichrist's Wrath.

[21] A suggested translation of Matt 24:40-41 would be: **Two men will be in the field; one will be received and the other left. Two women will be grinding with a hand mill; one will be received and the other left** (cf. Luke 17:34-35).

Received translates the Greek word *paralambanetai*. *BDAG* gives three definitions including: "to take into close association, *take (to oneself), take with/along*" (#1), "to gain control of, *receive*" (#2), "accept" (#3). All of these suggest a "taking" or "receiving" of someone personally.

The *NIDNTT* explains: "In the Gospels and Acts *paralambanō* ... frequently [means to] take someone with oneself" (III.751). This is a good description of the Church's Rescue (cf. 1 Thess 4:15-17).

Examples of this use of *paralambanō* in Matthew include **Jesus took with him Peter, James, and John** (17:1); **he took the Twelve aside** (20:17); and **He took Peter and the two sons of Zebedee along with him** (26:37). A NT use of *paralambanō* that specifically relates to its use in Matt 24:40-41 is Jesus' description of the very same event in John 14:3, **"I will come back and take [*paralēmpsomai*] you to be with me."** Matthew and Luke (cf. 17:34-35) intentionally used *paralambanō* here to communicate Jesus personally receiving someone to Himself.

Admittedly, all Bible versions translate *paralambanō* here as merely **taken**. This reflects and implies one possible meaning of the root word *lambanō* which can mean "to take hold of something" or "take away" (*BDAG* #1 & #2). But *paralambanō*, the specific word used here at Matt 24:40-41 and Luke 17:34-35, never means these things. And even *lambanō* can mean "to take up, receive" or "to enter into a close relationship" (*BDAG* #5 & #8).

Unfortunately, translating *paralambanō* as merely **taken** in Matt 24:40-41 (and Luke 21:34-35) makes Jesus' meaning unclear and leads to the common claim that He was speaking of people **taken** for punishment. But if *paralambanō* were better translated here, this incorrect meaning would be more readily recognized.

Left translates the Greek word *aphietai*. It means: "to dismiss or release someone or something from a place or one's presence ... send away" or "to move away ... causing a separation, *leave, depart from*" (*BDAG* #1 & #3). In contrast to *paralambanō* which means to receive someone, *aphietai* means to depart from someone. Again, if this translation were made more apparent in Bible versions, the common misunderstanding that Christ was referring to being "left behind" to enter God's kingdom would be less likely. Jesus was talking about leaving people on Earth for punishment.

Some have claimed that *paralambanō* here cannot mean "take with" as in Jesus taking the saints with Him. Verses used to support this is the use of this same word in Matt 27:27 describing the soldiers taking Jesus into the common hall after He had been scourged, and Matt 4:5, 8 describing

Satan taking Jesus to Jerusalem and to a high mountain. But such examples can easily be translated and interpreted as "take with," as in Matt 24:40-41.

Others claim that those "taken with" in Matt 24:40-41 are described in Matt 13:49-50 as the wicked who are separated from the righteous at the end of the age. But there is no evidence for that. The text simply says: **"The angels will come and separate the wicked from the righteous and throw them into the blazing furnace, where there will be weeping and gnashing of teeth"** (Matt 13:49-50). There is no "taken" language in this text as many assume, and therefore it is not describing those "taken with" in Matt 24:40-41.

Others point to Luke 17 to interpret Matt 24:40-41 to mean those being "taken with" will be taken to judgement. There Jesus says:

"**I tell you,** [of His Return, cf. vs. 22-24] **two people will be in one bed; one will be taken and the other left. Two women will be grinding grain together; one will be taken and the other left."** "Where, Lord?" they asked. He replied, "Where there is a dead body, there the vultures will gather." (Luke 17:34-37 NIV)

Some assume that when the disciples asked **"Where?"** they were asking where people will be **taken**. But the last thing Jesus said before their question referred to people being **left**. Therefore, it is much more likely that the disciples were asking where people would be **left** when He returned. Accordingly, Bock gives the right answer when he writes:

The most natural reading, based on the previous examples of Noah and Lot [vs. 26-30, just like Matt 24:37-39], is that one is taken for salvation (Ellis, Plummer, Fitzmyer, Marshall, Tiede). In addition, the final "where" question of 17:37 appears to look back to the image of death and judgment in the comparison with the gathered birds. If so, then those who are "left to the birds" experience judgment. Finally, this understanding matches Luke's use of aphiēmi (to leave) for judgment in 13:35 and of paralambanō ("close association") or "taking along" in 9:10, 28 and 18:31 (cf. Matt 24:31; Mark 13:27; John 14:3; 1 Thess 4:17; BAGD 619; BAA 1252). (1437)

This view would also fit Jesus' obscure proverb about vultures that will gather to a dead body (v. 37). This statement has understandably been understood in a variety of ways. Bock describes seven different views (1439-40). What seems to be the best interpretation is not even among those he lists. It seems in Luke this is a reference to the judgement that will occur at the Battle of Armageddon (cf. Rev 19:17-18, 21).

[22] *NIDNTT, III*.751; *BDAG* #1.

[23] The great majority of scholars agree with the view claimed in this chapter that those being **taken** (NIV, better **received**) in Matthew 24:40-41 are believers being rescued to be with the Lord (cf. Morris, Nolland, Bock, Davies and Allison, France, Gundry, Hagner, and Osborne. The latter says

this is the view of "the majority of commentators." Carson is non-committal). The endnote above regarding the suggested translation of Matt 24:40-41 is significant on this matter. For more on the translation of Matt 24:40-41 see *Additional Studies on the Endtimes*, ch. 8.

Chapter 5

The Sequence of Endtime Events According to the Apostle Paul

1 & 2 Thessalonians

Contents

A) Paul confirms what Jesus taught about the timing of Christ's Return & the Church's Rescue *1 Thess 4:13-17*

B) Paul confirms that the Church's Rescue does not occur until Christ's Return *2 Thess 1:6-10*

C) The Church's Rescue will not come until after the Antichrist's Claim to be God *2 Thess 2:1-4*

D) A summary of the sequence of Endtime events in 2 Thessalonians

Primary Points

- The most widely recognized description of the Church's Rescue ("rapture;" 1 Thess 4:13-17) is practically identical to Jesus' description of the same event in Matthew 24:31. Both describe a very loud and visible Return of Christ at the Church's Rescue.
- In 2 Thessalonians 1:6-10 the Apostle taught Christians not to expect rescue from persecution until the glorious appearing of Jesus Christ.
- 2 Thessalonians 2:1-4 clearly teaches the Church's Rescue will not occur until after Antichrist's Claim to be God in a Jewish temple which begins The Greatest Persecution.
- The Church's Rescue cannot happen "at any moment."
- Listen carefully Christian. If you are living when the Endtimes begin, you will experience The Beginning of Birth Pains. If you survive those, you will experience The Greatest Persecution. The Antichrist's Wrath on the Church comes before Christ's Return, the Church's Rescue, and Christ's Wrath on this world.

In the previous chapter a specific sequence of events that Jesus taught in His Endtimes Teaching was demonstrated. This chapter will look at the Apostle Paul's teaching on this topic. It will become clear that the Apostle taught the same sequence of events as his Lord.

A) Paul confirms what Jesus taught about the timing of Christ's Return & the Church's Rescue *1 Thess 4:13-17*

[Read 1 Thessalonians 4:13-17]

Most Christians believe this passage gives the clearest description of the Church's Rescue ("rapture") in the Endtimes. The Apostle begins his description of Christ's Return and the Church's Rescue with a curious statement that many overlook: **According to the Lord's own word** [*logō*] **we tell you...** (v. 15 NIV).

The Greek noun *logon* can refer to an entire speech. [1] In other words, the Apostle is telling the Thessalonians that his teaching regarding the Church's Rescue is **according to** a teaching of Christ on the same topic.

Did Paul possess a teaching from Jesus on Christ's Return and the Church's Rescue? Yes, in Christ's Endtimes Teaching discussed in the previous chapter. Compare **the Lord's own word** (1 Thess 4:15) in Matthew 24:29-31, with Paul's description of the same event in 1 Thessalonians 4:15-17. They are describing the same event. [2]

[Read Matthew 24:29-31 again. Then read 1 Thessalonians 4:15-17 again. Notice they are describing the same event.]

Let us notice at least seven obvious similarities in these teachings:

1) The general context is Christ's Return

Both Jesus and Paul were teaching about the Second Coming of Christ. Therefore, we would expect them to teach the same thing.

2) The specific context is severe persecution

The context of Jesus' teaching on His Return and the Church's Rescue was The Greatest Persecution of **God's elect people** (cf. Matt 24:9, 21, 29). The Apostle's teaching to the Thessalonians was also in the context of severe persecution (cf. 1 Thess 1:6; 2:2, 14-15; Acts 17:1-8). Martyrdom in the persecution may have been the cause of many of those who had died (cf. 1 Thess 4:13-14, 17).

3) The topic is the very public and visible Return of Christ

In the previous chapter (4) it was noted that many teach that the Church's Rescue will occur in a "secret and silent rapture." It was also explained there that Matthew 24:29-31 clearly refutes this idea.

So does the teaching of the Apostle. Paul says Christ's Return and the Church's Rescue will be LOUD. Indeed, it could be said this is the loudest passage in all of Scripture! 3 The Apostle said the Church's Rescue will include **a loud command, the voice of the archangel, and the trumpet call of God** (1 Thess 4:16 NIV). Accordingly, there is no verse in Scripture that describes Christ's Return or the Church's Rescue as "secret and silent." When Christ Returns to Rescue His Church, it will be bright and **loud** and witnessed by every person on Earth.

4) There is the presence of clouds

Jesus said, **the Son of Man** will be **coming on the clouds** (Matt 24:30). The Apostle said at Christ's Return and the Church's Rescue that Christians will **meet the Lord in the clouds** (1 Thess 4:17). In both passages this probably refers to the Glory Cloud that will accompany Christ at His Return.

5) There is the presence of Angels

Jesus said at His Return and the Church's Rescue, **"He will send His Angels ... and they will lift up and gather together God's elect people"** (Matt 24:31). Likewise, the Apostle said at the same event there will be **the voice of the archangel** (1 Thess 4:16 NIV). This certainly implies the presence of other Angels.

6) There is a trumpet call

This is perhaps the most obvious similarity between these two teachings. Anyone denying they are describing the same event exposes a distorting bias toward the text. 4 At Christ's Return and the Church's Rescue Jesus said, **"He will send out His angels with a loud trumpet sound"** (Matt 24:31). Likewise, the Apostle said at Christ's Return and the Church's Rescue there will be **the trumpet call of God** (1 Thess 4:16). Jesus and Paul are clearly describing the same event.

This is the same **trumpet** that **will sound** when **the dead will be raised imperishable, and we will be changed** (1 Cor 15:52 NIV) in the First Resurrection.

7) Believers will be gathered in the air to meet Christ

Jesus said, **angels ... will lift up and gather together God's elect people in the <u>sky</u>** when **the Son of Man** is **coming on the clouds of Heaven** (Matt 24:30-31). This will be for the purpose of meeting Christ in the air. Likewise, Paul said the Church, **will be caught up together ... to meet the Lord in the air** (1 Thess 4:17). Both Jesus and Paul are describing a gathering of the Church to meet Christ in the **sky** at His Return.

Important rules of biblical interpretation in which we compare Scripture with Scripture should clearly lead to the conclusion that both Jesus and the Apostle were teaching about Christ's Return and the Church's Rescue. Especially when we note that the Apostle described his teaching as being **According to the Lord's own word** (1 Thess 4:15). Why would we doubt that Paul is referring to one of the most famous and longest teachings Christ ever gave? Especially when Jesus and Paul were teaching on the very same topic, Christ's Return.

B) Paul confirms that the Church's Rescue does not occur until Christ's Return: *2 Thess 1:6-7*

[Read 2 Thessalonians 1:6-7. As you do, imagine the Thessalonian Christians in the midst of their persecution. Then ask yourself what they were instructed to look for when they received **relief** from their persecution.]

In the previous section regarding 1 Thessalonians 4, we noted that the context was severe persecution occurring in this church. There he offered them consolation by reminding them of Christ's Return and the Church's Rescue. When Paul wrote his second letter to them shortly afterwards, the persecution was continuing. And again, he seeks to encourage them by describing Christ's Return and the Church's Rescue:

> **We proudly tell God's other churches about your endurance and faithfulness in all the persecutions and hardships you are suffering. And God will use this persecution to show his justice and to make you worthy of his Kingdom, for which you are suffering. In his justice he will pay back those who persecute you.**
>
> **And God will provide rest** [*anasin*, NIV **relief**] **for you who are being persecuted and also for us when the Lord Jesus appears from heaven. He will come with his mighty angels, in flaming fire, bringing judgment on those who don't know God and on those who refuse to obey the Good News of our Lord Jesus.** (2 Thess 1:4-8 NLT)

Now here is the important question. **When** could these Christians expect **relief** from **being persecuted**? The Apostle said **This will happen when the Lord Jesus is revealed from heaven in blazing fire with his powerful angels** (NIV). Why would their **relief** from **being persecuted** happen then? Because Christ's very visible Return and the Church's Rescue will occur at that time.

Therefore, what did the Apostle teach the Thessalonians to expect when the Church's Rescue occurred? **The Lord Jesus is revealed from heaven in blazing fire with his powerful angels** (NIV). This again clearly refutes the popular belief of a "secret & silent rapture." [5]

Also notice that Christ's Wrath does not begin until <u>after</u> the very visible Return of Christ. It is only <u>after</u> **the Lord Jesus is revealed from heaven in blazing fire with his powerful angels** that **He will punish those who do not know God ... on the day he comes to be glorified** (2 Thess 1:7-8, 10 NIV). Again, contrary to popular teaching, Christ's Endtime Wrath does not begin until the very visible and very first appearing of Jesus Christ in glory to the whole world.

Also, notice again the similarities between Jesus and Paul on Christ's Return and the Church's Rescue. Like Matthew 24:30-31 and 1 Thessalonians 4:16, in 2 Thessalonians 2:6-10 Paul described the world-wide revelation of Christ and the presence of Angels at His Return and the Church's Rescue.

C) The Church's Rescue will not come until after the Antichrist's Claim to be God: *2 Thess 2:1-4*

[Read 2 Thessalonians 2:1-12. Focus especially on verses 1-4]

2 Thessalonians 2:1-4 is one of the clearest passages in Scripture regarding the sequence of Endtime events surrounding Christ's Return and the Church's Rescue. [6]

What is the context of the passage? Because of some false teaching, the Thessalonian Christians believed they had missed Christ's Return and the Church's Rescue that Paul had wrote about in his first letter to them (cf. 1 Thess 4:15-17). They understood that **the day of the Lord** (2 Thess 2:2) was the time of Christ's Wrath and would immediately follow Christ's Return. Therefore, they were **alarmed** (v. 2) they were going to experience Christ's Wrath because they had missed the "rapture" and had been "left behind." To correct this false teaching, the Apostle clearly teaches the following truths.

C.1) The Church's Rescue occurs simultaneously with Christ's Return

First, let us notice the topic of Paul's words. They were **with regard to the coming of our Lord Jesus Christ and our gathering together to Him** (v. 1 NASB [7]). It is obvious that by **the coming of our Lord Jesus Christ** the Apostle is speaking of the same visible Return of Christ he had just described in chapter 1 of the same letter as **when the Lord Jesus is revealed from heaven in blazing fire with His powerful Angels** (2 Thess 1:7 NIV).

Our gathering together to Him is speaking of the Church's Rescue. Above we noted that in Paul's first letter to this same church he described this same event as **we ... will be caught up together ... to meet the Lord in the air** (1 Thess 4:17). Likewise, Jesus said in Matthew 24 that His **angels ... will lift up and gather together God's elect people from one end of the sky to the other, from everywhere on Earth** (v. 31). In fact, both Jesus and Paul use the same Greek word to describe the Church's Rescue. [8]

Notice also that the Apostle saw these as two simultaneous events. [9] Therefore, when Paul writes, **with regard to the coming of our Lord Jesus Christ and our gathering together to Him** (v. 1), he is describing Christ's Return and the Church's Rescue as happening together. Sound familiar? We have already demonstrated that Matthew 24:29-31, 1 Thessalonians 4:13-17, and 2 Thessalonians 1:6-10 teach the same thing. So the first point Paul makes in this passage is that the Church's Rescue occurs simultaneously with Christ's visible Return.

C.2) The Church's Rescue will <u>not</u> occur until <u>after</u> Antichrist's Claim to be God

We have noted that the Thessalonians were **alarmed** (v. 2) that they had somehow missed **the coming of our Lord Jesus Christ and our gathering together to Him** (v. 1). How does Paul correct their error? He simply says:

> **Don't let anyone deceive you in any way, for that day** [the day of **the coming of our Lord Jesus Christ and our gathering together to Him** and the beginning of Christ's "Day of the Lord" Wrath] <u>**will not come until**</u> **the rebellion occurs and the man of lawlessness is revealed, the man doomed to destruction.**
>
> **He will oppose and will exalt himself over everything that is called God or is worshiped, so that he sets himself up in God's temple, proclaiming himself to be God.** (2 Thess 2:3-4 NIV)

That day (v. 3), refers to **the day of the Lord** (v. 2), which begins with the visible **coming of our Lord Jesus Christ and our gathering together to Him**, resulting in Christ's Wrath on His enemies remaining on Earth during the Trumpet and Bowl Punishments (cf. Rev chs. 8-9; 15-16). It is the same **day of the Lord** that Paul described in 1 Thessalonians where we read:

> **Now, brothers and sisters, about times and dates we do not need to write to you, for you know very well that** <u>**the day of the Lord**</u> **will come like a thief in the night** [for non-Christians]. **While people** [unbelievers] **are saying, "Peace and safety," destruction will come on them suddenly, as labor pains on a pregnant woman, and they will not escape.**

But you, brothers and sisters [Christians], **are not in darkness so that this day** [of the Lord and the destruction and wrath that will come with it] **should surprise you like a thief.** (1 Thess 5:1-4 NIV)

This is the same **day of the Lord** that Paul refers to in 2 Thessalonians above. Understandably, the Thessalonian Christians were concerned this **day** had already occurred and they had been left on the Earth to experience Christ's Wrath. [10]

Now, back to the critical text in 2 Thessalonians 2:1-4. The Apostle wrote that **the day of the Lord ... will not come until the rebellion occurs and the man of lawlessness is revealed** who **will oppose and will exalt himself over everything that is called God or is worshiped, so that he sets himself up in God's temple, proclaiming himself to be God**.

The meaning of **the rebellion** and **the man of lawlessness** being **revealed** will be discussed elsewhere. [11] The event when the Antichrist **sets himself up in God's temple, proclaiming himself to be God** is clearly what is referred to throughout the *Endtimes Essentials* as Antichrist's Claim to be God.

Jesus described this same event when He referred to a time **"When you see** [the Antichrist] **standing in the holy place** [of the Jewish temple] causing **'the abomination that causes desolation'"** (Matt 24:15 NIV; cf. Dan 9:26-27). It was immediately after this event that Jesus said His people should **flee** because The Greatest Persecution would begin (cf. Matt 24:16; cf. vs. 17-21). [12] Even though Antichrist's Claim to be God will occur in Jerusalem, Paul believed the Thessalonian Christians would know when it happened.

Therefore, the Apostle clearly taught that **the coming of our Lord Jesus Christ and our gathering together to Him** [the Church's Rescue] (v. 1), **will not come until** the Antichrist's Claim to be God in a rebuilt Jewish **temple**. Therefore, the Church's Rescue ("rapture") will not happen until <u>after</u> the Antichrist is active on Earth, well on his way to ruling it, and initiating The Greatest Persecution. [13]

C.3) Christ's Return and the Church's Rescue cannot happen "at any moment."

A popular teaching is that a "secret & silent rapture" of Christians could occur "at any moment." This is false. Paul clearly taught that **the coming of our Lord Jesus Christ and our gathering together to Him** [the "rapture"] ... **will not come until** a spiritual **rebellion occurs and the man of lawlessness is revealed** (vs. 1, 3).

Antichrist's Claim to be God in a rebuilt Jewish **temple** in Jerusalem is just one of many Endtime events that must occur before the Church's Rescue and Christ's Return. [14] Jesus of course described many more in His Endtimes Teaching.

D) A summary of the sequence of Endtime events in 2 Thessalonians

Therefore, the sequence of Endtime events in the Apostle Paul's Endtimes teaching to the Thessalonians is as follows:

1) First, there will be a spiritual **rebellion ... and the man of lawlessness** will be **revealed** and the Antichrist will **set himself up in God's temple, proclaiming himself to be God** (2 Thess 2:3-4).

2) Then, God's people will be **persecuted** and should not expect **relief** until **the Lord Jesus appears from heaven in blazing fire with his powerful Angels** (2 Thess 1:6-7).

3) Then, there will be **the coming of our Lord Jesus Christ and our gathering together to Him** for the Church's Rescue (2 Thess 2:1).

4) **Then He will be punishing those who do not know God and do not obey the good news of our Lord Jesus** (2 Thess 1:8).

Listen carefully Christian. If you are living when the Endtimes begin, you will experience The Beginning of Birth Pains. If you survive those, you will experience The Greatest Persecution. The Antichrist's Wrath on the Church <u>comes before</u> Christ's Return, the Church's Rescue, and Christ's Wrath on this world.

Therefore, the sequence of Endtime events taught in Thessalonians can be displayed and compared with Christ's Endtimes Teaching in the following table and graphics.

Endtime Events According to Jesus

#	Endtime Event	Description
1	The Beginning of Birth Pains	Wars, famines, plagues, and earthquakes. (Matt 24:4-8; Luke 21:11)
2	Antichrist's Claim to be God	The "abomination of desolation" when Antichrist enters a rebuilt Jewish temple and proclaims himself to be God. (v. 15)
3	The Greatest Persecution	Antichrist's wrath against God's people. (vs. 9, 16-21)
4	The Cosmic Signs	In the sun, moon, and stars signaling Christ's Return. (v. 29)
5	Christ's Return	His visible, glorious appearing. (v. 30)
6	The Church's Rescue	The "rapture" or lifting up of Christians who are still alive. (v. 31)
7	Christ's Wrath	God's wrath against His enemies on Earth. (vs. 37-41)

Endtime Events According to the Apostle Paul

#	Endtime Event	Description
1	Antichrist's Claim to be God	The "abomination of desolation" when the Antichrist enters a rebuilt Jewish temple and proclaims himself to be God. (2 Thess 2:3-4)
2	The Greatest Persecution	Antichrist's wrath against God's people. (2 Thess 1:6-7)
3	Christ's Return	His visible, glorious appearing. (2 Thess 1:6-7; 2 Thess 2:1)
4	The Church's Rescue	The gathering up of Christians who are still alive. (2 Thess 2:1)
5	Christ's Wrath	God's wrath against His enemies on Earth. (2 Thess 1:8)

Endtime Events According to Jesus

② Antichrist's Claim to be God

when you see standing in the holy place 'the abomination that causes desolation' (Matt 24:15)

④ Cosmic Signs / Christ's Return / Church's Rescue

Immediately after the completion of the greatest persecution ... He will send His Angels ... and they will lift up and gather together God's elect in the sky, from everywhere on earth (Matt 24:29-31)

① Beginning of Birth Pains

Antichrist's Rise

Wars, famines, plagues, & earthquakes. **All these are the beginning of birth pains** (vs. 4-8)

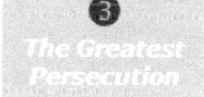

③ The Greatest Persecution

Antichrist's Wrath

<u>Then</u> you will be handed over to be persecuted... <u>Then</u> flee ... then there will be the greatest persecution (vs. 9, 16, 21)

⑤ Christ's Wrath

Just as it was in the days of Noah or Lot ... one will be received and the other left (Lk 17:26, 28, 34)

Endtime Events According to the Apostle Paul

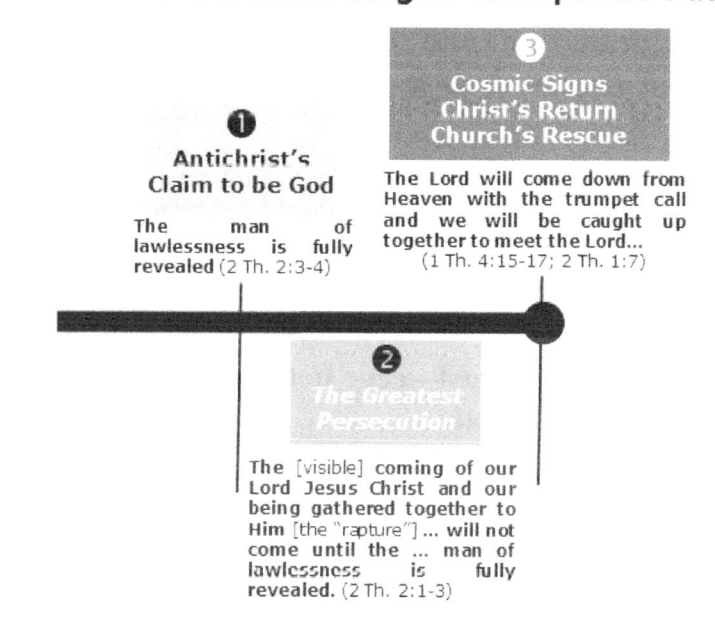

① Antichrist's Claim to be God

The man of lawlessness is fully revealed (2 Th. 2:3-4)

③ Cosmic Signs / Christ's Return / Church's Rescue

The Lord will come down from Heaven with the trumpet call and we will be caught up together to meet the Lord... (1 Th. 4:15-17; 2 Th. 1:7)

② The Greatest Persecution

The [visible] coming of our Lord Jesus Christ and our being gathered together to Him [the "rapture"] ... will not come until the ... man of lawlessness is fully revealed. (2 Th. 2:1-3)

E) Paul's correction of popular errors on the Endtimes

E.1) Christ's Return and the Church's Rescue will be visible to the whole world

A popular teaching in the Church is that the first "coming" of Christ will be "secret and silent" such that the world will not know what is happening. But the Apostle taught the Thessalonians not to expect **relief** from **being persecuted** until **The Lord Jesus appears from heaven in blazing fire with his powerful Angels** (1 Thess 1:6-7 NIV). When Christ returns to Rescue ("rapture") the Church, it will be a very obvious and loud event that the whole world will see and hear.

E.2) The Church's Rescue occurs after The Greatest Persecution

A popular teaching is that the Church's Rescue happens before The Greatest Persecution. But the Apostle taught:

> **Concerning the coming of our Lord Jesus Christ and our being gathered to him ... Don't let anyone deceive you in any way, for that day** [the day of the coming of our Lord Jesus Christ and our gathering together to Him, v. 1] **will not come until the rebellion occurs and the man of lawlessness** [Antichrist] **is revealed** [and] **sets himself up in God's temple, proclaiming himself to be God.** (2 Thess 2:1, 3 NIV)

Therefore, Christ's Return and the Church's Rescue will not happen until after the Antichrist's Claim to be God and The Greatest Persecution. The Last Generation Church will experience the Antichrist's Wrath.

E.3) Several events must occur before Christ's Return and the Church's Rescue

A popular teaching in the Church is that the "rapture" could happen at any moment. Even today. But again, the Apostle taught **the coming of our Lord Jesus Christ and our being gathered to** him ... will not come until ... the man of lawlessness [Antichrist] **is revealed.** Therefore, neither Christ's Return nor the Church's Rescue can happen "at any moment."

E.4) The biblical sequence of Endtime events is clear

As noted in chapter 1 the "apathetic" view on the Endtimes teaches that the biblical details of the sequence of Endtime events are unclear or unimportant. On the contrary, the Apostle rebuked the Thessalonians for not understanding the sequence of Endtime events. He asked them, **Don't you remember that when I was with you** for only about 3 weeks **I used to tell you these things?** (2 Thess 2:5 NIV). **These things** included the <u>timing</u> of **the coming of our Lord Jesus Christ and our being gathered to him** (v. 1).

Unfortunately, their ignorance caused them to be **easily unsettled or alarmed** (v. 2) by false teaching regarding Christ's Return. This "Thessalonian Panic" will be discussed further in chapter 16 (sec. B). This is why Paul corrected their ignorance by reminding them of the biblical sequence of Endtime events and wrote: **the coming of our Lord Jesus Christ and our being gathered to him ... will not come until ... the man of lawlessness** [Antichrist] **is revealed.** Therefore, <u>no</u> Christian should say the details or sequence of Endtime events is <u>not</u> important or is <u>not</u> clear.

E.5) Endtime prophecies will be fulfilled in a literal way, as in a physical event, person, or place

Many Christian teachers prioritize a metaphorical approach to interpreting Endtimes Scriptures (e.g. Amillennialism). As noted in chapter 3, this was reflected in a survey of Protestant Pastors where 50% of them denied or were unsure that Scripture predicts there will be a literal Antichrist in the future.

But the Apostle taught the Thessalonians: **the man of lawlessness** will be **revealed and will oppose and will exalt himself over everything that is called God or is worshiped, so that he sets himself up in God's temple, proclaiming himself to be God** (2 Thess 2:3-4). Contrary to 50% of Protestant Pastors, Paul believed in a literal Antichrist and his physical presence in a physical **temple**. Obviously, so did Jesus (cf. Matt 24:15).

Therefore, contrary to the popular practice of interpreting biblical prophecy in a metaphorical way, those concerning the Antichrist in Daniel and Revelation should be interpreted as predicting real, literal, actual events in the future.

---

[1] Vine's, 683.

[2] It is claimed in this section that when Paul said He was teaching about Christ's Return **according to the Lord's own word** (1 Thess 4:15), that Paul was referring to Christ's Endtimes Teaching. The similarities outlined make this evident.

Unfortunately, NT scholars are divided on this topic. In support of our position Calvin wrote: "It is probable that the word of the Lord means what was taken from his discourses." More recently, D. A. Carson writes regarding Matthew 24: "the [Olivet] discourse itself is undoubtedly a source for the Thessalonian Epistles" (*Matt*, underlining added). Likewise, Charles Wanamaker comments:

> The similarities between Mt. 24:29-31, 40f. in particular, and the images and language used in 1 Thess 4:16f. suggest that Paul was utilizing what he took to be the teaching of the Lord [in Matt 24] regarding the end of the age. (171)

John Piper has written:

> The number and specificity of the parallels between Paul's descriptions of the second coming and Jesus's descriptions are astonishing. I see at least fourteen, depending on how you count them. I find the conclusion inescapable that the end-time events that Paul describes are the same as those that Jesus describes... This points to conceptual unity, if not verbal dependence...
>
> [For example], notice how the parallels with Paul's view permeate the whole of Matt. 24: parousia (24:27), gathering (24:31), not alarmed (24:6), deception and loss of faith (24:4, 10, 11, 24), lawlessness (24:12), lovelessness (24:12), signs and wonders (24:24), clouds, power, glory, trumpet (24:30–31), birth pains (24:8). (217, 219-220).

Oddly, Walvoord does not even comment on the statement in his commentary on Thessalonians. Green is only willing to claim:

> The declaration of [1 Thess 4] vv. 15-17 corresponds in many respects with Matthew 24.29-31, 40-41, thus making it possible that Jesus' eschatological discourse was the source of this instruction" (*PNTC*, underlining added).

However, several other NT scholars disagree with the view in this chapter. The primary reason is described by John MacArthur:

> There are no close parallels to the present passage [1 Thess 4:16-17] in any of the Gospels. Nor is there any specific teaching in the Gospels to which Paul could be alluding. (*MNTC*)

Really? This is an odd and obviously erroneous statement coming from such a respected Bible teacher. Several "close parallels" are demonstrated in this section. But unfortunately such rightly respected NT scholars as Stott (*BST*) and Morris (*TNTC*) also deny there are any parallels between Matt 24:31 and 1 Thess 4:15-17.

Barnes, MacArthur, and Bruce (*WBC*) claim Paul was referring to another private revelation from Christ. But Paul uses the word *logon* ("speech, discourse") in Thess 4:15, not *apokalyptis* ("revelation") as he does when referring to a direct revelation from Christ in Galatians 1:11-12. In fact, Paul differentiates these very things in 2 Thessalonians 2:2 where he says a *logon* (**message** NASB) is something different from a revelation (**prophecy** NIV).

In the end, the similarities between Matt 24:29-31 and 1 Thess 4:16-17 make it rather certain that Paul was referring to Christ's Olivet Discourse when he wrote **according to the Lord's own word** (v. 15). It is humbly and respectfully suggested that those who deny this seem to demonstrate a distorting bias in their interpretation of these texts.

3 Gundry, loc. 1660.

4 Such a distorting bias on Christ's Endtimes Teaching is unfortunately demonstrated by the rightly respected Bible scholar Warren Weirsbe who writes: "We must not confuse the trumpet of Matthew 24:31 with the "trump of God" mentioned in 1 Thessalonians 4:16" (*BECW*). On the contrary, he seems to be the one who is "confused."

5 John Piper agrees with this interpretation, writing:
> The wording of 2 Thessalonians 1:5-8, when read carefully, shows that Paul, if he is alive at the coming of the Lord, expects to attain rest from suffering at the same time, and in the same event, that he expects the unbelievers to receive punishment— namely, at the revelation of Jesus with mighty angels in flaming fire... Which means that Paul did not expect a [Pre-tribulational] event at which he and the other believers would be given rest seven years before the glorious appearing of Christ in flaming fire. (208)

6 Unfortunately, Morris writes regarding 2 Thess 2:1-12:
> This passage is probably the most obscure and difficult in the whole of the Pauline writings and the many gaps in our knowledge have given rise to extravagant speculations (Morris, 125).

This is at best a great exaggeration and simply not true. But this perspective is common and is used as an excuse to not teach clearly what Paul wrote.

Greene is better when he comments on this passage: "Paul is keen to emphasize the order of future events throughout this section (vv. 3, 6-8)." (Green, 2 Thess 2).

7 Unlike some versions (NIV, NLT, NET), the Greek word *episynagōgēs* would be more fully translated by "gathered together" (*BDAG*) as it is in the NASB, ESV, GNT, KJV, NKJV, NCV. This is worth noting because "gathered together" obviously highlights the similarities between 2 Thess 2:1, 1 Thess 4:17, and Matt 24:31. In fact, as noted, the Greek words used in 2 Thess 2:1 and Matt 24:31 (*episynagōgēs* and *episynaxousin*) are "scarcely to be differentiated" (*BDAG*).

8 Piper writes:
> Paul uses the same word as Jesus does to describe the gathering of God's people at the coming of the Lord. Paul uses the noun form [*episynagōgēs*]; Jesus uses the verb form [*episynaxousin*]... Second Thessalonians 2:1 is the only place Paul uses this word (in either noun or verb form) in all his writings. (219)

Accordingly, Stott notes that Paul in 2 Thessalonians 2:1 is "describing how the angels will assemble God's people" according to Matt 24:31.

9 Even MacArthur who adheres to modern errors about Christ's Return notes regarding the coming of Christ and the gathering of believers here:
> The article ["the"] appears before *parousia* ["coming"] and is not repeated before *episunagoge* ["gathered"], indicating that these are complimentary elements in one event" (*MNTC*).

Seeing the meaning of this, Green remarks here: "These events are aspects of the same eschatological consummation and cannot be separated temporally or theologically, as some have suggested."

10 Piper writes regarding 2 Thess 2:1-3:
> It makes little sense to distinguish this "being gathered to [the Lord]" from "the day of the Lord." The flow of thought treats them as the same. The natural way to construe the gathering to the Lord is to see it in the light of 1 Thessalonians 4:17: "Then we who are alive, who are left, will be caught up together with them in the clouds to meet the Lord in the air, and so we will always be with the Lord." This is the same as "our being gathered together to him" in 2 Thessalonians 2:1. Which is the same as "the day of the Lord" in 2 Thessalonians 2:2 [and 1 Thess 5:1-4]. (209)

11 For more on Paul's reference to **the rebellion** and **the man of lawlessness** being **revealed** see *The Beginning of Birth Pains*, ch. 12.

12 What do other commentators say about the clear sequence of events Paul teaches in 2 Thessalonians 2:1-4? Walvoord writes:

Paul not only gave them assurance that they were not in this period [of God's Wrath], but he also gave them definite, discernible signs of the tribulation, which cannot occur while the church is still in the world. (*1 & 2 Thessalonians*).

Why not? Why can't Antichrist's Claim to be God and The Greatest Persecution occur "while the church is still in the world"? Walvoord does not explain.

MacArthur writes in his commentary on this passage:

[Paul] was not, of course, setting a posttribulational date for the Rapture; he did not tell his readers that they would live to experience the apostasy and the unveiling of the man of lawlessness. Paul's point was merely that the apostasy will precede the Day of the Lord.

On the contrary, Paul taught that "the apostasy" will also "precede" the "rapture." He taught: **the coming of our Lord Jesus Christ and our being gathered together to Him ... will not come until the ... man of lawlessness is revealed** (vs. 1, 3). Secondly, the reason Paul "did not tell his readers that they would live to experience the apostasy and the unveiling of the man of lawlessness," is because Paul did not know for certain the Endtimes would begin in their lifetime.

[13] Piper explains regarding 2 Thess 2:1-3:

If Paul were a pretribulationist, why did he not simply say in 2 Thessalonians 2:3 that the Christians don't need to worry that the day of the Lord has come because all the Christians are still here? They have not yet been raptured. But he does not say that. Instead, he talks just the way you would expect a posttribulational [or Pre Wrath Rescue] person to talk... "Let no one deceive you in any way. For that day will not come, unless the rebellion comes first, and the man of lawlessness is revealed, the son of destruction" (2 Thess. 2:3).

Paul tells them that they should not think that the day of the Lord is here, because the apostasy and the man of lawlessness have not appeared. In other words, he describes two events that must happen before the coming of the Lord, which we have seen is the same as the gathering of believers in 1 Thessalonians 4:17, when the "rapture" takes place. (209-210)

[14] Walvoord admits in an obscure footnote: "In 2 Thessalonians 2:1 Paul referred to the rapture as "our gathering together to him" (*Thessalonians*). However, he errs when he writes on the same passage: "all the passages clearly identified as referring to the rapture name no preceding events" ("Is a Posttribulational Rapture Revealed in Matthew 24?," *Grace Theological Journal* 6, no. 2 (1985): 258).

On the contrary, if "our gathering together to him" (2 Thess 2:1) refers to the "rapture," then Paul certainly taught there will be "preceding events" before the "rapture," including Antichrist's Claim to be God.

Chapter 6

The Sequence of Endtime Events According to Revelation 6-7

Contents

A) The Revelation of Jesus Christ is for the Church

B) The Beginning of Birth Pains, Christ's Return & the Church's Rescue in Revelation 6-7

Primary Points

- In Revelation, the description of saints being persecuted by the Antichrist refers to the Church.
- Revelation chapters 6-7 demonstrate the same sequence of Endtime events as Jesus taught in His Endtimes Teaching.
- The Church's Rescue is described in Revelation 7.

A) The Revelation of Jesus Christ is for the Church

Previously, we have confronted the popular view that Christ's Endtime Teaching (Matt 24) has no application for the Church (ch. 3, sec. D). Unfortunately, the Revelation is often viewed the same way. For example, Pre-tribulationism teaches that because the word "church" is not used after Revelation 3:22, that therefore, the Church has no part in any events described afterwards. [1]

However, there are many reasons to reject this view. This would include the fact that the word "church" is never used in the OT either. Are we to conclude from this that nothing in the OT applies to the Church? The OT predictions about Christ certainly do. Likewise, there are several reasons that the Revelation applies to the Church.

First, most will agree that the first 3 chapters of Revelation apply to the Church, including the seven letters to local churches. Likewise, most would agree the last 3 chapters of book apply to the Church, including the descriptions of the Resurrection (ch. 20) and the New Jerusalem (chs. 21-22). If such large parts of the beginning and end of the book clearly apply to the Church, then it seems questionable to assume that much of the remaining Revelation does not.

Secondly, let us note who the Revelation was written for. The first verse describes it as: **The revelation from Jesus Christ, which God gave him to show his servants** [*doulois*] **what must soon take place** (1:1 NIV). This is repeated in the last chapter of the book where we read: **The Lord ... sent his angel to show his servants** [*doulois*] **the things that must soon take place** (22:6 NIV).

This same Greek word (*doulos*) is translated throughout the NT over 30 times to refer to a **servant** (even slave) of **God**. [2] For example, we read, **Paul, a servant** [*doulos*] **of Christ Jesus, called to be an apostle** (Rom 1:1 NIV). Likewise, Peter writes, **Live as free people, but do not use your freedom as a cover-up for evil; live as God's slaves** [*douloi*] (1 Pet 2:16 NIV).

Therefore, **servants**, is practically a synonym for Church members throughout the NT. Therefore, Christ's **servants** in Revelation 1:1 and 22:6 certainly include the Church. This would be an odd way of introducing and summarizing the purpose of the Revelation if the vast majority of the book has nothing to do with the Church.

Granted, **the servants of our God** (Rev 7:3 NIV) can refer specifically to Jews or to **his servants the prophets** (Rev 10:7 NIV). But there are six other times the Revelation uses **servants** (*doulois*) to refer to a group of people and it is clear the term included the Church (cf. 1:1; 2:20; 11:18; 19:2, 5; 22:3). Therefore, when we read that the martyrs in Revelation 6 must wait **until the number of their fellow servants** [*syndouloi*] **and their brethren** [are] **killed** (v. 11 NIV), should we automatically deny these **servants** are members of the Church? No, we should not.

Likewise, it is odd how easily so many ignore the use of **the saints** throughout the Revelation. Again, throughout the NT the Greek word for **saints** (*hagios*) refers to members of the Church over 50 times. [3] For example, Paul writes: **To the church of God that is in Corinth, to those sanctified in Christ Jesus, called to be saints** [*hagiois*] (1 Cor 1:2 ESV). Likewise, in Revelation chapters 5 and 8 we read of **the prayers of the saints** [*hagiōn*] (5:8; 8:3, 4 NIV [4]). Does anyone want to deny that these include the prayers of Christians in the Church?

Later in chapter 11 we read: **The time has come for judging the dead, and for rewarding your ... <u>saints</u> [*hagiois*] and those who reverence your name, both small and great** (v. 18 NIV). Surely these **saints** to be rewarded include those in the Church.

In Revelation chapters 16-18, God is said to punish the world because **they poured out the blood of <u>saints</u> [*hagiōn*] and prophets** (16:6 NIV) and martyred **<u>saints</u> [*hagioi*] and apostles and prophets** (18:20 NIV; cf. **the saints** in 17:6; 18:24 NIV). Again, these **saints** certainly include the Church. In chapter 19 it is **the saints** [*hagiōn*] who participate in **the marriage supper of the Lamb** (vs. 8-9 NIV) and come to Earth **on white horses** (v. 14 NIV). The Church is mentioned repeatedly throughout the Revelation!

Where then does Pre-tribulationism want to exclude the Church in the Revelation? Any place the book mentions the suffering of God's people. Therefore, we can understand why this view is popular. It is tempting for modern interpreters of Revelation to find a way to exclude themselves personally from the warnings of great persecution. But **the saints** throughout the NT and the Revelation include the Church. And so do **the saints** in Revelation 13. The Church will be on the Earth for these events:

> **He** [the Antichrist] **was given power to make war against <u>the saints</u>** [*hagiōn*] **and to conquer them.** (Rev 13:7 NIV)
>
> **If anyone is to go into captivity, into captivity he will go. If anyone is to be killed with the sword, with the sword he will be killed. This calls for patient endurance and faithfulness on the part of <u>the saints</u>** [*hagiōn*]**.** (Rev 13:10 NIV)

So much for the common claim that the Church is absent from the Revelation after chapter 3! There are a total of 21 references to **saints** and **servants** referring to Christians in the Church in the Revelation. There is no biblical support for claiming otherwise. In fact, as we will see, the **saints** in the Revelation are the same Church members as **the elect** in the Christ's Endtimes Teaching. [5]

We can pause here and ask why the word "<u>church</u>" (*ecclesia*) is not used in the Revelation after chapter 3. First, let us notice where the word **church** <u>is</u> used in Revelation. In chapters 2-3 where it refers to the <u>local church</u> in various cities. But notice that many of the people in these churches were not real Christians. He describes those in **the church in Laodicea** as spiritually **wretched, pitiful, poor, blind and naked** (Rev 3:14, 17; cf. Rev 2:20; 3:1-6; esp. v. 3 with Matt 24:50).

That could <u>not</u> describe real Christians. Which is why Jesus essentially invites these church members to have a real relationship with Him when He says: **"be earnest and repent. Here I am! I stand at the door and knock. If anyone hears my voice and opens the door, I will come in and eat with that person, and they with me"** (vs. 19-20).

So why doesn't Revelation use the word "church" to describe who will be persecuted in The Greatest Persecution? First, it will not be local churches in general who will be persecuted. Many false Christians in churches will abandon their faith when the Antichrist's persecution begins (cf. Matt 24:9-10). It will only be the true **servants** and **saints** of God who will be persecuted. [6]

Secondly, the reason there are no references to the local church in much of Revelation is because it is describing The Greatest Persecution when local churches will be scattered and destroyed.

B) The sequence of Endtime events in Revelation 6-7

B.1) The Beginning of Birth Pains, The Greatest Persecution, & Christ's Return & Wrath in Revelation 6

The book of Revelation is, **The revelation of <u>Jesus Christ</u>, which God gave Him to show his servants** what will happen in the future (Rev 1:1 NIV). [7] Therefore, we would expect Christ's Endtimes Teaching in Revelation to be in harmony with His Endtimes Teaching in the Gospels. Both are on the exact same topic by the exact same Author.

This correspondence is precisely what we find when we compare the sequence of Endtime Events portrayed in Revelation 6 with that found in Matthew 24. Jesus is confirming Jesus. [8] Both of these texts reveal the same sequence of Endtime events: 1) The Beginning of Birth Pains, 2) The Greatest Persecution, and 3) Christ's Return.

[Stop and read Revelation 6:1-17]

In Matthew 24 Jesus said the first **birth pain** of the Endtimes would be **"many will come in My name, saying, 'I am the Christ,' and will mislead many"** (v. 5 NASB).

Likewise, **the first seal** describes a **rider** on **a white horse** emerging onto the world scene **bent on conquest** (Rev 6:2 NIV). It is rather clear that this **rider** will be attempting to imitate the **rider** on **a white horse** described in Revelation 19 (v. 11) who will be Jesus Christ. Therefore, the First Seal portrays the first **birth pain** of False Christs coming into the world. Elsewhere it will be argued that the emerging Antichrist will be the first and foremost False Christ. [9]

In Matthew 24 Jesus said the second **birth pain** would be unprecedented **wars** and **nation** rising **against nation** (vs. 6-7). Likewise, **the second seal** portrays a **rider** with **a large sword** who is **given power to take peace from the earth and to make people kill each other** (Rev 6:4 NIV). That is war.

In Matthew 24 Jesus said the third **birth pain** would be **famines and plagues** (Luke 21:11 NLT; cf. Matt 24:7). Likewise, **the third seal** describes a severe shortage of food when it will cost an entire **day's wages** for **two pounds of wheat** (Rev 6:4 NIV). With the opening of **the fourth seal** we read that **famine and plague** contribute to people living in **a fourth of the earth** being killed (v. 8 NIV).

In Matthew 24, Jesus said after these **beginning of birth pains**, **"Then you will be handed over to be persecuted and put to death"** (v. 9 NIV). Likewise, **the fifth seal** portrays **those who had been slain because of the word of God and the testimony** for Jesus **they had maintained** (Rev 6:9 NIV). This is The Greatest Persecution following The Beginning of Birth Pains. Then Jesus described what will happen **after the completion of the greatest persecution**:

> Immediately <u>after</u> the completion of the greatest persecution, <u>then</u> 'the sun will be darkened, and the moon will not give its light; the stars will fall from the sky and the heavenly bodies will be shaken.'
>
> **Then the sign that the Son of Man is coming will appear in the sky. And then all the peoples of the earth**

will mourn when they see the Son of Man coming on the clouds of heaven, with power and great glory. (29-30 [10])

Likewise, with the opening of **the sixth seal** in Revelation 6 we read:

The sun turned black like sackcloth made of goat hair, the whole moon turned blood red, and the stars in the sky fell to earth...

Then ... everyone ... called to the mountains and the rocks, "Fall on us and hide us from the face of him who sits on the throne and from the wrath of the Lamb! **For the great day of their** wrath has come, **and who can withstand it?"** (Rev 6:12-13, 15-17 NIV; cf. Isa 2:19-21)

This is describing the Cosmic Signs that will immediately precede Christ's Return and the beginning of Christ's Wrath. Revelation 6:16-17 makes this clear. With the appearance of the Cosmic Signs, unbelievers will recognize **"the wrath of the Lamb ... has come."**

Notice something very important. Many popular views on the Endtimes teach that all of the preceding Seals of Preparation will be Christ's Wrath. But this is impossible. The **fifth seal** includes The Greatest Persecution of God's people. This could never occur in the time of Christ's Wrath because Scripture promises we are to **wait for his Son from heaven ... Jesus, who rescues us from the coming wrath** (1 Thess 1:10 NIV).

Contrary to both Pre-tribulationism and Post-tribulationism, there will not be any members of the Church on the Earth during Christ's Wrath. This is why **the wrath of the Lamb** does not **come** until the opening of **the sixth seal** in Revelation 6. The nature and timing of Christ's Wrath will be further explained in chapter 14 of this book.

It is clear in both Christ's Endtimes Teaching and His Revelation that Jesus taught the Endtimes would begin with the first **birth pain** and **the first seal** of a False Christ(s), and be followed by **wars** and **famines** making up **the beginning of birth pains.** These then will be followed by Christians being **persecuted** in The Greatest Persecution with the opening of **the fifth seal**. In both accounts the Cosmic Signs, Christ's Return, and Christ's Wrath will follow in **the sixth seal**.

B.2) The Church's Rescue in Revelation 7

In Christ's Endtimes Teaching what did Jesus say would immediately follow the Cosmic Signs and Christ's Return? The Church's Rescue. Jesus taught:

He will send out His angels with a loud trumpet sound, and they will lift up and gather together God's elect people from one end of the sky to the other, from everywhere on Earth (Matt 24:31 [11])

Therefore, if the Cosmic Signs and Christ's Return were described at the end of Revelation chapter 6, then what would we expect to see described in Revelation chapter 7? The Church's Rescue before Christ's Wrath begins. And that is exactly what Jesus reveals.

[Read Revelation chapter 7. Notice especially verses 9 & 14]

Revelation 7 describes two events that occur at Christ's Return. The first event was not mentioned by Christ in His Endtimes Teaching. At Christ's Return, **144,000** Jews **from all the tribes of Israel** (v. 4 NIV) will be chosen to remain on the Earth and be **sealed** for protection. Why? Because Christ's Wrath to punish the world is about to begin, as described in Revelation chapter 8. These **144,000** Jews are described elsewhere as the **first fruits** (Rev 14:4 NIV) of God's Endtime plan to spiritually restore the nation of Israel. [12]

After this (Rev 7:9) John sees a **multitude** of Christians! from all over the world in Heaven. They are Christians who **have washed their robes and made them white in the blood of the Lamb** Jesus Christ (v. 14 NIV). They are the Church **from every nation, tribe, people, and language** (v. 9 NIV). Where did these Christians come from? The Angel tells John, **"These are they who have come out of the great persecution** [*thlipseōs*]**"** (v. 14). For reasons given earlier (ch. 3, sec. E), **persecution**, not "tribulation" is the best interpretation of the Greek word *thlipsis* here.

Therefore, notice where these Christians will come from. They were in The Greatest Persecution. They are among the same members of the Church depicted a few verses earlier as those **who had been martyred for the word of God and for being faithful in their testimony** for Jesus Christ (6:9 NLT).

Notice that both the martyrs in Revelation chapter 6 and **they who have come out of the great persecution** in chapter 7 are wearing **white robes**. These are the same people. They are **fellow servants** [*syndouloi*] of Christ and Christian **brothers and sisters** (6:11). Therefore, this **multitude** who had **washed their robes and made them white in the blood of the Lamb** and was **from every nation, tribe, people, and language** (7:9, 14) is describing the Church's Rescue after The Greatest Persecution. [13]

Finally, what would we expect to see next in the Revelation after the Church's Rescue? Christ's Wrath. And what do we read next starting in Revelation chapter 8?

> **The first angel sounded his trumpet, and there came hail and fire mixed with blood, and it was hurled down on the earth. A third of the earth was burned up, a third of the trees were burned up, and all the green grass was burned up.** (Rev 8:7 NIV)

That is the beginning of Christ's Wrath on the Earth.

B.3) Comparing the sequence of Endtime events in Matthew 24 & Revelation 6-7

It should be obvious that Jesus intended to teach a very specific sequence of Endtime events in both Christ's Endtimes Teaching and Christ's Revelation. It should also be obvious that the sequence He taught in Matthew 24 and Revelation 6-7 is the same.

Granted, there are some minor differences. In Matthew 24 Jesus mentions **earthquakes** as a part of The Beginning of Birth Pains, but **a great earthquake** is not mentioned in Revelation 6 until Christ's Return (v. 12). In Revelation 6 deaths by **wild beasts** are mentioned as part of The Beginning of Birth Pains, but this is not the case in Christ's Endtimes Teaching.

Likewise, Jesus did not talk about the sealing of the 144,000 Jews (Rev 7:2-8) in His Teaching. Christ's exclusion of this event in Matthew 24 is another reason to reject the popular view that it is primarily for the Jews and not the Church.

Likewise, in Revelation 6-7 Jesus did not reveal anything about Antichrist's Claim to be God (Matt 24:15). Although this event is described later in Revelation chapter 13 (cf. vs. 5-6). But the overall sequence of events in Matthew 24:4-31 and Revelation chapters 6-7 are identical. This can be summarized in the following table:

Sequence of Endtime Events in Matt 24 & Rev 6-7

	"These are the beginning of birth pains" (Matt 24:8)	
❶	**False Christ(s)**	First event: Matt 24:5 First Seal: Rev 6:1-2
❷	**Wars**	Second event: Matt 24:6-7 Second Seal: Rev 6:3-4
❸	**Famines**	Third event: Matt 24:7 Third Seal: Rev 6:5-6
❹	**Plagues**	Fourth event: Luke 21:11 Fourth Seal: Rev 6:8
	"Then you will be arrested, persecuted, and killed." (Matt 24:9 NLT)	
❺	**The Greatest Persecution**	After Antichrist's Claim to be God, **"then there will be the greatest persecution"** (Matt 24:21) Fifth Seal: Rev 6:9-11
	"Immediately after the completion of the greatest persecution" (v. 29)	
❻	**The Cosmic Signs**	Matt 24:29 Sixth Seal: Rev 6:12-14
❼	**Christ's Return**	Matt 24:30 Rev 6:15-16
❽	**The Church's Rescue**	Matt 24:31 Rev 7:9, 14
❾	**Christ's Wrath**	Matt 24:37-41 Rev 8:7ff

The similarities between Christ's Endtimes Teaching and Revelation 6-7 can be portrayed in the following graphics:

Endtime Events According to Jesus

② Antichrist's Claim to be God

when you see standing in the holy place 'the abomination that causes desolation' (Matt 24:15)

④ Cosmic Signs / Christ's Return / Church's Rescue

Immediately after the completion of the greatest persecution ... He will send His Angels ... and they will lift up and gather together God's elect in the sky, from everywhere on earth (Matt 24:29-31)

① Beginning of Birth Pains

Antichrist's Rise

Wars, famines, plagues, & earthquakes. All these are the beginning of birth pains (vs. 4-8)

③ The Greatest Persecution

Antichrist's Wrath

Then you will be handed over to be persecuted... Then flee ... then there will be the greatest persecution (vs. 9, 16, 21)

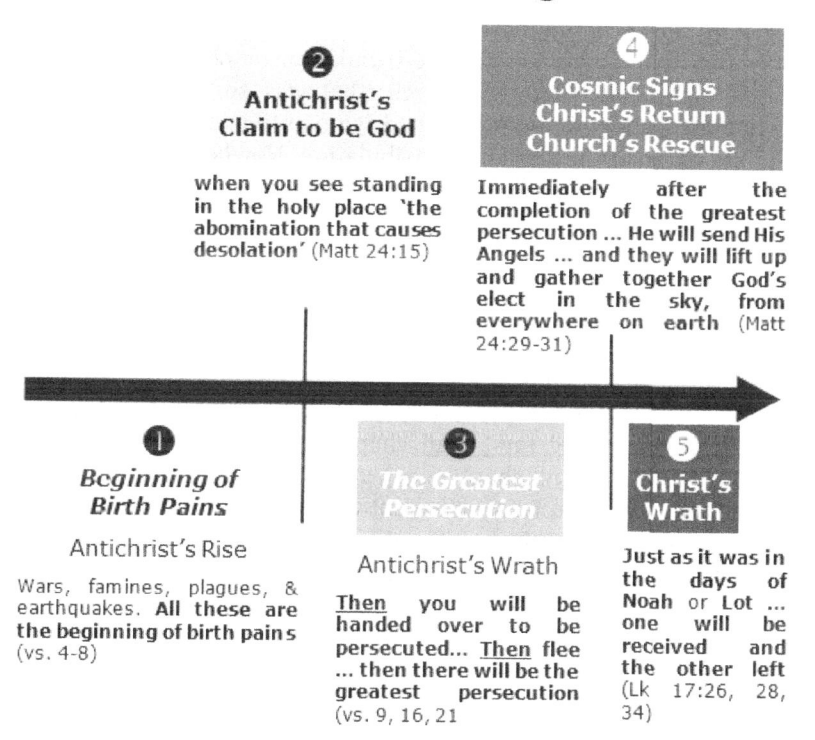

⑤ Christ's Wrath

Just as it was in the days of Noah or Lot ... one will be received and the other left (Lk 17:26, 28, 34)

Endtime Events According to Jesus in Rev 6-7

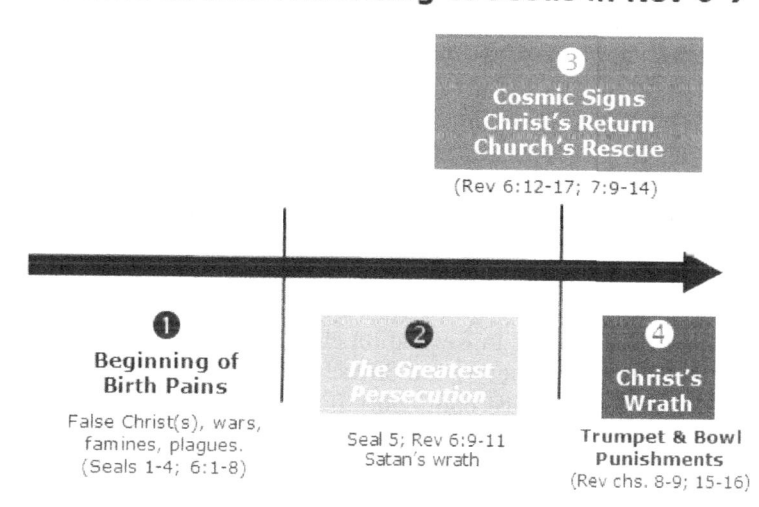

③ Cosmic Signs / Christ's Return / Church's Rescue

(Rev 6:12-17; 7:9-14)

① Beginning of Birth Pains

False Christ(s), wars, famines, plagues.
(Seals 1-4; 6:1-8)

② The Greatest Persecution

Seal 5; Rev 6:9-11
Satan's wrath

④ Christ's Wrath

Trumpet & Bowl Punishments
(Rev chs. 8-9; 15-16)

Seal Preparations for Christ's Wrath

[1] For example, the popular Pre-tribulation writer Mark Hitchcock writes: "Revelation is largely silent about the church, and 'the silence is deafening'" (quoted in Knoor). Likewise, the Pre-tribulationist John Walvoord writes:
> It is significant that the church, that was so prominent in [Rev] chapters 2 and 3, is not mentioned again until 22:16, except as the wife of the Lamb at the close of the tribulation. Nowhere in scenes of earth that describe the end time (chaps. 6–19) is the church pictured as involved in the earthly struggle. (*Rev*, loc. 1874)

On the contrary, Walvoord's point is not "significant" at all because "the church" is "pictured as involved in the earthly struggle" in chapters 6 and 12-14 as **servants** or **saints** in the Church experiencing The Greatest Persecution.

Finally, John MacArthur has written:
> For many reasons, the pre-tribulation view seems most faithful to New Testament teaching. First of all, chapters 2-3 of Revelation speak of the church on earth, and chapters 4-5 speak of the church in heaven. But beginning with chapter 6, which introduces the Tribulation, there is no further mention of the church until chapter 18. (*MNTC*, Matt 24)

Again, this is a false statement made by a rightly respected teacher.

[2] *BDAG*.

[3] Ibid.

[4] Unless otherwise noted, texts from Revelation in this section are from the NIV 1984 version because it retains the translation of *hagios* as **the saints**.

[5] Not surprisingly, it is difficult to find clear statements in commentaries that reflect the fact that these references in Revelation to **saints, bond-servants**, and those who proclaim **the word of God and the testimony of Jesus** are describing members of Christ's Church.

Osborne only refers to those making a **testimony** as a "Christian witness to the gospel message" (56). Thomas, a Pre-tribulationist, refers to "the testimony as a badge of allegiance to Christ" (723). MacArthur is willing to call those in Rev 6:9 "believers" (193). To most people these descriptions would refer to members of the Church. But as discussed in ch. 14 (sec. C), Pre-tribulationists oddly label these Christians in Revelation 6 as "post-rapture" Christians who are not members of the Church. Do not be deceived. The martyrs in Revelation chs. 6 and 13 are the Last Generation Church on the Earth before the Church's Rescue.

Interestingly, Mounce comments on Rev 6:9, "Note that John knows nothing of a 'rapture' of the church by which Christians are spared the tribulation that normally accompanies a godly life (cf. 2 Tim 3:12)" (147).

Walvoord makes an odd comment about the members of the Church who are "raptured" and **who have come out of the great persecution** described in Revelation 7:14:

> Though these are never described by the term "church," they are constantly called saints—those set apart as holy to God and saved through the sacrifice of Christ... They, like all others, must rest alone in that sacrifice that Christ provided for them. What is true for them is true for the saints of all ages; only the blood of Christ is able to wash away sin. (*Rev*, loc. 2159, 2301).

Those people are the Church, Dr. Walvoord. Likewise, the Pre-tribulationist Thomas Ice makes a similarly silly (and offensive, if not borderline heretical) statement:

> We are saying that the Holy Spirit will be present in His trans-dispensational ministry of bringing the elect of the tribulation to faith in Christ, even though they will not be part of the body of Christ—the Church. (quoted in Knoor, as "Ice, 2015e").

[6] Van Kampen adds to why Matt 24 and Rev differentiate between **elect**, **saints**, and **servants**, and using the term "church." Regarding the Revelation he writes:

> The fact that the word church is not used in the heart of the book [of Revelation] only validates once again the fact that it will not be the church in general that undergoes Antichrist's persecution. On the contrary, it will be the faithful remnant within the church that will stand true to Christ during these difficult times.
>
> That is why the word "saint" is used thirteen times in the heart of the book (see 5:8; 8:3–4; 11:18; 13:7, 10; 14:12; 16:6; 17:6; 18:20, 24; 19:8; 20:9). In fact, the book of Revelation isn't even addressed to the church in general, but to the true bond-servants of Christ. It is "the revelation of Jesus Christ, which God gave Him [Christ] to show to His bond-servants" (1:1). [This is why in Rev 2-3] Christ separates those "who have ears to hear"—genuine bond-servants of Christ who listen carefully to what the Spirit is telling these churches—from the specific church that He is reprimanding.

Likewise, regarding the Olivet Discourse, he writes:

> A possible explanation of why the term "church" is not used ... is that when the church is faced with the tribulation [better "persecution"] associated with Antichrist (Matt. 24:9; cf. vv. 21–22), it will not be the church in general that "endures to the end" (vv. 10–13); instead, it will be the genuine bondservants of Christ (His elect or saints) who will prefer to endure the wrath of Satan rather than the wrath of God (v. 9). This is why Christ refers to them as "you" throughout the teaching.
>
> The rest of the professing church will escape this terrible time of

persecution because they will "fall away" (v. 10) and their love for Christ "will grow cold" (v. 12) as they choose to worship Antichrist rather than die for the sake of the true Christ.

It will be the church in general that will fall away into apostasy in the last days. It is the elect of God (the saints) who will endure Antichrist's persecution. That is precisely why terms such as "the elect" and "the saints" are used instead of the word church to describe the faithful who will choose death over compromise! (*Rapture*, loc. 1836 ff.)

[7] The full text of Revelation 1:1 reads, **The revelation from Jesus Christ, which God gave him to show his servants what must <u>soon</u> take place** (NIV). The fact that Jesus said His predictions were to occur **soon** (v. 1) and the events were **near** (v. 3) is the primary reason that some (Preterist) believe most of the prophecies in Revelation have already been fulfilled. Admittedly, these are difficult statements, but a helpful answer is the near/far and double nature of prophecy fulfillment in Scripture. For more on this see ch. 12, sec. B.3.

[8] Joseph Jurgensmeier has noted regarding the comparison of Endtime events between Christ's Endtimes Teaching and His Revelation:

Something I noticed as I read Revelation 6-7 is that it specifically focuses on a heavenly viewpoint of the events while Matthew 24 seems focused on an earthly viewpoint. John is watching God decree and orchestrate the end times from heaven. We see riders leaving heaven (ch. 6) and saints being brought in (7:14). While in Matthew 24 the narrative is more focused on what an inhabitant of Earth will experience. The Antichrist will come, there will be persecution, but then Jesus will come to rescue his people and bring judgement on the Earth.

[9] For more on the meaning of the First Seal Preparation (cf. Rev 6:1-2) see *The Beginning of Birth Pains* (*BBP*), ch. 11.

[10] For an explanation of the suggested translation of Matt 24:29-30 see ch. 3, sec. E.

[11] For an explanation of the suggested translation of Matt 24:31 see ch. 4, sec. C.2.

[12] For more on God's plan for Israel during the Endtimes see Advanced Studies on the Endtime, ch. 11, available online at www.trainingtimothys.com.

[13] Regarding those described as **they who have come out of the great persecution** (Rev 7:14) commentaries are rather disappointing. Morris and Mounce take a symbolic (Idealist) approach suggesting it primarily applies to <u>all</u> persecuted saints throughout history (Morris, 114-15; Mounce, 164). Likewise, Beale writes: "it would be best to view them as

representative of all believers who must suffer" (433). But Jesus made it clear that the **great persecution** was a specific Endtime event (cf. Matt 24:21-22, 29-31).

Pre-tribulationists try to force the Church out of this passage. Walvoord believes "the multitude represents a different body of saints [than the Church]" (*Rev,* loc. 2254). Rather, he claims they are Christians who are saved <u>after</u> the Church has been "raptured" or "post-rapture" Christians. Again, this serious error will be addressed in ch. 14, sec. C.

Likewise, MacArthur is disappointing here, claiming, "the Rapture of the church is not in view in this verse" and adding, "If these believers were part of the church, why would the elder not have so identified them?" (230-1).

Contrary to MacArthur, "the elder" <u>did</u> identify them as "part of the church" by describing them as those who **have washed their robes and made them white in the blood of the Lamb**.

Likewise, Thomas reflects his Pre-tribulationism when he writes: "The best solution is to identify this vast crowd as Gentile and Jewish believers who have died either natural or violent deaths during the period of the first six seals and come out from the Great Tribulation" (792). He is substantially correct. But contrary to Thomas, Rev 7:9, 14 portrays the Church's Rescue which "Jewish believers" will not be a part of.

Osborne is better and writes:
> With the article ["the"] it does denote a particular "tribulation," and in the context of Revelation it most likely refers to the final war against the <u>saints</u> waged by the dragon (Rev 12). (324 underlining added)

Osborne interprets Rev 12 as describing the persecution of "the church ... in this final three-and-a-half-year period of history" (485).

Some have suggested those described in Rev 7:9, 14 represent the post-rapture evangelistic efforts of the 144,000, but even the Pre-tribulationist Thomas writes:
> ("After these things I looked") indicates a vision that is distinct from the preceding one (Alford; Ford). It is not a connective phrase advancing what John has just seen by way of a causal connection, i.e., the fruit of the ministry of the 144,000 being the Gentile multitude of the second vision. Conditions depicted in the two visions appear to be simultaneous rather than consecutive. (790)

Chapter 7

The Sequence of Endtime Events According to the Prophet Daniel

Daniel 7, 9, & 12

[Note: This chapter is considered supplemental. However, it will be especially helpful to those who have been taught the popular Pre-tribulation view of the Endtimes.]

Contents

A) Endtime Events According to Daniel 7

B) Endtime Events According to Daniel 9

C) Endtime Events According to Daniel 12

D) A summary of the sequence of Endtime events in Daniel

Primary Points

- Daniel chapters 7, 9, and 12 each describe the same sequence of Endtime events as Christ's Endtimes Teaching.
- The teaching in all of these chapters applies to the Church.
- The **saints** being persecuted by the Antichrist include the Church.
- Even Daniel's "70th week" includes God's plan for the Church, because the Church is certainly included in the first "69 weeks" predicting Christ's crucifixion.

As noted previously, it is common for Teachers to begin their presentation of the Endtimes in Daniel. However, for reasons given earlier (ch. 3, sec. C), it is best to start with Christ's Endtimes Teaching. This is because His NT teaching helps us accurately interpret Daniel's more obscure visions.

This will be demonstrated throughout this chapter. For example, Jesus provided commentary on Daniel 9:27 when He said, **"So when you see standing in the holy place 'the abomination that causes desolation,' spoken of through the prophet Daniel— let the reader understand"** (Matt 24:15 NIV).

Daniel is a very complex book of prophecy. It tells us many things about the Antichrist's Rise and Reign that will be discussed more in book #2 of the *Endtimes Essentials* series, *The Beginning of Birth Pains*. The focus of this chapter is primarily two things: 1) To establish Daniel's prophecies as revelation for what the Church will experience in the Endtimes; [1] 2) Recognize that the sequence of Endtime events in Daniel agrees with Jesus and Paul.

A) Endtime Events according to Daniel 7

[Read Daniel 7:1-27]

In Daniel chapter 7 the Prophet is given a vision of Endtime events and an interpretation of his vision. If we compare this to Christ's Endtimes Teaching, we again see the following four events being described: 1) The Beginning of Birth Pains, 2) Antichrist's Claim to Be God, 3) The Greatest Persecution, and 4) Christ's Return.

A.1) Daniel 7 is for the Church

This prophecy predicts a future **king will arise** who **will speak against the Most High and oppress his saints** (7:24-25 NIV [2]). This **king** will be the future Antichrist. In the Endtimes he will be **waging war against the saints and defeating them** (v. 21 NIV). **The saints will be delivered into his hands for a time, times and half a time** (NIV; 3.5 years; v. 25). These **saints** are referred to six times in this passage (vs. 18, 21, 22, 25, 27). Who are these **saints** whom the Antichrist will **war against**, be **defeating**, and **oppress** in the Endtimes? [3]

A popular view is that these **saints** are only Jews and do not include Christians in the Church. But three times the prophecy states these same **saints of the Most High will receive the kingdom and will possess it forever** (v. 18 NIV; cf. vs. 22, 27). The Church is certainly going to be a part of this eternal **kingdom**. Which is why verse 14 says this **kingdom** will include **all nations and peoples**, not just Jews. The **saints** who inherit the **kingdom** are the same **saints** who will be persecuted by the Antichrist. And those **saints** will not just be Jews, but will include Christians in the Church. [4]

The Hebrew word for **saints** in Daniel (*qaddish:* "holy ones, saints" [5]) means the same thing as the Greek word for **saints** in the NT (*hagios* "human beings consecrated to God" [6]). In the NT, the word **saints** consistently refers to the Church (almost 60 times). Therefore, NT revelation expands the biblical meaning of **saints** in the OT to include Christians from **all nations and peoples** (Dan 7:14 NIV).

Likewise, these **saints** in Daniel 7 who will be persecuted by the Antichrist are the same as **the elect** in Matthew 24 who **will be handed over to be persecuted** by the Antichrist (v. 9 NIV; cf. vs. 15, 21-22). And both references include the Church.

Therefore, contrary to popular teaching, this interpretation of Daniel 7 agrees with what we have seen in the previous three chapters. Both Jesus and Paul clearly taught the Church will experience The Beginning of Birth Pains, Antichrist's Claim to be God, and The Greatest Persecution. Therefore, Daniel's prophecy agrees with Jesus and Paul that **the elect** and **saints** in the Church will suffer the persecution of the Antichrist (cf. Matt 24:22, 24, 31).

A.2) The Beginning of Birth Pains in Daniel 7

In Christ's Endtimes Teaching Jesus said that a major part of The Beginning of Birth Pains would be **wars** (Matt 24:6-7). Daniel 7 also speaks of these Endtime wars when he writes: **The fourth beast is a fourth kingdom that will appear on earth. It will ... devour the whole earth, trampling it down and crushing it** (7:23 NIV). This future **fourth beast** depicts both the Antichrist and his Endtime Beast Empire. [7]

In Daniel chapter 8 it says of the Antichrist: **He will cause a shocking amount of destruction...he will destroy many without warning.** Elsewhere we read **He will attack the mightiest fortresses** and still **succeed in whatever he does** (8:24-25; 11:39 NLT). These prophecies reflect the unprecedented **wars** that Jesus predicted.

A.3) Antichrist's Claim to be God in Daniel 7

Christ taught that in the midst of these wars, His people will **see standing in the holy place 'the abomination that causes** desolation,' spoken of through the prophet Daniel** (Matt 24:15 NIV). As noted in a previous chapter, the Apostle Paul also described this event as when **the man of lawlessness is revealed** and **he sets himself up in God's temple, proclaiming himself to be God** (2 Thess 2:3-4 NIV).

Likewise, Daniel 7 says that an Endtime **king** [Antichrist] **will arise** and **speak against the Most High** (vs. 24-25 NIV; cf. vs. 8, 20-21). It is because of these biblical descriptions of **the abomination that causes desolation**, that it is referred to as Antichrist's Claim to be God throughout *Endtimes Essentials*.

A.4) The Greatest Persecution in Daniel 7

What did Jesus say would happen immediately after the Antichrist's Claim to be God in the Jerusalem temple? His people are to **flee** because then there will be The Greatest Persecution (cf. Matt 24:16-21). What did Daniel say would happen immediately after the Antichrist's Claim to be God? "**He** [the Antichrist] **will speak against the Most High and** then **oppress his saints** (v. 25 NIV). Earlier, the text said, **this horn was waging war against the saints and defeating them** (v. 21 NIV).

Daniel 7 states **The saints will be delivered into** [Antichrist's] **hands for a time, times and half a time** (v. 25 NIV). This corresponds to other references in Scripture that The Greatest Persecution will last 3.5 Jewish years. In Daniel 12:7 we read **It will be for a time, times and half a time. When the power of the holy people has been finally broken** (NIV). Likewise, in Revelation 13, **the saints** are persecuted by Antichrist for **42 months** (v. 5; cf. 11:2), all of which equal 3.5 Jewish years. [8]

A.5) Christ's visible Return will stop The Greatest Persecution because it will include the Church's Rescue

After the 3.5 years of The Greatest Persecution, Daniel says, "**his** [Antichrist's] **power will be taken away and completely destroyed forever**" (7:26 NIV). How and when is the Antichrist's power to persecute God's people **taken away**? Daniel saw, **one like a son of man, coming with the clouds of heaven** (7:13 NIV).

Christ's visible Return will stop The Greatest Persecution because it will include the Church's Rescue.

Likewise, Jesus said **the Son of Man** will be **coming on the clouds** for the Church's Rescue and to end The Greatest Persecution (Matt 24:30-31). Both Jesus and Daniel teach the Antichrist's persecution of God's **saints** and **elect** will be stopped by Christ's Return and **coming with the clouds of heaven** (Dan 7:13; cf. Dan 7:21-22; 25-27). This is because Christ's Return includes the Church's Rescue. Both Jesus and Daniel also taught Christ's Return would be visible to the whole world when He Rescues the Church.

Paul concurs with Daniel. He told the Thessalonians **God will provide rest** [*anasin*, NIV **relief**] **for you who are being persecuted and also for us when the Lord Jesus appears from heaven** (2 Thess 1:7 NLT). He added, **the coming of our Lord Jesus Christ and our gathering together to Him ... will not come unless the apostasy comes first, and the man of lawlessness is revealed** (2 Thess 2:1, 3 NASB). Jesus, Paul, and Daniel agree that the Antichrist persecutes God's **saints** before the real Christ rescues God's **saints**.

Therefore, in Daniel 7 we have the same sequence of Endtime events taught by Christ and the Apostle Paul. Wars will lead to Antichrist's Rise and his eventual Claim to be God. This will initiate The Greatest Persecution of God's **saints** (Dan 7:25) and **elect** (Matt 24:21-22), which will include the Church. Only after this time will The Greatest Persecution be stopped by Christ's visible Return.

B) Endtime Events according to Daniel 9

[Read Daniel 9:24-27]

In Daniel chapter 9 the Prophet is given another explanation of Endtime events. Verses 24-27 are some of the most well-known, controversial, and complex statements in Scripture. The primary purpose for discussing them here is again, 1) To establish Daniel's prophecies as revelation for what the Church will experience in the Endtimes; and 2) Recognize that the sequence of Endtime events in Daniel agrees with Jesus and Paul.

B.1) Daniel 9 is for the Church

Daniel 9:24-27 is a key text for those who claim Endtime events have little if anything to do with the Church. This is based on the Angel **Gabriel** (cf. v. 21) telling Daniel (a Jew) that the prophecy is **for your people and your holy city** (v. 24), and to **anoint the Most Holy Place** (NIV). This obviously refers to the Jews, Jerusalem, and a Jewish temple. Likewise, **the abomination that causes desolation ... at the temple** (v. 27 NIV) clearly applies to the Jews and Jerusalem. For these reasons many claim that Christians in the Church will not be present at all during Daniel's Last 7 Years ("70th week"). But there are clear problems with this view.

First, the prophecy of the "69 weeks" clearly includes God's plan for the Church. It culminates with **the Anointed One** (Christ) being **put to death** (v. 26). Does anyone want to claim that this prediction of the crucifixion of Christ does not apply to the Church in any way? [9] Of course not. Therefore, if the culmination of the "69 weeks" applies to the Church, then we can expect elements of the "70th week" to as well. There are no Scriptures that teach otherwise.

Secondly, it should be noticed that the very same **abomination that causes desolation** (Dan 9:27 NIV) is spoken of by Christ in the context of events that will include **God's elect people** (Matt 24:22, 24, 31), which includes the Church. Jesus taught that the Church will **"see ... the abomination that causes desolation, spoken of through the prophet Daniel"** (Matt 24:15 NIV).

Likewise, Paul taught the Church that:

> **The coming of our Lord Jesus Christ and our gathering together to Him ... will not come unless the apostasy comes first, and the man of lawlessness is revealed, the son of destruction, who opposes and exalts himself above every so-called god or object of worship, so that he takes his seat in the temple of God, displaying himself as being God.** (2 Thess 2:1, 3-4 NASB)

This is the very event being described in Daniel 9:27. Therefore, Paul taught that Christ's Return and the Church's Rescue will not happen until after: **In the middle of the 'seven' he** [Antichrist] **will put an end to sacrifice and offering. And at the temple**

he will set up an abomination that causes desolation (Dan 9:27 NIV). Jesus and Paul clearly taught that the Church is on Earth for this event, Antichrist's Claim to be God.

This illustrates something that should have been obvious. Gabriel <u>did not</u> say these events were <u>only</u> for the Jews as many assume. The fact that Gabriel says these events involve the nation of Israel <u>does not</u> require they cannot also apply to the Church. For example, he told Daniel the prediction of Christ's crucifixion was **for your people** the Jews (v. 24). But obviously that <u>did not mean it could not</u> also apply to other people. In fact, so far in history, Gabriel's prediction of Christ's crucifixion in Daniel 9 has applied much more to the Church than the nation of Israel.

To insist there can be no overlap in God's Endtime plan for the Church and Israel (Dispensationalism) is merely an unbiblical assumption that is nowhere supported by Scripture. In fact, the NT often melds God's plan for the Jews and the Church together (cf. Rom 11:1-25; Eph 2:11-22). These NT texts refute a great deal of the dogmatism in "dispensational" and Pre-tribulational views on prophetic Scripture. [10]

B.2) The Beginning of Birth Pains and Antichrist's Claim to be God in Daniel 9

Because Daniel 9 applies to God's Endtime plan for the Church, it describes several things that Jesus said applied to **God's elect people** in His Endtimes Teaching. First, there are two events described here that Jesus mentioned as well. Jesus said The Beginning of Birth Pains would include **wars** (cf. Matt 24:6-7). It is confirmed in Daniel 9 that **War will continue until the end** (v. 26 NIV).

Secondly, as noted, both Jesus and Paul taught the Church will be present for **'the abomination that causes desolation'** <u>spoken of through the prophet Daniel</u> (Matt 24:15; cf. Dan 9:27).

B.3) Understanding Daniel's Last 7 Years

Daniel 9 says **Seventy 'sevens' are decreed** (v. 24 NIV) for a certain part of God's prophetic plan. As most OT scholars explain, this OT language refers to seventy sets of seven years. [11] This equals a total of 490 years (70x7). The text goes on to explain what will happen within these 490 prophetic years.

First, there would be a decree **to restore and rebuild Jerusalem** (v. 25 NIV). This is referring to the decree of Artaxerxes recorded in the book of Nehemiah authorizing the rebuilding of the city (cf. Neh 2:1-8). This occurred in 445 B.C., about 100 years after Daniel received this prophecy.

Second, after this decree, we are told **there will be seven 'sevens,' and sixty-two 'sevens'** (v. 25 NIV). This equals 69 periods of seven years or 483 years (7x7 + 62x7=69 "7's").

Thirdly, the prophecy states at the end of that time, **the Anointed One will be put to death** (v. 26 NIV). This clearly refers to the crucifixion of Jesus Christ. Remarkably, it has been demonstrated that this prophecy was literally fulfilled, <u>perhaps even to the exact day</u>. [12]

Next, the prophecy states: **The people of the ruler who will come will destroy the city and the sanctuary** (v. 26 NIV). The near and partial fulfillment of this prediction occurred in A.D. 70 when the Roman general Titus destroyed Jerusalem and desecrated the Jewish temple. However, Luke 21:20 and Revelation 11:1-2, the latter written in the A.D. 90's, clearly describe the final and complete fulfillment of this prophecy.

Next, this prophecy states, **The <u>end</u> will come like a flood: War will continue until the <u>end</u>, and desolations have been decreed** (v. 26 NIV). This gives us a clue that the prophecy has fast-forwarded to the Endtimes. Indeed, what the prophecy says next definitely occurs in the Endtimes:

> **"He will confirm a covenant with many for one 'seven.' In the middle of the 'seven' he will put an end to sacrifice and offering. And at the temple he will set up an abomination that causes desolation, until the end that is decreed is poured out on him."** (Dan 9:27 NIV)

We know this prediction will be fulfilled in the Endtimes because in Christ's Endtimes Teaching He said the Last Generation Church will **see standing in the holy place 'the abomination that causes desolation,' spoken of through the prophet Daniel** (Matt 24:15 NIV). This event has been discussed in the previous section.

The point to notice here is that verse 27 describes the last seven years of the prophesied 490 years. This is typically called "Daniel's 70th Week" because the other "69 Weeks" of the prophecy were fulfilled at Christ's crucifixion. But it is more clearly "Daniel's Last 7 Years," and will be labeled this throughout the *Endtimes Essentials*.

Because Daniel's Last 7 Years occurs in the Endtimes, there has been an odd, but certain "gap" of almost 2,000 years between when **the Anointed One will be put to death** (v. 26), and what is being described in verse 27. Such "gaps" in what a biblical Prophet sees in the future is a feature of biblical prophecy. [13]

Therefore, Daniel indicates there is one more period of 7 years to be fulfilled. The prophecy predicts several important Endtime events will occur during this time.

First, a **ruler who will come** will make **a covenant with many** (vs. 26-27). As discussed further in the next volume, *The Beginning of Birth Pains*, this will probably be Antichrist's Religious Covenant with the unbelievers of the world.

The prophecy goes on to predict that **in the middle of the seven** years, or 3.5 years after making **a covenant with many**, the future Antichrist **will put an end to sacrifice and offering. And at the temple he will set up an abomination that causes desolation** (v. 27). This is what Jesus referred to as **"'the abomination that causes desolation,' spoken of through the prophet Daniel"** (Matt 24:15 NIV). This will be discussed further in book #4: *The Greatest Persecution*.

C) Endtime Events according to Daniel 12

[Read Daniel 12:1-13]

C.1) Daniel 12 is for the Church

A suggested translation for Daniel 12:1 would be:
"In the endtimes, the Archangel Michael, the great military commander who protects the sons of your people, will stop protecting them. Then the saints will experience the anguish of being attacked by an enemy. That anguish will be greater than any that has happened since nations have existed." [14]

The **anguish of being attacked by an enemy** translates the Hebrew word *tsarah* which can mean, "the anguish of a people besieged by an enemy." [15] The fact that this **anguish will be greater than any that has happened since nations have existed** clearly refers to The Greatest Persecution.

The sons of your people clearly refers to Israel. Therefore, some have used this text to claim that only the Jews will experience The Greatest Persecution. It is true that they will be a part of it. The Antichrist will persecute the Jews in Israel. This is why Jesus said after, **'the abomination that causes desolation,' spoken of through the prophet Daniel ... then let those** [Jews] **who are in Judea flee to the mountains** (Matt 24:15-16 NIV).

But God will miraculously protect Israel from the Antichrist (cf. Rev 12:15-16) and **then the dragon** Satan, who will indwell the Resurrected Antichrist will **wage war against the rest of** Israel's spiritual **offspring** the Church—**those who keep God's commands and hold fast their testimony about Jesus** (Rev 12:17 NIV). This text will be explained further elsewhere. [16]

The point is that just because Daniel describes the Antichrist persecuting the nation of Israel does not mean he will not persecute the Church. In fact, further revelation in Scripture clearly tells us this persecution will include the Church.

Even in Daniel 12 we see the Church mentioned. In verse 2 we read:

> **At that time, your people—everyone whose name is found written in the book —will be delivered. Multitudes who sleep in the dust of the earth will awake** (vs. 1-2 NIV).

A common error is to interpret **your people** here as only applying to Israel. But all of God's people have their **name ... written in the book** of life (cf. Exod 32:32; Luke 10:20; Phil 4:3; Heb 12:23; Rev 3:5; 13:8; 20:12; 21:27). The Book of Life is not just for the Jews. Likewise, this prophecy for **your** [Daniel's] **people** clearly describes the Resurrection, another event that certainly applies to the Church!

The full revelation of Scripture tells us these promises include the Church. If **your people** in Daniel 12 that are in the Book of Life and will be resurrected can include the Church, then **your people** in

Daniel 12 who will experience The Greatest Persecution can also include the Church.

C.2) The Greatest Persecution & the Church's Rescue in Daniel 12

Again, the text warns **the saints will experience the anguish of being attacked by an enemy. That anguish will be greater than any that has happened since nations have existed** (v. 1). This is the same **greatest persecution of God's elect people** that **will be greater than any persecution since the world began, and it will never be equaled again"** (Matt 24:21 [17]) that Jesus spoke of.

According to Jesus, what will happen **Immediately after the completion of the greatest persecution** (Matt 24:29)? **Christ will send out His angels with a loud trumpet sound, and they will lift up and gather together God's elect people from one end of the sky to the other, from everywhere on Earth** (Matt 24:31 [18]).

What does Daniel 12 say will happen when God's people experience **anguish** that **will be greater than any that has happened since nations have existed** (v. 1)?:

> **At that time every one of your people whose name is written in the book will be <u>rescued</u>.** [Also] **Many of those whose bodies lie dead and buried will <u>rise</u> up, some to everlasting life and some to shame and everlasting disgrace.** (Dan 12:1-2 NLT)

It would seem two events are being described here. First a rescue and then a resurrection. **Rescued** translates the Hebrew word *mālat*. Its "most prominent meaning is deliverance or escape from the threat of death." [19] There is no better Hebrew word to describe the Church's Rescue during The Greatest Persecution. Jesus warned the Church that after Antichrist's Claim to be God, **you will be handed over to be persecuted and put to death** (Matt 24:9 NIV). Daniel 12 seems to be describing the rescue of living saints from being killed by rescuing them.

In addition, the resurrection that occurs at the time of Christ's Return and the Church's Rescue also seems to be described in Daniel 12: **Many of those whose bodies lie dead and buried will <u>rise up</u>** (v. 2). Putting the Church's Rescue and Resurrection together fits Paul's description of the same event:

> **For the Lord Himself will come down from Heaven, with a loud command, with the voice of the archangel and with the trumpet call of God, and the dead in Christ will rise first.** (1 Thess 4:16 NIV)

Among the **Many of those whose bodies lie dead and buried** [and] **will rise up** (Dan 12:2), are the **dead in Christ** [who] **will rise first** (1 Thess 4:16). Although Paul immediately adds something that is not in Daniel 12: **After that, we who are still alive and are left will be caught up together with them in the clouds to meet the Lord in the air** [the Church's Rescue] (1 Thess 4:17 NIV). Daniel 12 is describing the same event as the Apostle Paul.

There is one more description of The Greatest Persecution in Daniel 12. The Angel says: **"It will be for a time, times and half a time [3.5 years]. When the power of the saints has been finally broken"** (Dan 12:7 NIV [20]). This repeats the duration given for The Greatest Persecution throughout Daniel and Revelation.

D) The sequence of Endtime events in Daniel

It was demonstrated above that Daniel chapters 7, 9, and 12 teach the same sequence of Endtime events that we have seen from the NT. This can be listed in the following table:

The sequence of Endtime events according to Daniel

#	Endtime Event	References in Daniel ch. 7	ch. 9	ch. 12
❶	The Beginning of Birth Pains (War)	v. 23	26	
❷	Antichrist's Claim to be God	vs. 24-25a	27	
❸	The Greatest Persecution	21, 25b		1, 7
❹	Christ's Return	26	27d	
❺	The Church's Rescue			1-2

Likewise, we can illustrate these things in the following graphic:

Endtime Events According to Daniel

❶ Antichrist's Religious Covenant (9:27)

❸ Antichrist's Claim to be God
Abomination of Desolation (7:25a; 9:27)

❺ Christ's Return
Church's Rescue & Resurrection

This horn was waging war against the saints until the Ancient of Days came (7:21-22; 12:1-2)

3.5 years (9:27) → 3.5 years (9:27) →

❷ Beginning of Birth Pains
Wars (Dan 7:21-24)

The fourth beast ... will devour the whole earth, trampling it down and crushing it. (Dan 7:23)

❹ The Greatest Persecution

"He will oppress His saints" for 3.5 Jewish years. (7:25; cf. 7:21; 12:1)

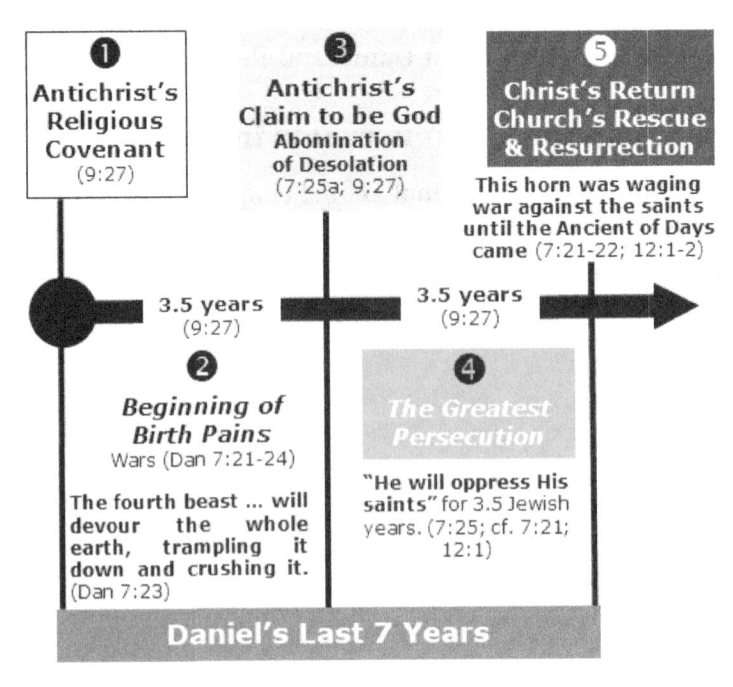

Daniel's Last 7 Years

1 It is very popular to claim that Daniel's descriptions of the Antichrist's activities have no relationship to the Church. For example, Walvoord writes on Daniel 9:24-27:
> [T]his chapter is specifically God's program for the people of Israel... To make this equivalent to the church composed of both Jews and Gentiles is to read into the passage something foreign to the whole thinking of Daniel. (*Daniel*, 220).

But Walvoord says at Dan 7:18, "Although there has been considerable discussion as to the reference of 'the saints,' it would seem to include the saved of all ages" (*Dan*, 172). So, the Church is in the prophecies of Daniel!

In addition, it is argued in this chapter that NT revelation can add elements to our interpretation of Daniel's prophecies. As noted above, Walvoord denies this regarding 9:24-27. But at 12:1 he admits:
> Here Daniel is ... revealing ... what has always been the hope of the saints [resurrection]. This, of course, is enlarged in the New Testament with the added truth of the rapture of living saints [the Church]" (285).

2 Throughout this chapter, the 1984 text of the NIV will be used where it translates the Hebrew *qaddish* as **saints**, just as the NASB does throughout Daniel. It is believed this helps us recognize that this is referring to the same **saints** referred to throughout the NT as including the Church.

3 It will be noted here that Daniel 2:4-7:28 were originally written in Aramaic, not Hebrew.

4 Young remarks on the use of **saints** in Daniel 7:
> These saints are not the Jews in distinction from the heathen (Maurer), nor "the Godfearing Jews who pass through the great tribulation" (Gaebelein)... The saints are the true members of the elect of God "the congregation of the New Covenant, consisting of Israel and the faithful of all nations; for the kingdom which God gives to the Son of Man will, according to v. 14, include those that are redeemed from among all the nations of the earth" (Keil). (157).

5 *BDB*.

6 *BDAG*.

7 For more on Antichrist's Beast Empire see *The Beginning of Birth Pains*.

8 Hill notes regarding the reference to **a time, times, and half a time** in Daniel: "The expression is generally taken to mean a period of three and a half years (so Collins, *Daniel*, 322; who notes the word "time" [Aramaic *'iddān*] can mean "year" on the basis of [Dan] 8:14 and 9:27)." The duration of The Greatest Persecution is discussed further in the book *The Greatest Persecution*.

9 Unfortunately, as a Pre-tribulationist, MacArthur <u>does</u> want to claim that this prediction of the crucifixion of Christ in Dan 9:26 does <u>not</u> apply to the

Church in any way. He writes: "That prophecy of Daniel was given to and about Israel, and it seems inappropriate to involve the church in the last week (the seven-year Tribulation) when it clearly was not involved in the first 69" (*Matt,* Matt 24).

But even the Pre-tribulationist Walvoord admits: "The natural interpretation of [Dan 9:26] is that it refers to the death of Jesus Christ on the cross" (229), which clearly applies to the Church.

[10] For more on the relationship between Israel and the Church in the Endtimes see "God's Endtime Plan for Israel & the Church" in *Advanced Studies on the Endtimes* (*ASE*), ch. 11, available online at www.trainingtimothys.com.

[11] For a detailed defense of the established opinion that the **sevens** in Daniel 9 refer to years, see Walvoord, *Daniel*, 216-220.

[12] For more on the fulfillment of this prophecy concerning the timing of Christ's crucifixion, see *God's Prophets*, chapter 9.8, section B.9 online in the scholar's section/divine revelation section of the website at www.trainingtimothys.com

[13] For more on time gaps in biblical prophecy see *Advanced Studies on the Endtimes*, ch. 3, sec. A; online at www.trainingtimothys.com.

[14] The suggested translation of Dan 12:1 is: **"In the endtimes, the Archangel Michael, the great military commander who protects the sons of your people, will stop protecting them. Then the saints will experience the anguish of being attacked by an enemy. That anguish will be greater than any that has happened since nations have existed."**

In the endtimes (**At that time** NIV) refers to the Endtime events described in the previous verses in Daniel chapter 11. These predict activities of the Antichrist **At the time of the end** (11:40).

Archangel Michael, the great military commander. Michael is not just any Angel, but an Archangel (see NLT). Most versions refer to him as a **prince** here (NIV, NASB). But the Hebrew word is *sar* which can mean "a military commander" (cf. Josh 5:14-15; Judg 4:2; 1 Sam 17:55). This fits the context of spiritual warfare best.

Will stop protecting them translates the Hebrew word *āmad* which is the "basic term for 'stand'" (*TWOT*, 673). However, *BDB* lists 12 times in the OT where *āmad* means: "stand still, stop, cease moving." That fits the context best here. Michael will stop protecting. For more on this see the discussion of "the Restrainer" in ch. 15, sec C.

The saints reflects the fact that the people being described as being persecuted here, are the same **saints** that the Antichrist will be **waging war against** (cf. Dan 7:21), will **oppress** (7:25), and who will be **delivered into** the Antichrist's **hands for a time, times and half a time** (7:25).

The anguish of being attacked by an enemy translates the Hebrew word *tsarah* which can mean, "the anguish of a people besieged by an enemy" (*TWOT*, 779; cf. Gen 32:7; Judg 2:15; 10:9).

[15] *TWOT*, 779; cf. Gen 32:7; Judg 2:15; 10:9.

[16] For more on Revelation 12 see appropriate section of book #4, *The Greatest Persecution*.

[17] For an explanation of the suggested translation of Matt 24:21 see ch. 3, sec. E.

[18] For an explanation of the suggested translation of Matt 24:29, 31 see ch. 3, sec. E and ch. 4, sec. C.

[19] *TWOT*, 507.

[20] This is the 1984 edition of the NIV which has **saints** instead of **holy people**.

Chapter 8

Conclusions on Christ's Endtimes Teaching

The Pre-wrath Rescue position

Contents

A) Summarizing the biblical substance and sequence of Endtime events in support of the Pre-wrath Rescue Position

B) 6 biblical beliefs of the Pre-wrath Rescue Position

C) The Church's historical testimony supporting the Pre-Wrath Rescue Position

Primary Points

- The view that best explains Christ's Endtimes Teaching is the Pre-wrath Rescue position. It teaches that the Church's Rescue occurs at Christ's Return and before Christ's Wrath. Accordingly, it is the "Pre-wrath Rescue" position. Therefore, the "rapture" is not "pre-tribulational" but pre-divine wrath.
- The biblical details of the sequence of Endtime events are important.
- The Church's Rescue occurs after the Antichrist's Claim to be God. Therefore, the Last Generation Church will suffer the Antichrist's Wrath in The Greatest Persecution.
- Christ's Return for the Church's Rescue will be visible to the whole world.
- The Church's Rescue will occur simultaneously with Christ's visible Return.
- Christ's Return will be preceded by multiple signs.
- The Greatest Persecution is not Christ's Wrath, but the Antichrist's Wrath.
- All Christian writers in the early Church who discuss the Endtimes believed the Church would suffer the persecution of the Antichrist.

A) Summarizing the biblical substance and sequence of Endtime events in support of the Pre-wrath Rescue Position [1]

A.1) 7 Primary Endtime Events in their biblical order

The previous chapters have demonstrated that when Christ's Endtimes Teaching is interpreted in its rather plain, literal sense, it provides a clear understanding of the biblical outline of Endtime events. The same approach to Paul's Thessalonian Epistles, Christ's Revelation, and Daniel's prophecies, confirms this interpretation. The sequence of Endtime events in these texts is summarized in the following table:

7 Primary Endtime Events According to Scripture

#	Endtime Event	Description
❶	The Beginning of Birth Pains	False Christ(s), wars, famines, plagues, and earthquakes. (cf. Matt 24:4-8; Luke 21:11; Rev 6:1-8; Dan 8:24-25)
❷	Antichrist's Claim to be God	The "abomination of desolation" when the Antichrist enters a rebuilt Jewish temple and proclaims himself to be God. (cf. Matt 24:15; 2 Thess 2:4; Rev 13:5-6; Dan 7:24-25; 9:27)
❸	The Greatest Persecution	Antichrist's wrath against God's people. (cf. Matt 24:9, 16-21; Rev 6:9-11; 12:7-17; 13:7-10; Dan 7:21, 25; 12:1, 7)
❹	The Cosmic Signs	The sun, moon, and stars signaling Christ's Return. (cf. Matt 24:29; Rev 6:12-13; Joel 2:30-31)
❺	Christ's Return	His visible, glorious appearing. (cf. Matt 24:30; Rev 6:14-16; 2 Thess 1:6-7; Dan 7:13-14; Tit 2:13)
❻	The Church's Rescue	Lifting up both living and dead Christians (cf. Matt 24:31; 1 Thess 4:13-18; 2 Thess 2:1; Rev 7:9-14; Dan 12:2).
❼	Christ's Wrath	God's wrath against His enemies on Earth. (cf. Matt 24:37-41; Rev 6:17; 1 Thess 1:6-7)

A.2) The biblical Pre-wrath Rescue position

The above biblical sequence of Endtime events reflects the Pre-wrath Rescue position. Simply put, the Pre-wrath Rescue position teaches that the Church's Rescue occurs at Christ's visible Return and before Christ's Wrath. Therefore, it is the Pre-wrath Rescue position. However, this view also teaches that the Last Generation Church will experience Antichrist's Wrath in The Greatest Persecution.

It is alarming that in a recent survey only 4% of Protestant Pastors claimed that the Pre-wrath view of Christ's Return and the Church's Rescue reflected their own view. [2] 4%! Some may assume this reflects the weakness of this position. But will all due respect, it is one more example of how confused even Pastors are about the doctrine of the Endtimes. The Pre-wrath Rescue position argued for in the previous chapters and summarized in this chapter, deserves a lot more careful Bible study than apparently 96% of Protestant Pastors have given it.

The biblical Pre-wrath Rescue position can be portrayed in the same graphic that has been used throughout the previous chapters to reflect the sequence of Endtime events taught in the many passages of Scripture that have been discussed.

The Biblical Pre-wrath Rescue Position
Confirmed by Christ's Endtimes Teaching, Revelation, & Paul

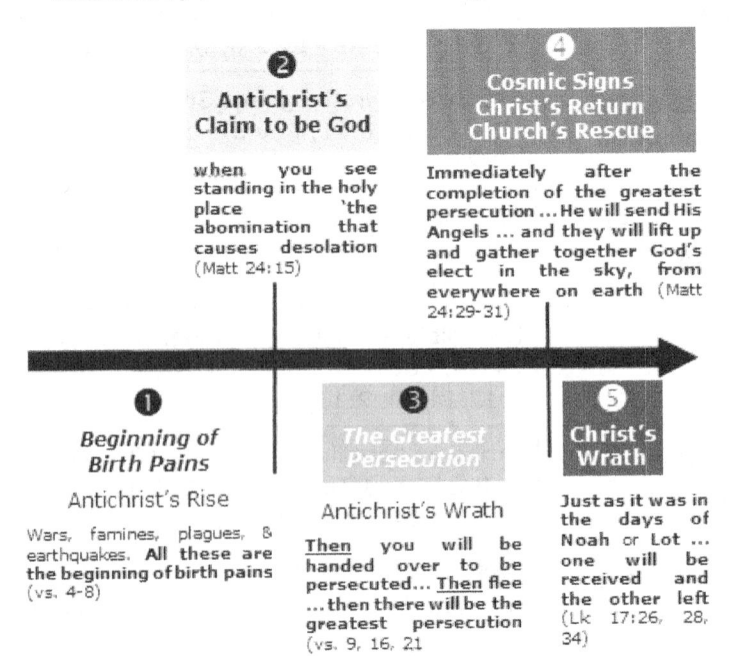

② Antichrist's Claim to be God
when you see standing in the holy place 'the abomination that causes desolation (Matt 24:15)

④ Cosmic Signs / Christ's Return / Church's Rescue
Immediately after the completion of the greatest persecution ... He will send His Angels ... and they will lift up and gather together God's elect in the sky, from everywhere on earth (Matt 24:29-31)

① Beginning of Birth Pains
Antichrist's Rise
Wars, famines, plagues, & earthquakes. All these are the beginning of birth pains (vs. 4-8)

③ The Greatest Persecution
Antichrist's Wrath
Then you will be handed over to be persecuted... Then flee ...then there will be the greatest persecution (vs. 9, 16, 21

⑤ Christ's Wrath
Just as it was in the days of Noah or Lot ... one will be received and the other left (Lk 17:26, 28, 34)

B) 6 biblical beliefs of the Pre-wrath Rescue position

Most of the points below have been thoroughly discussed and supported previously in *Christ's Endtimes Teaching*. This will be noted along the way. Some will find this chapter redundant. However, many will be learning the truths of Christ's Endtimes Teaching for the first time, and having several current beliefs challenged.

Therefore, repeating things in a summary fashion will be helpful. In addition, this section will summarize the primary beliefs of the Pre-wrath Rescue position.

B.1) The biblical details of the sequence of Endtime events are important

The disciples asked Jesus, **"what will be the sign of your coming and of the end of the age?"** (Matt 24:3 NIV). Jesus answered their question by telling them an entire series of Endtime events. He clearly intended to teach a specific sequence of Endtime events that He expects His people to understand. This is why He repeatedly used words like **then** (Matt 24:9, 10, 14, 21, 30), **when** (v. 15), **immediately after** (v. 29) and, **at that time** (v. 30). Based on this teaching, Christ expected His followers to **"Watch!"** current events in the world to recognize signs of the Endtimes (cf. Mark 13:5, 9, 23, 33, 34, 37).

Likewise, the Apostle Paul corrected the Thessalonians by telling them the biblical sequence of Endtime events. It was precisely because these Christians did not understand this, that they were vulnerable to being misled by false teaching (cf. 2 Thess 2:1-4). Therefore, belief #1 in the Pre-wrath Rescue position is clearly biblical: The biblical details of the sequence of Endtime events are important.

The error of denying this has been addressed earlier in a discussion of the "apathetic" view of the Endtimes (cf. ch. 1, sec. B.3). This view has also been labeled as Pan-tribulationism and is discussed further in chapter 11 (sec. A).

B.2) The Church's Rescue occurs <u>after</u> the Antichrist's Claim to be God. Therefore, the Last Generation Church will suffer the Antichrist's Wrath in The Greatest Persecution

After warning of the Antichrist's **abomination of desolation** (Matt 24:15) Christ said **"then there will be the greatest persecution [*thlipsis*] of God's elect people. It will be greater than any persecution since the world began, and it will never be equaled again"** (v. 21).

The Greek word *thlipsis* is used three times in Matthew 24. It clearly refers to the persecution of God's people in verse 9 and should be translated this way in verses 21 and 29 (cf. ch. 3, sec. E). The Greek word *eklektous* is also used three times in this passage (cf. vs. 21, 24, 31). It always includes the Church in the NT when referring to people (cf. ch. 3, sec. D). Therefore, Jesus taught that **God's elect people** (the Church), will experience The Greatest Persecution.

Accordingly, the Church's Rescue does not occur until after The Greatest Persecution is completed. Jesus taught us:

> "**<u>Immediately after the completion of the greatest persecution</u>** [*thlipsin*], **<u>then</u>** 'the sun will be darkened, and the moon will not give its light; the stars will fall from the sky and the heavenly bodies will be shaken.'
>
> **<u>Then</u> the sign that the Son of Man is coming will appear in the sky. And then all the peoples of the Earth will mourn when they <u>see the Son of Man coming</u> on the clouds of Heaven, with power and great glory.**
>
> **He will send out His angels with a loud trumpet <u>sound, and they will lift up and gather together God's elect people from one end of the sky to the other, from everywhere on Earth.</u>**" (Matt 24:29-31; cf. 1 Thess 4:13-17; 2 Thess 1:6-7).

The Church's Rescue that Jesus described in Matt 24:31 is also clearly described by Paul:

> **According to the Lord's word, we tell you that we who are still alive, who are left <u>until the coming of the Lord</u>, will certainly not precede those who have fallen asleep.**
>
> **For <u>the Lord himself will come down from heaven</u>, with a loud command, with the voice of <u>the archangel</u> and <u>with the trumpet call of God</u>, and the dead in Christ will rise first.**

After that, we who are still alive and are left <u>will be caught up together with them in the clouds to meet the Lord in the air.</u> (1 Thess 4:15-17 NIV)

Christ and the Apostle are describing the same event, the Church's Rescue. Jesus said it will not occur until **after the completion of the greatest persecution** (Matt 24:29). The Apostle confirmed this elsewhere when he wrote:

Concerning the coming of our Lord Jesus Christ and our being gathered to him [Christ's Return & the Church's Rescue] **... Don't let anyone deceive you in any way, for <u>that day will not come until</u> the rebellion occurs and <u>the man of lawlessness</u>** [Antichrist] **<u>is revealed</u>, the man doomed to destruction.**

He will oppose and will exalt himself over everything that is called God or is worshiped, so that he sets himself up in God's temple, proclaiming himself to be God (2 Thess 2:1, 3-4 NIV)

The Apostle clearly taught that **the coming of our Lord Jesus Christ and our being gathered to him**, (Christ's Return & the Church's Rescue), **will not come until ... the man of lawlessness** (the Antichrist) **is revealed** and in a rebuilt Jewish **temple proclaiming himself to be God** (Antichrist's Claim to be God; cf. ch. 5, sec. C).

This is also confirmed in Revelation that describes the same sequence of The Greatest Persecution occurring <u>before</u> the Church's Rescue. First, describing The Greatest Persecution we read:

When he [Christ] **opened the fifth seal, I saw under the altar the souls of those who had been <u>slain</u> because of the word of God and the testimony they had maintained. They called out in a loud voice, "How long, Sovereign Lord, holy and true, until you judge the inhabitants of the earth and avenge our blood?"**

Then each of them was given a white robe, and they were told to wait a little longer, until the full number of their fellow servants, their brothers and sisters, <u>were killed</u> just as they had been. (Rev 6:9-11 NIV)

Then in Revelation 7, after describing Christ's Return and impending Wrath (cf. Rev 6:12-17), we read a description of the Church's Rescue out of The Greatest Persecution:

> **After this I looked, and there before me was a great multitude that no one could count, from every nation, tribe, people, and language, standing before the throne and before the Lamb. They were wearing white robes** [the same as the Christian martyrs described in Rev 6:9-11] **and were holding palm branches in their hands...**
>
> **Then one of the elders asked me, "These in white robes —who are they, and where did they come from?" I answered, "Sir, you know."**
>
> **And he said, "These are they who have come out of the great persecution** [*thlipseōs*]**; they have washed their robes and made them white in the blood of the Lamb.**
> (Rev 7:9, 13-14)

These members of the Last Generation Church will **come out of the great persecution** because they will be <u>in</u> The Greatest Persecution (cf. ch. 6, secs. B-C).

This is confirmed later in Revelation 13 where we read that **the beast Antichrist will be given power to make war against <u>the saints</u> and to conquer them** (Rev 13:7 NIV). **Saints** is clearly used throughout the Revelation to refer to the Church (cf. 5:8; 8:3, 4; 11:18; 16:6; 17:6; 18:20, 24; 19:8-9, 14; cf. ch. 6, sec. A).

Therefore, belief #2 of the Pre-wrath Rescue position is clearly biblical: The Church's Rescue occurs <u>after</u> the Antichrist's Claim to be God. Therefore, the Last Generation Church will suffer the Antichrist's Wrath in The Greatest Persecution.

B.3) Christ's Return for the Church's Rescue will be visible to the whole world

Again, Matthew 24:29-31 makes this very clear. Jesus said:

> **"Immediately after the completion of the greatest persecution** [*thlipsin*]**, then 'the sun will be darkened, and the moon will not give its light; the stars will fall from the sky and the heavenly bodies will be shaken.'**

> **Then the sign that the Son of Man is coming will appear in the sky. And then all the peoples of the Earth will mourn when <u>they see the Son of Man coming</u> on the clouds of Heaven, with power and great glory.**
>
> [At that time] **He will send out His angels with a loud trumpet sound, and they will lift up and gather together God's elect people** [*eklektous*] **from one end of the sky to the other, from everywhere on Earth."** (Matt 24:29-31)

The idea of a "secret, silent rapture" is unbiblical. Accordingly, in Paul's description of the Church's Rescue, he said:

> **The Lord himself <u>will come down from heaven</u>, with <u>a loud command</u>, with the voice of the archangel and with <u>the trumpet call of God</u>, and the dead in Christ will rise first. After that, we who are still alive and are left will be caught up together with them in the clouds to meet the Lord in the air.** (1 Thess 4:16-17 NIV).

That is <u>not</u> describing a "secret, silent rapture."

Likewise, the Apostle taught Christians <u>not</u> to expect **relief** from their **persecution** until they saw the visible Return of Christ:

> **In his justice he will pay back those who persecute you. And <u>God will provide rest</u>** [*anasin*, NIV **relief**] <u>**for you who are being persecuted and also for us when the Lord Jesus appears from heaven**</u>**. He will come with his mighty angels, in flaming fire, bringing judgment on those who don't know God and on those who refuse to obey the Good News of our Lord Jesus.** (2 Thess 1:6-8 NLT)

Likewise, Paul taught elsewhere that **we** the Church **wait for the blessed hope—<u>the appearing</u> of the glory of our great God and Savior, Jesus Christ** (Tit 2:13 NIV).

This is why Christ said in Matthew 24:27: **"For as lightning that comes from the east is visible even in the west, so will be the coming of the Son of Man."** Likewise, in Revelation, His Return is described as being seen by everyone in the world (cf. Rev 6:12-17).

Therefore, belief #3 of the Pre-wrath Rescue position is clearly biblical: Christ's Return for the Church's Rescue will be visible to the whole world.

B.4) The Church's Rescue will occur simultaneously with Christ's visible Return

This is clearly taught in Matthew 24:30-31, 1 Thess 4:16-17, and 2 Thess 1:6-7 quoted above. In addition, Paul wrote: **Concerning the coming of our Lord Jesus Christ and our being gathered to him** (2 Thess 2:1). He was referring to Christ's Return and the Church's Rescue and implied they occur together (cf. ch. 5, sec. C.1).

Therefore, belief #4 of the Pre-wrath Rescue position is clearly biblical: The Church's Rescue will occur simultaneously with Christ's visible Return.

B.5) Christ's Return & the Church's Rescue will be preceded by multiple signs

This is clearly taught in Christ's Endtimes Teaching. Again, the Apostles asked, **"what will be the sign of your coming and of the end of the age?"** (Matt 24:3 NIV). Jesus answered their question by telling them an entire series of Endtime events that will precede His Return (cf. Matt 24:4-31).

Likewise, Paul taught **Concerning the coming of our Lord Jesus Christ and our being gathered to him ... that day will not come until the rebellion occurs and the man of lawlessness** [Antichrist] **is revealed** (2 Thess 2:1, 3 NIV; cf. ch. 5, secs. C.2-3). Both of these Scriptures clearly teach that multiple events and signs will occur before Christ's Return and the Church's Rescue.

Therefore, belief #5 of the Pre-wrath Rescue position is clearly biblical: Christ's Return and the Church's Rescue will be preceded by multiple signs.

B.6) The Greatest Persecution is not Christ's Wrath, but the Antichrist's Wrath

The **persecution** of **God's elect people** described in Christ's Endtimes teaching (Matt 24:9, 21), and the killing of the martyrs in His Revelation (cf. 6:9-11; 13:7), should <u>never</u> be defined as Christ's Wrath. Rather, The Greatest Persecution will be Antichrist's Wrath. Jesus clearly taught that in Matthew 24:29-31 quoted above that the Cosmic Signs are the sign that Christ's Wrath is about to begin.

These same Cosmic Signs are described in Revelation 6:12-14 when the world's people will cry out: **"hide us from the face of him who sits on the throne and from the wrath of the Lamb! For the great day of their wrath has come"** (Rev 6:16-17 NIV).

Therefore, in Joel that the Cosmic Signs will precede the beginning of Christ's Wrath: **The sun will be turned to darkness and the moon to blood <u>before</u> the coming of the great and dreadful day of the LORD** (2:31 NIV) which is an OT term for Christ's Wrath.

Therefore, both Matthew 24 and Revelation 6 clearly depict the events of The Beginning of Birth Pains, and The Greatest Persecution will occur <u>before</u> the Cosmic Signs (cf. Matt 24:4-30; Rev 6:1-17) and the beginning of Christ's Wrath. Therefore, these Endtime events are <u>not</u> a part of Christ's Wrath.

Therefore, belief #6 of the Pre-wrath position is clearly biblical: The Greatest Persecution is not Christ's Wrath, but the Antichrist's Wrath. The nature and timing of Christ's Wrath in the Endtimes will be discussed further in chapter 14.

C) The Church's historical testimony supporting the Pre-Wrath Rescue Position

The Pre-wrath Rescue position is certainly not new. The biblical outline of Endtime events summarized above was clearly the primary view of the Early Church (A.D. 100-300). The following is a sampling of leaders and Bible scholars in the Early Church who wrote as if the Church should expect to experience the Antichrist's Wrath and The Greatest Persecution.[3]

There are no hints anywhere in the literature of the Early Church suggesting otherwise. The Early Church did not view the following documents as apostolic Scripture. Still, they reflect the widespread belief of the Christian Church in the first 200 years after the Apostles.

> Hermas (c. A.D. 140):
> Happy are they who endure the great tribulation that is coming... Those therefore who continue steadfast, and are put through the fire of the great tribulation that is to come, will be purified by means of it... Wherefore cease not speaking these things into the ears of the saints. (*The Pastor of Hermas*, Vision 2, 4)

Irenaeus (c. A.D. 180):
And they [the ten kings]... shall give their kingdom to the beast [Antichrist], and put the Church to flight. (*Against Heresies*, V.26.1)

Tertullian (c. A.D. 200):
The beast Antichrist with his false prophet will wage war on the Church of God." (*On the Resurrection of the Flesh*, xxv).

When the times are fulfilled, and the ten horns spring from the beast in the last times, then Antichrist will appear among them. When he makes war against the saints, and persecutes them, then may we expect the manifestation of the Lord from heaven. (*On Daniel*, II.7).

Hippolytus (c. A.D. 220):
Now concerning the tribulation of the persecution which is to fall upon the Church from the adversary ... that refers to the one thousand two hundred and threescore days during which the tyrant is to reign and persecute the Church. (Ibid. 60, 61)

By A.D. 400 Roman Catholic influence had begun in the Church, along with a greater influence of the allegorical interpretation of Scripture. Nor was the threat of the Antichrist perceived as great because the Church had taken over the Roman Empire. However, some of the most influential Christian scholars of this time wrote the following.

Jerome (c. 400 A.D.):
I told you that Christ would not come unless antichrist had come before." (*Epistle 21*) [4]

Augustine (c. 400 A.D.):
But he who reads this passage [Daniel 12] even half asleep, cannot fail to see that the kingdom of antichrist shall fiercely, though for a short time, assail the Church." (*City of God*, XX, 23).

Accordingly, several modern scholars summarize the Church's historical testimony. Carson notes regarding the popular view that the Church will <u>not</u> experience the Antichrist and the Greatest Persecution:

Perhaps it is not surprising that [this view] finds no support until the nineteenth century. [This Pre-tribulational] approach to the Olivet Discourse must be judged historically implausible in reference to both the history of Jesus and the history of interpretation. [5]

Likewise, Alan Hultberg, Professor of NT at Talbot writes:

The earliest Christian writings we possess after the NT indicate no real question in the first three centuries of the church regarding the timing of the rapture... When the rapture was discussed at all, it was assumed to be simultaneous with the return of Christ to Earth to establish his kingdom...

At the very least, where they speak of it, the ante-Nicene fathers [A. D. 315 and earlier] consistently maintained that the church would witness the abomination of desolation and experience persecution under the Antichrist. [6]

George E. Ladd, former Professor of New Testament History and Biblical Theology at Fuller Theological Seminary concluded:

Every church father who deals with this subject expects the church to suffer at the hands of Antichrist... We can find no trace of Pre-tribulationism in the early church, and no modern Pre-tribulationist has successfully proved that this particular doctrine was held by any church fathers or students of the word before the nineteenth century...

Pretribulationism may be guilty of the danger of leaving the Church unprepared for tribulation when Antichrist appears. [7]

Likewise, NT scholar Robert Gundry has written:

We may fairly conclude that [those] who find imminence [the "any-moment" return of Christ] in the Ante-Nicene fathers [A. D. 315 and earlier], are grasping at straws. The early fathers uniformly expected a yet future persecution of antichrist [for the Church] prior to the Lord's return.

And so should we. [8]

A metaphorical interpretation of prophetic Scripture continued into the Protestant Reformation. Still, we can offer the following quotes that demonstrate popular views on Christ's Return and the

Church's Rescue were <u>not</u> supported by the Reformers.

John Wycliffe (c. 1380):
Wherefore let us pray to God that He keep us [Christians] in the hour of tribulation, which is coming upon all the world (as stated in) Revelation three. (*Writings of John Wickliff*, 155)

Martin Luther (c. 1530):
The book of Revelation is intended as a revelation of things that are to happen in the future, and especially of tribulations and disasters for the Church. (*Works of Martin Luther*, VI. 481)

John Calvin (c. 1560):
The calamity of the Church shall last through a time, times, and half a time (Daniel 7:25). (Commentary on Matthew, 24:15)

John Knox (c. 1570):
God has a great love towards His Church, whom he pleased to forewarn of dangers to come ... [meaning], the man of sin, the antichrist." (*The History of the Reformation*, I.76)

John Foxe (c. 1580):
There will be a second beast prophesied to come in the later time of the Church ... to disturb the whole Church of Christ." (*Acts and Monuments*, I)

It is much more difficult to find Christian authors in modern times who will support the view that the Church should expect The Greatest Persecution. However, here are a few. [9]

George Mueller (1890):
The Scripture declares plainly that the Lord Jesus will not come until the Apostasy shall have taken place, and the man of sin, antichrist ... shall have been revealed." (*Missionary Tours and Labours, Mrs. George Mueller*, 148)

Leonard Ravenhill (1907-1994):
There is a cowardly Christianity which ... still comforts its fainting heart with the hope that there will be a rapture--perhaps today--to catch us away from coming tribulation. (*Sodom Had No Bible, p. 94*)

Walter Kaiser (one of the most respected OT seminary professors in the world), has said:

> The Prewrath [Rescue] position is the prophetic position that best understands and properly applies Old Testament prophecy concerning the Day of the Lord as it relates to the second coming of Christ… If the fathers of dispensationalism had been able to choose between the Pre-tribulation and the Pre-wrath views, the Pre-wrath position would have received their vote, hands down. [10]

While the Pre-wrath Rescue position is not new in Church History, Pre-tribulationism is, relatively speaking. Speakman explains:

> The popularization of the Pre-Tribulation Rapture is a relatively recent phenomenon. In fact, there is no compelling evidence that this doctrine existed at all prior to the nineteenth century. The historical record strongly suggests that for the first 1,800 years of Christianity [this was the case]. [11]

Further refutations of Pre-tribulationism will be provided in chapters 13-16.

The Early Church understood they would face the Antichrist if the Endtimes began in their time. No doubt, this helped them be more prepared to glorify God if this happened. Unfortunately, the modern Church has largely lost this conviction, and it will cost God's people if it is not corrected before the Endtimes begin.

---

[1] The Pre-wrath Rescue position supported in the *Endtime Essentials* is slightly different than the more commonly recognized Pre-wrath Rapture view. While they are essentially the same, there is one difference.

The more commonly recognized Pre-wrath Rapture view claims that the "rapture" occurs at some unknown time after Antichrist's Claim to be God (**abomination of desolation**, Matt 24:15) and Christ's Return. However, the Pre-wrath Rescue position teaches that Christ's Return and the Church's Rescue will occur exactly 1,260 days after Antichrist's Claim to be God. This will be explained further in *The Beginning of Birth Pains*, ch. 14 sec. D.

2 This survey on the views of Protestant Pastors on the Endtimes can be found online at https://news.lifeway.com/2016/04/26/pastors-the-end-of-the-world-is-complicated/

3 Many of the original sources of these quotes can be read at www.ccel.org.

4 Admittedly, Jerome, Augustine, Luther, and Calvin often applied a metaphorical and Amillennial interpretation to biblical prophecy. Nonetheless, all of them demonstrate the claim that a belief that the Church would be spared The Greatest Persecution of Antichrist was not widely believed in their day.

5 Carson, *Matt*, Matt 24.

6 Hultberg, 14-15.

7 George E. Ladd, *The Blessed Hope*, (Eerdmans, 1990), 31, 164.

8 Such quotes from such respected NT scholars have been harmful to the Pre-tribulational view. Therefore, they have worked hard to find evidence that someone believed their view before it was popularized by John Nelson Darby (1800-1882).

Some have claimed such evidence is found in *The Shepherd of Hermas* (c. A.D. 180). But this document claims things that are never mentioned in Scripture, and seem unbiblical. For example, it claims that a person will "escape" the "tribulation" only if they are an exceptional Christian. The text in question states:

> Go therefore, and declare to the elect of the Lord His mighty works, and tell them that this beast is a type of the great tribulation which is to come.
>
> If therefore you prepare yourselves beforehand, and repent (and turn) to the Lord with your whole heart, you shall be able to escape it, if your heart be made pure and without blemish, and if for the remaining days of your life you serve the Lord blamelessly. (2[23]:5-6)

According to the author it will not be enough to simply be a Christian in order to "escape" "the great tribulation." You must be a "blameless" servant of God. Something that not all Christians will be. Therefore, there is not even any support for Pre-tribulationism here which claims all Christians are "raptured" before "the great tribulation."

For many years, the primary evidence offered for early Church evidence of Pre-tribulationism was one quote found in a document called Pseudo Ephrem. It is called "Pseudo" because it is believed to falsely claim to be written by the Syrian church leader Ephrem of Nisibis (someone that very few have even heard of anyway). Because scholars really do not know who wrote Pseudo Ephrem, or when, it is dated sometime between A. D. 300 and 625. However, there is really no way of knowing.

Nevertheless, Pre-tribulationists want to present this obscure document as evidence that the Early Church widely believed in Pre-tribulationism because of this one sentence: "All the saints and elect of God are gathered together before the tribulation, which is to come, and are taken to the Lord." Admittedly, this seems to reflect a Pre-tribulational view. But again, no one really knows who wrote it or when.

More recently, Tim Lahaye has written:
> For several years a popular argument against the pre-Tribulation theory ... is that it was invented by John Darby in the last century (1828) and was never seen or mentioned by the early Christian fathers for almost nineteen centuries of church history. That argument is simply not true! (*Revelation*, 109)

As proof, Lahaye can name one Baptist pastor, Morgan Edwards, who in 1742, "definitely taught that the Rapture occurs *before* the Tribulation" (Ibid.). Lahaye claims that in a book by Grant Jeffery, he "quotes many ... eighteenth century prophecy scholars" who believed in a Pre-tribulation Rescue. Lahaye adds: "Jeffrey's most important find was the electrifying discovery of a statement in an apocalyptic sermon" (110).

Perhaps there were some Pre-tribulationists before Darby. But the historical argument against this view remains. Whatever historical support Pre-tribulationists can find, is so obscure and sparse that biblical scholars such as Carson, Hultberg, Gundry, and Ladd have denied it even exists.

[9] Many add Charles Spurgeon to the list of respected Bible Teachers who taught that the Church would experience The Greatest Persecution. Dennis Swanson in his study: "Charles H. Spurgeon and Eschatology" writes:
> Spurgeon said little, if anything, about the rapture. He seems to have most likely equated this with the Second Coming. However, he did believe that the church would pass through a tribulation, thus any "rapture" in his thinking would be posttribulational.

However, Swanson is correct to add: "Given Spurgeon's notoriety and the volume of his writings, it is perhaps no wonder that almost every advocate of an eschatological viewpoint has attempted to bolster their position by appealing to Spurgeon as "being in their camp." (http://www.spurgeon.org/eschat.htm#ans-sum)

[10] This is Robert Van Kampen's "paraphrase" of a personal conversation with Dr. Kaiser (*Rapture*, loc. 2795ff.).

For additional modern support for important beliefs in the Pre-wrath Rescue position see the article at The Gospel Coalition website, "The Rapture Question" online at https://www.thegospelcoalition.org/essay/the-rapture-question/.

Although the author makes a mistake in claiming that the Pre-wrath position believes "that the rapture is a separate event from the second coming of Christ." This is misleading. The Pre-wrath position teaches that the rapture occurs at the initial appearing of Christ in His Second Coming. But unlike the Post-tribulationism the author of the article is supporting, the rapture will <u>not</u> occur after Christ's Wrath at the appearing of Christ for the Battle of Armageddon.

For more on the important differences between the Pre-wrath Rescue position and the Post-tribulational Rapture view, see ch. 11, sec. D.

[11] Speakman, 63. See 63-71 for refutation of other suggestions.

Chapter 9

The Nature of Christ's Return & the Church's Rescue

Contents

A) There will be two appearances of Christ during His Second Coming

B) The Church will know when Christ is coming: *Understanding Matthew 24:32-51*

Primary Points

- There is one Second Coming of Christ. But within His Coming, Christ will appear at two different times. Both appearances are described as visible.
- In Christ's first appearance He comes for the Church's Rescue (cf. Matt 24:29-31). In Christ's second appearance He comes with His Church for the Battle of Armageddon (cf. Rev 19:11-21).
- In between these two appearances of Christ on Earth, He remains in Heaven with the Church while His Angels execute His Wrath on Earth during a considerable but unknown period of time.
- Scripture does not tell us how much time elapses between Christ's two appearances, or how long Christ's Wrath lasts.
- If Jesus Christ visibly appeared to all the world right now, would He have come at an hour that you were not expecting Him? Do you understand that if that happened you would be going to Hell?
- It is impossible to live today expecting Christ's Return every hour of every day.
- As you read Matthew 24:32-25:46 keep one thing in mind: Christ was contrasting what His Return will be like for <u>believers</u> in comparison to <u>unbelievers</u>.
- Christians will know Christ's Return is near when all the events Christ described in His Endtimes Teaching occur.
- Unbelievers will be completely surprised by Christ's Return, but not Christians.

A) There will be two appearances of Christ during His Second Coming

There is some confusion over the nature of Christ's Second Coming. For example, Post-tribulationism teaches that there will be only one visible appearance of Christ during the Second Coming, occurring at the Battle of Armageddon. This view is necessary to support its claim that the Church is on Earth during Christ's Wrath, evidently right up to the time of this Battle. Likewise, Pre-tribulationism has a rather complicated view of Christ's appearances during His Second Coming (cf. ch. 13, sec. B.5). For example, one of his "comings" is in a "secret, silent" arrival to "rapture" the Church (cf. ch. 13, sec. B.3).

What does the Bible teach? Contrary to Post-tribulationism, Scripture describes two visible appearances of Christ during His Second Coming. Contrary to Pre-tribulationism, nowhere does Scripture teach a "secret, silent, rapture" or arrival of Christ.

Christ's two visible appearances in His Second Coming can be described in this way. In Christ's first appearance He comes for His Church. In Christ's second appearance He comes with His Church.

Christ's first visible appearance for His Church is described in Christ's Endtimes Teaching in the now familiar passage of Matthew 24:29-31. Jesus said:

> **"Immediately after the completion of the greatest persecution, then 'the sun will be darkened, and the moon will not give its light; the stars will fall from the sky and the heavenly bodies will be shaken.'**
>
> **Then the sign that the Son of Man is coming will appear in the sky. And then all the peoples of the Earth will mourn when they see the Son of Man coming on the clouds of Heaven, with power and great glory.**
>
> **He will send out His angels with a loud trumpet sound, and they will lift up and gather together God's elect people from one end of the sky to the other, from everywhere on Earth"** (Matt 24:29-31 [1])

Throughout the *Endtimes Essentials* this first visible appearance of Christ at His Second Coming is referred to as Christ's Return. Christ made it clear that His first visible appearance occurs **immediately after the completion of the greatest persecution** (v. 29) and immediately before the Church's Rescue and Christ's Wrath begin.

As explained elsewhere (ch. 6, sec. B), Revelation 6 describes the same sequence and Christ's first visible appearance. After The Beginning of Birth Pains (cf. Rev 6:1-8) and The Greatest Persecution (vs. 9-11), we read:

> **I watched as the Lamb broke the sixth seal, and there was a great earthquake. The sun became as dark as black cloth, and the moon became as red as blood. Then the stars of the sky fell to the earth like green figs falling from a tree shaken by a strong wind. The sky was rolled up like a scroll, and all of the mountains and islands were moved from their places.** [2]
>
> **Then everyone—the kings of the earth, the rulers, the generals, the wealthy, the powerful, and every slave and free person—all hid themselves in the caves and among the rocks of the mountains. And they cried to the mountains and the rocks, "Fall on us and hide us from the face of the one who sits on the throne and from the wrath of the Lamb. For the great day of their wrath has come, and who is able to survive?"** (Rev 6:12-17 NLT)

This is also describing Christ's first visible appearance. As in Christ's Endtimes Teaching, this appearance is immediately followed by the Church's Rescue described in Revelation 7:9-14. Notice in the above text that at Christ's first appearance, it is said **the wrath of the Lamb ... has come** (v. 16-17). Christ's Wrath begins at His first visible appearance.

Paul gave us another description of Christ's first appearance when he wrote:

> **For the Lord himself will come down from heaven, with a loud command, with the voice of the archangel and with the trumpet call of God, and the dead in Christ will rise first. After that, we who are still alive and are left will be caught up together with them in the clouds to meet the Lord in the air.** (1 Thess 4:16-17 NIV)

Other important descriptions of Christ's first appearance during His Second Coming include 2 Thessalonians 1:6-10 and 2:1-4. Notice some attributes of this first appearance of Christ for His Church:

1) Christ will come **immediately after the completion of the greatest persecution** (Matt 24:29; cf. Rev 6:12).
2) Christ will be accompanied by Cosmic Signs in the **sun, moon, and stars** (Matt 24:29; cf. Rev 6:12-13).
3) Christ will be **coming on the clouds of Heaven** (Matt 24:30; cf. 1 Thess 4:17).
4) Christ will be coming with **His angels** (Matt 24:31; cf. 1 Thess 4:16; 2 Thess 1:7).
5) **God's elect people** are **still alive and are left ... everywhere on Earth** (Matt 24:31; cf. 1 Thess 4:17).
6) **Angels ... will lift up ... God's elect people ... from everywhere on Earth into the sky** (Matt 24:31; 1 Thess 4:17)
7) **The dead in Christ will rise in the first resurrection** (1 Thess 4:17; Rev 20:5; cf. 1 Cor 15:52).
8) **Everyone—the kings of the earth ... the generals ...** will be **hiding themselves in the caves and among the rocks of the mountains** (Rev 6:15).
9) **The wrath of the Lamb** will have **come** and begun, including the Trumpet and Bowl Punishments (Rev 6:16-17; cf. chs. 8-9; 15-16)
10) **The throne of the beast** Antichrist, and his **kingdom** will continue to reign on Earth (Rev 16:10) after Christ's first appearance, even working to gather Christ's enemies at **Armageddon** (16:13-16).

Now let us look at a description of Christ's second visible appearance in Revelation 19:

> **I saw heaven standing open and there before me was a white horse, whose rider** [Jesus Christ] **is called Faithful and True. With justice he judges and wages war... The armies** [Resurrected Church] **of heaven were following him, riding on white horses and dressed in**

fine linen, white and clean...

Then I saw the beast [Antichrist] **and the kings of the earth and their armies gathered together to wage war against the rider on the horse and his army. But the beast was captured, and ... thrown alive into the fiery lake of burning sulfur.** (Rev 19:11, 14, 19-20 NIV)

Earlier in verse 8 it says **Fine linen, bright and clean, was given her** [the Church] **to wear**. So the **armies** coming with Christ are not Angels, but the Rescued and Resurrected Church. Notice that at this appearance **the kings of the earth and their armies** are **gathered together to wage war** (v. 19). The text makes it clear that this appearance occurs at the Battle of Armageddon at the end of Christ's Wrath (cf. Rev 16:12-16) when the Antichrist is finally destroyed.

The Apostle Paul also described the second appearance of Christ:

Then the man of lawlessness [Antichrist] **will be revealed, but the Lord Jesus will slay him with the breath of his mouth and destroy him by the splendor of his coming.** (2 Thess 2:8 NLT)

Here again the Antichrist is being destroyed at the Battle of Armageddon at this second appearance of Christ. Finally, Zechariah 14 also describes this second appearance of Christ when we read:

The LORD will go out and fight against those nations, as he fights on a day of battle [at Armageddon]. **On that day his feet will stand on the Mount of Olives, east of Jerusalem, and the Mount of Olives will be split in two** (vs. 3-4 NIV). [3]

There are many differences in the descriptions of these appearances. Some things are mentioned in some of the descriptions that are not in others. But an "argument from silence" is never best. It is possible to reconcile such differences. For example, just because the description of Christ's appearance in Matthew 24:29-31 does not mention that Christ **will stand on the Mount of Olives** and **split it in two**, would not necessarily mean that Zechariah could not be giving us additional information about the same appearance.

However, there are several differences in these descriptions that are difficult to reconcile into one appearance of Christ. Notice some differences between Christ's second appearance with His Church and His first appearance for His Church. In Christ's second appearance ...

1) Christ will appear at the Battle of **Armageddon** (Rev 19:11-20; cf. Rev 16:12-16), instead of **immediately after the completion of the greatest persecution** (Matt 24:29; cf. Rev 6:9-17).

2) Christ will be coming as a **rider** on **a white horse** (Rev 19:11), instead of **coming on the clouds of Heaven** (Matt 24:30; cf. 1 Thess 4:17).

3) Christ will be coming with the **armies [Church] of heaven**, instead of coming with **His angels** (Matt 24:31; cf. 1 Thess 4:16; 2 Thess 1:7).

4) The Church will be **following** Christ coming down from heaven (Rev 19:14), instead of still being **everywhere on Earth** (Matt 24:31; cf. 1 Thess 4:17).

5) The Church will be **following** Christ coming down from heaven (Rev 19:14), instead of being **lifted up ... from everywhere on Earth into the sky** to **meet the Lord in the air** (Matt 24:31; 1 Thess 4:17)

6) The Church will be **riding on white horses** (Rev 19:14), instead of being carried by **angels** (Matt 24:31).

7) The Church is already in their resurrected bodies, **dressed in fine linen, white and clean** (Rev 19:11), instead of being rescued and resurrected in their human bodies at Christ's first appearance (1 Cor 15:52).

8) **The kings of the earth and their armies** will be **gathered together to wage war** against Christ at **Armageddon** (Rev 19:19; 16:16), instead of **Everyone—the kings of the earth ... the generals ...** hiding **themselves in the caves and among the rocks of the mountains** (Rev 6:15) all over the world.

9) The **beast** Antichrist is **captured** and **thrown alive into the fiery lake of burning sulfur** (Rev 19:20; cf. 2 Thess 2:8), instead of being allowed to remain ruling on Earth (Rev 16:10).

It seems obvious that Matthew 24:29-31 and Revelation 19 are describing two different appearances of Christ. Let us draw some conclusions from the points made above on this rather complicated issue.

First, Revelation 16:12-21 and 19:11-21 make it clear that the Battle of Armageddon occurs at the end of the period of Christ's Wrath. Afterwards, Christ's 1,000-year Reign begins (cf. Rev 20:1-6). However, the appearance of Christ in Matthew 24:31 will occur **immediately after the completion of the greatest persecution** (v. 29), not the end of Christ's Wrath.

Therefore, Christ's first appearance described in Matthew 24:29-31 marks the beginning of Christ's Wrath on the unbelievers of this world. His second appearance in Revelation 19 marks the end of that Wrath.

Second, in Matthew 24 Christ returns with **Angels** to **gather together God's elect people in the sky** (v. 31). In Revelation 19 He is coming with **the saints** (vs. 8, 14) He Rescued and resurrected at His first appearance some extended time earlier, to kill a gigantic army and the Antichrist on the Earth. Therefore, the initial appearance of Christ described in Matthew 24:29-31 is not the same appearance described in Revelation 19 at the Battle of Armageddon. These above differences can be summarized in the following table:

Christ's Two Appearances During His 2ⁿᵈ Coming

Christ's 1ˢᵗ Appearance in Matthew 24	Christ's 2ⁿᵈ Appearance in Revelation 19
Occurs immediately after The Greatest Persecution at the beginning of Christ's Wrath.	Occurs at the time of the Battle of Armageddon at the end of Christ's Wrath.
Christians in the Church are still alive on the Earth.	Christians in the Church are no longer living on the Earth.
Christ appearing to rescue His Church.	Christ appearing to punish His enemies.
Angels lifting the Church from Earth to meet Christ in the sky.	White horses carrying the Church from Heaven to fight Christ's enemies.
Kings of the Earth hiding from Christ's Wrath.	Kings of the Earth gathering to fight Christ.
Antichrist continues to rule on Earth.	Antichrist is captured and eternally placed in Lake of Fire.

To summarize, in Christ's first appearance He comes for His Church in the Church's Rescue to begin His Wrath. In Christ's second appearance He comes to the Battle of Armageddon with His Church to consummate His Wrath.

In between these two appearances of Christ on Earth, He remains in Heaven while His Angels execute His Wrath on Earth. It is not Christ, but Angels who are described as releasing the Trumpet and Bowl Punishments (cf. Rev 8:2; 15:1).

Likewise, during Christ's Wrath on Earth the saints are **with the Lord** (1 Thess 4:17) in Heaven. This is what Jesus was describing when He said, **"I go and prepare a place for you** [and] **I will come back and take you** [in the Church's Rescue] **to be with me that you also may be where I am** [in Heaven]" (John 14:3 NIV). And because they are **with the Lord forever** (1 Thess 4:17) after the Church's Rescue, they will return to Earth with Christ for the Battle of Armageddon at the end of Christ's Wrath. They will also remain with Christ on the Earth during Christ's 1,000-year Reign (cf. Rev 20:4).

The time period between Christ's first appearance <u>for</u> His Church, and His second appearance <u>with</u> His church is <u>not</u> known. Scripture does not tell us the duration of Christ's Wrath in the Trumpet and Bowl Punishments.

Therefore, the following outline of Christ's appearances and subsequent events are suggested:

1) Christ appears <u>first</u> to Rescue His Church from The Greatest Persecution and begin His Wrath (cf. Matt 15-31; 1 Thess 4:15-17; Rev 6:12-17).

2) At the Church's Rescue the saints are translated to Heaven to be **with the Lord forever** (1 Thess 4:17; cf. John 14:1-4). Both Christ and the saints remain in Heaven during Christ's Wrath.

3) Christ's Wrath immediately follows Christ's first appearance, including the Trumpet and Bowl Punishments, and lasts for a considerable but unknown period of time (cf. Rev 6:12-17)

4) Christ appears a <u>second</u> time with the Church to consummate His Wrath at the Battle of Armageddon (cf. Rev 19:11-19; Zech 14:4; Isa 63:1).

5) Christ's 1,000-year Reign begins (cf. Rev 20:1-6).

6) The Great White Throne Evaluation occurs after the Millennium when Eternity has begun (cf. Rev 20:7, 11-15; Matt 25:31-46; 1 Cor 3:12-15; 2 Cor 5:10).

7) God the Father will come to live for Eternity in a new and perfect city on a new and perfect Earth (Rev 21:1-5).

For a complete outline of all Endtime events see Appendix B in *Endtimes Essentials* book #2, *The Beginning of Birth Pains*.

The two visible appearances of Christ during His Second Coming can be illustrated in the following graphic:

Christ's Two Appearances in His Second Coming

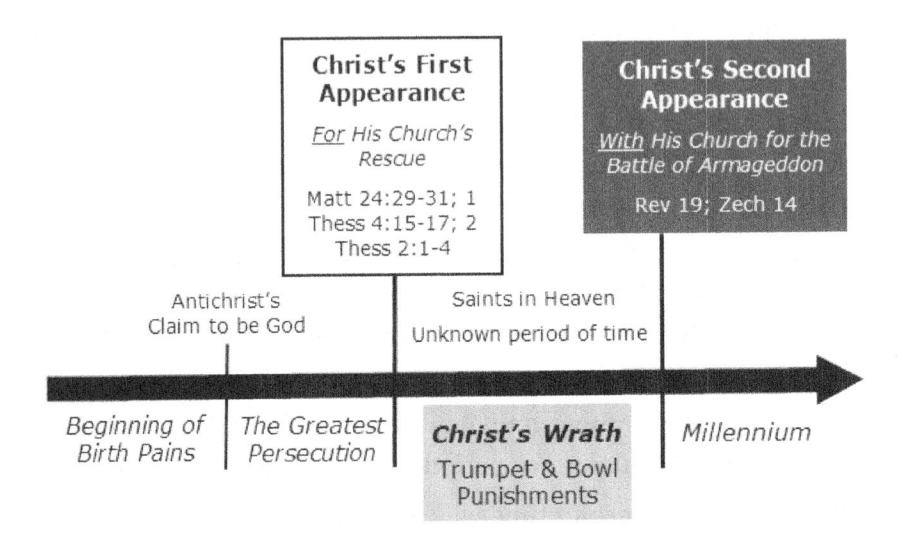

Christ's First Appearance
For His Church's Rescue
Matt 24:29-31; 1 Thess 4:15-17; 2 Thess 2:1-4

Christ's Second Appearance
With His Church for the Battle of Armageddon
Rev 19; Zech 14

Antichrist's Claim to be God

Saints in Heaven
Unknown period of time

Beginning of Birth Pains | *The Greatest Persecution* | **Christ's Wrath** Trumpet & Bowl Punishments | *Millennium*

The above corrects several common views on the Endtimes. Pre-tribulationism claims that there is only <u>one</u> visible appearance of Christ, at the Battle of Armageddon. Therefore, it further claims that the Church's Rescue being described in Matthew 24:31 is 1) The gathering of Israel on the Earth, or 2) The gathering of the Church in Heaven, which was "raptured" 7 years earlier, for the Battle of Armageddon. [4] Both of these views are unbiblical and are discussed later in this book (cf. ch. 13, sec. B.5; ch. 15, sec. E).

Likewise, <u>Post</u>-tribulationism claims there is only one visible appearance of Christ. Therefore, from this view His first appearance for the Church's Rescue before His Wrath, and His second appearance with His Church at the end of His Wrath <u>are the same event</u>. Therefore, in <u>Post</u>-tribulationism, the Church's Rescue described in Matthew 24:31 occurs at the same time as the Battle of Armageddon. But as we have seen, this is not biblical. <u>Post</u>-tribulationism will also be evaluated elsewhere. (cf. ch. 11, sec. D).

Because of the amount of confusion on this issue it may be helpful to point out that in 1 Thess 4:14-17 Paul actually described both appearances of Christ. He wrote:

For since we believe that Jesus died and was raised to life again, we also believe that when Jesus returns [at His second appearance for the Battle of Armageddon; cf. Rev 19:11-19], **God will bring back with him** [on white horses!] **the believers who have died** [and who were rescued alive or resurrected in Christ's first appearance].

We tell you this directly from the Lord [from Christ's Endtimes Teaching, Matt 24:30-31]**: We who are still living when the Lord returns** [at His first appearance] **will not meet him ahead of those who have died. For the Lord himself will come down from heaven** [at His first appearance, **on the clouds of Heaven**, Matt 24:30, not as a **rider** on **a white horse**, Rev 19:11] **with a commanding shout, with the voice of the archangel, and with the trumpet call of God.**

First, the believers who have died will rise from their graves [in **the first resurrection**, Rev 20:5]**. Then, together with them, we who are still alive and remain on the earth** [at Christ's first appearance] **will be caught up in the clouds to meet the Lord in the air** [for the Church's Rescue]**. Then we will be with the Lord forever** [including in Heaven while Angels execute Christ's Wrath on the Earth]. (1 Thess 4:14-17 NLT)

Admittedly, it is confusing that Paul described Christ's second appearance in verse 14 and His first appearance in verses 15-17. This confusion has led some [e.g. Post-tribulationists] to interpret Paul as saying that after the Church's Rescue the saints immediately return to Earth for the Battle of Armageddon. As explained elsewhere, this is not the best interpretation of these events (cf. ch. 11, sec. D). As the graphic above illustrates, the Trumpet and Bowl Punishments of Christ's Wrath occur between the two appearances of Christ. During this time, Christians in the Church on not on the Earth.

It is possible that the Apostle Paul was not aware of the above details about Christ's Second Coming. We should remember that there is "progressive revelation" in Scripture. The OT Prophets did not possess all the divine revelation of the NT Apostles.

Likewise, it is probable that the Apostle Paul, writing 1 Thessalonians around A.D. 50, [5] did not have the divine revelation that the Apostle John had over 40 years later when he wrote the Revelation (ca. A.D. 95 [6]). It is Revelation 19 that helps us most clearly understand there will be <u>two</u> visible appearances of Christ during His Second Coming. It is probably because Paul did not have this revelation that he put these appearances together in the text above.

B) The Church will know when Christ is coming
Understanding Matt 24:32-51

B.1) Illustrating the need for the Church to know when Christ is coming (Matt 24:50-51)

What are you doing at this moment? Reading this book, of course. Where are you? At home? Your office? Take a moment to think about where you are, and what you are doing right now.

Now imagine this. All of a sudden you hear a loud noise that sounds like a trumpet. It just keeps blowing. You go outside to see where it is coming from. As you do you immediately recognize that everything has gone completely black as if it is midnight. If it is during the day, you notice the sun has stopped shining. Not like a cloud is passing by, but the sun itself has gone dark. And if it is night right now, you notice that the moon is bright red in a way you have never seen before. And as you look up into the sky, you see something you were <u>not</u> expecting.

All of a sudden, a blinding bright light in the sky pierces the pitch darkness. And out of this bright light appears a Person shining with the glory of Heaven. You see His face and immediately recognize it is the Lord Jesus Christ. And you see millions of Angels streaking across the sky, picking up people... including YOU. And you realize-- this is THE DAY. The Day of Christ's Return and the Church's Rescue.

If all of that happened in the next few minutes would you be surprised? If Jesus Christ visibly appeared to all the world right now (even as you are reading about His Second Coming!), would He have come at an hour that you were not expecting Him? Do you understand that if that happened you would be going to Hell? Jesus said in His Endtimes sermon:

"The master of that [wicked, Matt 24:48] servant will come on a day when he does not expect him and at an hour he is not aware of. He will cut him to pieces and assign him a place with the unbelievers" (Luke 12:45-46 NIV; cf. Matt 24:51 [7]).

That is Hell. [8] And why do these people go to Hell? Because Christ came even **at an hour** they were not expecting Him.

This warning seems to put all of us in a very scary situation. We all probably have to agree that if Jesus Christ returned right now, we would not have been expecting Him at this very hour. So what is the point of this illustration? First, it demonstrates the importance of understanding an important section of Christ's Endtimes Teaching.

As explained in the previous chapters, Jesus gave the general sequence of Endtime events in the first portion of His Endtimes Teaching (cf. Matt 24:4-31). He then described how people will experience His Return (cf. vs. 32-51). And He concluded this section of His teaching with the serious warning quoted above. Accordingly, this portion of Scripture has been misinterpreted to teach that a real Christian could lose their salvation if they are not sufficiently watching for Christ's Return. Therefore, it is important that we accurately understand these verses.

Second, the illustration above exposes the error of the popular myth that the "rapture" could occur "at any moment," even right this very second. People who teach this misunderstand Christ's warning. Even for them, if Christ's Return and the Church's Rescue occurred today, it would have occurred **on a day** and even **at an hour** they were **not expect**ing. Nobody lives expecting Christ's Return every **hour** of every **day**. Not even the people who teach we should be living this way. It is simply not possible. And thankfully, not even Jesus expects us to live that way.

The solution to all the false teaching and confusion over these verses is to clearly understand them. And here is an important truth that will help you do that. As you read this section of Christ's Endtimes Teaching keep one thing in mind: Christ was contrasting what His Return will be like for believers in comparison to unbelievers.

[Read Matt 24:32-51. Again, notice how Christ contrasts believers with unbelievers.

B.2) How will we know Christ's Return and the Church's Rescue are near? (Matt 24:32-35)

In verses 32-35 Jesus said:

> **"Now learn this lesson from the fig tree: As soon as its twigs get tender and its leaves come out, you know that summer is near. Even so, when you see all these things, you know that it** [Christ's Return and the Church's Rescue, vs. 30-31] **is near, right at the door."**
>
> **Truly I tell you, this generation will certainly not pass away until all these things have happened. Heaven and earth will pass away, but my words will never pass away." (NIV)** [9]

What was Christ referring to when He said **it is near**? It was what He had described immediately before this in verses 30-31: Christ's visible Return and the Church's Rescue. Therefore, notice what Christ was saying. He expects His people to **know** when His Return and the Church's Rescue **is near**. The phrase, even **right at the door** suggests a very high level of immediacy and expectancy. In another teaching on this topic recorded by Luke, Jesus said regarding His Return:

> **"Be dressed ready for service and keep your lamps burning, like servants waiting for their master to return from a wedding banquet, so that when he comes and knocks they can <u>immediately</u> open the door for him."** (Luke 12:35-36 NIV)

Imagine the picture that Christ gives us. These servants are literally gathered together inside their **master**'s house **waiting** at **the** front **door** for him **to return from a wedding banquet**. They are not doing <u>anything</u> else. They are <u>only</u> focused on listening for their **master** to **knock** on the **door**, announcing His arrival so that **they can <u>immediately</u> open the door for him**. The only way these **servants** could have that kind of focus, readiness, and expectation is if they knew their **master** was **return**ing very soon. Like within a few minutes.

How will Christians know that Christ's Return is so close? How will they be able to have such an intense level of focus and expectation of

Christ's Return? The illustration above proved we cannot achieve or maintain such a focus hour after hour in our daily lives now. So how will Christians be able to expect Christ's Return on the exact **day** and even **hour** (Matt 24:51) it occurs? Jesus answered these questions when He said: **"When you see all these things, you** will **know that it** (His Return) **is near, right at the door"** (Matt 24:33).

What does **all these things** refer to? Probably not the Cosmic Signs and Christ's visible appearance described in the immediately preceding verses (30-31). If you are not expecting these things on the **day** they occur, it seems you will experience the punishment Christ warned of in verses 50-51 because Christ would have Returned **on a day** and **at an hour** you were not **expect**ing Him.

Therefore, **all these things** includes all the Endtime events Jesus described previously in His Endtimes Teaching. This included unprecedented **wars** and **famines** in **the beginning of birth pains** (Matt 24:6-8), the Antichrist's **abomination that causes desolation** in a rebuilt **holy place** (v. 15) or Temple in Jerusalem (cf. 2 Thess 2:3-4), and **the greatest persecution** (v. 21). When Christians **see all these things,** they will **know that** Christ's Return and the Church's Rescue, **is near, right at the door** (v. 33).

There is an additional reason that the Last Generation Church will **know that** Christ's Return and the Church's Rescue, **is near, right at the door** (v. 33), and will be **like servants waiting for their master to return from a wedding banquet, so that when he comes and knocks they can <u>immediately</u> open the door for him** (Luke 12:35-36). This is because Scripture tells us <u>8 times</u> that The Greatest Persecution will last <u>exactly 1,260 days</u> (cf. Dan 7:25; 9:27; 12:6-7; Rev 11:2, 3; 12:6, 14; 13:5). This often ignored biblical fact will be explained further in the book, *The Greatest Persecution.*

Jesus went on to say that the **generation** that will **see all these things** signaling Christ's Return, **will certainly not pass away until all these things have happened** (v. 34). Therefore, the Endtime events that Jesus described were not intended to refer to things that would occur to some degree throughout Church history. On the contrary, the events that will occur to signal Christ's Return will be unprecedented in their effect, and occur in one **generation**, when the Last Generation Church is on Earth. [10]

Jesus ended this section by saying: **"Heaven and earth will pass away, but my words will never pass away"** (v. 35). What **words**? The **words** He just used in His Endtimes Teaching to describe the events that will end this world as we know it. The fact that His **words** regarding the Endtimes **will never pass away** means there is nothing that will change them. These events and the end of this world will occur no matter what else happens.

B.3) Until Endtime events occur, no one can know the timing of Christ's Return (v. 36)

Next, Christ made the well-known statement: **"But about that day or hour** of His Return and the Church's Rescue (cf. vs. 30-31) **no one knows, not even the angels in heaven, nor the Son, but only the Father"** (v. 36 NIV). In chapter 1 it was noted:

> This is wrongly interpreted in many ways. Some think this means Christ's Return could happen at any time without any clear warning. Others misuse this statement to criticize those who would point to current events indicating the Endtimes are near.
>
> Misinterpreting Matthew 24:36 is probably why 45% of Evangelical Christians claim: "It is impossible to know the circumstances that will precede Jesus' return." In many ways, the apathetic view of the Endtimes is based on wrongly interpreting Christ's statement that no one knows the timing of His Return. (B.3)

It was pointed out there that many common mistakes are made when interpreting Matthew 24:36. For example:

> The first mistake is a failure to notice that **knows** (*oiden*) is in the <u>present tense</u>. This is missed by almost everyone who interprets this verse. Jesus <u>did not</u> say "no one will <u>ever</u> know the **day or hour**" of His Return. He said, when He was speaking with His disciples over 2,000 years ago, **"no one <u>now</u> knows about that day or hour."**
>
> Jesus gave us several signs of His Return that we are supposed to be looking for. Before those happen, no one can know the timing of His Return. But in a verse just before verse

36, Jesus said: **When you see all these things** [the signs of His Return]**, you know that it is near, right at the door**. (Matt 24:33 NIV).

And as noted above, if you do not **know** the **day or hour** of Christ's Return when He comes, you will be cast into Hell. So clearly, the Last Generation Church at some point will **know about that day or hour** of Christ's Return. In fact, as noted above, because Scripture states 8 times that The Greatest Persecution will last exactly 1,260 days, it will be argued elsewhere that the Last Generation Church will know the exact day Christ will Return and Rescue them.

The point here was summarized in chapter 1:
> Jesus did not intend to say that Christians will never know the timing of Christ's Return. It is only unbelievers that will not know the timing of Christ's Return. Christians will know the timing of Christ's Return because they will be watching for the signs of His Return in obedience to His commands. It is unbelievers who are expected to have an apathetic view on Christ's Return, not believers.

But again, until **all these things** in the Endtimes occur, **no one knows** ((*oiden*, present tense) the timing of Christ's Return.

Let it be added that it is possible that neither Christ nor the Angels still know the timing of Christ's Return. The Trinity is a perfect unity of Persons, but they have different roles. God the Son is under the authority of God the Father, and part of that relationship may be that **only the Father** still knows when He will send His Son back to Earth. As Christ later told His disciples, **"The Father alone has the authority to set those dates and times"** (Acts 1:7 NLT). However, it will be Christ who will open the **seven seals** of the **scroll** containing Endtime events (cf. Rev 5:6-7; 6:1). When that happens, Christ will surely **know about that day or hour** of Christ's Return.

B.4) When Endtime events occur, Christians will know Christ's Return is near (vs. 37-42)

Jesus went on in His Endtimes Teaching to describe the difference between how unbelievers and Christians will experience His Return. We read: **"As it was in the days of Noah, so it will be at the coming of the Son of Man"** (Matt 24:37 NIV).

Jesus said **the coming of the Son of Man** will be like **the days of Noah.** What was He referring to? For one thing, when God punished the Earth in the worldwide Flood, <u>Noah knew the exact day it would occur</u>, but the rest of the world had no idea.

In Genesis chapter 7 verse 1 we read: **The LORD then said to Noah, "Go into the ark, you and your whole family"** (NIV). Why? Because in verse 4 God says, **"<u>Seven days from now</u> I will send rain on the earth for forty days and forty nights, and I will wipe from the face of the earth every living creature I have made."** Notice then that **Noah** and his **family** knew the <u>exact day</u> that their rescue would begin, and God's wrath would begin. Accordingly, we read in verse 10: **after <u>the seven days</u> the floodwaters came on the earth.**

Jesus was using **Noah** and his **family** to illustrate how Christians will experience Christ's Return. Like **Noah**, they will **know that it is near, right at the door** because they will **see all these things** (v. 33) happen that Christ said would signal His Return.

As noted, with the example of the Flood, Jesus was contrasting what His Return would be like for Christians, as opposed to unbelievers. How did <u>unbelievers</u> in Noah's day experience the coming of God's wrath? Jesus went on to say:

"For in the days before the flood, people [the unbelievers] **were eating and drinking, marrying and giving in marriage, up to the day Noah** [and the believers] **entered the ark; and they** [the unbelievers] **knew nothing about what would happen until the flood came and took them all away. That is how it will be at the coming of the Son of Man."** (vs. 38-39 NIV)

We have already noted that **Noah** and his **family** knew exactly **seven days** beforehand that God's wrath was coming (Gen 7:1, 4). No doubt they were working frantically to make final preparations for the Flood to begin. But all the people of the world were going about their normal daily lives **in the days before the flood ... and they knew nothing about what would happen until the flood came and**

took them all away (vs. 38-39). Unbelievers were totally caught off guard by the coming of God's wrath in Noah's day. They were completely surprised. This will also be true for unbelievers before Christ's Return. They will be going about their daily lives having no idea that Christ and His Wrath are coming.

In verses 40-41 of Christ's Endtimes Teaching He continued to contrast what Christians and unbelievers would experience when He Returned. He said, **"Two men will be in the field; one will be taken** to be rescued, **and the other left** on the Earth to be punished. Likewise, when Christ Returns, **two women will be grinding with a hand mill; one will be taken** to be with Christ in the Church's Rescue, **and the other left** on Earth for Christ's Wrath. [11]

Some are confused that both believers and unbelievers are portrayed here doing the same things right before Christ's Return. There is an impression that both are experiencing normal life at this time. Such an interpretation fits into the Pre-tribulational view that the "rapture" will occur without warning, even for the believer.

But Jesus corrects this interpretation in this very passage. He said believers will experience His Return like **Noah** and his **family** experienced the coming of the Flood. Because they knew God's Wrath would begin soon, they were preparing for this very thing and living quite differently from others.

Therefore, how do we explain believers **in the field** or **grinding with a hand mill**, even though they will be experiencing **the greatest persecution** (v. 29) and **know that** Christ's Return **is near, right at the door"** (v. 33)? The simple answer is that even Christians in such circumstances will still need to eat. They will still need to be acquiring and preparing food.

Finally, in verse 42, Jesus essentially repeated what He said in verse 36: **"Therefore keep watch, because you do not know** [*oidate*] **on what day your Lord will come."** Again, present tense, neither we nor his disciples over 2,000 years ago, could **know on what day** our **Lord will come**. Which is precisely why Christ has wanted every generation of His people to **keep watch** for the signs of His Return that would enable them to **know that it is near, right at the door** (v. 33). This command to **watch** for signs of Christ's Return will be discussed further in the next chapter.

B.5) Christ's Return will come like a "thief in the night" for unbelievers, not Christians (v. 43)

Jesus continued in His Endtimes Teaching to illustrate the differences between believers and unbelievers at His Return:

> "**But understand this: If the owner of the house had known at what time of night the thief was coming, he would have kept watch and would not have let his house be broken into.**" (Matt 24:43: NIV)

Here Jesus introduced the well-known illustration of His Coming **like a thief in the night** (1 Thess 5:1). Many have used this statement to claim this is how Christians will experience Christ's Return. But notice again that Jesus said it is possible for **the owner of the house** to know **at what time of night the thief was coming** and to **have kept watch and ... not have let his house be broken into.** This illustrates the fact that Christians in the Last Generation Church will know when Christ is coming.

The Apostle Paul had Christ's Endtimes Teaching, probably in its written form. He knew Christ had used the illustration of a **thief coming** at **night** to refer to His Return. However, it would seem that like today, many in the Early Church had misunderstood Christ's statement. They too thought that even Christians would be surprised by the timing of Christ's Return, like a **thief** breaking into their **house** at **night**. But the Apostle corrected this misunderstanding when he wrote of Christ's Return:

> **Now concerning how and when all this will happen, dear brothers and sisters, we don't really need to write you. For you know quite well that the day of the Lord's return will come unexpectedly, like a thief in the night. When people** [unbelievers] **are saying, "Everything is peaceful and secure," then disaster will fall on them as suddenly as a pregnant woman's labor pains begin. And there will be no escape** [from Christ's Wrath].
>
> But **you** [Christians] **aren't in the dark about these things, dear brothers and sisters, and you won't be surprised when the day of the Lord comes like a thief.**
> (1 Thess 5:1-4 NLT)

The Apostle made the same distinction as Christ. The **day of the Lord's return will come unexpectedly, like a thief in the night** for the pagan **people** of this world. **But for brothers and sisters** in Christ, they will not **be surprised when the day of the Lord comes**. Therefore, as noted above, even in Matthew 24:43 Christ implied that **the owner of** a **house** can know **at what time of night the thief is coming** and to **not have his house be broken into.**

B.6) Unbelievers will be completely surprised by Christ's Return, but not Christians (vs. 44-51)

We noted above that the key to understanding Matthew 24:32-51 was to recognize that Jesus was repeatedly contrasting what His Return would be like for believers and unbelievers. This helps us correctly understand the difficult statement in verse 44. Christ said to His disciples: **"So you also must be ready, because the Son of Man will come at an hour when you do** not **expect him"** (v. 44).

Why is this a difficult statement? Because everything Christ had said before this about the **fig tree** (v. 32) and **the days of Noah** (v. 37), made it clear that He expected His people to **know** when His return **is near, right at the door** (v. 33). So how could Jesus later say, **the Son of Man will come at an hour when you do not expect him**? The **you** seems to refer to the disciples He was talking to, and would extend to Christians in the Church.

There is another problem with this statement that was introduced above. Jesus said a few verses later:

> **"The master of that servant will come on a day when he does not expect him** and at an hour he is not aware of. **He will cut him to pieces and assign him a place with the hypocrites** [Hell], **where there will be weeping and gnashing of teeth"** (vs. 50-51; cf. Luke 12:46)

As explained above, if Christ Returns even **at an hour** that surprises you, you will go to Hell. So how do we reconcile this with Christ's statement in verse 44 that **the Son of Man will come at an hour when you do not expect him**?

Fortunately, Jesus taught on these things in another teaching recorded by Luke.

[Stop reading and read Luke 12:35-46]

As noted above, there Christ said, **"Be dressed ready for service and keep your lamps burning, like servants waiting for their master to return from a wedding banquet, so that when he comes and knocks they can immediately open the door for him"** (Luke 12:35-36). Again, this communicates a very high level of expectancy for Christ's Return. The only way that **servants** could be **waiting** like this, is if they knew <u>when</u> **their master** was to **return**.

The disciples who were listening to this teaching understood that the above illustration about **servants** communicated a very high level of expectancy for Christ's Return. Therefore, they were puzzled when Christ said a little later in this teaching: **"You also must be ready, because the Son of Man will come at an hour when you do not expect him"** (Luke 12:40; cf. Matt 24:44). For the disciples, this seemed to imply something different than the high level of expectancy Christ had described for His disciples concerning His Return.

Accordingly, Peter interrupted Jesus to ask a very important question. Luke records that Jesus said, **"You also must be ready, because the Son of Man will come at an hour when you do not expect him"** (Luke 12:40). Then Luke records: **Peter asked, "Lord, are you telling this parable to us, or to everyone?"** (v. 41). In other words, Peter is asking, does your warning that people will <u>not</u> be **expect**ing your Return at the **hour** it occurs, apply **to us**, your followers, or to **everyone** else, the unbelievers?

Jesus goes on in Luke to contrast a **faithful and wise manager** (v. 42) who is a Christian, as opposed to a **servant** who **begins to beat the other servants ... and get drunk** (v. 45), like an unbeliever. In answer to Peter's question, Jesus explains **The master of that wicked servant will come ... at an hour he is not aware of. He will cut him to pieces and assign him a place with the unbelievers** (v. 46). So in Luke's version, who was Jesus referring to when He said, **"You also must be ready, because the Son of**

Man will come at an hour when you do not expect him" (Luke 12:40)? He was referring to unbelievers, who will not be expecting Christ to Return at the **hour** it occurs and will be sent to Hell.

It is admitted that Christ's repeated use of **you** in the text seems to imply that this warning was directed toward the disciples. This is especially true of Matthew's and Mark's versions where only a few disciples heard this teaching (cf. Matt 24:3; Mark 13:3). But Luke tells us that Jesus made this same statement during another teaching **when a crowd of many thousands had gathered** (Luke 12:1). Therefore, it makes sense that Christ would address both believers and unbelievers in this teaching. Therefore, Jesus intended to do the same in the version of this teaching given in Matthew and Mark.

Luke's version of this teaching helps us to better understand the same statement in Matthew 24:44. Jesus was referring to unbelievers when He said, **"So you also must be ready, because the Son of Man will come at an hour when you do not expect him."** This is why in the verses that immediately follow, Christ also clearly distinguishes between how believers and unbelievers will experience His Return. Just as in Luke 12:42-46, in Matthew 24:45-49 Jesus again contrasts **the faithful and wise servant** (v. 45) who is the Christian, as opposed to a **servant** who is **wicked** and **begins to beat his fellow servants and to eat and drink with drunkards** (vs. 48-49) like an unbeliever. He then concludes:

> **The master of that [wicked, v. 48] servant will come on a day when he does not expect him and at an hour he is not aware of. He will cut him to pieces and assign him a place with the hypocrites, where there will be weeping and gnashing of teeth**. (Matt 24:50-51)

Just as Jesus explained in Luke's version of this teaching, those for whom Christ's Return **will come at an hour when you do not expect him** (Matt 24:44), are the same unbelievers who will be like a **wicked servant** for whom his **master ... will come ... at an hour he is not aware of** (v. 50) and go to Hell. Again, unbelievers will be completely surprised by Christ's Return, but not Christians (vs. 43-51).

You were warned in chapter 1 that the Bible's teaching on the Endtimes is rather complicated!

[1] For an explanation of the suggested translation of Matt 24:29-31 see ch. 3, sec. E. and ch. 4, sec. C.

[2] It is suggested that Rev 6:12-14 is primarily referring to events that will occur with Christ's Return at His first appearance. However, biblical prophecy is complicated enough that there may also be allusions to the end of Christ's Wrath here and Christ's second appearance at the Battle of Armageddon (cf. 16:20).

Some claim Rev 6:12-17, and especially v. 14 is only describing the very end of Christ's Wrath and is parallel to Rev 16:20: **Every island fled away and the mountains could not be found** (NIV). It is agreed by most this last reference is describing the end of Christ's Wrath. The view that Rev 6:14 and 16:20 are describing the same event seems supported by the NIV translation of 6:14, **every mountain and island was removed from its place**. Accordingly, Beale writes that 6:12-17 is describing "the final judgment and the very end of the world" (398; cf. Osborne, 293).

However, it is more likely that Revelation 6 and 16 describe a progression of the destruction of the Earth's **islands** and **mountains** (cf. MacArthur, *Rev*, 207; Thomas, 737-8). First, one of Beale's arguments is that, "The whole of the sun, moon, and stars are destroyed in 6:12-13" (399). But that is not at all what the text says. Rather, the appearance of the sun and moon are simply and temporarily changed. Likewise, based on Rev 8:12, it does not seem that Rev 6 is even describing that all **the stars fell to the earth**.

Second, even NIV's **removed from its place** could mean merely "moved" rather than completely "removed" from the Earth.

Third, there is only one instance in the NT where the relatively rare Greek word in this text (*ekinēthēsan*) probably means to "completely remove" (cf. Rev 2:5). However, simply **move** is by far its most common meaning in the NT (cf. Matt 23:4; Acts 17:28). It can even refer to people **shaking their heads** (Matt 27:39; Mark 15:29). It seems best to translate *ekinēthēsan* in Rev 6:14 to mean **all of the mountains and islands were moved from their places** (NLT, NASB), rather than completely removed from the Earth.

Fourth, merely (!) moving the **islands** and **mountains** would be the expected result of the **great earthquake** (6:12) that will be occurring at this same time, rather than completely removing them.

Therefore, we see a progression of destruction of the Earth's **islands** and **mountains** in Rev 6 and 16. At the beginning of Christ's Wrath, they are simply **move**d. At the end of His Wrath they are removed. This would reflect the general progression of destruction portrayed throughout the Trumpet and Bowl Punishments described in Revelation.

[3] A third biblical description of Christ's second appearance on Earth to complete His Wrath is Isa 63:1 that describes Christ as **coming from**

Edom, from Bozrah, with his garments stained crimson ... robed in splendor, striding forward in the greatness of his strength.

4 Speakman notes:
> Some [Pre-tribulational] scholars, however, argue that the "gathering of the elect" described in Matthew 24:31 refers not to the Rapture but to the calling together of God's heavenly armies—including, perhaps, believers raptured seven years earlier, prior to the Great Tribulation—for the Battle of Armageddon. (39)

Apparently, these Pre-tribulationists would have the same view of Matt 24:29-31 as Post-tribulationists. Still, both views seem to ignore the biblical arguments in this section.

5 *An Introduction to the New Testament,* D. A. Carson, Douglas J. Moo, Leon Morris (Zondervan, 1992), 347.

6 Carson, Moo, and Morris conclude after a detailed discussion: "We are inclined, then, to follow the oldest tradition [from Irenaeus] on this point and date Revelation in the last years of [the Roman Emperor] Domitian" (476), whose reign was A. D. 81-96 (474) (*Introduction*). For more on this see the evaluation of Preterism in chapter 12, sec. B.

7 Matthew's version refers to the damned as **hypocrites** perhaps not making it as clear that they are sent to Hell. However, Morris adds: "The wailing and grinding of teeth ... stands for the anguish and suffering of those who are finally lost" (*Matthew*, 618).

8 Wiersbe misses the fact that Christ is only addressing unbelievers in Matt 24:50-51, and believes church leaders are the subject. He writes:
> If the spiritual leader is obediently doing his job when the Lord returns, he shall be rewarded. But if that leader is not doing his job when the Lord returns, he will be dealt with in a severe way. I prefer to translate Matthew 24:51: "And shall punish him severely and appoint him his portion with the hypocrites.".. [This] suggests loss of reward and loss of opportunity. (at Matt 24:45)

On the contrary, Jesus is describing sending unbelievers to Hell (cf. Luke 12:46).

9 Christ's illustration of a **fig tree** blossoming in Matt 24:32-33 has probably been widely misunderstood. It has been common to teach that Jesus was giving a prophecy here, and that Israel becoming a nation in 1948 was its fulfillment. OT illusions to Israel being a fig tree are used to support this.

But it is doubtful there is any truth to this. Granted, Israel becoming a nation in 1948 and fending off an overwhelming army of its enemies in the Six Day War (1967), seem only possible with divine intervention. God was certainly enabling these events in preparation for Endtime prophecies concerning the nation of Israel.

However, there is no indication that Jesus intended such a prediction by using the illustration of a **fig tree** (v. 32). Second, 1948 is now over 70 years ago, which stretches the limit of the meaning **near, right at the door** (v. 33). Thirdly, Christ said His Return would be **near ... when you see <u>all</u> these things.** As noted in this section, **these things** include The Beginning of Birth Pains and The Greatest Persecution. Jesus never explicitly mentioned the establishment of Israel as a nation in His Endtimes Teaching.

[10] For more on **this generation** (Matt 24:34) see ch. 12, sec. B.2.

[11] For more on Matt 24:40-41 see chapter 4, sec. C.3.

Chapter 10

Commands in Christ's Endtimes Teaching

Contents

A) "Watch out that no one misleads you"

B) "Guard yourself against fear and make sure you are not alarmed"

C) "Always be ready for action"

D) "Watch!"

E) Wait

F) Work

Primary Points

- The very first words of Christ's Endtimes Teaching were a command: **"Watch out that no one misleads you."** Unfortunately, popular views on the Endtimes have led to this very thing.

- COURAGE will be needed for Christians to LIVE in the Endtimes in a God-glorifying way. But Christian COURAGE is also needed to face and properly interpret what God has revealed for His Church in Christ's Endtimes Teaching.

- The only way to practically obey Christ's command to **"Watch!"** is to monitor current events in our world and compare them with the first signs of the Endtimes in biblical prophecy.

- God wanted signs of the Endtimes to occur in every generation because He wanted every generation of Christians to believe they could be the Last Generation of Christians.

- Christ is expecting Christians to live with two very different perspectives about their life on Earth: believing that the Endtimes could begin tomorrow, or not for another 1,000 years. It is the tension between watching expectantly and waiting patiently for His Return.

- A purpose of Christ's Endtimes Teaching is to encourage us to have an eternal perspective on our life and to faithfully work for the rewards of serving His Kingdom and His people.

A) "Watch out that no one misleads you" *Matt 24:4*

The very first words of Christ's Endtimes Teaching were a command: **"Watch out that no one misleads you"** (Matt 24:4 [1]). This warning primarily applies to not being deceived by the False Christs described in the next verse. This is discussed elsewhere. [2]

But why would Christians be deceived by such people claiming to represent Christ? One reason may be they do not understand the biblical sequence of Endtime events that Jesus subsequently taught in His Endtimes Teaching. They believe the lie that the real Christ comes before the False Christ(s).

The Apostle Paul gave the same command to the Thessalonians: **Do not let anyone deceive you in any way** (2 Thess 2:3). Again, deceived about what? The sequence of Endtime events he had taught them as young converts, and repeated in this passage of Scripture (cf. ch. 5, sec. C).

Therefore, Christian, **"Watch out that no one misleads you"** about the substance and sequence of Endtime events. That is Christ's command to you. This has been a primary purpose of this book, *Christ's Endtimes Teaching*.

B) "Guard yourself against fear" *Matt 24:6*

In Christ's Endtimes Teaching He warned:

> **You will hear reports of devasting wars and riots, but guard yourself against fear and make sure you are not alarmed. These horrific conflicts must happen, but My coming and the end of the age will not follow immediately.** (Matt 24:6 [3])

The suggested translation reflects the seriousness that Jesus intended in this command. His command against **fear** was specifically in the context of the **devastating wars** that **must happen** in **the beginning of birth pains** (v. 8). These **wars** will be so **horrific** that Christians will be tempted to be **alarmed**. But Jesus will want you to **guard yourself against fear and make sure you are not alarmed** by the **devastating wars**, and not deceived to think **the end** is imminent. Because **Such things must happen, but the end** and more painful events are **still to come** (v. 6).

The **devastating wars** will only be the beginning of **the beginning of birth pains**. They will lead to unprecedented **famines** and **earthquakes** and **plagues** so that the people living in **one fourth of the earth** will die (Matt 24:7; Luke 21:11, Rev 6:8).

But again, these will only be **the beginning of birth pains** (Matt 24:8). They will simply set up the world to be dominated by the Antichrist who will unleash **the greatest persecution of God's elect people. It will be greater than any persecution since the world began, and it will never be equaled again** (Matt 24:21 [4]).

Persecutions of Christians occurring in the past and today have shown us the truly terrible things God has allowed persecutors to do to His children. Enduring such things in a God-glorifying way will require a supernatural COURAGE that can only be experienced by being controlled by the Holy Spirit. This is discussed in chapter 16.

COURAGE will be needed for Christians to LIVE in the Endtimes in a God-glorifying way. But Christian COURAGE is also needed to face and properly interpret what God has revealed for His Church in Christ's Endtimes Teaching. This was explained fully in chapter 1. There you read:

> If your view of what Scripture teaches about the Endtimes does not shock and deeply sadden you, because of what YOU and the Christians you love may experience, then may I humbly suggest that you need to re-evaluate your view...
>
> Another reason for the widespread error, neglect, and confusion on this topic is that what God says about the Endtimes is painful. Therefore, we must also endure this doctrine with a brave heart. Fear will keep you from properly understanding God on this biblical topic. You will never understand the Endtimes if you are afraid to do so. (sec. B.1)

Indeed, FEAR in American Christianity is one reason for all of the popular and rather "painless," but unbiblical views of the Endtimes. That fear has driven some teachers to develop complicated schemes of interpretation to deceive many Christians to believe Christ's Endtimes Teaching has no relevance for the Church. And fear of what Christ predicted has driven many to **look for teachers who will tell them whatever their itching** [and fear-controlled] **ears want to hear and reject the truth and chase after myths** (2 Tim 4:3-4 NLT).

It is especially fear of persecution that has driven too many Christians to ignore or distort Christ's Endtimes Teaching. This is because in that teaching He predicted The Greatest Persecution for **God's elect people** which will include the Church (Matt 24:21-22). But what did Jesus say should be our response to persecution?

> **"Happy are those who are persecuted because of their righteousness, because they are fortunate that the Kingdom of Heaven belongs to them... Be happy and very joyful about being persecuted, because great is your reward in Heaven"** (Matt 5:10, 12; 5 cf. 2 Cor 12:10; 1 Pet 3:14; 4:14).

Jesus expected His people to be **happy and very joyful** about being **persecuted**. Instead, many are so fearful of it that they ignore or distort Christ's Endtimes Teaching to avoid any warning of it.

Likewise, in the context of persecution, the Apostle Peter told Christians, **Do not fear their threats; do not be frightened** (1 Pet 3:14). But again, false teachers play upon the fears Christians have of being persecuted to make their teachings attractive. The false prophets in Scripture did the same. Instead of telling people the truth about the danger that God wanted them warned about, false prophets would tell people what they wanted to hear.

Do not be afraid (Luke 1:13) is the most repeated command in Scripture. The Apostle Paul repeated it when he wrote: **Do not be anxious about anything** (Phil 4:6), including the Endtimes. Christians like to deny it, but worry is a sin. Even worry about living in the Endtimes. Fear is the opposite of faith.

Christian, never interpret Scripture with sinful fear, but with God-trusting faith. Never respond to Scripture's Endtimes teaching in sinful fear, but God-pleasing faith. Regarding the Endtimes, God wants us to be alert, but not alarmed. Fear will always lead you into more sin, and actually more danger, because it will always lead you outside of God's will.

All of this is why Jesus commanded in His Endtimes Teaching, **"Guard yourself against fear and make sure you are not alarmed"** (Matt 24:6).

C) "Always be ready for action" *Luke 12:35*

In another Endtimes teaching in Luke 12:35-38, Jesus said:

Always be ready for action, serving, and fleeing. And keep your lamps burning, like servants waiting for their master to return from the wedding feast, so that when he comes and knocks they can immediately open the door for him.

It will be good for those servants whose master finds them watching when he comes... It will be good for those servants whose master finds them ready.

Always be ready for action, serving, and fleeing translates the literal Greek which reads, **"Let your loins be girded"** (KJV). But as NT scholar Wayne Grudem explains:

> The phrase ... in [literal] Greek [is] an almost meaningless phrase for modern readers unfamiliar with the ancient Oriental custom of gathering up one's long robes by pulling them between the legs and then wrapping and tying them around the waist, so as to prepare for running, fast walking, or other strenuous activity (see 1 Ki. 18:46; 2 Ki. 4:29; 9:1). [6]

Accordingly, the NASB has **be dressed in readiness** and the ESV has **Stay dressed for action** (Luke 12:35; cf. NRSV). The GNT has, **Be ready for whatever comes, dressed for action.** Nolland writes it is "a sign of readiness for departure on a journey." [7] Morris adds: "The girding of the loins is a step toward preparedness." [8] Bock translates the statement to mean "a state of constant readiness to act." [9] Hagner writes that "gird up your loins" in Luke 12:35 means: "let the long, ankle-length robe be adjusted by a waist-belt to ensure readiness for action or departure." [10]

The NET translation notes explain: "'Let your loins be girded,' is an idiom referring to the practice of tucking the ends of the long cloak into the belt to shorten it in preparation for activities like running, etc." [11] Therefore, the suggested translation: **Always be ready for action, serving, and fleeing.**

Likewise, scholars explain that the second phrase, **"keep your lamps burning"** means to be ready for action even in a time of darkness. [12]

This is an especially appropriate command for the Endtimes. Why do Christians need to **<u>Always</u> be ready for action, serving, and fleeing**? Because the Endtimes could begin TODAY! Are you and your family and your church **ready** for that?

Why must we **Always be ready for <u>action</u>** and **<u>serving</u>**? Because God will have much for us to do in the Endtimes. Why must we **Always be ready for ... fleeing**? Because Christians will be hunted in The Greatest Persecution, and God will want us to stay alive to be **serving** Him and His people. This is why, when The Greatest Persecution begins, Jesus commanded His people to immediately **"flee to the mountains. Let no one on the housetop go down to take anything out of the house"** (Matt 24:16-17).

Are Christians **"ready for action, serving, and fleeing"** in the Endtimes? Most are not because they have been taught the rather "painless" views of the Endtimes which falsely exempt them from the coming Greatest Persecution. This too will be discussed further in chapter 16. Contrary to popular views, there is a reason that Christ commanded in the context of the Endtimes: **"Always be ready for action, serving, and fleeing."**

D) "Watch!"

In chapter 2 of *Christ's Endtimes Teaching* you read:

There are also several practical reasons God wants us to understand the Endtimes. First, He wants His Church to be watching and ready for it when it begins. We read: **Later, Jesus sat on the Mount of Olives. His disciples came to him privately and said, "Tell us, when will all this happen? What sign will signal your return and the end of the world?"** (Matt 24:3 NLT).

In response Jesus very carefully and intentionally described many signs and events that will signal His Return.

This is why throughout Christ's sermon on the Endtimes He said: **"Be on guard! Be alert!"** ... **"keep watch"** ... **"What I say to you, I say to everyone: 'Watch!'"** (Mark 13:33, 34, 37 NIV). **Watch!** for what? Current events in our world that would signal the beginning of the Endtimes, and that Christ's Return is near. (sec. B)

Elsewhere, Christ rebuked the Pharisees for not understanding biblical signs. He said, **"You know how to interpret the appearance of the sky** [to predict the weather], **but you cannot interpret the signs of the times"** (Matt 16:1-3 NIV) to recognize Christ's First Coming. Likewise, Christ would confront Christians today who **cannot interpret the signs** of His Second Coming.

Christ could not have been clearer. A repeated command in His Endtimes Teaching was to **"Watch!"** current events so that we would recognize the beginning of the Endtimes. Unfortunately, this command is widely ignored in the Church today. As discussed further in chapter 16 (sec. C), popular views on the Endtimes discourage this very thing. It is the popularity of these teachings on the Endtimes that has led to the statistic that 45% of American Evangelical Christians claim: "it is impossible to know the circumstances that will precede Jesus' return." [13] Therefore, it is impossible for such Christians to intelligently obey Christ's command to **"Watch!"**

E) Wait   *Matt 25:1-13*

It is easy to forget that Christ's Endtimes Teaching takes up two entire chapters in Matthew. In the first part of the sermon He taught the biblical outline of Endtime events (cf. 24:4-31). In the second part of the sermon He encouraged His people to **"Watch!"** (Mark 13:5) and **be ready** (Matt 24:44) for those Endtime events to begin (v. 42, 44). But in the third part of the sermon He warned His people that these events may be **a long time in coming** (Matt 25:5).

[Read Matthew 25:1-13]

This parable contrasts believers and unbelievers. It is only to unbelievers that the **Lord** will say, **"I don't know you"** (vs. 11-12). The **wise virgins** represent believers who **took oil in jars along with their lamps** (25:1, 4). These are like the **wise servant** in the previous verses who is faithfully watching for his master's return (24:45). So in a sense, the purpose of this parable is also to encourage watchfulness for Christ's Return. Indeed, Jesus ended the parable by repeating: **"Therefore keep watch"** (25:13).

Accordingly, Carson comments on this passage: "In light of the entire parable, the dominant exhortation of this entire discourse is repeated: Be prepared! Keep watching!" [14]

But the parable recognizes that **The bridegroom** may be **a long time in coming** (25:5). Likewise, later in the sermon, Jesus shares another parable about His Return and says, **"After a long time the master of those servants returned and settled accounts with them"** (25:19 NIV).

Much of what is said here is repeated by Christ in another teaching and parable recorded in Luke. There we read:

> **While they were listening to this, he went on to tell them a parable, because he was near Jerusalem <u>and the people thought that the kingdom of God was going to appear at once</u>. He said: "A man of noble birth went to a <u>distant</u> country to have himself appointed king and then to return.** (Luke 19:11-12)

Christ implied here that **the kingdom of God was <u>not</u> going to appear at once**. Therefore, Christ taught that we are to live with this tension between <u>watching expectantly</u> and <u>waiting patiently</u> for His Return. [15] Accordingly, you read in chapter 2:

> [H]ere is a hard truth: Endtime events could literally begin TODAY, or not for another 1,000 years. That is the biblical truth. Scripture's teaching on the Endtimes presents it this way. This is because God has wanted every generation of Christians to believe they <u>could be</u> living in the Last Generation Church.
>
> God wants us to live with this challenging tension between <u>expectant watching</u> and <u>patient waiting</u>. On one hand, to plan on living a long life. But also not be surprised if the Endtimes begin TODAY. (sec. B)

Therefore, Christians can err in two ways regarding Christ's Return. Like unbelievers or skeptics, they can ignore Christ's command to **"Watch!"** expectantly for the signs of His Return. On the other hand, in the rest of the sermon, Jesus rebukes those who would be distracted from service because of their watching.

In essence, Christ is expecting Christians to live with two very different perspectives about their life on Earth. On one hand, to **"keep**

watch, because you do not know on what day your Lord will come" (Matt 24:42 NIV). This is to live as if the Endtimes could begin Today. It is the kind of short-sighted outlook on life that the Apostle Paul encouraged when he wrote:

> **The time that remains is very short. So from now on, those with wives should not focus only on their marriage. Those who weep or who rejoice or who buy things should not be absorbed by their weeping or their joy or their possessions. Those who use the things of the world should not become attached to them. For this world as we know it will soon pass away.** (1 Cor 7:29-31 NLT)

The difficulty with Paul saying this over 2,000 years ago is addressed elsewhere. [16] Nevertheless, such a lens on life would discourage any long-term planning for your life on Earth. Why get married, have children, develop a career, or plan for retirement if the Endtimes are to begin tomorrow? Indeed, in some sense, Jesus expects us to live this way with such an eternal perspective on life that is expecting His soon Return.

But Jesus did not end His Endtimes Teaching there. He went on to provide balance to only a short-sighted view of life. He shared a parable that warned Endtimes events may be **a long time in coming** (Matt 25:5). Therefore, Jesus also encouraged a long-term view of life, with the possibility that Christ's Return will <u>not</u> occur in your lifetime. This would call for Christians to plan accordingly, seeking to make the most of a long life on this Earth.

It is biblical to live with both a short-term and long-term view on our life. This is what God wants. To be both <u>watching expectantly</u> and <u>waiting</u> patiently for Christ's Return. But these are two very different ways to live, and pursuing both is difficult and requires wisdom. Jesus provided such wisdom in what He said next.

F) Work *Matt 25:16*

How are we supposed to live while we are both <u>watching expectantly</u> and <u>waiting patiently</u> for Christ's Return? We are to be diligently serving our Lord and His people.

[Read Matthew 25:14-46]

Jesus again contrasts believers with unbelievers. At Christ's Return the latter will be treated as a **worthless servant** and cast **into the darkness, where there will be weeping and gnashing of teeth** (25:30 NIV, Hell). This fate parallels that of the unbelieving **wicked servant** Jesus had spoken of earlier in the sermon (24:48-51).

Believers in the parable are described as those who **put** the master's **money to work and gained** something **more** (25:16). The point of the parable is obvious. Jesus wants us to be making the most of our life and time while we wait for His Return. This same point was made with the earlier example of **"the faithful and wise servant, whom the master has put in charge of the servants in his household to give them their food at the proper time"** (24:45 NIV).

What kind of work does Christ want us doing until His Return? Earlier in the sermon He said, **this gospel of the kingdom will be preached in the whole world as a testimony to all nations, and then the end will come** (Matt 24:14 NIV). Obviously, Christ wants us to be committed to fulfilling His Great Commission before His Return.

Later in the sermon Jesus shared other kinds of works He expects us to do. This includes simple acts of kindness for even **the least of** Christ's **brothers and sisters** (25:40; cf. vs. 35-36). Obviously, all of these things will become even more important for Christians in the Endtimes.

Jesus ends His Endtimes Teaching with a literal description of future events and not a parable. At The Great White Throne Evaluation **the King will say to** believers, **"Come, you who are blessed by my Father; take your inheritance, the kingdom prepared for you since the creation of the world"** (v. 34). **Then he will say to** unbelievers **"Depart from me, you who are cursed, into the eternal fire prepared for the devil and his angels"** (v. 41 NIV).

At this point, we will have entered Eternity. Jesus ends His Endtimes Teaching by saying: **"Then** the unbelievers **will go away** to eternal punishment, but the righteous to eternal life" (v. 46).

Therefore, a purpose of Christ's Endtimes Teaching is to encourage us to have an eternal perspective on our life. We experience this as we both expectantly <u>watch</u> for the signs of His Coming, and patiently <u>wait</u> and faithfully <u>work</u> for the rewards of serving His Kingdom and His people.

---

[1] **Misleads** (NASB, NET, DEV) is probably a better translation then simply **deceive** (NIV). The Greek word (*planaō*) can mean more than just cause people to believe the wrong things, but rather cause them to live and act in the wrong way. Luke's **"Do not follow them"** (21:8) confirms this meaning.

[2] The most important command that Christ gave in His Endtimes Teaching was a warning <u>not</u> to be mislead by False Christs and false prophets in the Endtimes. This topic is discussed further in the "Challenges" section of *Endtimes Essentials* book #4: *The Greatest Persecution*.

[3] For an explanation of the suggested translation of Matt 24:6 see *BBP* ch. 14, sec. B.

[4] For an explanation of the suggested translation of Matt 24:21 see ch. 3, sec. E.

[5] The suggested translation of Matt 5:10, 12 is: **"Happy are those who are persecuted because of their righteousness, because they are fortunate that the kingdom of heaven belongs to them... Be happy and very joyful about being persecuted, because great is your reward in heaven."**

Happy ... fortunate translates the Greek word *makarios* which means, "pertaining to being fortunate or happy because of circumstances, fortunate, happy" (*BDAG*). It is unfortunate that most versions translate *makarios* here as **blessed**. This misses half the meaning of what Jesus intended. To most people, "blessed" merely means to be "fortunate."

But there were Greek words available that only meant fortunate or blessed. Neither Matthew nor Luke used those words in their rendering of the Beatitudes. Instead, they used *makarios* which primarily means to feel **happy**.

Accordingly, the full meaning of *makarios* is explained by NT scholar Darrell Bock who writes that it "refers to a sense of inner happiness because of good fortune" (571). Therefore, the NLT is especially insufficient when it has **God blesses those who are persecuted**, with no reference to how Christ expected such people to feel.

Likewise, in v. 12 most versions translate *chairete* as **rejoice**. But many people interpret this as meaning "give praise." However, the word actually means, "to be in a state of happiness" (*BDAG*) and is a synonym for the other word used in the sentence (*agalliasthe*) which means, "to be exceedingly joyful." Thus, the suggested translation of **very joyful**.

6 Grudem, *1 Peter*, loc. 746 at 1:13, underlining added. For other uses of the idiom of "girding your loins" see Luke 17:8, Acts 12:8, and Eph 6:14. For the same idea but different Greek wording see 1 Peter 1:13.

7 Nolland, *Luke*, 535.

8 Morris, *Luke*, 237.

9 Bock, 1174.

10 Hagner, 987. He adds:
> This instruction may be an allusion to that given to the Israelites at the first celebration of the Passover: to be in readiness for a hasty exodus from Egypt and the arrival of the destroying angel (Exod 12:11, 22-23). But the expression became in the OT a common instruction for readiness to service. See 1 Kgs 18:46; 2 Kgs 4:29; 9:1; Job 38:3; 40:7."

11 Luke 12:35 NET notes.

12 Bock writes of **"keep your lamps burning"**: "shows someone's readiness to move about during darkness" (Exod. 27:20; Lev. 24:2; Matt 25:1-13)" (1174; cf. Nolland, 535).

13 https://www.pewresearch.org/fact-tank/2022/12/08/about-four-in-ten-u-s-adults-believe-humanity-is-living-in-the-end-times/

14 Carson, *Matt*, 577.

15 Osborne notes: "The foolish bridesmaids live only for the moment and give little thought to contingencies. They ... do not prepare for a lengthy wait" (1321). Likewise, Hagner comments on Matt 24-25: "Running through the prophecies of eschatological ... events in the Gospel of Matthew are strands of imminence and delay" (711).

16 For more on the NT Church's view that Christ's Return was near see *Advanced Studies on the Endtimes*, ch. 15; online at www.trainingtimothys.com.

Part III

Biblically Evaluating Endtime Views

Including 13 popular myths taught by Pre-tribulationism

[Note: This section is considered supplemental and not essential to understanding the material in Christ's Endtimes Teaching. *However, it will be especially helpful to those who have been taught popular views of the Endtimes.]*

Chapter 11

A Biblical Evaluation of Various Views of the Endtimes

Contents

A) Pan-tribulationism denies any view

B) Pre-millennialism is biblical but often misused

C) Post-millennialism is attractive but unbiblical

D) Post-tribulationism rightly corrects Pre-tribulationism, but has several biblical problems

Primary Points

- The Pre-wrath Rescue position argued for in *Christ's Endtimes Teaching* is Pre-millennial in its view of Christ's Return and Reign.
- Post-millennialism has been supported by several rightly respected Bible scholars, but is very difficult to prove from Scripture.
- Post-tribulationism claims that the Church's Rescue occurs at the end of Christ's Wrath ("tribulation") at the time of the Battle of Armageddon.
- <u>Post</u>-tribulationism, like <u>Pre</u>-tribulationism, confuses "the tribulation" with Christ's Wrath.
- Post-tribulationism fails to distinguish between the two appearances of Christ during His Second Coming.
- The clearest biblical reason to reject the unique claims of Post-tribulationism is this: The NT clearly promises that the Church will be <u>rescued from</u>, not <u>protected in</u> Christ's Endtime Wrath.

In chapter 1 of *Christ's Endtimes Teaching*, 14 distinct views on the Endtimes and interpreting prophetic Scripture were listed.[1] In the same chapter it was said that this book would begin with Scripture instead of all these various views. Thus far, that approach has been emphasized. Conclusions of our Bible study have been summarized in a previous chapter (8).

However, several unbiblical aspects of Historicism were addressed in chapter 3 (sec. B). Historicism is the view that Christ's predictions of The Beginning of Birth Pains and The Greatest Persecution (and the prophecies in Revelation) have essentially already been fulfilled throughout Church history. This is a very popular view amongst Christian scholars, and it often diminishes the need to obey Christ's command to **"Watch!"** for signs in current events for His Return (Mark 13:33, 34, 37)

Among other problems, it was pointed out that:
The "historical" view ignores what the disciples asked Jesus. The disciples did not ask Jesus, "What catastrophes will occur throughout Church history?" They asked Him, **"What sign will signal your return and the end of the world?"** (Matt 24:3 NLT). Contrary to the "historical" view, Christ answered their question with **sign**s of His **return and the end of the world**. (ch. 3, sec. B)

Additional "academic" views on the Endtimes will be addressed in this chapter and those following. This chapter (11) will briefly address several popular views. Chapter 12 will focus on the more complex views of Amillennialism and Preterism. Chapters 13-15 will be an evaluation of Pre-tribulationism. Chapter 16 will discuss how the popular but false views of the Endtimes will harm the Last Generation Church.

There is some truth in most of the popular views on the Endtimes. But unfortunately, when those truths are overly emphasized, even more important truths get ignored or denied. We want to emphasize what the Scriptures do, not what proponents of various views do.

Some of these views discussed in the following chapters are rather complex. Still, there will be an effort to keep arguments as succinct and simple as possible. Unfortunately, while you can state the truth well in a paragraph, it requires many pages to refute error. The following arguments may not be sufficient to persuade those who are entrenched in these popular views. More could be said to biblically confront them, but that would require another whole book.

It is hoped that as Endtime events unfold, an increasing number of Christians will realize their errors in time to be prepared for the Endtime events that will follow.

It should be noted that most of those who believe the views critiqued in these chapters are real Christians. This is true of both the scholars and our friends who would support these views. Therefore, as God's people they deserve our great respect.

However, the biblical conclusions provided in the previous chapters of *Christ's Endtimes Teaching* clearly suggest there are unbiblical elements in many popular views of the Endtimes that should be confronted and corrected in order to honor Christ and His Word and protect God's people.

A) Pan-tribulationism denies any view

In chapter 1 (sec. B.3), the "apathetic" view on the Endtimes was addressed rather thoroughly. However, more can be added here.

Many have called this view Pan-Tribulationism. The "pan" part of the term refers to the idiom, "it will all pan out in the end." "Tribulationism" refers to the **great tribulation** that Jesus predicted will occur in the Endtimes (Matt 24:21 NASB). Pan-tribulationism is certainly a rather apathetic view of the doctrine of the Endtimes in Scripture. Andersen has written of the popularity of essentially Pan-tribulationism:

> By far the prevailing view of eschatology among Bible scholars and pastors today is that the end could come suddenly at any moment, that no one knows when this will happen or what events will precede it, and that there are no specific references in biblical prophecy to anything that is happening in the world today—the point of view that I have called "eschatological agnosticism."
>
> This is the view of most Catholics, Lutherans, Presbyterians, and Baptists, regardless of whether they may be amillennial or premillennial. Thus, all of these Christian leaders are completely in the dark with regard to how God is working His plan in the world today, what will happen, and how Christians ought to respond. In fact, they are vehemently opposed to attempts to understand what the Bible prophesies about events in the world today. [2]

As noted in chapter 1:
> What prompted this sermon of Christ [on the Endtimes]? The disciples asked Jesus, **"What sign will signal your return and the end of the world?"** (Matt 24:3). Listening to many Christians today, you would think that Jesus simply answered: "Guys, the details don't matter. All I want you to know is that I'm coming back." But that is not what our Lord said! And to act and talk as if He did dishonors our Savior. (sec. B.3)

This is because Christ makes it clear throughout the sermon that He was intentionally and clearly revealing a specific and connected sequence of Endtime events. This is why He repeatedly used words like **then** (Matt 24:9, 10, 14, 21, 30), **when** (v. 15), **immediately after** (v. 29) and, **at that time** (v. 30) in this sermon.

Also, those promoting Pan-tribulationism generally ignore Christ's repeated command to **"Watch!"** current events in the world to recognize signs of the Endtimes (cf. Mark 13:5, 9, 23, 33, 34, 37; ch. 10, sec. D). For all of these reasons, popular Pan-tribulationism dishonors Christ.

God gave us hundreds of verses of Scripture about the Endtimes. To everyone who has been infected with apathetic Pan-tribulationism, you are encouraged to not dishonor God by putting any of His word into trash cans labeled "too hard," "too complex," "too obscure," "too controversial," or "too scary."

If we love God, the Author of those prophetic Scriptures, then we will obey His command to: **Work hard so you can present yourself to God and receive his approval. Be a good worker, one who does not need to be ashamed and who correctly explains the word of truth** (2 Tim 2:15 NLT). Including **the word of truth** in all of the many passages of Scripture on the doctrine of the Endtimes.

The potential harm of Pan-tribulationism is demonstrated by the experience of the Thessalonians discussed in chapter 16 (sec. B).

B) Pre-millennialism is biblical but often misused

This and the next two sections deal with various views on the timing and nature of Christ's 1,000-year Reign on Earth, or the

Millennium. The Pre-millennial view of Christ's Reign states that Christ's Return occurs before Christ's Reign on Earth for a literal 1,000 years. Therefore, it is Pre-millennialism.

The biblical value of this view is that it promotes a literal interpretation of biblical prophecies, including those concerning the **one thousand years** in Revelation 20. The Pre-wrath Rescue position argued for in this book is Pre-millennial in its view of Christ's Return and Reign.

Unfortunately, Pre-tribulationism often implies that Pre-millennialism practically proves its view. It is common for Pre-tribulationism to biblically disprove Amillennialism and Post-millennialism (discussed below), and then claim that because Pre-millennialism is biblical, that so is Pre-tribulationism.

But Pre-tribulationism is not the only Pre-millennial view of the Endtimes available. The Pre-wrath Rescue position is also a Pre-millennial view of the Endtimes. It is true that there are serious biblical problems with other millennial views, but the same is true of Pre-tribulationism. These will be discussed in future chapters.

C) Post-millennialism is attractive but unbiblical

Post-millennialism claims that Christ's Return occurs after Christ's Reign has been established on Earth. Therefore, it is Post-millennialism. It believes that some time in the future the Gospel will be accepted by the vast majority of people on the Earth and the whole world will become essentially Christian, before the Second Coming of Christ.

Therefore, this view has often encouraged Christians to pursue (and even depend on?) political activism to change the world. Post-millennialism also promotes the idea that the "bad stuff" in Christ's Endtimes Teaching and Revelation concerning the Antichrist and The Greatest Persecution has already occurred or is occurring in the world now.

For obvious reasons, this view is attractive. And it has been promoted by respected Christian leaders including John Owen in the 1600's, Jonathan Edwards in the 1700's, and Charles Hodge and B. B. Warfield in the 1800's. [3] However, two World Wars in the 1900's made Post-millennialism quite unpopular. In fact, the popularity of the view tends to follow how Christianity or world prosperity is going at the time. [4]

But Post-millennialism has always been a very minor view in the Church. As Erickson puts it, "Today postmillennialists are, if not an extinct species, at least an endangered species." [5] This is because it is very difficult to prove from Scripture. Much of it is based on the metaphorical interpretations of Amillennialism and Preterism which are both refuted in the next chapter.

One verse that Post-millennialism cannot explain away is Christ's own statement about the effect of the Gospel during the Church Age:

"You can enter God's Kingdom only through the narrow gate. The highway to hell is broad, and its gate is wide for the many who choose that way. But the gateway to life is very narrow and the road is difficult, and only a [relatively] few ever find it." (Matt 7:13-14 NLT)

Contrary to Post-millennialism, Christians will always be a minority in the Church Age. Indeed, there is coming a day when: **The kingdom of the world has become the kingdom of our Lord and of his Messiah, and he will reign for ever and ever** (Rev 11:15). But the book of Revelation clearly teaches this prophecy will only be fulfilled after Christ's Return and the literal fulfillment of the Trumpet and Bowl Punishments. Contrary to Post-millennialism, this world will never be a Christian world until after Christ's Return. [6]

D) Post-tribulationism rightly corrects Pre-tribulationism, but has several biblical problems

D.1) Theological problems in Post-tribulationism

Post tribulationism claims that the Church's Rescue occurs at the end of Christ's Wrath ("tribulation") at the time of the Battle of Armageddon. It suggests that God somehow protects Christians as they are on the Earth during the Trumpet and Bowl Punishments. Therefore, this view also believes that the entire "tribulation" period is Christ's Wrath. Accordingly, Post-tribulationism claims that the Church's Rescue does not occur until the end of the "tribulation" or Christ's Wrath. Therefore, it is the Post-tribulational Rapture view. [7]

Post-tribulationism agrees with some important points of the Pre-wrath Rescue position explained in this book, *Christ's Endtimes Teaching*. Accordingly, its supporters have been among the foremost opponents to Pre-tribulationism.

However, there are several problems with Post-tribulationism. Several of these have already been thoroughly addressed.

First, Post-tribulationism, like Pre-tribulationism, confuses "the tribulation" with Christ's Wrath. As explained elsewhere, "tribulation" (*thlipsis*) in the NT and Christ's Endtimes Teaching means "persecution," not suffering in general or God's wrath (cf. ch. 3, sec. E).

Accordingly, Revelation 7 reflects the Church's Rescue as both Post-Persecution and Pre-Wrath when it describes **a great multitude that no one could count, from every nation, tribe, people and language, standing before the throne and before the Lamb ... wearing white robes ... who have come out of the great persecution** [*thlipseōs*] (vs. 9, 14 [8]). Contrary to Post-tribulationism, Revelation 7 depicts the Church's Rescue occurring before Christ's Wrath begins in Revelation 8. Defining Christ's Wrath and its timing will be addressed further in chapter 14.

Second, Post-tribulationism fails to distinguish between the two appearances of Christ during His Second Coming. As discussed previously (ch. 9, sec. A), in Christ's first appearance He comes for His Church before His Wrath. After a significant but unspecified period of time, in Christ's second appearance He comes with His Church at the end of His Wrath at the Battle of Armageddon. Post-tribulationism claims these two events happen virtually at the same time. [9]

This leads to a third problem in Post-tribulationism. Richard Mayhue, Professor of Theology at The Master's Seminary explains:

> A post-tribulational rapture demands that the saints meet Christ in the air [at the "rapture"] and immediately descend to earth [for the Battle of Armageddon] without experiencing what the Lord promised in John 14. Since John 14 refers to the rapture, [the Post-tribulational view does not allow] raptured saints to dwell for a meaningful time with Christ in His Father's house. [10]

Accordingly, the Pre-wrath Rescue position corrects the Post-tribulational view. As explained earlier in chapter 9 (sec. A), the

Rescued Church will be with the Lord during Christ's Wrath, giving them "meaningful time with Christ in His Father's house."

Accordingly, John 14 seems to imply some time between these events. Jesus said, **"If I go and prepare a place for you, I will come back and take you to be with me that you also may be where I am"** (John 14:3 NIV).

Again, this implies some time with Christ in Heaven during the period of Christ's Wrath on Earth after Christ's Return.

Contrary to Post-tribulationism, the Church will <u>not</u> be on the Earth during the Trumpet and Bowl Punishments or when the Battle of Armageddon is occurring. On the contrary, the Church's Rescue will occur a considerable time before the Battle of Armageddon and the Church will have already been in Heaven.

This is why the Church is described as **following** Christ <u>coming from</u> **heaven, riding on white horses** (Rev 19:11, 14), returning to Earth to join Christ in the Battle of Armageddon. There is no mention in Revelation 19 of the Church being "raptured" from the Earth at the Battle of Armageddon (cf. Rev 19:11-19). [11] Again, this was discussed thoroughly elsewhere in the book (cf. ch. 9, sec. A).

D.2) Exegetical problems with Post-tribulationism

A fourth problem with <u>Post</u>-tribulationism, is that like <u>Pre</u>-tribulationism, perhaps its most important verse is Revelation 3:10. There Jesus told the church in Philadelphia:

> **"Because you have obeyed my command to persevere, I will protect you from the great time of testing that will come upon the whole world to test those who belong to this world"** (NLT).

<u>Post</u>-tribulationism has invested a lot in trying to prove that **I will protect you from** (*tērēsō ek*) actually means, "I will protect you while you remain <u>in</u>." This supposedly supports the claim that the Church will be protected on Earth during Christ's Wrath. Not surprisingly, <u>Pre</u>-tribulationism has made just as much effort to prove that *tērēsō ek* means "to rescue <u>from</u>." This supposedly supports its claim that Revelation 3:10 promises the Church's Rescue before any Endtime events, including The Greatest Persecution.

This debate illustrates an important truth in biblical interpretation. When a significant number of equally skilled and respected Greek scholars disagree over the precise meaning of the grammar of a Greek word or phrase, then very little weight should be given to the issue in terms of correctly interpreting the text. Other considerations become decisive, such as the immediate context, and the broader context of the teaching of Scripture as a whole.

Elsewhere, Pre-tribulationism's interpretation of Revelation 3:10 will be addressed, and an alternative offered (cf. ch. 15, sec. D). Here, "the broader context of the teaching of Scripture as a whole" will help us evaluate Post-tribulationism's interpretation of Revelation 3:10. As a result, it will become evident that the effort Post-tribulationism has made to argue a particular meaning for the grammar of *tēresō ek* in Revelation 3:10 is of questionable value.

The clearest biblical reason to reject the unique claims of Post-tribulationism is this: The NT clearly promises that the Church will be rescued from ever experiencing Christ's Endtime Wrath.

For example, Paul writes that we **wait for ... Jesus, who rescues us from the coming wrath** (1 Thess 1:10 NIV). **From** translates the Greek preposition *ek* which means: "marker denoting separation, *from, out of, away from.*" [12] The definition of the Greek verb translated **rescues** (*rhyomenon*) is: "to rescue from danger, *save, rescue, deliver.*" [13] It means to take someone out of a dangerous situation, not to protect them while remaining in danger.

For example, Paul uses the same word when he writes: **For he has rescued** [*rhysato*] **us from** [*ek* "out of"] **the dominion of darkness and brought us into the kingdom of the Son he loves** (Col 1:13). God has not left Christians within **the dominion of darkness** while protecting them. Rather, we have been completely removed from **the dominion of darkness**.

Likewise, using the same Greek word, Paul writes: **Who will set me free from** [*rhysetai ek*] **the body of this death? Thanks be to God through Jesus Christ our Lord!** (Rom 7:24-25 NASB). Paul is not saying that in the Resurrection we will remain "preserved" in our current bodies. On the contrary, we will be removed from them.

Finally, using the same Greek word, and writing metaphorically, Paul wrote, **I was rescued out of** [*rhysthēn ek*] **the lion's mouth**

(2 Tim 4:17 NASB; cf. 2 Cor 1:10). Again, the Apostle was not saying he was "protected" while remaining in the metaphorical **lion's mouth**, but rather, he was completely removed from it.

If the Apostle had meant that **Jesus will protect us in the coming wrath**, there are several Greek words that he used elsewhere to mean "protect" or "guard."

For example, he wrote in the same Thessalonian epistles, **the Lord is faithful, and he will strengthen you and protect [*phlaxei*] you from the evil one** (2 Thess 3:3 NIV). [14] Here, Paul meant God will **protect** us while we remain in a world controlled by the evil one (cf. 1 John 5:19; John 17:11, 15). Therefore, if Paul meant "protect" in 1 Thessalonians 1:10, why didn't he use the same word (e.g. *phlaxei*) he used in 2 Thessalonians 3:3? Because he meant **Jesus rescues us from the coming wrath**, not that He will "protect" or "preserve" us in it.

Paul wrote that **Jesus rescues us from the coming wrath** with the Church's Rescue before that **wrath** begins. He clearly meant that Christ will remove His Church from the Earth before He punishes those remaining on the Earth.

However, Post-tribulationism suggests the Church's experience on Earth during the Trumpet and Bowl Punishments will be like several OT stories. These include Noah's protection in the Ark while God punished the world, or the Israelite's protection while God punished the Egyptians. These are wonderful stories about God's protection, but they do not illustrate what the Apostle meant when he wrote **Jesus rescues us from the coming wrath**.

There is another Bible story that is more applicable to what Paul meant by **Jesus rescues us from the coming wrath**. Its description in the NT again uses the same Greek word Paul used in 1 Thessalonians 1:10. We read in 2 Peter:

> **God condemned the cities of Sodom and Gomorrah and turned them into heaps of ashes. He made them an example of what will happen to ungodly people. But God also rescued [*rhysato*] Lot out of Sodom.** (2:6-7 NLT)

Again, God did not protect or preserve **Lot** while he remained in **Sodom**. Rather, Angels completely removed **Lot** from **Sodom** before God's wrath punished it (cf. Gen 19:16-17). Elsewhere, Jesus said, "**the day Lot <u>left</u> Sodom, fire and sulfur** [God's wrath] **rained down from heaven and destroyed them all.**" And then He said, "**It will be <u>just like this</u> on the day the Son of Man is revealed**" and the Church is Rescued from Christ's Wrath at Christ's Return (Luke 17:29-30 NIV).

Accordingly, Jesus elsewhere described His Church being removed from the Earth by Angels at Christ's Return and the Church's Rescue before Christ's Wrath begins on Earth (cf. Matt 24:29-31; *CET* ch. 4). Once again, the graphics on the following page produced from our study of Christ's Endtimes Teaching will summarize these things and demonstrate a correction to Post-tribulationism.

The Biblical Pre-wrath Rescue Position
Confirmed by Christ's Endtimes Teaching, Revelation, & Paul

② Antichrist's Claim to be God

when you see standing in the holy place 'the abomination that causes desolation (Matt 24:15)

④ Cosmic Signs Christ's Return Church's Rescue

Immediately after the completion of the greatest persecution ... He will send His Angels ... and they will lift up and gather together God's elect in the sky, from everywhere on earth (Matt 24:29-31)

① Beginning of Birth Pains

Antichrist's Rise

Wars, famines, plagues, & earthquakes. **All these are the beginning of birth pains** (vs. 4-8)

③ The Greatest Persecution

Antichrist's Wrath

Then you will be handed over to be persecuted... **Then** flee ... then there will be the greatest persecution (vs. 9, 16, 21)

⑤ Christ's Wrath

Just as it was in the days of Noah or Lot ... one will be received and the other left (Lk 17:26, 28, 34)

Christ's Two Appearances in His Second Coming

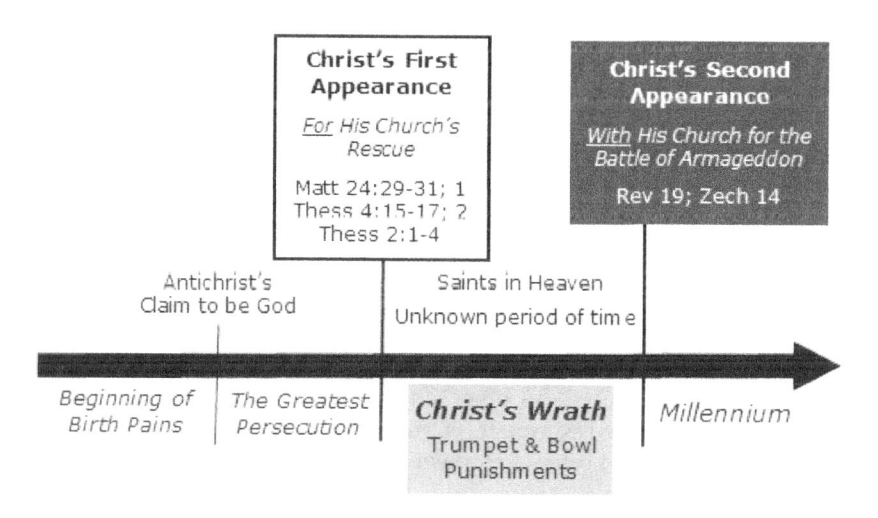

Christ's First Appearance

For His Church's Rescue

Matt 24:29-31; 1 Thess 4:15-17; 2 Thess 2:1-4

Christ's Second Appearance

With His Church for the Battle of Armageddon

Rev 19; Zech 14

Antichrist's Claim to be God | Saints in Heaven Unknown period of time

Beginning of Birth Pains | The Greatest Persecution | **Christ's Wrath** Trumpet & Bowl Punishments | Millennium

1 Millard Erickson's *A Basic Guide to Eschatology* (Baker, 1998), is a helpful introduction to several Endtimes views.

2 Andersen, 54.

3 Erickson adds that the Lutheran "Augsburg and [Reformed] Westminster Confessions are basically postmillennial" (*Guide*, 61).

4 Current supporters of Post-millennialism include rightly respected Christian teachers like Douglas Wilson and James White.

5 Erickson, 62.

6 For a thorough refutation of Post-millennialism see https://cbtseminary.org/theonomic-postmillennialism-critiqued-sam-waldron/ These articles are by Sam Waldron, President and Professor of Systematic Theology at Covenant Baptist Theological seminary. Unfortunately, Waldron himself is an Amillennialist.

7 Post-tribulationism is supported by several very respected NT scholars including G. E. Ladd, Robert Gundry, Douglas Moo, Grant Osborne, and John Piper.

8 The suggested translation of Rev 7:9, 14 follows the NIV except for translating *thlipseōs* as **persecution**.

9 For example, Piper illustrates his Post-tribulational collapsing of the two separate appearances of Christ when he writes that the Church's Rescue described in 2 Thess 2:1, will occur on the same "day" as when **the Lord Jesus will overthrow** the Antichrist **with the breath of his mouth and destroy by the splendor of his coming** (2 Thess 2:8 NIV) (cf. 209).

But as demonstrated in *CET* ch. 9, sec. A, there is a considerable gap between these events. It is understandable that Paul is at times interpreted to mean there will only be one appearing of Christ in His Second Coming. But as noted elsewhere, the Book of Revelation, written about 40 years after the Thessalonian epistles, probably gives us more information about the Endtimes, and Christ's Second Coming, than Paul had (cf. *CET* ch. 9, sec. A).

10 Richard Mayhue, "Why a Pretribulational Rapture?," *Masters Seminary Journal*, Vol. 13, No. 2 (Fall 2002).

11 Piper uses an additional argument to support Post-tribulationism. 1 Thess 4:17 says the Church will **meet** [*apantēsin*] **the Lord in the air**. Piper writes:

> The word translated "to meet" in the ESV occurs in only two other places in the New Testament [cf. Acts 28:15-16; Matt 25:6], and in both of them, the word refers to a meeting in which people go out to meet a

dignitary and then [immediately] accompany him in to the place from which they came out. (207)

Piper is claiming the use of this word in 1 Thess 4:17 reflects a rather immediate return to Earth after the Church's Rescue. Piper's claim regarding *apantēsin* in the NT is true. However, as he admits, its use in the NT is very limited.

In addition, this word was used more commonly in ancient Greek pagan literature and the Greek OT (LXX). *BDAG* defines it in these cases as merely "meeting" without the specific meaning Piper points out in the NT.

Therefore, it would seem unwise to derive too much from the nuance of *apantēsin* in the NT. In addition, the Pre-Wrath Rescue position also reflects the idea of meeting Christ at the Church's Rescue from the Earth and then returning to the Earth with Him. It just reflects the more biblical teaching that there is a considerable gap between these events.

[12] *BDAG* #1.

[13] *BDAG*. Oddly, it adds that *rhyomenon* may mean "preserve." But none of the NT examples of this word being used mean this. If they do, the "preserving" comes through rescuing.

[14] This same Greek word (*phlaxei*) is translated **kept them safe** (John 17:12 NIV); **protect** (1 Tim 6:20; 2 Tim 1:12, 14 NET); and **guard** (1 John 5:21 NASB).

Chapter 12

A Biblical Evaluation of Amillennialism & Preterism

Contents

A) A biblical evaluation of Amillennialism

B) A biblical evaluation of Preterism

Primary Points

- Amillennialism is named after its belief that there is not a literal Millennium or 1,000-year Reign of Christ on the Earth.
- Amillennialism emphasizes interpreting the fulfillments of biblical prophecy in merely metaphorical and spiritual realities instead of literal and physical people, places, and events.
- Amillennialism is a prime promoter of the apathetic view which claims the biblical specifics on the substance and sequence of Endtime events do not matter.
- Amillennialism does very little to help the Church be prepared for the physical realities that are coming in the Endtimes.
- So how should biblical prophecy be interpreted? With common sense.
- The debate is not really about how biblical prophecy is to be interpreted. Rather, the debate is about how biblical prophecy will be fulfilled.
- The real debate is between the expectation of a "spiritualized" versus physical fulfillment of biblical prophecy.
- The very great majority of biblical prophecies are both communicated and fulfilled in a literal way.
- The metaphorical approach of many Bible scholars today would have led them to misunderstand a great deal about Christ's First Coming. The same metaphorical approach will lead them to also misunderstand a great deal about Christ's Second Coming.
- A common strategy used to diminish the literal meaning of biblical prophecy is to label it as "apocalyptic" literature.

- Almost <u>600</u> biblical prophecies have been identified as already being fulfilled in history. <u>Every single one</u> of them was fulfilled in a physical way by a person, place, or event. <u>None</u> of them were fulfilled in the way Amillennialism claims all or most prophecies will be fulfilled in the future.
- Even when a prophecy is <u>communicated</u> in a symbolic way, we should still expect it to be <u>fulfilled</u> in a physical person, place, or event.
- Metaphorical interpreters need to be asked, "When did God abandon His repeated practice of fulfilling biblical prophecy in a physical and literal way?" Contrary to the popular metaphorical view, God has <u>not</u> changed the way He will fulfill biblical prophecy.
- We also have a <u>moral</u> reason to <u>not</u> haphazardly interpret biblical prophecies in merely a metaphorical way. Such an approach makes it more difficult to be certain God is keeping His promises.
- The spiritualized approach often drastically alters how it claims a promise of God will be fulfilled, in relation to the original promise given by God. In the process, <u>they would make God a liar</u> if He actually <u>did</u> fulfill the promise in the way metaphorical interpreters claim He will.
- There are several reasons that Amillennialism's interpretation of Revelation 20 and the Millennium is unbiblical and unreasonable.
- Preterism is the view that almost everything predicted in Christ's Endtimes Teaching and even Revelation has already occurred in the past.
- Preterism misinterprets what Jesus meant by **"the end of the age"** and **"this generation"** in His Endtimes Teaching.
- Preterism completely depends on the unlikely claim that Revelation was written before A.D. 70.
- Preterism ignores the literal and multiple fulfillment nature of biblical prophecy.

A) A Biblical evaluation of Amillennialism

A.1) The perspectives and problems in Amillennialism

Amillennialism is named after its belief that there is not a literal Millennium. Therefore, it is called A-millennialism. This view claims that the **thousand years** of Christ's **reign** (Rev 20:1-7) on Earth began with His Resurrection and is being fulfilled now during the Church Age, or will be fulfilled in Eternity. [1] Obviously, Amillennialism largely depends on a metaphorical, rather than literal, interpretation of Scripture.

For example, how will the prophecies about the coming Antichrist be fulfilled? In the book, *The Beginning of Birth Pains*, it will be argued that he will be a future physical person. But as noted in chapter 1 of *Christ's Endtimes Teaching*, a recent survey claimed that 50% of Protestant Pastors deny or are not sure that Scripture predicts there will be a literal and physical Antichrist in the future. [2]

Some of these Pastors believe the biblical prophecies about the Antichrist simply refer to the spiritual reality of growing evil in the Endtimes. In other words, this view expects the biblical prophecies about the Antichrist to be fulfilled in a "spiritualized" way rather than in a physical way. This is a foundational perspective of Amillennialism that will be discussed more below.

Amillennialism also claims that the OT prophecies about Israel prospering in the future have already been, or will be, completely fulfilled in a spiritualized way by the Church. This can be called "Replacement Theology." It means the Church has eternally replaced Israel as the recipient of the unfulfilled promises God made to the nation in the OT. For example, Amillennialism claims that promises made to Israel to inherit geographical land need to be spiritualized and refer to the Church in Heaven, not literal land on Earth.

Therefore, this metaphorical approach to the fulfillment of biblical prophecy expects they will be completely fulfilled in spiritual realities, rather than in physical people, places, and events. As Millard Erickson puts it, "The amillennialist tends to expect no literal fulfillment of prophecy at some future time." [3] This is one of the most common views taught in American seminaries and scholarly Bible commentaries and has been especially promoted by Reformed theology.

But understanding Amillennialism is not that simple. For example, some Amillennialists claim the Antichrist will be a literal person in the future. In other words, Amillennialists are divided and obscure about what they interpret literally and what they interpret merely spiritually. Therefore, it is rather difficult to clearly understand what Amillennialists believe. As Erickson also notes:

> There are several obstacles to a clear understanding of it... So many explanations of ... amillennialism have been offered that it tends to be a bit confusing, to say the least. At times one almost wonders if one is dealing with subtypes of a single basic view or with different views. 4

This lack of unity among Amillennialists is one reason it is rare that they will offer a specific and clear view on the substance and sequence of Endtime events. Which is also why Amillennialism is a prime promoter of an apathetic and Pan-tribulational view of the Endtimes which claims the biblical specifics on this doctrine do not matter.

As noted, Amillennialists sometimes do expect a future and physical fulfillment of a biblical prophecy. But their approach does not sufficiently value this. Amillennialism overwhelmingly prioritizes finding spiritual meanings in prophetic Scripture and saying relatively little about their future physical fulfillment.

As a result of all this, Amillennialism does very little to help the Church be prepared for the physical realities that are coming in the Endtimes. This will be further discussed in chapter 16 (sec. E).

The priorities of Amillennialism remind us of Jesus' statement to the Pharisees: **"You have neglected the more important matters of the law... You blind guides! You strain out a gnat but swallow a camel"** (Matt 23:23-24). The Pharisees were prioritizing minor insights they thought they were discovering in Scripture (**a gnat**), but neglecting the much more important teachings of Scripture (compared to **a camel**). Amillennialism does the same with prophetic Scripture and also ends up being **blind guides** for those wanting to clearly understand important things God wanted to teach His people regarding the Endtimes. 5

A.2) How are we to interpret the meaning and fulfillment of biblical prophecy? *"Spiritualized" versus physical meaning*

This section introduces a complex topic in biblical interpretation. Often the issue is described as the debate between the metaphorical versus the literal interpretation of biblical prophecy. But this is too simple. For example, many biblical prophecies are communicated in very symbolic language that should not be interpreted literally. This is true of the very first prophecy in Scripture where **the Lord God said to the serpent**:

> **"And I will cause hostility between you and the woman, and between your offspring and her offspring. He will strike your head, and you will strike his heel."** (Gen 3:14-15 NLT)

A common interpretation of this prophecy is that it refers to Satan injuring Christ (**strik**ing **his heel**) at His crucifixion, and Christ eventually destroying Satan (**strik**ing his **head**, cf. Rev 20:10). Even if this is the meaning of this prophecy, it must be admitted that it is communicated in very symbolic and metaphorical language. For example, we have no record of a **serpent**, or even Satan literally **strik**ing Christ's **heel**.

Therefore, it is not correct to simply say all biblical prophecy should be interpreted "literally." So how should biblical prophecy be interpreted? With common sense. There is hardly a better way to say it. And common sense dictates that some biblical prophecies should be interpreted in a symbolic and metaphorical way. But common sense also dictates that most biblical prophecies should be interpreted literally. This will be discussed further below.

Still, the debate is not really about how biblical prophecy is to be interpreted. Rather, the debate is about how biblical prophecy will be fulfilled. Even then, saying that biblical prophecy should always be fulfilled in a "literal" way is not true. Again, Genesis 3:15 was not fulfilled in a "literal" way. The prediction that the **serpent**, symbolizing Satan would **strike** Christ's **heel** was probably fulfilled in Christ's crucifixion.

So how can we simply and clearly distinguish the two ways people expect biblical prophecy to be fulfilled? It is suggested the real debate is between the expectation of a "spiritualized" versus physical fulfillment of biblical prophecy. The term "physical" seems more accurate than "literal." Genesis 3:15 was not literally fulfilled, but it was fulfilled by a physical person and event. And this is what the metaphorical or spiritualized view of biblical prophecy wishes to consistently diminish or deny. The above examples of spiritualizing the biblical prophecies about the Antichrist, or Israel's land demonstrate this.

A.3) Interpret the meaning and fulfillment of a biblical prophecy in a literal way when there is no biblical or reasonable basis to do otherwise

Two rules of interpretation can be suggested regarding biblical prophecy. First: Interpret the meaning and fulfillment of a biblical prophecy in a literal way when there is no biblical or reasonable basis to do otherwise. *Webster's* defines "literal" as "adhering to the ordinary or primary meaning of a term or expression." It is common to encounter complicated discussions about what "literal" interpretation means. Prophecy scholar Robert VanKampen explains it well:

> *The first principle* is that all Scripture is to be understood in its most natural, normal, customary (i.e., literal or face value) sense. Of course, we allow for obvious figures of speech, which includes both symbols and expressions. Almost always these are explained in the same passage or elsewhere in Scripture...
>
> This principle has special relevance in the study of prophecy. It finds strong confirmation in the [literal and physical] way Old Testament prophecy was fulfilled in the life of Christ. [6]

Again, an important rule for interpreting biblical prophecy is: Interpret the meaning and fulfillment of a biblical prophecy in a literal way when there is no biblical or reasonable basis to do otherwise. One reason for this is that the very great majority of biblical prophecies are both communicated and fulfilled in a literal way. For example, God promised in the OT through the Prophet Micah:

But you, Bethlehem Ephrathah, though you are small among the clans of Judah, out of you will come for me one who will be ruler over Israel (Mic 5:2 NIV).

Was **Bethlehem** meant to be merely a metaphor for something that was <u>not</u> a physical town? Of course not. The prophecy was fulfilled literally by a physical place. What if we applied the merely spiritualized view of the meaning and fulfillment of biblical prophecy to this prediction? We would conclude that Micah was <u>not</u> predicting Jesus would be born in a literal physical town. And we would be wrong.

For the same reason, those who incorrectly interpret the meaning of a biblical prophecy, or its future fulfillments, in merely a metaphorical way will be wrong. The metaphorical approach of many Bible scholars today would have led them to misunderstand a great deal about Christ's First Coming. The same spiritualized interpretations will lead them to also misunderstand a great deal about the events surrounding Christ's Second Coming.

For example, as noted, 50% of Protestant Pastors deny, or are not sure, that the prophecies concerning the Antichrist will be fulfilled in a literal way. However, writing of Antichrist's Claim to be God, Paul wrote of when:

> **the <u>man</u>** [*anthrōpos*, "a human being" [7]] **of lawlessness is revealed, the <u>son</u>** [person] **of destruction, who opposes and exalts <u>himself</u> above every so-called god or object of worship, so that <u>he</u>** [*auton* "self" a person] **takes his <u>seat</u> in the temple of God, displaying <u>himself</u> as being God** (2 Thess 2:3-4 NASB).

The Apostle Paul clearly believed the Antichrist will be a literal, physical man. Why are 50% of Protestant Pastors unclear about this? It would seem a priority of metaphorical interpretation has invaded the Church and created a distorting bias against the literal interpretation of biblical prophecy.

Amillennialism wants to claim that the Apostles and early Church expected OT prophecies to be fulfilled primarily in a spiritualized, rather than literal or physical way. But this claim is severely challenged by the example of the Gospel of Matthew. In this Gospel there are 14 references to Christ fulfilling an OT prophecy. Every single one of these 14 prophecies were both <u>communicated</u> in <u>literal</u> language and <u>fulfilled</u> in a <u>literal</u> way. These 14 prophecies and their fulfillments are as follows:

1) The virgin will conceive and bear a child (cf. Matt 1:22-23; Isa 7:14).
2) Bethlehem will be the birthplace of the coming 'King of the Jews' (cf. Matt 2:5-6; Mic 5:2).
3) "Out of Egypt I called my Son" (cf. Matt 2:15; Hos 11:1).
4) Weeping over the dead children after Herod's slaughter of the infants in Bethlehem (cf. Matt 2:16-18; Jer 31:15).
5) Jesus would be called a Nazarene (cf. Matt 2:23; Isa 53:3). [8]
6) Jesus based his ministry out of Galilee (cf. Matt 4:13-16; Isa 9:1-2).
7) He took up our infirmities and bore our diseases (cf. Matt 8:17; Isa 53:4).
8) Jesus' meekness and strength (cf. Matt 12:17-21; Isa 42:1-4). [9]
9) Jesus would speak to the people in parables (cf. Matt 13:34-35; Ps 78:2).
10) Jesus would enter Jerusalem riding on a donkey (cf. Matt 21:4-5; Zech 9:9).
11) Jesus would be struck down and His disciples would be scattered (cf. Matt 26:31; Zech 13:7).
12) Jesus' betrayal would literally fulfill prophecy (cf. Matt 26:52-54).
13) Jesus' capture would literally fulfill prophecy (cf. Matt 26:55-56).
14) The priests used the 30 pieces of silver to buy the potter's field (cf. Matt 27:9-10; Zech 11:12-13).

All of these OT prophecies that Matthew recorded Christ fulfilling were to be interpreted in a <u>literal</u> way and were fulfilled in a <u>literal</u> way by a physical person, place, or event. This is how the Apostles and early Church expected OT prophecy to be interpreted and fulfilled. And this is how God wants the very great majority of biblical prophecies and their fulfillment to be interpreted.

For reasons that seem unclear, unreasonable, and unbiblical, Amillennialism simply refuses to value the future, physical, and literal fulfillment of biblical prophecy. The problem with such a bias can be illustrated in the biblical prophecy that was given to Noah.

God said to him: **"Look! I am about to cover the earth with a flood that will destroy every living thing that breathes.**

Everything on earth will die" (Gen 6:17 NLT). We know this prophecy was literally fulfilled. Of course, it would seem sea creatures survived the Flood. But only those people and animals who were <u>not</u> on **earth** but floating above the **earth** in a boat survived. Therefore, **everything on earth** literally **die**d.

If this prophecy was about the Endtimes, or in prophetic Scripture, many Bible scholars today would be very tempted to interpret it metaphorically rather than literally. The idea of a world-wide flood making **<u>Everything</u> on earth die** would be deemed an exaggeration requiring only a spiritual or symbolic meaning.

Likewise, the "weirdness" of a literal 1,000-year reign of Christ on Earth seems to be one reason Amillennialists deny it will happen. But that perspective would have been misleading in correctly interpreting the prophecy of a literal world-wide flood. Therefore, we should not deny a literal interpretation of a biblical prophecy simply because it seems to be exaggerated. God can and will do things that will challenge our understanding of what is possible or appropriate.

Later God told Noah: **"<u>Seven</u> days from now I will send rain on the earth for <u>forty</u> days and <u>forty</u> nights"** (7:4 NIV). Again, if this was a biblical prophecy about the future, many interpreters today would assume these numbers are only symbolic and not to be taken literally. This is what is done with the six references to **one thousand years** in Revelation 20. But what happened in Noah's day? Exactly and literally **"After the <u>seven</u> days the floodwaters came on the earth"** (7:10). For how long? Exactly and literally, **"rain fell on the earth <u>forty</u> days and <u>forty</u> nights"** (7:12). Therefore, we should interpret the <u>meaning</u> and <u>fulfillment</u> of a biblical prophecy, including numbers, in a literal way when there is no biblical or reasonable basis to do otherwise.

A common strategy used to diminish the literal meaning of biblical prophecy is to label it as "apocalyptic" literature. Based on this label, it is further claimed that such a genre is intended to be interpreted differently than the rest of Scripture. Specifically, it is claimed that we should expect "apocalyptic" literature to only be speaking about spiritual realities and rarely or clearly predicting future and physical events. There are several errors in this approach. [10]

First, the distinctions between prophetic and "apocalyptic" Scripture are not as clear or important as many would claim. [11] Second, these same scholars of "apocalyptic" literature all label significant portions of Daniel in this way. And yet, the "apocalyptic" prophecies of the **large statue** (Dan 2:31) and the **four great beasts** (Dan 7:3), were all physically fulfilled in the emergence of the Babylonian, Persian, Greek, and Roman Empires. In other words, Daniel is proof that even prophetic Scripture that some would label "apocalyptic," needs to be expected to be fulfilled in a physical way by a person, place, or event.

A.4) Expect a biblical prophecy to be fulfilled in a physical way by a person, place, or event when there is no biblical or reasonable basis to do otherwise

This leads to a second rule for interpreting the meaning and fulfillment of biblical prophecy. Expect a biblical prophecy to be fulfilled in a physical way by a person, place, or event, when there is no biblical or reasonable basis to do otherwise. [12]

This rule of interpretation is generally denied or diminished in Amillennialism. As noted by Erickson above, "The amillennialist tends to expect no literal fulfillment of prophecy at some future time." [13] It is also true that this view tends to expect no "physical" fulfillment of prophecy at some future time. Amillennialism seems to completely ignore how God has fulfilled biblical prophecy in the past.

OT scholar J. B. Payne has provided what is probably the most detailed study of biblical prophecy available. In his *Encyclopedia of Biblical Prophecy* he identified 592 OT and NT prophecies that have already come true in history. [14] Every single one of these almost 600 biblical prophecies was fulfilled in a physical way by a person, place, or event. [15] None of these prophecies were fulfilled in merely a metaphorical or spiritualized way.

It is possible that Payne did not document every single biblical prophecy that has been fulfilled in all of history. Perhaps he missed a few. But the 592 he did identify clearly represent almost every fulfilled biblical prophecy in the history of the world. And none of them were fulfilled in the way Amillennialism claims all or most prophecies will be fulfilled in the future.

Note that it is _not_ being claimed here that _no_ biblical prophecy can have a spiritualized meaning to its fulfillment. Perhaps there are some clear examples of this. But Amillennialism rather dogmatically claims that most or all biblical prophecies in the future will be fulfilled in only or primarily a spiritualized way. Therefore, this view seems to be ignoring the overwhelming historical precedent God Himself has established.

This is true even in the many instances when God communicates a biblical prophecy in metaphorical language. The example of Genesis 3:15 was already noted above. Again, this prophecy was communicated in symbolic language (i.e. **the serpent would strike** Christ's **heel**). But it was fulfilled by a physical person and event (Christ's crucifixion), not a spiritualized reality.

Likewise, in Daniel, the Greek Empire of Alexander the Great was predicted and described as the **chest and arms of silver** on **a large statue** (2:31-32) and a **beast that looked like a leopard** (7:6). But obviously these symbolic prophecies were fulfilled in a very physical kingdom on this Earth. Therefore, even when a prophecy is communicated in a symbolic way, we should still expect it to be fulfilled in a physical person, place, or event.

Metaphorical interpreters need to be asked, "When did God abandon His repeated practice of fulfilling biblical prophecy in a physical way?" Contrary to the popular metaphorical view, God has not changed the way He will fulfill biblical prophecy.

Unfortunately, Amillennialism does claim God has radically changed the way He fulfills prophecy. For example, the influential Amillennialist Kim Riddlebarger says those who would value how God has consistently fulfilled prophecy in the past, "downplay or ignore how Old Testament passages are interpreted by the authors of the New." [16] He writes, "A specific example of what I mean might help to clarify the issue." It seems probable then that Riddlebarger would offer one of Amillennialism's best examples of how God has changed the way He fulfills prophecy. Acts 15 and the "Jerusalem Council" is the example he offers. There we read:

> **The whole assembly became silent as they listened to Barnabas and Paul telling about the signs and wonders God had done among the Gentiles through**

them. When they finished, James spoke up. "Brothers," he said, "listen to me. Simon has described to us how God first intervened to choose a people for his name from the <u>Gentiles</u>. <u>The words of the prophets are in agreement with this</u>, as it is written:

"'After this I will return and rebuild David's fallen tent. Its ruins I will rebuild, and I will restore it, that the rest of mankind may seek the Lord, even all the <u>Gentiles</u> who bear my name, says the Lord, who does these things' — things known from long ago." (Acts 15:12-18 NIV)

What is Riddlebarger's interpretation of James' intent? He writes: James saw the [entire] prophecy as fulfilled in Christ's resurrection, exaltation, and in the reconstitution of his disciples as the new Israel. The presence of both Jew and Gentile in the church was proof that the prophecy of Amos had been [entirely] fulfilled. David's fallen tent had been rebuilt by Christ. [17]

That seems to be a lot of assumptions. Riddlebarger's interpretation is also a classic example of "Replacement Theology" and the denial that God plans any future for the nation of Israel. There are several problems with Riddlebarger's common interpretation.

First, it ignores God's overwhelming precedent of fulfilling prophecy in a physical and even literal way. If Amillennialists want to claim God has radically changed this, then they need a great deal more evidence than this.

Secondly, Amillennialism is reading far too much into this text in order to support its view. James' primary (if not only) point was that OT prophecy predicted that God would save **Gentiles** and not just the Jews. James himself made it clear that the issue being debated was whether or not God has **intervened to choose a people for his name from the Gentiles** (v. 14). To argue this was the case, James said, **"The words of the prophets are in agreement with this"** (v. 15). He then quoted a prophecy from Amos that predicted in the future **the rest of mankind** will **seek the Lord, even all the Gentiles** (v. 17). [18] That was clearly James' primary (if not only) point. [19]

But Amillennialism wants to dogmatically claim that James also believed that the salvation of the **Gentiles** fully fulfilled God's promise to **rebuild David's fallen tent**. But again, such a merely spiritualized fulfillment of an OT promise is a radical change from how God fulfilled at least 592 biblical prophecies in the past. And there is no indication in the text that James thought everything in Amos' prophecy was being fulfilled in the salvation of the **Gentiles**.

Amos' original prophecy stated:

"In that day I will restore the fallen house of David. I will repair its damaged walls. From the ruins I will rebuild it and restore its former glory" (Amos 9:11 NLT).

Contrary to Amillennialism, this promise from God was not fulfilled in a spiritualized way by Gentiles being saved in the first century. It more obviously refers to the hundreds of Bible verses predicting the physical and spiritual restoration of the nation of Israel, and even **the city of David** (1 Kgs 11:27), Jerusalem. All of this will occur during Christ's 1000-year Reign on Earth that Amillennialism wishes to deny will ever exist (cf. Rev 20:1-6).

Again, if Amillennialism wants us to believe God has radically changed how He expects us to interpret hundreds of Bible verses predicting the physical restoration of the nation of Israel, then it needs a lot more clear biblical proof than it provides.

Also contrary to Amillennialism, the OT prophecies of Gentiles being saved will not be finally and completely fulfilled in the NT Church Age, but in the Millennium. Amillennialism completely ignores a proven attribute of biblical prophecy. Many of them will have more than one fulfillment.

It is possible that God intended to have some prophecies initially and partially fulfilled in a spiritualized way. But Amillennialism has no biblical or historical proof that these prophecies will never be finally and completely fulfilled in a physical and even more literal way. In other words, we have no clear examples where a merely spiritualized application of a biblical prophecy completely replaced an additional and physical fulfillment. The multiple fulfillment nature of biblical prophecy is discussed further below to also correct Preterism.

The point here is that a primary example that Amillennialism puts forth to claim God has radically changed the way He fulfills prophecy

(Acts 15:12-18), does not even come close to clearly proving this. Likewise, the relatively few other examples offered by Amillennialism do not seem to prove its foundational way of interpreting prophetic Scripture either. The fact is that God fulfilled 592 prophecies in the past in a physical and often literal way, and Amillennialism falls far short of providing biblical evidence that God has or will change this.

A.5) Metaphorical interpretations of biblical prophecy make it more difficult to be certain God is keeping His promises

We can ask another important question that Amillennialism seems to ignore. Why does God consistently fulfill biblical prophecy in such a literal, physical, and obvious way? Because prophecies are promises. For example, God said:

> **"When seventy years are completed for Babylon, I will come to you and fulfill my good promise to bring you back to this place"** (Jer 29:10 NIV).

Did you notice that God said this prophecy was **my good promise**? In fact, all biblical prophecies are a **promise** from God. Also notice that God fulfilled His **good promise** in a very literal and physical way. The Book of Ezra describes God literally **bring**ing the Jews **back to** the land of Israel after exactly **seventy years** of captivity in **Babylon**.

But imagine prior to its fulfillment, Amillennialism claimed this promise was not to be interpreted literally (especially the **seventy years**). More than that, it was claimed this promise was fulfilled in a spiritualized way, and not a physical way. It must be admitted it would be much more difficult to be certain God kept His **good promise.** Literal and physical fulfillments are the best way we can be certain a prophecy and promise from God was fulfilled.

Therefore, we also have a moral reason to not haphazardly interpret biblical prophecies in merely a metaphorical way. Such an approach makes it more difficult to be certain God is keeping His promises. For example, God promised regarding those in **the first resurrection** that **they** will **reign with Christ for a thousand years** (Rev 20:5 NLT). Amillennialism claims this promise cannot be interpreted literally, and is already being fulfilled <u>now</u> in a spiritualized way by Christ and saints reigning in Heaven. If so, can we be certain God has kept his promise that those in **the first resurrection** will **reign with Christ for a thousand years**?

No, we cannot. And Amillennialism's complicated and obscure arguments to claim we should be certain God is already keeping His promise about the Millennium are not convincing enough for such a serious question. When God makes a promise we rightly expect it to be fulfilled in an obvious way, not the ambiguous way Amillennialism claims God keeps His promises.

Even more seriously, the spiritualized approach often drastically alters how it claims a promise of God will be fulfilled, in relation to the original promise given by God. In the process, <u>they would make God a liar</u> if He actually <u>did</u> fulfill the promise in the way metaphorical interpreters claim He will. If you think this is an exaggeration, consider an example.

As noted above, Amillennialism claims that promises made to Israel to inherit land need to be spiritualized and will be fulfilled by the Church living in Heaven, not literal land on Earth. Read the following promises from God and ask yourself this question: If these promises are fulfilled by Christians living in Heaven, wouldn't a reasonable person conclude God is a liar? For example, we read:

On that day the LORD made a covenant [a promise!] **with Abram and said, "To your descendants** [the Jews] **I give <u>this land</u>, from the Wadi of Egypt to the great river, the Euphrates** [in modern day Iran] (Gen 15:18 NIV; cf. 12:7; 13:14-17; 48:4).** [20]**

If instead, as Amillennialism claims, this promise is fulfilled by <u>not</u> giving **Abram**'s physical **descendants** real, literal, physical **land** as far east as Iran, then can we still clearly claim that God keeps His promises? No, we cannot. Again, Amillennialism's view of how God keeps His promises requires some rather obscure and complicated explanations that diminish a clear and simple claim that God keeps His promises.

Of course, Christians have been united with Israel as God's chosen people (cf. Eph 2:11-22) and are Abraham's spiritual descendants (cf. Rom 9:8; Gal 3:8, 14, 17, 29). But Paul clearly explains this specifically refers to promises of <u>salvation</u> first given to Abraham (cf. Gen 12:3). Nowhere does the NT teach that <u>all</u> the promises given to Abraham or Israel have been fulfilled or replaced by Christ or the Church.

In fact, Paul points out, **The agreement God made with Abraham could not be canceled 430 years later when God gave the law to Moses** [the Old Covenant]. **God would be breaking his promise** (Gal 3:17). Likewise, **The agreement** and promises of land that **God made with Abraham could not be canceled** about 2,000 **years later when God gave** us the New Covenant through Christ. Otherwise, **God would be breaking his promise.** [21]

God repeated this promise when He spoke of the future:
This is what the Sovereign LORD says: "Divide <u>the land</u> in this way for the twelve tribes of <u>Israel</u>... I took a solemn oath and swore that I would give <u>this land</u> to your physical **ancestors, and it will now come to you as your possession.** (Ezek 47:13-14 NLT). [22]

But Amillennialism essentially claims this will never happen. As a result it <u>does not</u> seem to adequately respect the promises and word of God. He said to the Jews, <u>not</u> Christians, **"I took a solemn oath and swore that I would give <u>this land</u> to your** physical **ancestors."** If He <u>does not</u> literally **give land** to the Jews in the Endtimes, then most reasonable people would rightly conclude God's promise was at least misleading. Certainly, the Jews would! If anyone made a promise to an Amillennialist and fulfilled it the way they claim God fulfills promises, there is no doubt they would think the person was a liar too.

In general it can be said that Amillennialism has a great disrespect for the promises God has made to the nation of Israel. Its teaching can actually lead to a disdain for God's people, the Jews. This very thing happened during the Protestant Reformation, specifically because of Luther's theological and even eschatalogical views. [23] It seems that God loves the Jews more than many Amillennialists, and that is not a good thing for them. They would do well to read the OT Prophets and notice how they are all focused on one nation of people, and therefore, be reminded of how much God loves Israel.

One more thing can be said about Amillennialism's rejection of any literal future for the nation of Israel. In Acts we read:

Then they [the Apostles] **gathered around him** [Jesus] **and asked him, "Lord, are you at this time going to <u>restore the kingdom</u> [and land!] to [the nation and people of] Israel?" He said to them: "It is not for you to know the times or dates the Father has set by his own authority"** [to do that very thing!] (Acts 1:6-7 NIV)

Jesus surely wanted the Apostles to have a correct understanding of what they were asking about concerning the literal and physical nation of **Israel**. If Amillennialism's view of the future of **Israel** were correct, it seems very probable that Jesus would have corrected the Apostles right here. In that case, He would have said something "Amillennial" like: "The kingdom will <u>not</u> be restored to Israel as you understand it, but will be fulfilled in the Church which you are the foundation of." But Jesus said no such thing. In fact, by <u>not</u> correcting their belief that the **Lord** is **going to restore the kingdom to** the literal nation of **Israel**, He confirmed the Apostles' belief that this is precisely what will happen in the Endtimes.

For all the reasons above, the fulfillment of biblical prophecies needs to be expected to occur in a literal or physical way. And in general, even prophetic Scripture should be interpreted literally, except when symbolism is obviously being used. Therefore, a well-known rule for interpreting the Bible says: "When the plain sense, makes common sense, seek no other sense." This is how God intended Scripture to be interpreted, including prophetic Scripture. Therefore, throughout the *Endtimes Essentials* you will be encouraged to interpret even prophetic Scripture in its plainest, most literal sense, when there is no biblical or reasonable basis to do otherwise.

A.6) Amillennialism's unbiblical interpretation of Revelation 20:1-3

As noted, Amillennialism argues that many Endtime events are currently being fulfilled <u>now</u> throughout Church history in a spiritual and metaphorical way. This includes the events predicted during the Millennium in Revelation 20. As also noted, Amillennialism rejects a literal interpretation of the **thousand years** of Christ's **reign** on the Earth (Rev 20:1-7). In general, it believes this is already being fulfilled as Christ spiritually reigns over His Church from Heaven.

A fundamental question for the doctrine of the Endtimes is this: is the following prophecy being fulfilled <u>now</u> during the Church Age in a spiritualized way, or will it be fulfilled in the future in a physical and rather literal way. In Revelation 20:1-7 we read:

> **And I saw an angel coming down out of heaven, having the key to the Abyss and holding in his hand a great chain. He seized the dragon, that ancient serpent, who is the devil, or Satan, and bound him for <u>a thousand years</u>. He threw him into the Abyss, and locked and sealed it over him, to keep him from deceiving the nations anymore until <u>the thousand years</u> were ended. After that, he must be set free for a short time.**
>
> **I saw thrones on which were seated those who had been given authority to judge. And I saw the souls of those who had been beheaded because of their testimony about Jesus and because of the word of God. They had not worshiped the beast or its image and had not received its mark on their foreheads or their hands.**
>
> **They came to life and reigned with Christ <u>a thousand years</u>. (The rest of the dead did not come to life until <u>the thousand years</u> were ended.) This is the first resurrection. Blessed and holy are those who share in the first resurrection. The second death has no power over them, but they will be priests of God and of Christ and will reign with him for <u>a thousand years</u>.**
>
> **When <u>the thousand years</u> are over, Satan will be released from his prison.** (Rev 20:1-7 NIV)

For Amillennialism to be true, it must <u>deny</u> that this promise from God will be fulfilled in a physical way. But there are clear and biblical reasons to reject Amillennialism's interpretation of this promise.

First, as noted above, God has established an overwhelming historical precedent for fulfilling biblical prophecy in a physical, and often literal way. Again, every one of the almost 600 biblical prophecies that have already been fulfilled in history, were fulfilled in a physical way by a person, place, or event. Revelation 20 will not be an exception to the rule God Himself has demonstrated.

Second, notice that six times in the span of six verses the text reads a **thousand years**. Do you think God is wanting to emphasize something here? If he merely meant the **thousand years** to be a symbol for something, would He repeat a **thousand years** in every one of the six verses in this prophecy? Probably not. But in spite of God's own emphasis on a literal meaning for the **thousand years**, Amillennialism still ignores it.

Third, there is no clear reason in the text of Revelation 20, or elsewhere in Scripture, to deny God intended this prophecy to be interpreted literally. There are no statements in Scripture that would contradict a belief in a literal one **thousand** year Reign of Christ on this Earth. In fact, some Scriptures seem to clearly describe this period of time (cf. Isa 65:19-25). This includes all the OT predictions about the restoration of Israel at this time. The only way Amillennialism can find what it claims to be contradictions to a literal **thousand** year Reign of Christ, is to interpret all these OT promises as spiritual metaphors. Which, again, is not how God fulfills His promises.

Fourth, another serious problem with the Amillennial view of Revelation 20 is verses 1-3. The prophecy states that **Satan** will be **bound** (*edēsen*, v. 2). The Greek word is used many times in the NT to mean preventing the activity of someone with chains or prison. The obvious sense here is that at some point in time Satan will be **bound** such that he is not active at all outside of **the Abyss**.

This is confirmed by the fact that He will be cast **into the Abyss** which will be **locked and sealed ... over him** (v. 3). The **Abyss** is the place where the dead and demons are confined (cf. Rom 10:7; Luke 8:31). The prophecy is clear that during this **thousand years** the **devil** will not be active or present on Earth or in Heaven at all.

One result will be that **Satan** will not be **deceiving the nations anymore until the thousand years were ended** (v. 3). **Deceiving** is Satan's essential nature and activity. Jesus said of him:
> **He has always hated the truth, because there is no truth in him. When he lies, it is consistent with his character; for he is a liar and the father of lies.** (John 8:44 NLT)

If **Satan** will not be **deceiving** during **the thousand years**, then this is more evidence he will not be doing anything during this time. Therefore, being **bound** in **the Abyss** and not having any presence or activity on Earth or in Heaven would obviously prohibit **the devil** from other activities described in Scripture.

This completely refutes the Amillennial claim that Revelation 20:1-3 is being fulfilled during the Church Age. Scripture itself denies this. In fact, the Apostles Peter, Paul, and John did not believe in this foundational claim of Amillennialism. They wrote the following texts even after Christ's Death and Resurrection. As you read them, ask yourself the question: Is it reasonable or biblical to believe **Satan** could do the following things if he was **bound** in **the Abyss** and having it **locked and sealed ... over him** so that he cannot be **deceiving** people?

> **Be alert and of sober mind. Your enemy the devil prowls around like a roaring lion looking for someone to devour** [by deception!]. **Resist him** [because he is very active on Earth], **standing firm in the faith, because you know that the family of believers throughout the world is undergoing the same kind of sufferings** [from the attacks of Satan]. (1 Pet 5:8-9 NIV)

> **Put on all of God's armor so that you will be able to stand firm against all strategies of the devil** [to deceive!]. **For we are not fighting against flesh-and-blood enemies, but against ... evil spirits in the heavenly places** [including Satan]. (Eph 6:11-12 NLT)

> **And even if our gospel is veiled, it is veiled to those who are perishing. The god of this age [Satan] has blinded** [deceived!] **the minds of unbelievers, so that they cannot see the light of the gospel that displays the glory of Christ** (2 Cor 4:3-4 NIV)

> **We know that we are children of God, and that the whole world is under the control** [and deception!] **of the evil one.** (1 John 5:19 NIV)

> That ancient serpent called <u>the devil, or Satan</u>, who leads the whole world astray [by deception!], God would be breaking his promise God would be breaking his promise the accuser of our brothers and sisters, who accuses them before our God [in Heaven!] day and night (Rev 12:9-10 NIV)

It does not seem reasonable to believe, as Amillennialism claims, that **Satan** can be doing all of this in Heaven and on Earth if he is currently **bound** in **the Abyss** and having it **locked and sealed ... over him** so that he cannot be **deceiving** people. You can be assured that all the complicated arguments and additional metaphorical interpretations of Scripture that Amillennialism uses, <u>do not</u> refute the clear, literal, and obvious meaning of the verses cited above.

How does Amillennialism attempt to overcome these biblical arguments against its view? Only by severely limiting the binding and confining imposed on **Satan** described in Revelation 20 and forcing its meaning to fit this view. Amillennialism would claim that instead of being **bound** in **the Abyss**, and having it **locked and sealed ... over him**, that Satan is still present and active on the Earth and in Heaven, doing all the things the above Scriptures describe.

In addition, Amillennialism attempts to limit Satan's **deceiving** to only **deceiving** <u>some</u> people in **the nations** about <u>only</u> the Gospel. But even that is refuted by Paul's claim above that during the Church Age **the god of this age** [Satan] **has blinded** [deceived!] **the minds of unbelievers, so that they cannot see the light of the gospel** (2 Cor 4:4).

Even the label Amillennialism is founded on its claim that there will be no literal 1,000-year Reign of Christ on this Earth. Therefore, the very foundation of Amillennialism in not biblical.

B) A biblical evaluation of Preterism

In chapter 3 (sec. B) the popular but faulty view of "Historicism" was discussed. This claims that the biblical prophecies Christ gave us in His Endtimes Teaching have essentially been fulfilled throughout Church history and have little relevance for the future. A related view is Preterism which is addressed in this section.

B.1) Understanding "the end of the age" & refuting Preterism *Matt 24:3*

Another view of the Endtimes that is particularly common in scholarly Bible commentaries is Preterism. [24] The term comes from the Latin word *praeter* which can refer to something that is in the past. Therefore, the fundamental view of Preterism is that NT prophecies have already been fulfilled in the first century.

For example, Preterism claims the predictions of Antichrist's **abomination of desolation** (Matt 24:15) and **the greatest persecution** (v. 21) in Christ's Endtimes Teaching were fulfilled in A.D. 70 when the Roman army destroyed Jerusalem and the temple. Likewise, Preterism claims the prophesies in Revelation were fulfilled in the ancient Roman Empire.

First, like Historicism, Preterism ignores the question the Apostles asked to prompt Christ's Endtimes Teaching. We read:

> **Jesus left the temple and was walking away when his disciples came up to him to call his attention to its buildings. "Do you see all these things?" he asked. "Truly I tell you, not one stone here will be left on another; every one will be thrown down."**
>
> **As Jesus was sitting on the Mount of Olives, the disciples came to him privately. "Tell us," they said, "when will this happen** [the destruction of the temple]**, and what will be the sign of your coming and of the end of the age?"** (Matt 24:1-3 NIV).

Preterism claims that by **the end of the age**, the Apostles meant only the destruction of the **temple** and not Christ's physical Return. Therefore, Preterism also claims that the Apostles believed **the beginning of birth pains** (v. 8), the **greatest persecution** (v. 21), and even in some symbolic way, the Cosmic Signs, Christ's Return, and the Church's Rescue (vs. 29-31) all occurred in A.D. 70!

It is true that the disciples probably believed the destruction of the **temple** would occur at **the end of the age** when Christ Returned. But why would Jesus confirm their error as Preterism claims? Contrary to Preterism, what the Apostles did understand, and what Jesus taught, was that at **the end of the age** Christ would physically return. Both their understanding of **the end of the age** is reflected earlier in Matthew when Jesus had shared a parable and explained:

> **The harvest is <u>the end of the age</u>, and the harvesters are angels. As the weeds are pulled up and burned in the fire, so it will be at <u>the end of the age</u>. The Son of Man will send out his angels, and they will weed out of his kingdom everything that causes sin and all who do evil** [probably by means of the Church's Rescue, cf. Matt 24:31]. (Matt 13:39-41 NIV; cf. v. 49)

Likewise, in the Great Commission given in Matthew, Jesus said:

> **Therefore go and make disciples of all nations, baptizing them in the name of the Father and of the Son and of the Holy Spirit, and teaching them to obey everything I have commanded you. And surely I am with you always, to the very <u>end of the age</u>."** (Matt 28:19-20 NIV)

Therefore, when the disciples asked, **"what will be the sign of your coming and of the end of the age?"** did they mean something different than the **end of the age** described elsewhere by Jesus in the hearing of the disciples as Preterism claims? No they did not. Both Jesus and the Apostles knew that the disciples were asking what was going to happen immediately before Christ's physical Return. And contrary to Preterism, Jesus answered their question. [25]

The claim of Preterism that Matthew 24:4-35 only applies to the first century is also clearly refuted by Christ's statement in verse 14 where Jesus said, **"And this gospel of the kingdom will be preached in the whole world as a testimony to all nations, and <u>then the end will come</u>"** (NIV). According to a Preterist perspective, this prophecy was also fulfilled before A.D. 70. [26] Again, that is not true.

B.2) Understanding "this generation" & refuting Preterism
Matt 24:33-34

A key text for Preterism is Christ's statement:

> **When you see all these things** [the events described throughout Christ's Endtimes Teaching], **you know that it**

[Christ's Return] **is near, right at the door. Truly I tell you, <u>this generation</u> will certainly not pass away until all these things have happened** (Matt 24:33-34).

Preterism interprets **this generation** to refer to the first century in which Jesus was speaking. But this is impossible. Jesus said the **generation** He was referring to would **see all these things**. **All these things** included the Cosmic Signs, Christ's Return, and the Church's Rescue described in the immediately preceding verses.

In the first century, **the stars** <u>did not</u> **fall from the sky, all the peoples of the Earth** <u>did not</u> **see the Son of Man coming on the clouds of Heaven, with power and great glory**, and Jesus <u>did not</u> **send out His angels with a loud trumpet sound, and ... lift up and gather together God's elect people from one end of the sky to the other, from everywhere on Earth** (Matt 24:29-31).

Accordingly, most Preterists claim that **all these things** <u>does not</u> include the above events, but only Antichrist's Claim to be God and The Greatest Persecution described earlier in the text (vs. 15-21). But Jesus said the **generation** He was referring to would experience **all** [*panta*] **these things**.

In order to support their view, Preterists depend on the same faulty view of prophecy fulfillment as Amillennialism. It claims that at least some of the above predictions were fulfilled in merely a spiritual or symbolic way, not in a literal physical event. But as noted above, this approach ignores the fact that every one of the almost 600 biblical prophecies that have already been fulfilled in history, were fulfilled in a physical way in a person, place, or event.

Therefore, it is rather clear to understand **this generation** to be the Last Generation living when Christ Returns. They will be **the generation** who will **see all these things** that Christ predicted that will lead up to His Return. <u>That</u> **generation will certainly not pass away until all these things have happened**. In other words, all of the Endtime events described by Christ will occur within one generation, the Last Generation. [27]

Christ confirms this when He describes several Endtime events in Luke's version of His Endtimes Teaching and then concludes: **For this is the time of punishment in fulfillment of <u>all</u> that has**

been written (Luke 21:22 NIV). Was all biblical prophecy fulfilled in A.D. 70? Clearly not.

When proponents of the Preterist ("historical") view also claim most of the events in Revelation have already been fulfilled, their view becomes even more unbelievable. When did a fourth of humanity perish? (cf. 6:8). When did every person on Earth see **the face of Him who sits on the throne and ... the wrath of the Lamb** (cf. 6:15-17). When has **a third of the sea turned into blood** and **a third of the living creatures in the sea died** (8:8-9)?

Obviously, dozens of examples from Revelation could be given. And again, the only way Preterism can make their view work is to suggest merely spiritual fulfillments of prophecy in the Revelation and abandon God's precedent for fulfilling His promises with physical events, people, and places.

In addition, Preterism's interpretation of **this generation** requires that the book of Revelation was written before A.D. 70. Otherwise, John was simply describing events that had already happened. Accordingly, the influential Preterist Kenneth Gentry has admitted that if Revelation was written after A.D. 70 then the Preterist view would "go up in smoke." [28] If your theological view depends on the correct and rather precise dating of a NT document, then you have a very questionable foundation.

Unfortunately for Preterism, the clearest and most authoritative statement ever made in the Early Church about the dating of any NT document, was written about Revelation. The "Early Church Father" Irenaeus wrote in his *Against Heresies* that the Book of Revelation "was [first] seen not long ago, but almost in our own generation, at the end of the reign of Domitian." [29]

Irenaeus (c. A.D. 130-200) had personally heard the teaching of Polycarp (c. A.D. 70-155), [30] who was a personal disciple of the Apostle John (c. A.D. 10-100). Therefore, Irenaeus was in a unique position to know when Revelation was written. Roman historical records state that "Domitian was assassinated on September 18, A.D. 96." [31] This means that the "end of the reign of Domitian" would date John's writing of Revelation in A.D. 96.

Accordingly, Carson, Moo, and Morris agree with the vast majority of Revelation scholars, and conclude after a detailed discussion: "We are inclined, then, to follow the oldest tradition [from Irenaeus] on this point and date Revelation in the last years of [the Roman Emperor] Domitian." [32] In fact, it is essentially only Preterist scholars who even suggest otherwise.

B.3) Preterism ignores the fact that many biblical prophecies have more than one fulfillment *Isa 7:14-16; Rev 1:1-3*

What else is Preterism based on? There were some events in Jerusalem in A.D. 70 that were partial fulfillments or "foreshadowings" of predictions in Christ's Endtimes Teaching. For example, Roman soldiers brought an image of the Roman Emperor into the temple area and made sacrifices to it, therefore certainly "desecrating" it.

But no one did what the Apostle Paul said will happen in the complete and final fulfillment of the **abomination of desolation**. The Apostle said the future Antichrist **will oppose and will exalt himself over everything that is called God or is worshiped, so that he sets himself up in God's temple, proclaiming himself to be God.** (2 Thess 2:4). Again, none of the fanciful and metaphorical explanations of Preterism should convince a reasonable person that this actually happened in A.D. 70.

Also, Preterism tries to make the case that what the Jews experienced in the Roman destruction of Jerusalem, rather fully fulfilled Jesus' prediction that **there will be the greatest persecution of God's elect people. It will be greater than any persecution since the world began, and it will never be equaled again** (Matt 24:15, 21). The persecution of the Jews by the Romans was horrific, but it was <u>not</u> **the greatest persecution of God's elect people** there will ever be. Contrary to Preterism, the Antichrist will be worse than the Romans.

Preterism ignores an important biblical principle for interpreting prophetic Scripture. Many biblical prophecies have a near/partial fulfillment before their final/complete fulfillment. God intends these to be a "down payment" on His plan for the ultimate fulfillment of these prophecies. So, of course the events in A.D. 70 "foreshadowed" the final and complete fulfillment of Christ's predictions.

But contrary to Preterism, first century events were not the ultimate or most important fulfillment of those events. [33] Some of Jesus' predictions were to have more than one fulfillment. [34]

There are many examples of the near/far nature of biblical prophecy. One of the first and clearest regards Christ's birth. In Isaiah we are told that **Pekah, the king of Israel**, formed an army to attack the kingdom of **Judah**, led by **king Ahaz** (cf. 7:1-2). The Prophet Isaiah was told by God to tell Ahaz the battle **"will not happen"** (vs. 3-9). Then God said He would give king Ahaz a miraculous **sign** to prove this prophecy will come true. We read in verses 14 and 16:

> **Therefore, the Lord himself will give you a sign: The virgin will conceive and give birth to a son, and will call him Immanuel... Before the boy knows enough to reject the wrong and choose the right, the land of the two kings you dread will be laid waste.** (NIV)

Therefore, sometime around 700 B.C. a real **virgin** miraculously conceived a child and gave birth to a **son** who was named **Immanuel**. **Before the boy** was old enough to understand **right** from **wrong**, [35] the **two kings** attacking Judah were destroyed. That was God's promise and God's proof of His promise to Ahaz.

Unfortunately, many modern Bible scholars want to deny this happened. But if this prophecy was not literally fulfilled in Ahaz's time, then God was a liar, and the king had no reason to believe Isaiah was speaking for God.

Obviously, the **virgin** birth of this baby named **Immanuel** around 700 years before Christ was not the final, nor the most important, fulfillment of this prophecy. Matthew wrote regarding Jesus Christ's birth by the virgin Mary:

> **All this took place to fulfill what the Lord had said through the prophet** [in Isaiah 7]**: 'The virgin will conceive and give birth to a son, and they will call him Immanuel'" (which means "God with us")"** (Matt 1:22-23 NIV).

This was the final, complete, and most significant fulfillment of this prophecy about 700 years after it was given. But its near and partial fulfillment in Ahaz's time should not be ignored.

Why did God communicate prophecy and plan its fulfillment in this way? Most scholars recognize what the eminent prophecy scholar Dwight Pentecost said many years ago: "It was the purpose of God to give the near and far view so that the fulfillment of the one should be the assurance of the fulfillment of the other." [36] Accordingly, the miraculous birth of a baby from a virgin mother ca. 700 B.C. was a confirming sign that it would happen again in a much more important way.

Indeed, what was the <u>most important</u> fulfillment of this prophecy? Was it in the time of Ahaz in 700 B.C., or what happened in Christ's birth ca. 1 B.C? The answer is obvious. But what a Preterist perspective would do is focus on what happened in 700 B.C. and claim that virtually all of the prophecy was fulfilled then, or at least its most important fulfillment occurred then. As a result, they would miss the more important meaning of the prophecy of Christ's First Coming. This will be the case for Preterism's understanding of Christ's Second Coming.

Other examples of multiple fulfillments of biblical prophecy include predictions of the Antichrist in Daniel fulfilled in the 2nd century B.C. by Antiochus, and predictions of the destruction of the Jewish temple by Jesus in His Endtimes Teaching. This latter phenomenon has confused many about how to interpret these passages. Jesus gave His Endtimes Teaching 40 years before Rome attacked Jerusalem and destroyed the temple. Therefore, it is clear that Jesus was predicting these events.

Some claim that Luke's version of Christ's Endtimes Teaching (21:5-36) uniquely emphasizes this. Therefore, it is legitimate to find elements of Christ's prophecy that were fulfilled in A.D. 70. But Preterism is wrong to claim these events were the final and complete fulfillment of Christ's predictions. This view ignores the multiple fulfillment nature of biblical prophecy.

The multiple fulfillment nature of biblical prophecy helps us understand the difficult statements at the beginning of Revelation:

The revelation from Jesus Christ, which God gave him to show his servants what must <u>soon</u> take place... blessed are those who hear it and take to heart what is written in it, because <u>the time is near</u>. (Rev 1:1, 3 NIV)

The fact that Jesus said His predictions in the Revelation were to occur **soon** (v. 1), and the events were **near** (v. 3), is a primary reason that Preterism believes most (if not all) of the prophecies in Revelation have already been fulfilled. Admittedly, these are difficult statements, but a helpful answer is the near/far nature of prophecy fulfillment in Scripture.

Some of the prophecies in Revelation did occur in the first century. For example, Jesus warned many first century churches of painful consequences that would occur if they did not repent (cf. Rev 2:5, 16, 21-23; 3:16). No doubt, these churches experienced these things in the first century. Likewise, this prophecy to the church in Smyrna was certainly fulfilled **soon** (Rev 1:1) after the Revelation was given:

> **Do not be afraid of what you are about to suffer. I tell you, the devil will put some of you in prison to test you, and you will suffer persecution for ten days.** (Rev 2:10)

That happened **soon** after this church received the Revelation. But again, because of the multiple fulfillment nature of biblical prophecy, there is no reason to believe that Revelation 1:1-3 is saying that all of Revelation was fulfilled in the first century.

One argument for Preterism is that biblical prophecy must be made applicable and meaningful for those who initially received it. That is not true. The Apostle Peter wrote:

> **Concerning this salvation** [that was prophesied in the OT] **the** [OT] **prophets, who spoke of the grace that was to come to you, searched intently and with the greatest care, trying to find out the time and circumstances to which the Spirit of Christ in them was pointing when he predicted the sufferings of the Messiah and the glories that would follow. It was revealed to them that they were not serving themselves but you** [in the far future] (1 Pet 1:10-12 NIV)

Contrary to Preterism, a lot of OT prophesies had no practical relevance for those who initially received or heard them. God regularly gave prophesies that were for people living many hundreds of years later. The Book of Revelation is an example.

Preterism has some value in helping us understand the **near** (Rev

1:3) fulfillments of biblical prophecy. But like Amillennialism, Preterism also **strains out a gnat but swallows a camel** (Matt 23:23-24). This is because it focuses on past, partial, metaphorical, and often questionable fulfillments of biblical prophecies, and ignores the more important, literal, future, and final fulfillments. As a result, Preterism also ends up being a **blind guide** to helping the Church to understand and be prepared for the Endtimes. [37]

---

[1] Of course there are spiritual realities about the Kingdom of God that were initiated by Christ's First Coming. Therefore, there is some sense in which God's Kingdom on Earth and the Endtimes began with this (cf. Matt 12:28; Luke 17:20-21, Rom 14:17; 1 Cor 10:11; 1 John 2:18). Theologians call this "realized eschatology" or the "already not yet" aspect of God's Kingdom on Earth.

Christ's First Coming and the indwelling of the Holy Spirit have initiated some things that will be consummated in Christ's Second Coming and even after the completion of His 1,000 year Reign on Earth. This is also related to the near/final and partial/complete nature of the fulfillment of biblical prophecy discussed in section B.3 in this chapter.

Unfortunately, some (such as Amillennialism) focus so much on what can be included in "realized eschatology" that they neglect a biblical understanding of what is still to be fulfilled in biblical prophecy. For more on "realized eschatology" see *Additional Studies on the Endtimes* (*ASE*), ch. 3.

[2] The survey of Protestant Pastors on the Endtimes can be found online at https://news.lifeway.com/2016/04/26/pastors-the-end-of-the-world-is-complicated/. See explanation of statistics in endnotes in ch. 1.

[3] Erickson, *Guide*, 84.

[4] Ibid., 73.

[5] For more on biblical principles for interpreting biblical prophecy see chapters 1 4 in *Advanced Studies on the Endtimes*; online at www.trainingtimothys.com.

[6] Van Kampen, 6.

[7] *BDAG*.

[8] The prediction that Christ **would be a Nazarene** (Matt 2:23) is nowhere explicitly stated in Scripture. Carson seems to reflect the best explanation when he reminds us that in the first century the town of Nazareth "was a despised place (Jn 7:42, 52)." Therefore:

Matthew is not saying that the OT Prophets foretold that the Messiah would live in Nazareth; he is saying that the OT prophets foretold that the Messiah would be despised (cf. Pss 22:6-8, 13; 69:8, 20-21; Isa 11:1; 49:7; 53:2-3, 8; Dan 9:26)… In other words Matthew gives us the substance of several OT passages, not a direct quotation. (124-5)

9 Matt 12:15-16 help us understand how Matthew viewed these events as a fulfillment of the OT prophecy in Isa 42:1-4. In v. 15 we read that **he healed all who were ill**. Such feats usually drew large and demanding crowds (cf. Matt 8:4; 9:30). This was burdensome for Christ. So much so that He told the healed **not to tell others about him** (12:16).

In other words, Christ's ministry, including His healings, were demanding. Therefore, Matthew recalled the prophecy in Isaiah which described a meek **servant** of God would be empowered by God's **Spirit on him** (Isa 42:1; cf. Matt 12:18). Accordingly, Carson writes on Matt 12:15-21: "Jesus' conduct under these pressures, Matthew perceives, was nothing less than the fulfillment of the Scriptures … of the Suffering Servant" (330).

10 See endnote #5 above.

11 Contrary to the distorting emphasis many scholars place on Revelation by labeling it an "apocalypse," Osborne writes:

> It is impossible to distinguish ultimately between prophecy and apocalyptic, for the latter is an extension of the former… John calls his work a prophecy five times (1:3; 22:7, 10, 18, 19)… Revelation is a symbolic book, but that does not mean the symbols do not depict literal events, like the "great tribulation" (7:14), as well as the various depictions of the "three and a half years"… or the "beast" for the Antichrist. (13-16)

Even the influential Amillennialist, Gregory Beale, writes: "Too much distinction has typically been drawn between the apocalyptic and prophetic genres" (37).

12 An example of a prophecy predicting a spiritual event is Ezek 36:

> **I will give you a new heart and put a new spirit in you; I will remove from you your heart of stone and give you a heart of flesh. And I will put my Spirit in you and move you to follow my decrees and be careful to keep my laws.** (Ezek 36:26-27 NIV)

This prophecy has been fulfilled in a rather <u>literal</u> way by a spiritual event. When a Christian is regenerated and indwelled with God's Spirit at conversion, they literally receive in a spiritual way **a new heart** and **a new spirit**. God explained the spiritual reality He predicted when He added, **I will put my Spirit in you**. In other words, there is no need to guess what the metaphorical language in the prophecy meant. God explained it. And this is the same in the vast majority of prophetic Scripture. God provides an explanation of the symbols and metaphors in the prophecy.

In addition, the promise of spiritual regeneration in Ezekiel 36:26-27 is a good example of the multiple fulfillment nature of biblical prophecy. Unfortunately, metaphorical interpreters of biblical prophecy consistently ignore this proven attribute of prophetic Scripture. For example, this promise of the Spirit's indwelling has already been <u>partially</u> fulfilled in the Church Age. But it will be completely and <u>finally</u> fulfilled in the spiritual restoration of Israel in the Endtimes. For a similar example see Acts 2:14-21 (cf. Joel 2:28-32).

It is suggested that Ezekiel 36 is one of the very rare cases that we should expect a biblical prophecy to be fulfilled in a spiritual rather than physical way. But this is because <u>the prophecy clearly and literally predicted a spiritual event</u>. Of course, metaphorical interpreters of the fulfillment of biblical prophecy suggest many examples of biblical prophecy will be fulfilled in a spiritual reality, rather than a physical one in the future. But, unlike Ezekiel 36, the prophecies in question are <u>not</u> clearly promising a spiritual reality.

[13] Erickson, *Guide*, 84.

[14] Payne, 653. In spite of Payne's exhaustive work, including his "Summaries," it is difficult to determine helpful data. The claim of 592 prophecies fulfilled to date comes from having to distinguish past and future fulfillments under Payne's category "church." Past fulfillments seem to stop at #591, but then he lists the remembrance of "Mary's act of anointing Jesus" throughout the Church Age (cf. Matt 26:13). Thus, we suggest 592 prophecies fulfilled to date. Payne lists 737 total prophecies in Scripture, with 145 remaining to be fulfilled.

Payne's numbers will seem low to many because they have heard things like "There are over 300 prophecies about Christ's First Coming and over 2,000 remaining for His Second Coming." But such statistics are referring to the total number of biblical <u>references</u> to individual prophecies. For example, Payne lists 12 <u>places</u> in the OT that refer to the <u>one</u> prediction that Christ "will be from the household of David." (646).

[15] Of course the only way for the reader to verify this conclusion is to obtain Payne's book and evaluate the prophecies in the "Summaries" section for yourself. But in this author's opinion, every single one of the 592 fulfilled prophecies Payne identified were fulfilled in a physical way by a person, place, or event.

[16] Riddlebarger, 39.

[17] Ibid. It is admitted that many respected NT scholars would agree with Riddlebarger on the interpretation and application of Acts 15:12-18 (cf. Stott, *Acts*; Bruce, 293; Marshall, 252; Peterson, *PNTC*).

[18] James' use of Amos 9:11-12 is complicated by the fact that he used the ancient Greek translation of the OT (Septuagint, or LXX) instead of the Hebrew text used by modern Bibles. Therefore, James' quote of the prophecy is quite different from the text of our Bibles.

[19] MacArthur is in agreement with the interpretation of Acts 15:12-18 argued for in this section:
> The Amos passage speaks of the millennial kingdom. It is then that God **will rebuild the tabernacle of David which has fallen, ... rebuild its ruins, ... and restore it**. In the millennial kingdom, **the rest of mankind** will **seek the Lord, and all the Gentiles who are called by My name, says the Lord, who makes these things known from of old**. Gentiles will be saved as Gentiles, without first becoming Jews, or else verse 17 would make no sense...
>
> James reassured his Jewish audience that the inclusion of Gentiles into the church did not abrogate God's plan for Israel. In fact, in the kingdom they will be the messengers to bring Gentiles to God (Zech. 8:20–23). (loc. 9090; cf. Longenecker, *Acts*, 242.)

[20] Some have suggested this promise was fulfilled in the time of David. But the promise was forever. Earlier in Genesis we read:
> **The LORD said to Abram after Lot had parted from him, "Look around from where you are, to the north and south, to the east and west. All the land that you see I will give to you and your offspring <u>forever</u>.** (Gen 13:14-15 NIV)

Likewise God told Abraham:
> **"I will establish my covenant as an everlasting covenant between me and you and your descendants after you for the generations to come, to be your God and the God of your descendants after you. The whole land of Canaan, where you now reside as a foreigner, I will give as an <u>everlasting possession</u> to you and your descendants after you; and I will be their God."** (Gen 17:7-8 NIV)

Accordingly, David Jeremiah writes:
> The land promised to Abraham and his descendants was described with clear geographical boundaries. It takes in all the land from the Mediterranean Sea as the western boundary to the Euphrates River as the eastern boundary. The Prophet Ezekiel fixed the northern boundary at Hamath, 100 miles north of (Syrian) Damascus (Ezek 48:1), and the southern boundary at Kadesh, about 100 miles south of Jerusalem (v. 28).
>
> If Israelis were currently occupying all the land that God gave to them, they would control all the holdings of present-day Israel, Lebanon, and the West Bank of Jordan, plus substantial portions of Syria, Iraq, and Saudi Arabia...

Israel has never, in its long history, possessed anywhere near this much land—not even at the height of its glory days under David and Solomon. (https://davidjeremiah.blog/the-promised-land-of-israel/)

[21] For more on the relationship between Israel and the Church see *Additional Studies on the Endtimes*, ch. 11, online at www.trainingtimothys.com.

[22] Amillennialism is especially prone to claim that the prophecies of Ezekiel, starting in chapter 40, cannot be fulfilled literally. For scholarly arguments to the contrary, see *K&D*.

[23] For evidence of anti-semitism being promoted in the Protestant Reformation based on theological, and even eschatological beliefs, see Martin Luther's *On the Jews and Their Lies*.

[24] There is a recognized difference between "full Preterism" and "partial Preterism." The "full" variety claims that virtually all biblical prophecy has already been fulfilled, including the Resurrection. Most rightly regard this view as heretical based on Paul's condemnation of **Hymenaeus and Philetus**, whom the Apostle said, **have departed from the truth. They say that the resurrection has already taken place, and they destroy the faith of some.** (2 Tim 2:17-18 NIV).

The "partial" variety claims that most of the predictions in Christ's Endtimes Teaching have already been completely fulfilled, including the Antichrist's Claim to be God and The Greatest Persecution. However, they believe Christ's Return and the Resurrection are still to come.

Prominent proponents of "partial Preterism" include the highly respected Reformed theologian R. C. Sproul, the NT scholar N. T. Wright, and Hank Hanegraaff of "The Bible Answer Man" radio program.

[25] Piper writes in response to Preterism's belief about Christ's Endtimes Teaching:

> When the disciples used the phrase "end of the age" (συντελείας τοῦ αἰῶνος, Matt. 24:3), they were very likely using it the way Jesus had used it in their hearing, namely, to signify the very end of this age marked by the judgment on unbelievers... (Matt 13:39-43; cf. 13:49; 28: 20)...
>
> It is unlikely that as Jesus began to speak in Matthew 24, the disciples would have understood verses 4–35 to be unrelated to this "end of the age" [as Preterism claims] (229-230).

[26] Piper describes the Preterist view when he writes:

> Those who believe that the events prophesied in Matthew 24:4-35 should be limited to the events leading up to AD 70 argue that the mission to the nations prophesied in verse 14 was fulfilled by that date...

> Sam Storms [an Amillennialist who therefore must depend on Preterist interpretations] says:
>> As far as Jesus' prophecy in Matthew 24:14 is concerned, his point is that following his resurrection the gospel will be preached outside the boundaries of Judea, such that the Gentile nations in the inhabited world known as the Roman Empire will hear the testimony of his redemptive work. Only thereafter, says Jesus, will the 'end' of the city and temple occur [and this prophecy of the **gospel** being **preached in the whole world** will be fulfilled]...
>> [Regarding] The Great Commission in Matthew 28 ... My point ... is simply that Matthew 24:14 is not concerned with that task. (Sam Storms, *Kingdom Come: The Amillennial Alternative* (Mentor, 2013), pp. 242-44) (232)
>
> With all due respect, this seems to be an example of an arrogant attempt to twist Scripture into a preconceived theology.

27 Accordingly, MacArthur supports the correct view of **this generation**: "This generation," that is, the generation living during the time of those end-time events, "will not pass away until all these things take place" (v. 34). The signs of Matthew 24 will all be fully experienced within one generation, a generation that could be no other than the generation living when Christ returns. (*MNTC*, loc. 42713; cf. Bock, 1691-2)

28 Kenneth L. Gentry, "The Days of Vengeance: A Review Article," *The Counsel of Chalcedon*, Vol. IX, No. 4., p. 11.

29 Eusebius, *Church History* 3.18.3.

30 Irenaeus, *Against Heresies* 4.14.1-8; 5.33.4. *Letter to Florinus*. Irenaeus writes, "I can remember the events of that time... so that I am able to describe the very place where the blessed Polycarp sat... and the accounts he gave of his conversation with John and with others who had seen the Lord" (Irenaeus as quoted by Eusebius, *Church History* 5.20.5-6).

31 https://www.evidenceunseen.com/bible-difficulties-2/nt-difficulties/jude/date-of-revelation/#_ftnref1. This is a good website for the refutation of Preterism's claim that Rev was written before A.D. 70.

32 *An Introduction to the New Testament*, D. A. Carson, Douglas J. Moo, Leon Morris (Zondervan, 1992), 476.

33 Many names for the near/far nature of biblical prophecy fulfillment have been used. They include "prophetic foreshortening," "prophetic telescoping" and a myriad of others. For more on this see *ASE* ch. 3.

34 Against Preterism, Piper explains how the near/far aspect of the fulfillment of biblical prophecy helps to explain Christ's Endtimes Teaching:
> Therefore, to argue from this presumed [Preterist] structure that Matthew 24:4-35 relates only to the first century (pre-AD 70) and the

rest of the chapter (24:36-51) describes the yet-future second coming, is, I think, unwarranted. I suggest that both the disciples' questions (Matt. 24:3) and Jesus's answer reflect what I have called "prophetic perspective" (see chapter 8, note 1). The near and distant mountain ranges of the future are seen as a whole. (229).

[35] The prophecy stated that **Before the boy knows enough to reject the wrong and choose the right, the land of the two kings you dread will be laid waste** (Isa 7:16). How old was this child when the prophecy was fulfilled? According to the Association for Psychological Science: "Children know the difference between right and wrong before they reach the age of two, according to new research published today." online at https://www.psychologicalscience.org/news/research

[36] Dwight Pentecost, *Things to Come* (Zondervan, 1958), 47.

[37] For a resource for refuting Preterism, see online at http://www.according2prophecy.org/Preterism.html.

Perhaps unfortunately, all the authors noted there are Pre-tribulationists.

Chapter 13

A Biblical Evaluation of Pre-tribulationism

Contents

A) Introduction to Pre-tribulationism

B) 8 Pre-tribulation myths already addressed in Christ's Endtimes Teaching

Primary Points

- The Pre-tribulation Rapture teaching is a significant fulfillment of Paul's prophecy that **myths** would arise in the Church.
- Pre-tribulationism is one of the most influential false teachings to invade the Church in its entire history.
- There is not a single verse in Scripture that teaches what Pre-tribulationism claims.
- All the arguments for the most popular view of the Endtimes are all **myths**, rather than biblical doctrine.
- It is a myth that the events described in the first 28 verses of Christ's Endtimes Teaching have nothing to do with the Church.
- It is a myth that the Church will never encounter the Antichrist or experience The Greatest Persecution.
- It is a myth that Christ will come in a "secret & silent rapture."
- It is a myth that the Church is not mentioned in Revelation chapters 5-18 as being on Earth.
- It is a myth that Christ's Return for the Church and His visible Coming are described as two different events in Scripture, separated by 7 years.
- Matthew 24:31 is <u>not</u> describing a gathering of Jews at the Battle of Armageddon as Pre-tribulationism claims.
- It is a myth that God's Endtimes plan for Israel and the Church are completely separate and do not overlap in any way.
- It is a myth that a literal interpretation of prophetic Scripture leads to the Pre-tribulational view.

A) Introduction to Pre-tribulationism

In chapter 1 you were reminded of the Apostle Paul's prediction and warning to the Church:

> **The time will come when they** [Christians] **will not endure sound doctrine; but wanting to have their ears tickled, they will accumulate for themselves teachers in accordance to their own desires, and will turn away their ears from the truth and will turn aside to myths.** (2 Tim 4:3-4 NASB)

The next several chapters will explain and refute several popular **myths** about the Endtimes. These are primarily promoted by the view known as the Pre-tribulation Rapture. It is important that we recognize that many of those who teach and believe this view are genuine Christians. No unnecessary offense is intended as we biblically evaluate the view.

But unfortunately, the Pre-tribulation Rapture teaching is a significant fulfillment of Paul's prophecy that Christians would **accumulate for themselves teachers in accordance to their own desires, and ... turn away their ears from the truth and ... turn aside to myths.** To call the biblical errors in Pre-tribulationism **myths**, is a nicer way of saying they are actually false teaching. In fact, given the popularity of these **myths**, it will be demonstrated that Pre-tribulationism is one of the most influential false teachings to ever invade the Church in its entire history.

Let us be reminded of what the Pre-tribulational Rapture view claims. It teaches that the Church's Rescue ("rapture") will occur before the "tribulation." Thus, it is labeled Pre-tribulationism. You read in chapter 3:

> Pre-tribulationism claims that the Church is "raptured" from the Earth before any other Endtime events occur. In other words, it is claimed that the Church will not experience any of the events Jesus described in His Endtimes Teaching. Therefore, Pre-tribulationism claims no Christians in the Church today can experience or witness the **wars**, and **famines** of **the beginning of birth pains**, or Antichrist's **abomination of desolation**, or the **greatest persecution** (Matt 24:4-7, 15, 21, 24).

Obviously, this is a very attractive view. In a survey, 36% of Protestant Pastors claimed Pre-tribulationism best reflected their beliefs on the Endtimes. That was significantly higher than the percentage for any other views. This view has been especially promoted by the *Left Behind* fictional novels which have sold over 65 million copies worldwide. Again, these novels are fiction. Still, they have had more impact on the Church's Endtimes beliefs than any other resource. (sec. D)

As demonstrated in chapter 8 (sec. C), this view was not taught in the Early Church, nor in about 1900 years of Church history. It was not until the 1920's that it grew in popularity. Since then it has been adopted by some very influential American seminaries and teachers. [1]

It is obvious why Pre-tribulationism is an attractive view of the Endtimes. It promises that Christians living today cannot experience the Antichrist and his Greatest Persecution. For example, Mark Hitchcock, one of the most popular teachers of Pre-tribulationism writes:

> If the Rapture occurs in your lifetime, your future will be very different depending on which view is correct. Will you be here to see the Antichrist? Will you be forced to choose whether to take his mark?.. Or will you be in heaven during this time, experiencing a glorious fellowship with the Lamb and His sheep? [2]

It is obvious which alternative is more attractive. We would all rather avoid what Jesus called **the greatest persecution** of His people that will ever occur in the history of humanity (Matt 24:21). But as Paul warned us in 2 Timothy above, we cannot determine **sound doctrine ... in accordance** with our **own desires**. If we do, we **will turn away ... from the truth and will turn aside to myths.**

This is precisely what has happened in the Church's response to the Pre-tribulation Rapture teaching. Perhaps the primary reason it is so popular is because it promises we will not have to experience the suffering that Christ said would occur in the Endtimes.

It is feared that one motivation for teaching Pre-tribulationism is to please people rather than God. If so, then they are among those teachers that enable Christians to **accumulate for themselves teachers in accordance to their own desires** (2 Tim 4:3).

This dysfunctional and unbiblical dynamic in Pre-tribulational churches has resulted in what Van Kampen described when he wrote:

> There is, however, one other element that contributes to the reluctance of some of these Christian leaders to change their view on the timing of Christ's return for His own, even if they know in the depths of their hearts that their pretribulation position is either wrong or, at best, weak.
>
> Teachers gain significance through what they teach. And if for years they have taught something as truth—and in some cases written books about it—then no matter how overwhelming the argument against their position becomes, it is hard for them to say, "I was wrong."
>
> Like [the very influential 20th century Bible teacher Donald G.] Barnhouse, they may admit reservations privately, but not publicly. Scores of men in Christian leadership have told me that if they were to publicly teach the Prewrath Rapture position, they would lose their jobs. [3]

Because of Pre-tribulationism's popularity, the reader might be wondering what Bible verses are used to support it. It is not exaggerating to say <u>there is not a single verse in Scripture that teaches what Pre-tribulationism claims</u>. Again, its teaching is this: The very first event of the Endtimes is a "secret and silent" Return of Christ to "rapture" the Church so that it does not experience The Beginning of Birth Pains or the Antichrist and his Greatest Persecution. Again, there is not a single verse in Scripture that teaches this.

In fact, the Pre-tribulationist Mark Hitchcock admits: "No single verse says Jesus is coming to rapture His saints before the seven-year Tribulation." [4] That is a remarkable statement. But it is true.

And this fact about Pre-tribulationism can be contrasted with the many NT Scriptures that clearly teach the Pre-wrath Rescue position explained in this book. As demonstrated in previous chapters, these include Christ's Endtimes Teaching, Paul's Thessalonian epistles, and Revelation chapters 6-7. All of these consistently teach that The Beginning of Birth Pains and The Greatest Persecution all occur <u>before</u> the Church's Rescue. Therefore, it would seem the best argument for Pre-tribulationism is the Church's fear of suffering, not something in God's Word.

The following are 13 primary **myths** taught by Pre-tribulationism. They represent its most popular and foundational arguments: [5]

Myth #1: The events described in the first 28 verses of Christ's Endtimes Teaching have nothing to do with the Church.

Myth #2: The Church will never encounter the Antichrist or experience The Greatest Persecution.

Myth #3: Christ will come in a "secret & silent rapture."

Myth #4: The Church is not mentioned in Revelation chapters 4-17 as being on Earth.

Myth #5: Christ's Return for the Church and His visible Coming are described as two different events in Scripture, separated by 7 years.

Myth #6: Christ's Return and the Church's Rescue described in Christ's Endtimes Teaching is merely a gathering of Jews at the Battle of Armageddon.

Myth #7: God's Endtimes plan for Israel and the Church are completely separate and do not overlap in any way.

Myth #8: A literal interpretation of prophetic Scripture leads to Pre-tribulationism.

Myth #9: The "tribulation" is Christ's Wrath which we are promised to be rescued from.

Myth #10: The Rapture will happen at any moment, without any warning signs.

Myth #11: Unbelievers will be experiencing "peace and safety" before Christ's Return

Myth #12: The "Restrainer" of the Antichrist in 2 Thessalonians 2:6-7 is the Holy Spirit, and His removal refers to the "Rapture" of the Church

Myth #13: Revelation 3:10 describes the Church's Rescue.

Pre-tribulation **myths** #1-#8 above will be briefly discussed in this chapter because they have already been refuted in previous chapters of *Christ's Endtimes Teaching*. Myth #9 regarding the nature and timing of Christ's Wrath is a fundamental issue in disproving Pre-tribulationism and will be explained in chapter 14. Myths #10-#13 are addressed in chapter 15. Finally, the practical and spiritual harm of Pre-tribulationism and other views is discussed in chapter 16.

Obviously, this is a lot of information. That is why 3 entire chapters are devoted to explaining and biblically refuting Pre-tribulationism. Again, you can explain the truth well in a paragraph. But it requires pages to refute error. As a result of this study, it will become clear that all the arguments for the most popular view of the Endtimes are all **myths**, rather than biblical doctrine.

B) 7 Pre-tribulation myths already addressed in *Christ's Endtimes Teaching*

B.1) Myth #1: The events described in the first 28 verses of Christ's Endtimes Teaching have nothing to do with the Church

This myth is required to be true for Pre-tribulationism to have any validity. As discussed thoroughly in chapter 3 of *Christ's Endtimes Teaching*, if there is even one Endtime event described by Christ in Matthew 24:4-31, that Christians in the Church will experience on Earth, then Pre-tribulationism completely falls apart.

Contrary to Pre-tribulationism, Jesus said three times that His Endtimes Teaching applied to **the elect** (Matt 24:22, 24, 31), a term used for God's people in the Church throughout the NT. Therefore, this essential Pre-tribulational myth is proven to be unbiblical.

Myth #1 in Pretribulationism is that the events described in the first 28 verses of Christ's Endtimes Teaching have nothing to do with the Church. The truth is this: All of Christ's Endtimes Teaching applies to the Church because the Last Generation Church will experience everything Jesus described in his sermon.

B.2) Myth #2: The Church will never encounter the Antichrist or experience The Greatest Persecution

Again, this is probably the most attractive thing about Pre-tribulationism: It's promise that the Church will never experience the events of the "tribulation." However, chapters 3-8 of this book clearly and biblically refute this myth of Pre-tribulationism. Specific Scriptures that clearly refute it are Matthew 24:29-31 and 2 Thessalonians 2:1-4.

This popular myth claims that the Real Christ comes to Rescue the Church <u>before</u> the Antichrist comes to persecute the Church. That is not biblical. Instead, Jesus and Paul taught that the Antichrist comes to <u>persecute</u> the Church <u>before</u> the Real Christ comes to Rescue the Church.

Myth #2 in Pretribulationism is that the Church will never encounter the Antichrist or experience The Greatest Persecution. <u>The truth</u> is this: The Last Generation Church will suffer the greatest persecution in the history of humanity.

B.3) Myth #3: Christ will come in a "secret & silent rapture"

It is difficult to understand how Pre-tribulationism even came to this belief in Scripture. This is a foundational theme of Lahaye's *Left Behind* novels and Pre-tribulationism. The fictional books are famous for portraying Christians instantly and mysteriously missing from airplanes, cars, etc. This false teaching is that the unbelieving world will be clueless as to where all the Christians have gone after the "rapture."

Such an idea may make a wonderful storyline for fictional novels. However, there is <u>not</u> a single verse of Scripture that describes Christ's Return or the Church's Rescue as a "secret, silent" event. Therefore, without this foundational argument, Pre-tribulationism is completely false. The truth is that Christ's Return for the Church's Rescue will be visible to the whole world. Even the classic "rapture" text states:

> **For <u>the Lord himself will come down from heaven</u>** [and be seen by the whole world], **with a <u>loud</u> command, with the voice of the archangel and with the <u>trumpet call</u> of God, and the dead in Christ will rise first. After that, we who are still alive and are left will be caught up together with them in the clouds to meet the Lord in the air.** (1 Thess 4:16-17 NIV)

Contrary to a fundamental claim of Pre-tribulationism, this is <u>not</u> describing a "secret, silent rapture" but a very visible and **loud** Rescue of the Church. The Bible consistently describes Christ's Return for His Church in this way (cf. Matt 16:27; 24:27-31; Acts 1:9-11; 1 Thess 4:15-17; 2 Thess 1:6-7; 2 Tim 4:8; Tit 2:13; 1 Pet 1:13; Rev 1:7; 6:16-17).

The most common Scripture offered to suggest a "secret & silent rapture" is 1 Corinthians 15:51-52 where Paul writes:

> **But let me reveal to you a wonderful secret. We will not all die, but we will all be transformed! <u>It will happen in a moment, in the blink of an eye</u>, when <u>the last trumpet is blown</u>. For <u>when the trumpet sounds</u>, those who have died will be raised to live forever. And we who are living will also be transformed.** (NLT)

Obviously, this passage describes the Church's Rescue and the First Resurrection. It also describes the transformation of our bodies happening quickly as **in a moment, in the blink of an eye**. Pre-tribulationism claims that because our bodies **will all be transformed ... in the blink of an eye** during the "rapture," that this means the "rapture" is a "secret and silent" event.

First, just because the transformation of our bodies will occur <u>quickly</u> in the "rapture," does not mean it will happen "secretly and silently."

Secondly, those who teach this seem to intentionally ignore something very clear in the text. The Apostle adds that when the First Resurrection occurs **the last trumpet** will be **blown** and make **trumpet sounds**. This is the same **trumpet call of God** that Paul describes in 1 Thessalonians 4:16 that will occur with the "rapture." It is also the same **loud trumpet sound** that Jesus said would occur when **He will send out His angels** to **lift up and gather together God's elect people in the sky, from everywhere on Earth** (Matt 24:31).

Myth #3 in Pretribulationism is that Christ will come in a "secret & silent rapture." <u>The truth</u> is this: Christ's Return for the Church's Rescue will be visible and known to the whole world. As Jesus said: **For as lightning that comes from the east is visible even in the west, so will be the coming of the Son of Man** (Matt 24:27 NIV) when He Rescues His Church. [6]

B.4) Myth #4: The Church is not mentioned in Revelation chapters 4-17 as being on Earth

Many supporters of Pre-tribulationism suggest this is among the most important reasons to accept this view. For example, John MacArthur writes:

> For many reasons, the pre-tribulation view seems most faithful to New Testament teaching. <u>First of all</u>, chapters 2-3 of Revelation speak of the church on earth, and chapters 4-5 speak of the church in heaven. But beginning with chapter 6, which introduces the Tribulation, there is no further mention of the church until chapter 18. [7]

Frankly, one is astounded with a statement like this from such a rightly respected Bible teacher. As demonstrated earlier, the many mentions of **bond-servants** and **saints** throughout the NT and the Revelation clearly refer to members of the Church (cf. ch. 6, sec. A). It seems the only places in Revelation that Pre-tribulationism wants to exclude the Church is where it describes Christians being persecuted by the Antichrist in chapters 12-13 of the book.

Again, Pre-tribulationism is the popular view that the Church is "raptured" before any of the painful events in Revelation occur. One of the most common verses to support this view is Revelation 4:1-2:

> **After this I looked, and there before me was a door standing open in heaven. And the voice I had first heard speaking to me like a trumpet** [Jesus Christ] **said, <u>"Come up here, and I will show you what must take place after this</u>." At once I was in the Spirit, and there before me was a throne in heaven with someone sitting on it.** (NIV)

Many supporters of Pre-tribulationism have claimed this is one of the clearest verses in Scripture supporting their view that the "rapture" occurs before any of the subsequent events in the Revelation. For example, Tim Lahaye writes:

> Inasmuch as John was the last remaining apostle and a member of the universal Church, his elevation to heaven is a picture of the Rapture of the Church just before the Tribulation begins. [8]

What is a primary reason Lahaye gives for reading so much into the command **"Come up here"**? He writes: "The absence of any mention of the Church in the rest of Revelation." [9] But that has been clearly demonstrated above to be simply false.

Contrary to Lahaye, we do not have the freedom to simply insert whatever meaning we want into the text in order to fit our preconceived scheme.

The text itself explains why Jesus told the Apostle to **"Come up here."** Jesus said to him, **"I will show you what must take place after this."** The Apostle was elevated to Heaven to receive the rest of the Revelation. That's it.

It is interesting to note that the two Endtime Prophets are given the identical heavenly command to **"Come up here"** (Rev 11:12). Pre-tribulationism never claims this has anything to do with the "rapture."

As explained in chapter 6 (sec. B.2), Revelation 7:9, 14 is a much better description of the "rapture." It would seem the only reason it is rejected as such by Pre-tribulationism is because it describes the Church's Rescue occurring after **the great persecution** (v. 14), something Pre-tribulationists cannot accept. [10]

Myth #4 in Pre-tribulationism is that the Church is not mentioned in Revelation chapters 4-17 as being on Earth. The truth is that Revelation chapters 12-13 describe Christ's **bond servants** and God's **saints** who will be the Last Generation Church, being persecuted by the Antichrist on Earth.

B.5) Myth #5: Christ's Return for the Church and His visible Coming are described as two different events in Scripture, separated by 7 years

Pre-tribulationism claims the initial appearance of Christ's Return occurs separate from the Church's Rescue. More than that, this false teaching claims that Christ's visible Return occurs 7 years after the Church's Rescue. This is because it is claimed that the Church's Rescue occurs in a "secret, silent, rapture" at the beginning of what can be called "Daniel's Last 7 Years" ("70th Week"). And then it is claimed that Christ's first appearance occurs at the end of those 7 years.

Indeed, Pre-tribulationism is rather complicated. Instead of trying to explain its errors more clearly, let us be reminded of the truth about Christ's Second Coming.

Earlier in chapter 9 (sec. A) the following primary points were demonstrated:

- There is one Second Coming of Christ. But within His Coming, Christ will visibly appear at two different times.
- In Christ's <u>first</u> appearance He comes <u>for</u> the Church's Rescue (cf. Matt 24:29-31). In Christ's <u>second</u> appearance He comes <u>with</u> His Church for the Battle of Armageddon (cf. Rev 19:11-21).
- In between these two appearances of Christ on Earth, He remains in Heaven with the Church while His Angels execute His Wrath on Earth during a considerable but unknown period of time. The Pre-wrath Rescue position does <u>not</u> teach that the Church immediately returns to Earth after its Rescue.
- Scripture does <u>not</u> tell us how much time elapses between Christ's two appearances, or how long Christ's Wrath lasts.

These biblical conclusions were illustrated in the following graphic:

Christ's Two Appearances in His Second Coming

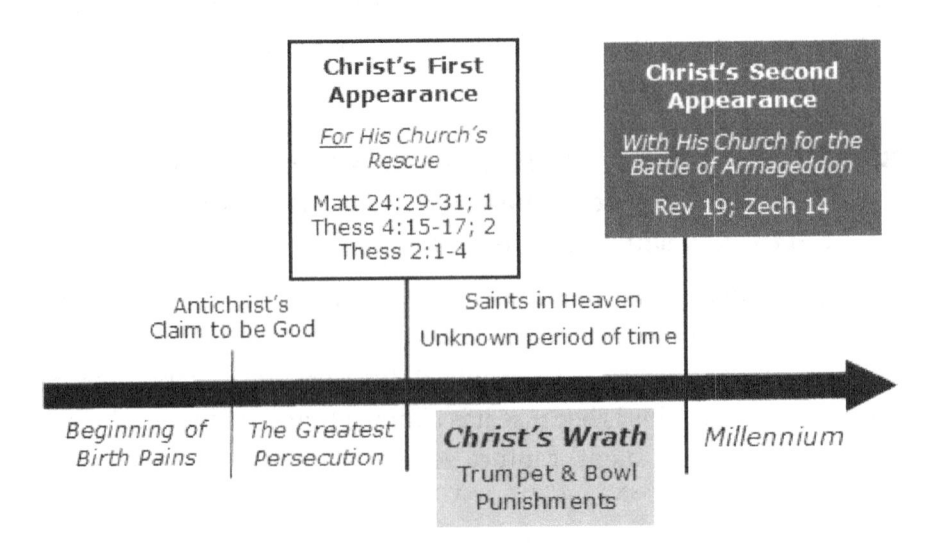

Christ's First Appearance	Christ's Second Appearance
For His Church's Rescue	*With* His Church for the Battle of Armageddon
Matt 24:29-31; 1 Thess 4:15-17; 2 Thess 2:1-4	Rev 19; Zech 14

Antichrist's Claim to be God

Saints in Heaven — Unknown period of time

Beginning of Birth Pains | The Greatest Persecution | **Christ's Wrath** — Trumpet & Bowl Punishments | Millennium

With these biblical truths, we can address more errors in Pre-tribulationism. For example, Hitchcock writes:
> There are three key future events that comprise God's distinct prophetic plan for the church: the Rapture, the judgment seat of Christ, and the marriage of the Lamb. The church will be caught up to the Father's house, each believer will be rewarded, and then the bride will be presented to her Bridegroom. <u>All this will happen before the church returns with Christ to earth at His second coming</u> [7 years later at the Battle of Armageddon]. [11]

Not only are these statements complicated, like most of Pre-tribulationism, they are unbiblical. Let's again go to Scripture.

Pretribulationism places The Great White Throne Evaluation between the two appearances of Christ, suggesting it occurs during "Daniel's Last 7 Years" ("70th Week"). But the Bible does <u>not</u> require this and argues against it. Let us remember how Paul described this event:

For we must <u>all</u> appear before the judgment seat of Christ, so that <u>each of us</u> may receive what is due us for the things done while in the body, whether good or bad. (2 Cor 5:10)

Jesus Christ will personally meet with every single person who has ever lived and evaluate everything in their life (cf. the **books**; Rev 20:11-13). How many people will that be? One source suggests that would be "about 117 billion" humans if the world ended today. [12] If Christ spends even one hour with each person that would require over 320 million "years." All of this is why The Great White Throne Evaluation occurs <u>after</u> Eternity begins.

This is implied in Revelation chapters 20-21. After a description of the end of the 1,000 year Millennium (cf. Rev 20:7-10) we read: **Then I saw a great white throne** [where The Great White Throne Evaluation will occur] **and him who was seated on it. The earth and the heavens fled from his presence, and there was no place for them** (Rev 20:11).

The absence of the **earth and the heavens** in Revelation 20 suggests at this point that **the first earth had passed away** and **a new heaven and a new earth** exist at this point in "time" as described in chapter 21 (v. 1). But there really is no "time" at this point because Eternity has begun.

Therefore, it would seem that perhaps for the first several million "years" of Eternity, The Great White Throne Evaluation will be occurring. Why would this seem impractical? This event is very important to Christ, and again, time has no meaning at all in eternity!

This explanation is better than how Pre-tribulationism describes this. It claims "the Judgment Seat of Christ" occurs during some supposed 7 years between the Church's Rescue and Christ's second appearance at the Battle of Armageddon. To make such a view practical, Tim Lahaye in his fictional novels suggests Jesus supernaturally meets personally with millions of people <u>all at the same time</u>.

Such a fanciful explanation is <u>not</u> necessary if we understand The Great White Throne Evaluation, which is "the Judgment Seat of Christ" occurs after Eternity begins. [13] But more importantly, it does <u>not</u> reflect the personal and individual nature of our evaluation with Christ described in 2 Corinthians 5:10.

In addition, the Pre-tribulational teaching that Daniel's Last 7 Years ("70th Week") begins with the Church's Rescue is not biblical. Daniel's Last 7 Years begins with Antichrist's Religious Covenant with many (Dan 9:27). This will occur sometime during The Beginning of Birth Pains, seven years <u>before</u> Christ's Return to Rescue His Church. This will be discussed further in the book, *The Beginning of Birth Pains*.

Another error of Pre-tribulationism is to claim that NT references to "the day of Christ" can be clearly distinguished between references to "the day of the Lord." It is further claimed that the "Christ" references refer to Christ's "secret, silent, rapture" and the "Lord" references to His second appearance at the Battle of Armageddon.

Common sense would tell us such a distinction between "Christ" and "Lord" is very unlikely. In fact, when one studies the relevant verses, it becomes obvious there is no clear distinction at all. NT scholar Robert Gundry has provided a lengthy study of the issue and summarizes his research as follows:

> A distinction is often made between a pre-tribulational "day of Christ" and a following "day of the Lord." The phrases "day of

Christ" and "day" with a compound appellative appear in 1 Cor. 1:8; 5:5 (perhaps); 2 Cor. 1:14; Phil. 1:6, 10; 2:16.

The arbitrariness of the proposed distinction becomes evident in the following observations: In not one passage is the "day of Christ" construed with the rapture or a pre-tribulational coming of Christ (as Pretribulationism claims).

In the one reference where Paul connects the phrase with other eschatological terms (1 Cor. 1:8), those terms are at least ambiguous if not weighted on the post-tribulational [rapture] side…

Of the remaining five occurrences, there are four different combinations of the component names in the full title of Christ: "day of our Lord Jesus Christ" (1 Cor. 1:8); "day of our Lord Jesus" (2 Cor. 1:14); "day of Christ Jesus" or "Jesus Christ" (Phil. 1:6; but again manuscripts vary); "day of Christ" (Phil. 1:10; 2:16). The variations suggest that we do not have a single technical phrase in contradistinction to the day of the Lord, but an expansion of the basic term "day of the Lord." [14]

Myth #5 in Pre-tribulationism is: Christ's Return for the Church and His visible Coming are described as two different events in Scripture, separated by 7 years. The truth is that there will be an initial appearance of Christ to Rescue the Church (cf. Matt 24:29-31), and then after an unspecified period of time at the end of Christ's Wrath (and the Trumpet and Bowl Punishments), Christ will appear again, with the Church, for the Battle of Armageddon (cf. Rev 19:11-21).

B.6) Myth #6: Christ's Return and the Church's Rescue described in Christ's Endtimes Teaching is merely a gathering of Jews at the Battle of Armageddon

In Christ's Endtimes Teaching He said:

"He will send out His angels with a loud trumpet sound, and they will lift up and gather together God's elect people from one end of the sky to the other, from everywhere on Earth." (Matt 24:31 [15])

As demonstrated throughout *Christ's Endtimes Teaching*, Pre-tribulationism completely misinterprets this Scripture and practically ignores it. This would seem to be because of a bias against it. In chapter 3 (sec. A) there was a warning against the distorting effect of approaching Endtime texts with a preconceived bias.

That distorting bias would seem to be illustrated by the eminent Dallas Theological Seminary Professor John Walvoord when he wrote regarding the correct interpretation of Matthew 24:

> What is often overlooked in the discussion [of Endtime events] is that we lack a specific statement that the rapture of the church occurs at the time of Christ's second coming to set up his kingdom. [16]

On the contrary, in Matthew 24:31 Jesus could hardly be clearer that He is describing a "rapture" of **God's elect people** (*eklektous*) at the time of His coming.

Likewise, it is difficult to understand how Walvoord can write:

> The two essentials of the rapture of the church are resurrection of the dead in Christ and translation of living Christians, as brought out clearly in central passages such as 1 Thess 4:13–18 and 1 Cor 15:51–58.
>
> The prophecy in Matthew [24], however, says nothing of either resurrection or <u>translation</u> [into the sky] and refers only to the gathering of the elect [on the Earth?]. [17]

On the contrary, Christ was describing a gathering in **the sky**, not on the Earth. Also, Walvoord ignores that Jesus mentions a **loud trumpet sound**, just as Paul does in his description of the "rapture" (cf. 1 Thess 4:16), and the resurrection (cf. 1 Cor 15:52).

Unfortunately, Pre-tribulationism typically interprets Matt 24:31 in the following way: 1) This is describing only a gathering of Jews on the Earth; 2) This is Christ's Return at the Battle of Armageddon. This latter claim was thoroughly refuted in chapter 9 (sec. A) and illustrated in the graphic above of Christ's two appearances.

Regarding the claim that Matthew 24:31 is only describing a gathering of Jews on the Earth, more can be said. Scripture does predict a world-wide gathering of saved Jews after Christ's Return (cf. Deut 30:4; Isa 27:12-13; Jer 32:37; Ezek 34:11-13). But there are several reasons to distinguish the gathering of Jews described in the OT, from the gathering of the Church described in Matthew 24:31.

First, it was demonstrated earlier that Matthew 24:31 and 1 Thessalonians 4:13-17 are describing the same event (cf. ch. 5, sec. A). No Pre-tribulationists contend that Paul was describing a mere gathering of Jews in Thessalonians. Therefore, they are in error to claim this is the case with Matthew 24:31.

Second, the gathering of the Church in Matthew 24:31 lifts His people **to meet the Lord in the air** to **be with the Lord forever** (1 Thess 4:17). As reflected in the OT verses referenced above, the gathering of Jews predicted in the OT will bring them to the nation of Israel.

Myth #6 in Pre-tribulationism is: Christ's Return and the Church's Rescue described in Christ's Endtimes Teaching is merely a gathering of Jews at the Battle of Armageddon. The truth is this: Matthew 24:31 is describing Christ's Return for the Church.

B.7) Myth #7: God's Endtimes plan for Israel and the Church are completely separate and do not overlap in any way

This is a foundational belief of Pre-tribulationism. Lahaye writes: Separating Israel and the Church is one of the major keys to rightly understanding Bible prophecy... If you do not make that distinction, it is unlikely you will see a pre-Tribulation Rapture of the Church." [18]

That's quite true. If you do not completely separate God's Endtime plan for Israel and the Church, then you will not "see a Pre-Tribulation Rapture of the Church." The fact is that the Scriptures clearly teach that both the Church and the Jews will be persecuted by the Antichrist in the Endtimes. For example, Jesus said The Greatest Persecution would involve **God's elect people** (Matt 24:22, 24, 31) which includes the Church. However, it will begin in **Jerusalem** (Luke 21:21, 24) and **Judea** (Matt 24:15-16) and include the Jews.

This is confirmed in Revelation 12 which says of the Satan-indwelled Antichrist: **he pursued the woman** [Israel] **who had given birth to the male child** [Jesus] (v. 13). Clearly he will be persecuting the Jews in Israel. However, the prophecy goes on to state that after Israel is miraculously rescued from the Antichrist (cf. vs. 14-16) He will **wage war against the rest of her** [Israel's spiritual]

offspring [the Church]—**those who keep God's commands and hold fast their testimony about Jesus** (v. 17).

The only way Pre-tribulationism can argue against this is to conveniently claim that passages referring to Endtime persecution have nothing to do with the Church, but only Israel.

This foundational argument for Pre-tribulationism (and its theological parent, Dispensationalism [19]) has been disproven multiple times in previous chapters of *Christ's Endtimes Teaching*. In chapters 3, 6, and 7 sections were provided proving that Christ's Endtimes Teaching (Matt 24), Revelation (chs. 6-7, 12-13), and Daniel (chs. 7, 9, 12), all apply to the Church. This is devastating to the Pre-tribulation position.

For example, perhaps the most foundational claim by Pre-tribulationism is that Daniel 9:24-27 has no application for the Church. More specifically, it is often stated that the "69 weeks" predicted in this passage does not apply to the Church. Therefore, it is claimed that Daniel's "70th week," describing activities of the Antichrist, cannot apply to the Church. But as stated earlier:

> First, the prophecy of the "69 weeks" clearly includes God's plan for the Church. It culminates with **the Anointed One** (Christ) being **put to death** (v. 26). Does anyone want to claim this prediction of Christ's crucifixion of does not apply to the Church in any way? (ch. 7, sec. B.1)

Unfortunately, as a Pre-tribulationist, MacArthur does want to claim that this prediction of the crucifixion of Christ in Dan 9:26 does not apply to the Church in any way. He writes:

> That prophecy of Daniel [that Christ would be killed] was given to and about Israel, and it seems inappropriate to involve the church in the last week (the seven-year Tribulation) when it clearly was not involved in the first 69. [20]

On the contrary, if the culmination of the "69 weeks" was Christ's death and applies to the Church, then we can expect elements of the "70th week" to as well. There are no Scriptures that teach otherwise. Even the Pre-tribulationist Walvoord admits: "The natural interpretation of [Dan 9:26] is that it refers to the death of Jesus Christ on the cross." [21]

Pre-tribulationism seems to completely ignore what the NT teaches on the relationship between the Church and Israel. The Apostle Paul wrote:

> **Don't forget that you Gentiles** [in the Church] **used to be outsiders... You were excluded from citizenship among the people of Israel, and you did not know** [nor were you participants in] **the covenant promises God had made to them** [Israel, including promises about the Endtimes]...
>
> **But now you have been united with Christ Jesus... He made peace between Jews** [Israel] **and Gentiles** [the Church] **by creating in himself one new people from the two groups.** (Eph 2:11-13, 15 NLT)

Granted, the relationship between God's Endtimes plan for Israel and the Church is one of the most complex topics of Scripture. [22] But contrary to Pre-tribulationism (and Dispensationalism), Israel and the Church have been united in at least some elements of God's Endtimes plan for them. Any view of the prophetic Scriptures that automatically and completely separates God's Endtimes plan for Israel and the Church is not biblical. [23]

The unity of Israel and the Church is clearly portrayed in Revelation. For example, **twenty-four elders** in Heaven are mentioned five times. They are introduced in chapter 4 where we read: **Surrounding the throne** [of God] **were twenty-four other thrones, and seated on them were twenty-four elders. They were dressed in white and had crowns of gold on their heads** (v. 4). Not surprisingly, there has been considerable debate about who these elders are. But the best interpretation seems to be that they represent the 12 OT Patriarchs and the 12 NT Apostles. This is confirmed in Revelation 21 where we read of the New Jerusalem:

> **It had a great, high wall with twelve gates... On the gates were written the names of the twelve tribes** [Patriarchs] **of Israel... The wall of the city had twelve foundations, and on them were the names of the twelve apostles of the Lamb.** (Rev 21:12, 14 NIV).

Clearly, the consummation of God's plan is to bring Israel and the Church together for all of eternity. It is suggested this unity is also portrayed in the **twenty-four elders**.

Pre-tribulationism itself seems to violate a complete distinction between Israel and the Church in the Endtimes in its interpretation of the **144,000 from all the tribes of Israel** who will be **sealed** at Christ's Return (Rev 7:4). According to Pre-tribulationism, these Jews will be super-evangelists who lead a multitude of new Christians into the New Covenant. Of course, the claim is that these Christians are <u>not</u> members of Christ's Church, which is clearly not biblical. Nevertheless, the suggested mixture of Jews and Christians at this time argues against the typical (and Dispensational) view that God's program for these two groups is completely separate.

Why does Pre-tribulationism want to completely separate God's Endtime plan for Israel and the Church? For one reason, it allows them to claim the first 28 verses of Christ's Endtimes Teaching has nothing to do with the Church.

Myth #7 in Pretribulationism is that God's Endtimes plan for Israel and the Church are completely separate and do not overlap in any way. <u>The truth</u> is this: Both the Church and Israel will be persecuted by the Antichrist, which is one example of God's Endtimes plan for them overlapping in some way.

B.8) Myth #8: A literal interpretation of prophetic Scripture leads to Pre-tribulationism

Fortunately, Pre-tribulationism has been a foremost defender of interpreting prophetic Scripture literally. Lahaye writes:

> Never should one resort to a figurative, symbolic, or secondary meaning of any passage of Scripture unless there is warrant for the same in the context. [24]

This is good advice. Accordingly, Pre-tribulationism has provided many legitimate critiques of only interpreting prophetic Scripture metaphorically or symbolically. As a result, they have correctly exposed many biblical errors in other views including Amillennialism (i.e. fulfillment of prophecy is primarily spiritual) and Preterism (i.e. prophecy has already been fulfilled).

However, Pre-tribulationism has assumed that after disproving these views, that their position is the only one that reflects a literal and logical approach to prophetic Scripture. In other words, it is often implied that by merely demonstrating the importance of interpreting Scripture literally, and disproving other views that ignore this, that Pre-tribulationism is proven to be biblical.

In response, two things can be said. First, Pre-tribulationism at times violates their own rules of hermeneutics. An example is the belief that the command to John in Revelation 4 to **"Come up here"** (v. 1) is the "rapture" of the Church. The Pre-tribulationist Lahaye was quoted above to say: "Never should one resort to a ... secondary meaning of any passage of Scripture unless there is warrant for the same in the context." Yet as noted above, (see B.4), Lahaye violates his own rule of interpretation.

The second thing that can be said about the myth that a literal interpretation of prophetic Scripture leads to Pre-tribulationism is this. The Pre-wrath Rescue position explained in *Christ's Endtimes Teaching* also emphasizes a literal interpretation of prophetic Scripture.

Myth #8 in Pre-tribulationism is that a literal interpretation of prophetic Scripture leads to the Pre-tribulational view. The truth is that a literal interpretation of prophetic Scripture also leads to the more biblical Pre-wrath Rescue position.

---

[1] Seminaries and Bible Colleges especially promoting Pre-tribulationism include Dallas Theological Seminary, The Master's Seminary, Talbot School of Theology, Grace Theological Seminary, and Liberty University. Prominent teachers promoting Pre-tribulationism include John MacArthur, John Walvoord, and many popular radio teachers including Charles Swindoll and David Jeremiah.

[2] Hitchcock, *End*, 135.

[3] Van Kampen, *Rapture*, Kindle loc. 2675ff.

[4] Ibid. 136.

[5] Just to make sure that all the important arguments for Pre-tribulationism are addressed, we will note those proposed by Dr. Richard Mayhue. He is

the Research Professor of Theology Emeritus at The Master's Seminary where the rightly respected Bible teacher John MacArthur also serves.

In the Master's Seminary journal (vol. 10, num. 2) Mayhue writes an article entitled "Why a Pretribulational Rapture?" Because of his standing as a Bible scholar one would expect the very best arguments for Pre-tribulationism in his article. One section is entitled: "Will the 'Rapture' be Pre-, Mid-, or Post-Daniel's 70th Week?" Notice he does not even include the Pre-wrath Rescue position in his article.

Mayhue has seven arguments he claims will support Pre-tribulationism. #1 is: "The Church Is Not Mentioned in Revelation 6-18 as Being on Earth." This argument was refuted earlier in ch. 6, sec. A, and in this chapter (12, sec. B.4) where it was pointed out that God's **servants** and **saints** are repeatedly mentioned throughout Revelation and clearly refer to the Church.

Arguments #2 and #5 from Mayhue are meant to refute Post-tribulationism (#2: "The Rapture Is Rendered Inconsequential if it is Posttribulational First; #5: "John 14:1-3 Parallels 1 Thessalonians 4:13–18). The Pre-wrath Rescue view would generally agree with Mayhue on these points. However, his arguments against Post-tribulationism do nothing to refute the Pre-wrath Rescue position.

Mayhue's third argument is: "The Epistles Contain No Preparatory Warnings of an Impending Tribulation for Church-Age Believers." First, Mayhue completely ignores the warnings to the Church in Christ's Endtimes Teaching as all Pre-tribulationists do. Secondly, Paul wrote: **But mark this: There will be terrible times in the last days** including people who would be **brutal** and **treacherous** (2 Tim 3:1, 3-4 NIV) toward other people, certainly including Christians. Thirdly, if there is a lack of "warnings" regarding a "tribulation" in the NT epistles, it may be because the early Church believed it was already experiencing Endtime events. Therefore, they did not need a "preparatory warning" of "tribulation." This was certainly the case in the Thessalonian epistles.

Mayhue's fourth argument is: "First Thessalonians 4:13–18 Demands a Pretribulational Rapture." He supports this by stating:

> One would expect the Thessalonians to be joyous over the fact that loved ones are home with the Lord and will not have to endure the horrors of the tribulation. But the Thessalonians are actually grieving because they fear their loved ones have missed the rapture. Only a pretribulational rapture accounts for this grief.

This is not true. These Christians were grieving because their loved ones had died. And why would these Christians "fear their loved ones had missed the rapture" if their loved ones were already dead?

Secondly, Mayhue writes:
> One would expect the Thessalonians to be grieving over their own impending trial rather than grieving over loved ones [why? They died]. Furthermore, they would be inquisitive about their own future doom. But the Thessalonians have no fears or questions about the coming tribulation.

This is only presumption, and they certainly had "fears" and "questions" when Paul wrote his second letter to them (cf. ch. 2).

Mayhue goes on:
> Third, one would expect Paul, even in the absence of interest or questions by the Thessalonians, to have provided instructions and exhortation for such a supreme test, which would make their present tribulation seem microscopic in comparison. First Thessalonians 4 fits only the model of a pretribulational rapture. It is incompatible with any other time for the rapture.

Mayhue ignores the fact that in Paul's second letter to this same church he "provided" considerable "instructions and exhortation" about The Greatest Persecution (cf. 2 Thess 1:6-10; 2:1-11). The reason the Apostle went into so much detail about the Antichrist in 2 Thess 2 was because he clearly anticipated that the Church will experience these things (cf. esp. 2 Thess 2:1-4). Mayhue's last statement above is false.

Mayhue's sixth argument for Pre-tribulationism is: "Revelation 3:10 Promises that the Church Will Be Removed Before Daniel's 70th Week."

Unfortunately, this fine scholar makes the classic Pre-tribulational mistake of defining "Daniel's 70th Week" as Christ's Wrath. "Daniel's 70th Week," the last half of which is after Antichrist's Claim to be God, will include The Greatest Persecution (cf. Matt 24:15-22). Therefore, "Daniel's 70th Week" is not synonymous with Christ's Wrath. In fact, "Daniel's 70th Week" will end with Christ's Return and the beginning of Christ's Wrath. As argued elsewhere in ch. 15, sec. D, Rev 3:10 seems to be promising Endtimes Christians divine protection from the damning temptation of worshipping the Antichrist.

Mayhue's last argument is that: "The Nature of Events at Christ's Posttribulational Coming Differs from that of the Rapture." Again, some of his points refute Post-tribulationism but not the Pre-wrath Rescue position which would agree with some of his points. For example, he concludes: "These differences demand that the rapture occur at a time significantly different from that of the final event [and appearance] of Christ's second coming." Indeed, there are differences between Christ's first appearance to Rescue the Church, and a second appearance sometime later where the Church joins Him for the Battle of Armageddon. This is discussed further in *CET* (ch. 9, sec. A).

However, Mayhue makes several statements here that are not biblical. For example, he writes: "At the rapture, Christ gathers His own (1 Thess 4:16-17), but at the final event of the second coming, angels gather the elect (Matt 24:31). Because of his misunderstanding of Matt 24:31, he thinks there is a difference between Christ's "own" and "the elect." This Pre-tribulational myth will be addressed in ch. 3, sec. E and ch. 15, sec. E.

Secondly, Mayhue misinterprets Matt 24:40-41 which is discussed thoroughly in ch. 4, sec. C.3.

Thirdly, Mayhue shows his dependence on denying that Christ's Endtimes Teaching applies to the Church when he writes:

> Finally, the rapture is not mentioned in either of the most detailed second coming texts—Matthew 24 and Revelation 19. This is to be expected in light of the observations above, because the pretribulational rapture will have occurred seven years earlier.

How such an otherwise fine Bible scholar cannot see "the rapture" in Matt 24:31 is difficult to understand.

[6] The respected Baptist theologian Millard Erickson writes in response to the idea that there will be a "secret" return of Christ: "There seems little doubt, upon examining the biblical data, that Jesus' return will be personal and bodily and thus perceivable and unmistakable" (*EDT*, 993).

G. Campbell Morgan, one of the most respected Bible teachers of the last century stated emphatically:

> The phrase 'secret Rapture' has to me for a longtime been a very objectionable one, and utterly unwarranted in its wording, and in what it is made to stand for by the teaching of Scripture. (quoted in *The Blessed Hope*, George E. Ladd, p. 55)

[7] MacArthur, *MNTC*, Matt 24, underlining added.

[8] Lahaye, *Revelation*, 99.

[9] Ibid. 100.

[10] Gundry shares another reason that Pre-tribulationism's view of John's translation to Heaven is incorrect:

> John does not maintain his heavenly viewpoint throughout Revelation, as we see from 10:1; 11:1ff.; 13:1; 14:1; 18:1. He was transported back and forth between heavenly and earthly settings. Has John suddenly lost his symbolic value as representative of the Church? Or will the Church be raptured only to commute between heaven and earth during the tribulation? There is no convincing reason why the seer's being 'in the Spirit' and being called into heaven typifies the rapture of the church any more than his being taken into the wilderness to view Babylon indicates that the church is there in exile. (*Tribulation*)

[11] Hitchcock, *End*, 224.

[12] https://www.prb.org/articles/how-many-people-have-ever-lived-on-earth/#:~:text=No%20demographic%20data%20exist%20for,ever%20been%20born%20on%20Earth.

[13] The timing of **the wedding supper of the Lamb** (Rev 19:9) is described in a text describing the second appearance of Christ before the Battle of Armageddon.

However, the Revelation is known to not always describe events in chronological order. Surely this event will include all of the Church and therefore be after the Second Resurrection. Therefore, it too will occur at the beginning of Eternity.

[14] Gundry, *Tribulation*, loc. 1569.

[15] For an explanation of the suggested translation of Matt 24:31 see ch. 3, sec. E and ch. 4 sec. C.

[16] Walvoord, "Is a Posttribulational Rapture Revealed in Matthew 24?," *Grace Theological Journal* 6, no. 2 [1985], 258)

[17] Ibid., 262. Underlining added.

[18] Lahaye, 110. The order of the sentences quoted is reversed for greater clarity.

[19] Dispensationalism is a popular theological framework that believes there are clear divisions of covenants that God has made with people, and there is virtually no relationship between them. Therefore, they believe God's redemptive and eschatalogical plan for Israel and the Church are completely separated.

[20] MacArthur, *Matt,* at Matt 24.

[21] Walvoord, *Rev*, 229.

[22] The relationship between God's Endtimes plan for Israel and the Church is discussed further in *Additional Studies on the Endtimes*, chapter 11, available online at www.trainingtimothys.com.

[23] Unfortunately, Amillennialism uses Eph 2:11-15 to claim the Church has symbolically fulfilled <u>all</u> of God's intended meaning of His promises to Israel and there is no literal or future meaning for all of OT prophecies. Such "replacement theology" completely ignores the fact that <u>almost 600 biblical prophecies that have already been fulfilled in history, were fulfilled in a physical way by a person, place, or event</u>, (cf. ch. 12, sec. A.2).

[24] Lahaye, 117.

Chapter 14

When Does Christ's Endtime Wrath Begin?

The Cosmic Signs

[Note: See the Glossary in Appendix B for Christ's Wrath, Trumpet and Bowl Punishments.]

Contents

A) Myth #9 in Pretribulationism: The "tribulation" is Christ's Wrath which we are promised to be rescued from

B) Defining Christ's Wrath

C) Christ's Wrath is not the persecution of Christians

D) The Cosmic Signs mark the beginning of Christ's Wrath

E) The Seals of Preparation prepare the world for Christ's Wrath

F) What is the "blessed hope"? (Tit 2:13)

Primary Points

- Christ's Endtimes Wrath is defined as the period of time when Christ executes His punishment of unbelievers remaining on Earth after Christ's Return and the Church's Rescue. It is made up of the Trumpet and Bowl Punishments.

- Unfortunately, Pre-tribulationism perverts the promise that Christians will be rescued from this wrath (1 Thess 1:10) and even claims this promise will not apply to all Christians in the Endtimes.

- Myth #9 in Pretribulationism is that the "tribulation" is Christ's Wrath which we are promised to be rescued from. The truth is this: Christ's Wrath begins after the Cosmic Signs, Christ's Return, and the Church's Rescue.

- Pre-tribulationism fails to distinguish Christ's Wrath against unbelievers, from Antichrist's Wrath against believers.

- Pre-tribulationism concludes that The Greatest Persecution is Christ's Wrath! This is both biblically and morally wrong. What makes Pre-tribulationism's view even worse is that it also claims

there are "post-rapture" Christians on the Earth during Christ's Endtime Wrath.
- The repeated teaching of Scripture is that the Cosmic Signs indicate Christ's Return and the beginning of Christ's Endtime Wrath.
- Pre-tribulationism claims that all of the Seals described in Revelation 6 are Christ's Wrath. This is clearly false because one of those Seals unleashes The Greatest Persecution on the Church which cannot be Christ's Wrath.
- The **scroll** (Rev chs. 5-6) contains Christ's Wrath. The **seals** on the **scroll** prepare the world for Christ's Wrath. After all **seven seals** are opened, Christ's Wrath will begin.
- The **blessed hope** (Tit 2:13) is not to be exempted from The Greatest Persecution as Pre-tribulationism claims. Rather, it is the better promise to be rescued from Christ's Wrath.

A) Myth #9 in Pretribulationism: The "tribulation" is Christ's Wrath which we are promised to be rescued from

This myth is most clearly refuted by answering the question posed in the title of this chapter: When does Christ's Endtime Wrath begin? The biblical answer to this question clearly reveals the difference between the biblical Pre-wrath Rescue position and the unbiblical Pre-tribulation Rapture view.

Christ's Wrath throughout the *Endtimes Essentials* is what Revelation refers to as **the wrath of the Lamb!** (Rev 6:16 NIV). It is defined as the period of time when Christ executes His punishment of unbelievers remaining on Earth after Christ's Return and the Church's Rescue. It is made up of the Trumpet and Bowl Punishments (cf. Rev chs. 8-9, 15-16, 19). Therefore, it can be further distinguished as Christ's Endtimes Wrath.

Thankfully, the NT promises that before Christ's Endtime Wrath begins, the Church's Rescue will occur with Christ's Return. This is why the Apostle Paul tells Christians **to wait for his Son from heaven ... Jesus, who rescues us from the coming wrath** (1 Thess 1:10 NIV; cf. 5:9; Rom 5:9; Col 3:6). This is a precious, repeated promise in Scripture that the Church will not suffer Christ's punishing

Endtime Wrath but will be **rescue**d by Jesus <u>before</u> it occurs.

Unfortunately, Pre-tribulationism perverts this promise and even claims this promise will <u>not</u> apply to all Christians in the Endtimes. It does this by redefining Christ's Endtimes Wrath as the entire "tribulation" period. Therefore, it claims that Christ's Wrath will include The Beginning of Birth Pains and The Greatest Persecution of Christians. This redefining of *thlipsis* ("tribulation") as Christ's Wrath, leads to the claim that the Church is "raptured" before any of the Endtime events in Christ's Endtimes Teaching occur. This fundamental error in Pre-tribulationism was discussed thoroughly in chapter 3 (sec. E).

Contrary to the popular Pre-tribulation Rapture view, the Pre-wrath Rescue position teaches that the Church's Rescue occurs <u>after</u> The Greatest Persecution and Antichrist's Wrath against God's people. Therefore, the "rapture" is not "pre-tribulational" but pre-divine wrath. The differences between these two views can be illustrated in the following graphics.

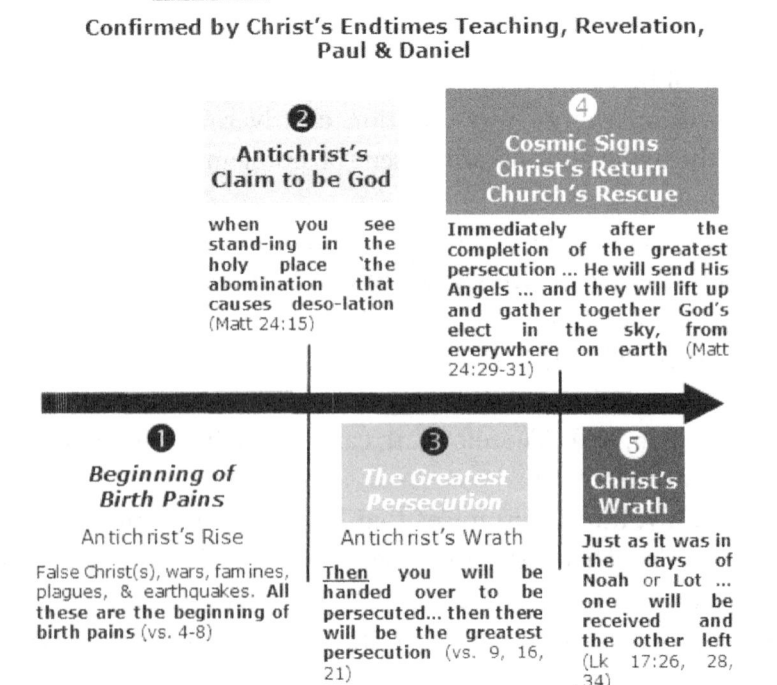

The <u>Biblical</u> Pre-wrath Rescue Position
Confirmed by Christ's Endtimes Teaching, Revelation, Paul & Daniel

❷ Antichrist's Claim to be God

when you see stand-ing in the holy place 'the abomination that causes deso-lation (Matt 24:15)

❹ Cosmic Signs / Christ's Return / Church's Rescue

Immediately after the completion of the greatest persecution ... He will send His Angels ... and they will lift up and gather together God's elect in the sky, from everywhere on earth (Matt 24:29-31)

❶ Beginning of Birth Pains

Antichrist's Rise

False Christ(s), wars, famines, plagues, & earthquakes. All these are the beginning of birth pains (vs. 4-8)

❸ The Greatest Persecution

Antichrist's Wrath

<u>Then</u> you will be handed over to be persecuted... then there will be the greatest persecution (vs. 9, 16, 21)

❺ Christ's Wrath

Just as it was in the days of Noah or Lot ... one will be received and the other left (Lk 17:26, 28, 34)

The <u>Unbiblical</u> Pre-tribulation View

The very first event of the Endtimes is a "secret and silent rapture" of the Church

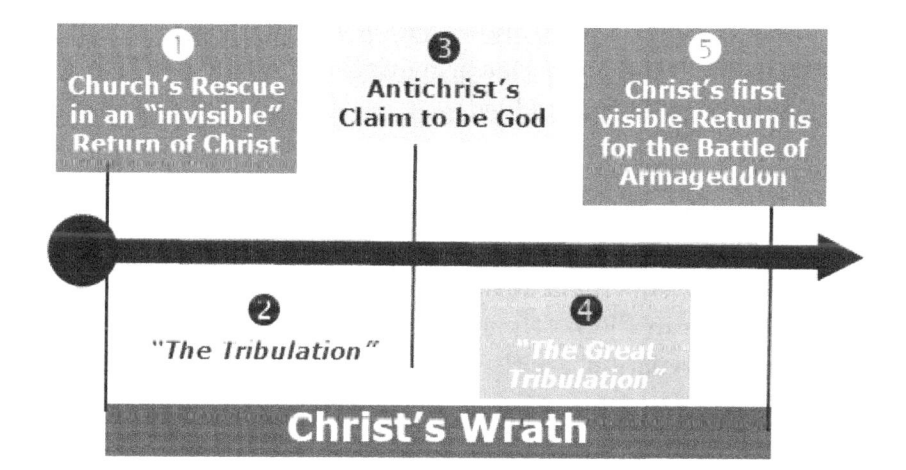

① Church's Rescue in an "invisible" Return of Christ

③ Antichrist's Claim to be God

⑤ Christ's first visible Return is for the Battle of Armageddon

② "The Tribulation"

④ "The Great Tribulation"

Christ's Wrath

Redefining Christ's Wrath as including The Beginning of Birth Pains and The Greatest Persecution is essential to Pre-tribulationism. Accordingly, the Pre-tribulationist Mark Hitchcock writes:

> While no single verse says Jesus is coming to rapture His saints before the seven-year <u>Tribulation</u>, there are clear statements that He is coming to deliver His people from the coming <u>wrath</u> [notice how the author equates "Tribulation" and "wrath"] (1 Thess 1:10; 5:9; Rev 3:10). Thus, it stands to reason that God will use the Rapture to accomplish this promise...

More could be said about this view [the Pre-wrath Rescue position taught in the *Endtimes Essentials*]. Its validity rises and falls on the interpretation of when God's wrath begins [true!]. <u>If God's wrath doesn't begin</u> until <u>the seventh seal of Revelation</u>, as proponents [of the Pre-wrath Rescue position rightly] suggest, then this view could be right [that's one reason it is].

If, however, God's wrath unfurls from the start of the Tribulation [even before the first seal of Revelation as Pre-tribulationism claims], then this view [Pre-wrath Rescue position] falls to pieces. One must decide which interpretation makes more sense.

> In my opinion, the wrath of God does not begin near the end of the Tribulation, but at the very beginning. The <u>seal judgments in Revelation 6</u> are opened by the Lamb (Jesus Christ) at the very beginning of the Tribulation (Revelation 6:1-2). He is the source of these judgments. <u>To argue that they are the wrath of man and Satan, ignores that the One bringing these judgments forth is the Lamb.</u> [1] (Underlining added)

Hitchcock is right to recognize that the timing of Christ's Wrath is a pivotal issue between the biblical Pre-wrath Rescue position and the unbiblical Pre-tribulation Rapture view. However, the author makes several biblical errors in the text above.

First, notice in the first paragraph that Hitchcock equates "the seven-year Tribulation" with "the coming wrath." Again, this fundamental error of Pre-tribulationism was addressed earlier (cf. ch. 3, sec. E). There it was concluded that 1) "tribulation" in English means "persecution" not "God's wrath"; and 2) Jesus described the periods of the Endtimes as **the beginning of birth pains** and **the greatest persecution of God's elect people** (Matt 24:8, 21 [2]).

Referring to these events with the general term "tribulation" is misleading. Pre-tribulationism's "great tribulation" is not Christ's Endtime Wrath to punish unbelievers. Rather, "the great tribulation" is The Greatest Persecution (*thlipsis*; cf. Matt 24:9, 21, 29) of **God's elect [*eklektous*] people**. In no way should The Beginning of Birth Pains and The Greatest Persecution be referred to as Christ's Wrath. This error will be discussed further below.

Second, notice that Hitchcock's confusion of "the Tribulation" with "the coming wrath" results in placing **the greatest persecution of God's elect people** (Matt 24:21) during Christ's Wrath. Therefore, Pretribulationism claims that a period of time when Christians are being persecuted and murdered, should be understood as the wrath of God. This is not only biblically wrong, but morally wrong. And it is the clearest reason to reject their view on the timing of Christ's Wrath. This is discussed further in section C below.

Third, in the second paragraph, Hitchcock <u>rejects</u> the biblical teaching that "God's wrath doesn't begin until the seventh seal of Revelation." On the contrary, this truth will be demonstrated below in section D.

Fourth, Hitchcock's claim that the Pre-wrath Rescue position believes "the wrath of God" begins "near the end of the Tribulation" is false. Christ's Wrath begins with the opening of the 7th Seal, but will include all of the Trumpet and Bowl Punishments.

Finally, in the last sentence above, Hitchcock claims that "To argue that" the Seals described in Revelation chapter 6 are not Christ's Wrath "ignores that the One bringing these judgments forth is the Lamb." This seems to be the author's strongest argument for his view. It can be dealt with fairly easily.

First, Hitchcock again seems to forget that the martyrdom of Christians is revealed in the Fifth Seal (cf. Rev 6:9-11). Therefore, even Pre-tribulationism needs to answer the question of why the demonic genocide of God's people is unleashed when Christ opens the Fifth Seal. The answer is something else Hitchcock seems to forget. God's sovereignty and plan can include the actions of Satan and the worst disasters for His people.

Myth #9 in Pretribulationism is that the "tribulation" is Christ's Wrath which we are promised to be rescued from. The truth is this: As depicted in the graphic above, Christ's Wrath begins after the Cosmic Signs, Christ's Return, and the Church's Rescue.

Jesus said **Immediately after the completion of the greatest persecution when the heavenly bodies will be shaken ... And then all the peoples of the Earth will ... see the Son of Man** then **He will send out His angels with a loud trumpet sound, and they will lift up and gather together God's elect people from one end of the sky to the other, from everywhere on Earth.** (Matt 24:29-31; cf. Rev 6:12-17).

Therefore, neither The Beginning of Birth Pains, nor The Greatest Persecution is **the coming wrath** that **Jesus** is coming **from heaven** to **rescues us from** (1 Thess 1:10). Particularly, The Greatest Persecution should never be labeled as Christ's Wrath. The biblical truth is that The Greatest Persecution will be Antichrist's Wrath against God's people, not Christ's Wrath. Therefore, the Church's Rescue ("rapture") is Pre-wrath, not Pre-tribulational.

Again, God promises that the coming of **Jesus ... rescues us from the coming wrath** (1 Thess 1:10). But, contrary to Pre-tribulationism, the Church has been promised it will experience "tribulation." Pre-tribulationism <u>denies</u> that Christ's Endtimes Teaching places the Church in the **great tribulation** [*thlipsis*] (Matt 24:21 NASB). But using the same Greek word, Jesus promised His Church elsewhere, **"In the world you will have tribulation** [*thlipsin*]" (John 16:33 ESV). More will be said about this in the next chapter (15).

The next section (B) will more specifically define what Christ's Endtime Wrath is. Section C will further discuss the unbiblical and even immoral claim of Pre-tribulationism that real Christians will be on Earth during Christ's Endtimes Wrath. Section D will answer the question, "When does Christ's Endtime Wrath begin?" Section E will demonstrate these truths by further explaining the Seals of Preparation. Finally, section F will rescue the biblical **blessed hope** (Tit 2:13) from the false teaching of Pre-tribulationism.

B) Defining Christ's Endtime Wrath

Paul tells Christians **to wait for ... Jesus, who rescues us from the coming wrath** (1 Thess 1:10 NIV). This Endtime **coming wrath** of Christ was defined above as: the period of time when Christ executes His punishment of unbelievers remaining on Earth after Christ's Return and the Church's Rescue. It is made up of the Trumpet and Bowl Punishments (cf. Rev chs. 8-9, 15-16, 19).

Christ's Endtime Wrath needs to be distinguished from other expressions of God's wrath and human catastrophes. Of course, God chooses to punish sinners on Earth in His wrath now. **God is a righteous judge, a God who displays his wrath every day** (Ps 7:11; cf. Rom 1:18; 13:4; Eph 5:6). Perhaps some wars, famines, plagues, and catastrophes in human history have been directly caused by God exercising His wrath. Unfortunately, there can be times that God's own people are caught up in these divine judgments.

In both Christ's Endtimes Teaching and Revelation 6, The Beginning of Birth Pains is described as a time of unprecedented wars, famines, and plagues killing people on one fourth of the Earth. Surely some of those people will include Christians in the Church. Therefore, will this be Christ's Wrath on unbelievers? Of course not. Scripture repeatedly says the Church will be on Earth during this time.

Therefore, we cannot label these catastrophes as Christ's Wrath. Rather, they are better labeled Seals of Preparation for Christ's Wrath. This will all be confirmed below when we clearly see when Christ's Wrath begins in the book of Revelation. The Scriptures clearly teach that Christ's Endtime Wrath is the period of time when Christ executes His punishment of unbelievers remaining on Earth after Christ's Return and the Church's Rescue. It is **the coming wrath** that **Jesus ... rescues us from** (1 Thess 1:10).

The Bible often refers to Christ's Endtimes Wrath as a part of "The Day of the Lord." For example, we read in Isaiah:

See, the day of the LORD is coming—a cruel day, with wrath and fierce anger—to make the land desolate and destroy the sinners within it... I will punish the world for its evil, the wicked for their sins... I will make the heavens tremble; and the earth will shake from its place at the wrath of the LORD Almighty, in the day of his burning anger (13:9, 11, 13 NIV).

Likewise, Paul referred to **the day of God's wrath, when his righteous judgment will be revealed** (Rom 2:5 NIV). Revelation chapter 6 introduces the arrival of **the wrath of the Lamb** (Rev 6:16) in the sequence of Endtime events. The **wrath of the Lamb** (Christ) is what is referred to as Christ's Wrath throughout the *Endtimes Essentials* series.

Revelation goes on in chapters 8-9 and 15-16 to describe in more detail **the wrath of the Lamb** in the Trumpet and Bowl Punishments. For example, starting in Revelation 8:7 we read:

The first angel sounded his trumpet, and there came hail and fire mixed with blood, and it was hurled down on the earth. A third of the earth was burned up, a third of the trees were burned up, and all the green grass was burned up. (NIV)

Revelation goes on to tell us that Christ's Endtime Wrath includes: The Earth's water turning to blood and killing every sea creature (cf. 8:8-9; 15:3-6); locusts from the Abyss stinging people and causing enough pain to make them seek death but they will not die (cf. 9:1-11); and an army of horses with lion's heads killing people with fire coming from their mouths (cf. 9:13-19).

That is the supernatural Endtime Wrath of Christ to punish unbelievers remaining on the Earth after the Church's Rescue. It is concluded with the Battle of Armageddon, **the battle on the great day of God Almighty** (Rev 16:14; cf. 15:1; 19:15). [3]

Those defeated are described as **grapes ... loaded into the great winepress of God's wrath** which will be **trampled** such that **blood** [will] **flow from the winepress in a stream about 180 miles long and as high as a horse's bridle** (Rev 14:19-20 NLT [4]). This is because Christ, **treads the winepress of the fury of the wrath of God Almighty** (Rev 19:15). This is **the coming wrath** that the Church is promised **Jesus** will rescue it from (1 Thess 1:10).

Unfortunately, Pre-tribulationism fails to distinguish Christ's Wrath against unbelievers, from Antichrist's Wrath against believers. The Antichrist's Wrath will begin immediately after Antichrist's Claim to be God and the resulting Greatest Persecution (cf. Matt 24:15-29; Rev 12:7-17; 13:1-17; 14:9-13). Antichrist's Wrath will be ended with Christ's Return and the Church's Rescue. Following these, Christ's Wrath on the unbelievers remaining on Earth will begin and then end with the Battle of Armageddon. [5] Again, this is portrayed in the graphic above of the biblical Pre-wrath Rescue position.

C) Christ's Endtime Wrath is not the persecution of Christians

Scripture encourages the Church **to wait for ... Jesus, who rescues us from the coming wrath** (1 Thess 1:10). Again, Pretribulationism claims that this **rescue** occurs before The Greatest Persecution. Therefore, it also claims that The Greatest Persecution is Christ's Wrath! This is perhaps the most alarming and even immoral conclusion of Pre-tribulational teaching.

It is alarming how many teachers are willing to claim that the Antichrist's persecution of **the elect** (Matt 24:22) and **the saints** (Dan 7:25; Rev 13:5-10) is during Christ's Endtime Wrath. Those who carelessly define the **great tribulation** (Matt 24:21 NASB) as God's wrath seem to intentionally ignore the fact that the persecution of Christians is described as occurring at that time.

What makes Pre-tribulationism's view even worse is that it also claims there are "post-rapture" Christians on the Earth during Christ's Endtime Wrath. Pre-tribulation comes to this complicated conclusion by claiming: 1) "the tribulation" will be Christ's Wrath; and 2) There is a massive revival of Christianity after the Church's Rescue.

This latter error is based on interpreting the **144,000 from all the tribes of Israel** (Rev 7:4 NIV) as worldwide evangelists whom God uses to convert a massive number of people during the Endtimes. According to the error of Pre-tribulationism, this "post-rapture revival" and these "post-rapture Christians" are described later in Revelation 7 where we read:

> **After this I looked, and there before me was a great multitude that no one could count, from every nation, tribe, people, and language, standing before the throne and before the Lamb...**
>
> **Then one of the elders asked me, "These in white robes —who are they, and where did they come from?" I answered, "Sir, you know." And he said, "These are they who have come out of the great tribulation; they have washed their robes and made them white in the blood of the Lamb.** (Rev 7:9, 13-14 NIV)

As a result of Pre-tribulationism's complex scheme, Lahaye writes: Revelation 7:9 indicates that during the first part of the Tribulation [after the "rapture"] the greatest soul harvest in all history will take place." [6]

There are several biblical problems with claiming that Revelation 7:9-14 is not describing the Church's Rescue, but a multitude of Christians getting saved after the "rapture."

First, this completely ignores the sequence of Endtime events that Christ gave us in His Endtimes Teaching. The **great persecution** (*megalēs thlipseōs*) mentioned in Revelation 7:14 is the same **greatest persecution** (*megalē thlipsis*) that Christ spoke of in Matthew 24:21. And Christ made it clear that the **greatest persecution** will occur before the Church's Rescue (cf. Matt 24:29-31). Therefore, it is impossible for this **great persecution** in Revelation 7 to occur after the Church's Rescue as Pre-tribulationism claims.

Second, contrary to Lahaye, there is no clear biblical evidence of any kind of Christian revival among Gentiles after Christ's Return and the Church's Rescue. There is some evidence that God begins to work in Israel during this time. [7]

For the above reasons it is unbiblical and even perverted for Pre-tribulationism to claim there will be Christians on the Earth during Christ's Wrath. Frankly, supporters of this view do not think through the ramifications of their teaching.

Why are these so-called "post-rapture" Christians disqualified from God's promise to rescue them **from the coming wrath** (1 Thess 1:10)?

These Christians are described as **those who had been slain because of the word of God and the testimony they had maintained** (Rev 6:9). They are **fellow servants** of Christ and **brothers and sisters** in Christ (v. 11). **These are they who have come out of the great persecution; they have washed their robes and made them white in the blood of the Lamb** (7:14).

We ask again, what is inferior about these Christians that denies them membership in the Church of Christ and to be rescued by Christ from the time of Christ's Endtime Wrath on Earth? Proponents for this view have no good answer for that. [8]

Many seem so desperate to exempt themselves and the Church from The Greatest Persecution that they have invented a separate category of Christians who are disqualified from God's promise to **rescue us from the coming wrath** (1 Thess 1:10). This false teaching has separated the Church into Christians who are exempt from Christ's Endtime Wrath, and those who will experience it.

And of course, those teaching this view are among those who are exempt. Ironically, some of those promoting this false teaching are also false Christians and will in fact experience Christ's Endtime Wrath and even God's eternal wrath.

The persecution of Christians should NEVER be labeled as the time of Christ's Endtime Wrath. Rather, The Greatest Persecution will be Antichrist's Wrath against God's people, including the Church. [9]

D) The Cosmic Signs mark the beginning of Christ's Wrath

Scripture encourages the Church **to wait for ... Jesus, who rescues us from the coming wrath** (1 Thess 1:10). When will this **rescue** occur in the Endtimes? We can answer that question by answering another one. How will we know when Christ's Endtime Wrath is just about to begin?

The repeated teaching of Scripture is that the Cosmic Signs indicate Christ's Return and the beginning of Christ's Endtime Wrath. Many times in Scripture, the Cosmic Signs signal God's Wrath (cf. Isa 13:10; 34:4; Ezc 32:7; Joel 2:10,31; Zep 1:15; Rev 6:12,13). We will discuss three of these descriptions.

First, the Prophet Joel described the Cosmic Signs as marking the beginning of the Endtime "day of the Lord" wrath. God says:

> **I will cause wonders in the heavens** [stars] **and on the earth—blood and fire and columns of smoke. The <u>sun</u> will become dark, and the <u>moon</u> will turn blood red <u>before</u> that great and terrible day of the LORD arrives.** (2:30-31 NLT)

The Cosmic Signs are **wonders in the heavens** or stars, including the **sun** turning **dark** and the **moon** turning **blood red**. These are consistently the Cosmic Signs throughout Scripture. The **great and terrible day of the LORD** is a biblical term for Christ's Wrath against His enemies. Therefore, notice the sequence in Joel: the Cosmic Signs are immediately **<u>before</u> that great and terrible day of the LORD arrives**. Accordingly, the Cosmic Signs immediately precede Christ's Endtime Wrath.

This same purpose for the Cosmic Signs is revealed in Christ's Endtimes Teaching. Jesus said:

> <u>**Immediately after the completion of the greatest persecution, then**</u> [there will be Cosmic Signs] **'the sun will be darkened, and the moon will not give its light; the stars will fall from the sky and the heavenly bodies will be shaken.'**
>
> **Then the sign that the Son of Man is coming will appear in the sky. And then all the peoples of the earth**

will mourn when they see the Son of Man coming on the clouds of heaven, with power and great glory.

He will send out His angels with a loud trumpet sound, and they will lift up and gather together [rescue] **God's elect people from one end of the sky to the other, from everywhere on Earth."** (Matt 24:29-31 [10]).

We see that the Church's Rescue rather immediately follows the Cosmic Signs. Why? Because at this point, with Christ's Return, Christ's Wrath is about to begin.

Of course, there are many Christian Teachers who claim these Cosmic Signs are merely symbolic and not to be understood in a literal way. But Jesus made it clear that the physical appearance of these phenomena will mark His Return. As discussed previously (ch. 12, sec. A), God usually fulfills biblical prophecy in a literal and physical way. [11] The Bible teaches that these Cosmic Signs will mark the beginning of Christ's Wrath on Earth.

All of this perfectly agrees with Revelation 6 where the Apostle John says:

I watched as he opened the sixth seal. There was a great earthquake. The <u>sun</u> turned black like sackcloth made of goat hair, the whole <u>moon</u> turned blood red, and the <u>stars</u> in the sky fell to earth. (vs. 12-13)

Then we are told that unbelievers in the world at that time will be desperate to **hide ... from the wrath of the Lamb!** (v. 16). Christ's visible Return following the Cosmic Signs marks the beginning of Christ's Endtime Wrath. This is why v. 17 says: **For <u>the great day of their wrath has come</u>,** the Greek referring to an event that has just begun or is about to appear. [12]

Revelation 6:16 is the first time God's **wrath** or anger is mentioned in the book of Revelation, followed by 15 more times. However, Pre-tribulationism teaches that the first 5 Seals of Preparation described previously in Revelation 6:1-11 is Christ's Endtimes Wrath. If this were true, why are the Christian martyrs in verse 10 asking, **"How long, Sovereign Lord, holy and true, until you judge the inhabitants of the earth and avenge our blood?"**? They are asking this because Christ's Endtime Wrath and

His punishment of unbelievers on the Earth has not occurred yet in the sequence of Endtime events. Their martyrdoms and The Greatest Persecution they will experience will not be the wrath of God.

Therefore, Revelation 6-8 makes it clear when Christ's Endtime Wrath begins in the sequence of Endtime events. Revelation 6:1-11 describes the first 5 Seals of Preparation, including the wars and famines of The Beginning of Birth Pains and martyrdoms that will occur during The Greatest Persecution. Then when The Greatest Persecution is completed, the sixth Seal of Preparation will be opened, and the Cosmic Signs will occur signaling that **the wrath of the Lamb ... has come** (vs. 16-17). Next Revelation chapter 7 describes the Church's Rescue (vs. 9, 14) because Christ's Wrath is about to begin.

After the Church's Rescue described in Revelation chapter 7, chapter 8 begins a description of Christ's Wrath. The **seventh seal** of Preparation is **opened** and there is an ominous **silence in heaven for about half an hour** (v. 1). In verse 7 we read **the first angel sounded his trumpet** and **a third of the earth was burned up, a third of the trees were burned up, and all the green grass was burned up**. That is the beginning of Christ's Wrath, signaled by the Cosmic Signs described at the end of Revelation chapter 6.

E) The Seals of Preparation prepare the world for Christ's Wrath

Pre-tribulationism claims that all the Seals described in Revelation chapter 6 is Christ's Wrath. This has been thoroughly demonstrated to be false. Again, one reason is that one of those Seals unleashes The Greatest Persecution on the Church which cannot be Christ's Wrath.

Therefore, what is the meaning of this scroll that is being opened? Its first mention is in Revelation chapter 5 where John wrote:

> **Then I saw a scroll in the right hand of God the Father Who was sitting on the throne. There was writing on the inside and the outside of the scroll, and it was sealed with seven seals.** (Rev 5:1 [13])

What does this **scroll** represent? What is contained within it? Christ's Endtime Wrath on this world. When all **seven seals** of

Preparation are broken and the **scroll** is opened, Christ's Wrath will be unleashed.

As noted above, after **the seventh seal** is **opened** (v. 1) "all Hell breaks loose." Rather immediately **a third of the Earth** will be **burned up** by **hail and fire mixed with blood** being **hurled down on the Earth** (v. 7 NIV). This is the beginning of Christ's Wrath.

So what do the previous six **seals** on the **scroll** represent? They are events that prepare the world for Christ's Wrath. In the ancient world important legal announcements from a ruler were written on such scrolls. Then they were sealed with a piece of wax imprinted with the signet ring of the ruler. Often times each seal represented a condition that needed to be met before the scroll was to be opened.

Likewise, the events unleashed by the **seals** prepare the world for the contents of the **scroll** which is Christ's Endtime Wrath. These events will include The Greatest Persecution of God's people in the Fifth Seal (cf. Rev 6:9-11). This will certainly be one thing that prepares the world for Christ's Wrath (cf. Rev 6:10; 16:6; 18:20; 19:2).

This is why these events are referred to as Seal Preparations throughout the *Endtimes Essentials* studies. They prepare the world for Christ's Wrath. For reasons given above, the Seal Preparations themselves are not Christ's Wrath. Christ's Endtime Wrath does not begin until all **seven seals** of the **scroll** are broken. But, when all **seven seals** are opened, Christ's Wrath will be unleashed. This is because Christ's Wrath is the contents of the **scroll**. It contains the Trumpet and Bowl Punishments described in Revelation chapters 8-9 and 15-16. The end of the **scroll** and Christ's Wrath will be the Battle of Armageddon (cf. Rev 16:12-21; 19:11-21). [14]

F) What is the "blessed hope"? *(Tit 2:13)*

The Scriptures say: **we wait for the blessed hope—the appearing of the glory of our great God and Savior, Jesus Christ** (Tit 2:13 NIV). Unfortunately, Pre-tribulationism claims **the blessed hope** is being exempted from The Greatest Persecution by a "secret and silent rapture." This view further claims that any view of the Endtimes that places the Church in The Greatest Persecution, steals our **blessed hope**. There are at least three errors in this view.

First, the biblical **blessed hope** is not some "secret and silent rapture." It is rather surprising how Pre-tribulationists completely ignore how Paul describes the "rapture" in Titus 2:13. The Apostle said, **we wait for the blessed hope—the appearing of the glory of our great God and Savior, Jesus Christ**. Again, that is not a "secret, silent, rapture" as Pre-tribulationism claims. Lahaye tries to solve this problem by claiming Paul is referring to two different appearances of Christ in this one verse. He writes:

> The "blessed hope" [refers to] that day just before the Tribulation when we will be gathered together ... to meet the Lord in the clouds [for the "rapture"]. The "glorious appearing" obviously refers to His [visibly] coming to the earth in "power and great glory." To those who take the Bible literally, this interpretation passes the test of "making common sense" out of Scripture. [13]

On the contrary, Titus 2:13 is not describing two different appearances of Christ. The verse simply says: **we wait for the blessed hope—the appearing of the glory of our great God and Savior, Jesus Christ** (Tit 2:13). Contrary to what Lahaye, the Apostle clearly believed that **the blessed hope was the appearing of the glory of our great God and Savior, Jesus Christ.** These will not be two separated events.

This is confirmed by the Apostle's teaching in 2 Thessalonians 1:6-7. There he told the persecuted Christian not to expect **relief** until **the Lord Jesus is revealed from heaven in blazing fire with his powerful angels** (NIV; cf. ch. 5, sec. B).

Our **blessed hope** is something even better than being exempted from The Greatest Persecution and Antichrist's Wrath. Our **blessed hope** is **to wait for his Son from heaven ... who rescues us from the coming wrath** of God (1 Thess 1:10)! The Antichrist's Wrath will be minor and very temporary compared to the powerful anger and eternal punishment of God Almighty. Which one would you rather be rescued from? The Antichrist's temporary persecution, or God Almighty's eternal Wrath?

As Jesus said, **"Do not be afraid of those who kill the body** [in persecution, for example] **but cannot kill the soul** [like God]. **Rather, be afraid of the One who can destroy both soul and**

body in hell forever (Math 10:28 NIV). Indeed, it is a very **blessed hope** to **wait for his Son from heaven … Jesus, who rescues us from the coming wrath** of God!

---

[1] Hitchcock, *End*, 136, 143.

[2] For an explanation of the suggested translation of Matt 24:21 see ch. 3, sec. E.

[3] Evidence for the claim that the end of Christ's Wrath (and the end of the world) occur at the Battle of Armageddon include the following. First, a description of Christ's 1,000-year Reign in Revelation 20 follows a description of the end of the Battle in chapter 19.

Secondly, this text from Isaiah describes both the Battle and the end of this world:

> **Come near, you nations, and listen; pay attention, you peoples! Let the earth hear, and all that is in it, the world, and all that comes out of it! The LORD is angry with all nations; his wrath is on all their armies. He will totally destroy them, he will give them over to slaughter. Their slain will be thrown out, their dead bodies will stink; the mountains will be soaked with their blood. All the stars in the sky will be dissolved and the heavens rolled up like a scroll; all the starry host will fall like withered leaves from the vine, like shriveled figs from the fig tree.** (Isa 34:1-4 NIV)

[4] For arguments that Revelation 14:19-20 is referring to the Battle of Armageddon and can be interpreted literally see Thomas.

[5] This section contains the simple and biblical explanation of Christ's Endtime Wrath. However, it needs to be reconciled with the following prophecy from Luke's version of Christ's Endtimes Teaching:

> **"When you see Jerusalem being surrounded by armies, you will know that its desolation is near. Then let those who are in Judea flee to the mountains, let those in the city get out, and let those in the country not enter the city. For this is the time of punishment in fulfillment of all that has been written.**
>
> **How dreadful it will be in those days for pregnant women and nursing mothers! There will be great distress in the land and wrath against this people. They will fall by the sword and will be taken as prisoners to all the nations. Jerusalem will be trampled on by the Gentiles until the times of the Gentiles are fulfilled."** (Luke 21:20-24 NIV)

This is a complex prophecy. First, it should be noticed that elements of it were fulfilled in A. D. 70 when **Jerusalem** was **surrounded by armies** from Rome and the city became a **desolation** (v. 20). However, Luke's version of Christ's Endtimes Teaching makes it clear that the final and ultimate fulfillment of this prophecy will occur immediately before **"There will be signs in the sun, moon and stars** and **people ... will see the Son of Man coming"** (vs. 25-27). In other words, Luke 21:20-24 will occur during The Greatest Persecution.

It has been argued in this section that The Greatest Persecution will not be Christ's Endtime Wrath. This would violate God's promise that the Church is **to wait for ... Jesus, who rescues us from the coming wrath** (1 Thess 1:10). In addition, as also demonstrated in this section, Christ's Endtimes Wrath will not begin until after The Greatest Persecution, the Cosmic Signs, Christ's Return, and the Church's Rescue.

However, the text above predicts that during The Greatest Persecution of the Church, **There will be great distress in the land** of Israel **and wrath against this people** (v 23) the unbelieving Jews. **This** will be **the time of punishment in fulfillment of all that has been written** (v. 22) in the OT about God's Endtime plan for Israel. It seems that during The Greatest Persecution that the Jews and Jerusalem will **finish their rebellion ... put an end to their sin ... atone for their guilt** and **bring in everlasting righteousness** (Dan 9:24 NLT).

Therefore, we have another example of the complex differences between God's Endtime plan for the Church and Israel. During The Greatest Persecution, Christians in the Church will be experiencing Antichrist's Wrath as an opportunity to glorify their Savior.

But during the same time, unbelieving Jews will be experiencing God's punishment for their sin, in preparation for restoring them after Christ's Return and during "the day of the Lord."

For more on the relationship between Israel and the Church in the Endtimes see chapter 11 in *Additional Studies on the Endtimes* (*ASE*). The point here is this. The fact that unbelieving Jews will be experiencing God's wrath during The Greatest Persecution does not mean that the saved, forgiven believers in the Church will be experiencing the same. The Church will be experiencing Antichrist's Wrath and afterwards **Jesus** will come **from heaven to rescue us from the coming wrath** (1 Thess 1:10) of God.

[6] Tim Lahaye, *Revelation Unveiled* (Zondervan, 1999), 153.

[7] For more on the question, "Will people get saved in the Endtimes?" see chapter 10 in *ASE*.

[8] Others recognize that The Beginning of Birth Pains and The Greatest Persecution contained in the first 5 Seals of Revelation 6 should not be considered Christ's Endtime Wrath in the "Day of the Lord." Morris writes:

> The first four seals ... show us the self-defeating character of sin. When the spirit of selfishness and conquest is operating, all God needs to do is let events take their course and sinners will be inevitably punished. (*Rev*)

Likewise, Osborne writes of the "four horsemen" of Rev 6:1-8: "God is not so much pouring down judgment on the earth-dwellers as allowing their depravity to come full circle" (274).

Finally, Van Kampen notes: "The wrath of God is never equated with the persecution of God's elect" (*Sign*, 19).

[9] The error of confusing "the tribulation" and persecution of Christians with "the day of the Lord" and Christ's Endtime Wrath is illustrated in the following. MacArthur writes regarding the alarm the Thessalonians had about the false claim that **the day of the Lord has already begun** (2 Thess 2:2):

> The Thessalonians' fears that they were in the Day of the Lord and thus had missed the Rapture imply that the Rapture precedes the Tribulation [Day of the Lord & Christ's Wrath]. If the Thessalonians knew that the Rapture came at the end of the Tribulation, persecution would not have caused them to fear they had missed it. Instead, that persecution would have been a cause for joy, not concern.(*Thessalonians*, 124)

There are several problems with this interpretation. In the first sentence MacArthur confuses "the Day of the Lord" with "the Tribulation" claiming the latter is Christ's Endtime Wrath. We have argued against this in detail in this book. In chapter 3, it was noted that "tribulation" in both Greek and English means "persecution," not "wrath" (cf. sec. E). In this chapter it has been demonstrated that Christ's Wrath does not begin until after the Cosmic Signs, Christ's Return, and the Church's Rescue. Contrary to MacArthur, the "rapture" is pre-wrath, not pre-tribulational.

The second and third sentences of MacArthur's statement are true. They express the biblical view of the sequence of Endtime events and if the Thessalonians had understood it, they would not have been alarmed, but anticipating the Church's Rescue.

But MacArthur claims the "pre-wrath rapture" cannot be true because the Thessalonians were afraid. On the contrary, the reason they were afraid is because they believed the same error as MacArthur: that their persecution ("the tribulation") was the wrath of God.

[10] For an explanation of the suggested translation of Matt 24:29-31 see ch. 3, secs. E & F and ch. 4, sec. C.

[11] Piper addresses the common error of interpreting the Cosmic Signs in merely a symbolic way when he writes:

We should be slow to treat the signs accompanying the second coming as metaphorical. Jesus and the apostles give no hint that they are not describing cosmological reality... The prophets' use of such language is regularly in contexts marked by what I have called "prophetic perspective" in which a near event (like the destruction of Babylon) and a distant event (like the universal judgment) are spoken of with no temporal distinction.

One would need to be careful, therefore, not to assume that a reference to stars and sun being darkened (e.g., Isa. 13:10) is metaphorical in such a context, when in fact it may have a literal fulfillment at the last day. (241, 245)

[12] **Has come** in Revelation 6:17 translates the Greek verb *ēlthen* in the aorist tense and indicative mood. Unfortunately, many scholars claim the aorist tense here means Christ's Endtime Wrath has already been happening throughout the Seals (cf. Thomas, Osborne). This is based on the fact that the aorist tense often refers to something that has been completed in the past.

However, NT scholar D. A. Carson notes in his classic book, *Exegetical Fallacies* regarding the Greek aorist:

> The problem [is that] competent scholars deduce from the presence of an aorist verb that the action was "once for all" or "completed." The problem arises in part because the aorist is often described as the punctiliar tense. Careful grammarians, of course, understand that this does not mean the aorist could be used only for point actions.
>
> The aorist, after all, is well-named: it is aorist, without a place, undefined. It simply refers to the action itself, without specifying whether the action is unique, repeated, ingressive, instantaneous, past, or accomplished. (Baker, 1996, 69-70; cf. A. T. Robertson, *A Grammar of the Greek New Testament* [Broadman, 1934], 835, 846).

Likewise, Bible scholar Paul Feinberg, who is a committed Pre-tribulationist, commented on the use of *ēlthen* at Revelation 6:17:

> The aorist verb *ēlthen* is either an ingressive or dramatic aorist. The ingressive or inceptive aorist expresses a state or condition *just entered*. On the other hand, the dramatic or proleptic aorist functions like a future, taking place after the realization of some condition. This would mean with the sixth seal the wrath of God has just begun or is about to appear. (*The Rapture: Pre-, Mid-, or Post-Tribulational* [Zondervan, 1984], 59).

Another Bible scholar, Gary Cohen, has described the use of *ēlthen* here as meaning God's wrath "is an overhanging event about to occur" (*Understanding Revelation* [Wipf & Stock, 2001]).

For an example of the Greek verb *ēlthen* in the same aorist indicative tense, see Mark 14:41 where we read Jesus saying to His disciples in the

Garden of Gethsemane: **The hour has come. Look, the Son of Man is delivered into the hands of sinners. Rise! Let us go! Here comes my betrayer!** Christ being **delivered into the hands of sinners** had not yet occurred, but was just about to occur.

As noted above, additional evidence for this is that Revelation 6:9-10 describes the martyrdom of Christians and their request for Christ's wrath. Therefore, at this point in the sequence of Endtime events, before 6:17, Christ's Endtime Wrath has not yet begun.

Likewise, this understanding is proven by the fact that Revelation 7:9, 14 depicts Christians on the Earth during **the great persecution**. Therefore, the wrath of God could not have commenced before this.

13 The fact that the **Lamb** Who **had been slain** (Rev 5:6) is portrayed as the One Who **took the scroll from the right hand of him who sat on the throne** (v. 7), makes it clear that the One **on the throne** in both Rev 5:1 and 7 is **God the Father**. This is reflected in the suggested translation.

14 Not surprisingly, there are many rather odd suggestions from scholars about what the **scroll** contains. Thomas addresses and refutes five of them and rightly concludes: "in this scroll is a comprehensive account of the future wrath of the Lamb (cf. 6:17)" (625). Along the same lines, Osborne writes: "The seven seals are preliminary judgments on the earth that prepare for the trumpets and bowls... [After the seals are opened] the contents of the scroll are concerned more with the trumpets and bowls [i.e. Christ's Wrath]" (269).

15 Lahaye, 105-6.

Chapter 15

Refuting More Myths in Pre-tribulationism

Imminency, the Restrainer, & Rev 3:10

Contents

A) Myth #10: The Rapture will happen at any moment, without any warning signs

B) Myth #11: Unbelievers will be experiencing "peace and safety" before the Church's Rescue

C) Myth #12: The "Restrainer" of the Antichrist is the Holy Spirit, and His removal refers to the "Rapture" of the Church (2 Thess 2:6-7)

D) Myth #13: Revelation 3:10 is promising the Church's Rescue before the "tribulation"

Primary Points

- Matthew 24:4-31 and 2 Thess 2:1-4 clearly disprove Pre-tribulationism's belief in the "imminency" of the Church's Rescue.

- The NT makes it clear that the early Church was not expecting the Church's Rescue "at any moment."

- The beginning of the Endtimes could begin at any time and is therefore "imminent." But not Christ's Return and the Church's Rescue.

- Contrary to Pre-tribulationism, Christ makes it clear that the world will be desperately seeking "peace and safety" before His Return, not experiencing it.

- Contrary to Pre-tribulationism, the "Restrainer" (cf. 2 Thess 2:6-7) is not the Holy Spirit, but probably the Archangel Michael.

- Contrary to Pre-tribulationism, there is not a single promise in Scripture that the Church will be exempted from persecution. This includes Revelation 3:10. On the contrary, the NT promises the Church persecution.

- The Last Generation Church is promised exclusion from the wrath of God, but it has been promised exposure to the wrath of men and the Antichrist.

- It seems Revelation 3:10 is a promise to **protect** Christians **from the great time of temptation ... that will tempt those who belong to this world** to worship the Antichrist, take his **mark**, and be eternally damned.

A) Myth #10: The Rapture will happen at any moment, without any warning signs

Because of the influence of Pre-tribulationism, many believe that the Church's Rescue ("rapture") could occur at "any moment," including today. [1] For example, Lahaye writes: "Properly taught, prophecy emphasizes the 'imminent' return of Christ—that He could come at any moment." [2] Likewise, the popular Pre-tribulationist Mark Hitchcock writes:

> No sign signals the Rapture. Signs are for Christ's return, not the church's rapture. The Rapture is an imminent, sign-less event. It's an event that could occur at any moment without warning. [3]

Pre-tribulationism supports this by claiming the Church's Rescue is the very first event in the Endtimes, occurring before any of the events Christ described in His Endtimes Teaching. In theological discussions this foundational belief of Pre-tribulationism is known as Imminency. When an event is said to be "imminent," it means there is nothing that needs to take place before that event will occur. In other words it is "signless," without warning, and it could literally happen at "any moment."

This foundational teaching of Pre-tribulationism has been thoroughly disproved in previous chapters of *Christ's Endtimes Teaching*. Both Jesus and Paul clearly taught that several Endtime events will occur before the Church's Rescue (cf. Matt 24:4-31; 2 Thess 2:1-4). For example, in Christ's Endtimes Teaching He gave us many signs of His Return leading right up to its immediate occurrence (see especially Matt 24:29). Only when the Last **generation** Church sees **all these things** will they **know that** Christ's Return **is near, right at the door"** (Matt 24:33-34).

In addition, it is clear that the early Church was <u>not</u> expecting the Church's Rescue "at any moment." Just a few examples of many will be offered here.

First, Jesus had given them the Great Commission to **"go and make disciples of all nations** until **the very end of the age"** (Matt 28:19-20 NIV). Such an endeavor would require a considerable amount of time. It has now required almost 2,000 years and the task Jesus gave the Church is evidently still not complete. The Church's Rescue could not occur "at any moment" until this task was completed.

The Apostle Peter did not expect the "rapture" to happen at "any moment." The Lord clearly prophesied to Peter that he would live to be an old man and die in a painful way (cf. John 21:18-19). This did not happen until the mid-60's A.D. over 30 years after Christ predicted it. It would seem absurd to claim that Peter expected the Church's Rescue before Christ's words were fulfilled.

The Apostle Paul never expected the Church's Rescue to happen at "any moment" and without warning signs. He told the Thessalonians:

Concerning the coming of our Lord Jesus Christ and our being gathered to him [the "rapture"] ... **Don't let anyone deceive you in any way, for that day <u>will not come until</u> the rebellion occurs and the man of lawlessness is revealed, the man doomed to destruction.** (2 Thess 2:1-3)

In light of Paul's clear instruction to the Thessalonians, no believer should be expecting the Church's Rescue (the "rapture") until at least Antichrist's Claim to be God in a rebuilt temple in Jerusalem.

Accordingly, NT scholar D. A. Carson writes:

> On what is the "any second" view of imminency based and how well does it withstand close scrutiny? The truth is that the biblical evidence nowhere clearly endorses the "any second" view and frequently militates against it.
>
> First, all the relevant NT verbs for "looking forward to" or "expecting" or "waiting for" have a semantic range including necessary delay. Secondly, many NT passages also implicitly rule out an "any second" imminency (Matt 24:45-51; 25:5, 19; Luke 19:11-27: John 21:18-19; Acts 9:15; 22:21; 23:11; 27:24).
>
> Yet the terms "imminent" and "imminency" retain theological usefulness if they focus attention on the eager expectancy of the Lord's return characteristic of many NT passages, a return that could take place soon, i.e. within a fairly

brief period of time, without specifying that the period must be one second or less! This is not so rigid as the "any second" view, and it more fairly represents the exegetical evidence. [4]

Indeed, the beginning of the Endtimes could begin at any time and is therefore "imminent." But not Christ's Return and the Church's Rescue.

So how does Pre-tribulationism support an "any moment rapture"? Under the subtitle: "The Rapture Could Come At Any Moment" Lahaye writes, "Many of the texts cited above for the Rapture of the Church teach an imminent coming of Christ." [5] On a previous page he lists 26 verses that are labeled "Rapture Passages." However, most of the passages do not specifically mention the Church's Rescue at all.

Next, Lahaye apparently quotes the Scripture that he thinks most clearly supports "imminency." He writes:

> Take, for example, one of the first teachings of the Rapture in 1 Thessalonians 1:9-10: ...
>
>> "for they themselves report what kind of reception you gave us. They tell how you turned to God from idols to serve the living and true God, and to wait for his Son from heaven, whom he raised from the dead —Jesus, who rescues us from the coming wrath."
>
> These Thessalonian Christians were not sitting around waiting for the Rapture, they were "serv[ing] the living and true God" in an attitude of expectancy "to wait for his Son." [6]

This is the best argument the pre-eminent teacher of Pre-tribulationism can suggest for an "any moment rapture"? The fact that these Christians were simply **wait**i**ng for ... Jesus** "in an attitude of expectancy" does not at all imply they believed nothing needed to happen before Jesus returned.

Because the biblical evidence for an "any moment rapture" is lacking, it is common for Pre-tribulationism to make a practical appeal for it. As Knoor puts it: "If we knew what events had to occur before He would return, then we could live carelessly, instead of in eager expectation of His return." [7] On the contrary, you do not need to believe the "rapture" could happen any second, in order to not "live carelessly." Nor do we need the doctrine of "imminency" to eagerly wait for Christ's Return. Jesus commanded us to **"Watch!"** (Mark 13:37) for signs of His Return, and if we love Him we will obey Him.

Finally, even Pre-tribulationists themselves do not live expecting the "rapture" to occur at any moment. Do any of them regularly wake up every morning believing the "rapture" could happen that very day? This is doubtful. And that is a huge problem for Pre-tribulationism because Jesus said if He comes **on a day when** you do **not expect him and at an hour** you are **not aware of** then **He will cut** you **to pieces and assign** you **a place with the unbelievers** which is Hell (Luke 12:46 NIV; cf. Matt 24:50-51).

As demonstrated in an illustration given in chapter 9 (sec. B.1), Pre-tribulationism's "imminency" places us all in danger of such condemnation because none of us were probably expecting Christ's Return at this very hour. Therefore, the popular view of an "any moment rapture" is not only unbiblical, but impossible.

Harmful myth #10 in Pre-tribulationism is: The Rapture will happen at any moment, without any warning signs. The biblical truth is: Multiple signs will occur before Christ's Return and the Church's Rescue so that Christians in the Last Generation will not be surprised by the day and even the hour these events occur (cf. ch. 9, sec. B).

B) Myth #11: Unbelievers will be experiencing "peace and safety" before the Church's Rescue

The Pre-tribulationist Mark Hitchcock writes:

> A key problem with [the Pre-wrath Rescue position taught in *Endtimes Essentials*] is that according to 1 Thessalonians 5:1-3 the Day of the Lord comes unexpectedly while people everywhere are saying, "Peace and safety" (NASB)...
>
> According to the pre-wrath view, the sixth seal [of Christ's Wrath] will just have been broken, which will result in earthquakes and great cosmic disturbances that will cause incredible terror to the inhabitants of the earth (Revelation 6:12-17). In fact, more than one-fourth of the world's population will have been recently destroyed by famines, disease, and widespread warfare on the earth [4th Seal, Rev 6:8].

It does not seem likely that the people of the world will be saying "Peace and safety" when more than a billion people have recently perished, and incredible cosmic disturbances are taking place. No one will be saying, "Peace and safety," at that time.

Placing the beginning of the Day of the Lord and therefore the Rapture at that point in the Tribulation doesn't make sense.
8

Therefore, Pre-tribulationism is claiming that because the world will be experiencing "peace and safety" right up to "the Rapture," then the "rapture" must occur before all the "bad stuff" happens. This results in Myth #11 of Pre-tribulationism: Unbelievers will be experiencing "peace and safety" before the Church's Rescue. But such a myth does not fit the biblical data.

The first vital mistake Hitchcock makes is completely ignoring Christ's Endtimes Teaching as a source for his teaching. Christ clearly taught that The Beginning of Birth Pains and The Greatest Persecution of the Church will occur <u>before</u> Christ's Return and the Church's Rescue. If he understood that Christ's Endtimes Teaching applies to the Church and refers to Christ's first appearance to Rescue His Church, his argument above would cease to exist.

In addition, Christ said some things in His Endtimes Teaching that argue against the myth that unbelievers will be experiencing "peace and safety" before the Church's Rescue.

Speaking of the Endtimes <u>before</u> His Return and the Church's Rescue, Jesus said: **"If those days had not been cut short, no one would survive"** (Matt 24:22 NIV). One reason is that the **wars, famines,** and **plagues** (Matt 24:6-7; Luke 21:11) of The Beginning of Birth Pains will continue throughout the Endtimes. As we read in Daniel, **War will continue until the end, and desolations have been decreed** (9:26). In Luke's version of Christ's Endtimes Teaching Jesus predicted before His Return, **"On the earth, nations will be in anguish"** (21:25 NIV). Contrary to Pre-tribulationism, that is not a world experiencing "peace and safety."

Some suggest that later in Christ's Endtimes Teaching He taught the world would be experiencing peace and prosperity right before His Return. There we read:

> **As it was in the days of Noah, so it will be at the coming of the Son of Man. For in the days before the flood, people were eating and drinking, marrying, and giving in marriage, up to the day Noah entered the ark; and they knew nothing about what would happen until the flood came and took them all away.**
>
> **That is how it will be at the coming of the Son of Man... men will be in the field ... women will be grinding with a hand mill** (Matt 24:37-41 NIV)

Jesus said right up to **the coming of the Son of Man** people will be **eating and drinking** and **marrying** and working. Most scholars understand rightly that Jesus is simply describing ordinary and even essential human practices for living. Therefore, the NLT over-translates when it suggests Jesus said: **"the people were enjoying banquets and parties."** [9] No, Jesus simply said they were **eating and drinking** as normal activities of life.

The context of Christ's statement was His desire to communicate the unbelieving world will be surprised by Christ's Return. His prediction that they will be continuing normal human activities illustrates this. It does not suggest a period of peace and prosperity. Carson puts it well when he writes regarding the Endtimes: "Despite the distress, persecutions, and upheavals (vv. 4-28), life will go on: people will eat, drink, and marry." [10]

Now we have a biblical context to properly interpret 1 Thessalonians 5:3. Paul predicted concerning the Endtimes: **While people are saying** [*legōsin*, "utter in words" [11]], **"Peace and safety," destruction will come on them suddenly, as labor pains on a pregnant woman, and they will not escape** (1 Thess 5:3 NIV). Green explains what the **peace and safety** referred to:

> The word peace described ... both the absence of war and a social concord that was a guarantee of tranquility that brought joy and prosperity to a people. The political safety (*asphaleia*) was the condition of those who were saved from any kind of harm and the security and stability under which people could live. [12]

Is this what the world will be experiencing at the time of Christ's Return? Not at all. Instead of "the absence of war," **War will**

continue until the end (Dan 9:26). Will people be "saved from any kind of harm" during that time? No. Jesus said, **"If those days had not been cut short, no one would survive"** (v. 22).

Therefore, it becomes obvious that Pre-tribulationism is misinterpreting the Apostle in 1 Thessalonians 5:3. It is not that **people** will be **saying, "Peace and safety,"** because they will be experiencing and enjoying these things. On the contrary, the **people** of the world will be desperately begging, asking, and seeking for **"Peace and safety"** because they will not be experiencing it. Or as the NASB has it, they will be **saying, "Peace and safety!"** Perhaps the exclamation point was intended to reflect their desperation.

But the **people** of the world will not get the **"Peace and safety!"** they seek. Instead, **destruction will come on them suddenly** with Christ's Return and the beginning of Christ's Wrath. [13]

It is true that the Antichrist will probably accomplish some level of peace in this world, particularly during his initial Rise to power. This is probably portrayed in the First Seal of Preparation (cf. Rev 6:1-2).

However, this temporary peace is shattered by the breaking of the Second Seal of war (cf. Rev 6:3-4). Accordingly, the Scriptures shared above indicate the Antichrist will never be able to completely accomplish peace and prosperity in this world. Only the Return of Jesus Christ will truly accomplish this.

Myth #11 of Pre-tribulationism is that unbelievers will be experiencing "peace and safety" before the Church's Rescue. The truth is that **on the earth, nations will be in anguish** and begging for "peace and safety."

C) Myth #12: The "Restrainer" of the Antichrist is the Holy Spirit, and His removal refers to the "Rapture" of the Church (2 Thess 2:6-7)

The Apostle Paul told the Thessalonians that at some point in the Endtimes the Antichrist, **will oppose and will exalt himself over everything that is called God or is worshiped, so that he sets himself up in God's temple, proclaiming himself to be God** (2 Thess 2:4 NIV). Why hasn't this occurred yet? The Apostle wrote:

> **And you know what restrains him now, so that in his time he will be revealed. For the mystery of lawlessness**

is already at work; only he who now restrains will do so until he is taken out of the way. (2 Thess 2:6-7 NASB)

The Apostle is describing something or someone who currently **restrains** the Antichrist from committing **the abomination of desolation** (Matt 24:15; cf. Dan 9:27). Thus, we refer to this entity as the "Restrainer." Pre-tribulationism insists the "Restrainer" is the Holy Spirit. Then it further claims that the removal of the Holy Spirit is somehow a reference to the "rapture" before the Antichrist emerges in the world. For example, the Pre-tribulationist Warren Wiersbe writes on the passage quoted above:

> Many Bible students identify this restrainer as the Holy Spirit of God... When the church is raptured, the Holy Spirit will not be taken out of the world (otherwise nobody could be saved during the tribulation), but He will be taken out of the midst [of the Church] to allow Satan and his forces to go to work. [14]

Even if the Restrainer is the Holy Spirit, interpreting His being **taken out of the way** (2 Thess 2:7) as the "rapture" is an unwarranted conclusion. Still, Pre-tribulationism's interpretation of this passage is a very popular argument for it.

Many scholars state that it is rather impossible to determine who the Restrainer is. The claim is that the Thessalonians had information that is not available to us, but was so commonly understood that the Apostle did not explain further. Contrary to this common belief, the Prophet Daniel probably identified the Restrainer for us, and the Apostle was simply pointing to this.

As explained previously, Daniel 12:1-2 is describing The Greatest Persecution (cf. ch. 7, sec. C.2). But it also describes something occurring immediately <u>before</u> The Greatest Persecution. In a suggested translation, the Angel tells Daniel:

> **"In the endtimes, the Archangel Michael, the great military commander who protects the sons of your people, will stop protecting them. Then the saints will experience the anguish of being attacked by an enemy. That anguish will be greater than any that has happened since nations have existed."** (Dan 12:1 [15])

In the endtimes (**At that time** NIV) refers to the Endtime events described in the previous verses in Daniel chapter 11. These predict activities of the Antichrist **at the time of the end** (11:40). [16] The **anguish of being attacked by an enemy** translates the Hebrew word *tsarah* which can mean, "the anguish of a people besieged by an enemy." [17]

During the time of Antichrist's activities, the **Archangel Michael ... will stop protecting ... the saints** from being persecuted. The Hebrew word here is *āmad* which basically means "to stand'." [18] However, *BDB* lists 12 times in the OT where *āmad* means: "stand still, stop, cease moving." Examples include the following:

> **The moon stopped** [*āmad*, "cease moving"], **till the nation avenged itself on its enemies, as it is written in the Book of Jashar. The sun stopped** [*āmad*, "cease moving"] **in the middle of the sky and delayed going down about a full day.** (Josh 10:13 NIV)

> **So Joab blew the trumpet, and all the troops came to a halt** [*āmad*]**; they no longer pursued Israel, nor did they fight anymore.** (2 Sam 2:28 NIV; cf. 2 Kgs 4:6)

We see that *āmad* can mean to stop something. In 2 Samuel 2:28 it referred to David's men ceasing to chase their enemy and **fight anymore**. This seems to be the meaning of *āmad* in Daniel 12:1. The Archangel **Michael will stop** doing something in the realm of spiritual warfare. He **will stop protecting ... the saints** from **the anguish of being attacked by an enemy**.

What does the text in Daniel say will be the result? **Then the saints will experience ... anguish** that **will be greater than any that has happened since nations have existed.** Of course, this is exactly the language used by Christ to describe The Greatest Persecution that will occur after the Antichrist is indwelled by Satan and Claims to be God (cf. Matt 24:15, 21). So, Daniel 12:1 is predicting that the Archangel **Michael ... will stop protecting ... the saints** and then they **will experience the anguish of being attacked by an enemy** which will be The Greatest Persecution.

Who is this **enemy** that **Michael** is currently restraining from attacking God's people? Satan. Remarkably, Revelation 12 describes in greater detail what is happening at this time. This passage is describing what will happen in the spiritual realm just before Satan incarnates the Antichrist and begins The Greatest Persecution:

> **Then war broke out in heaven. Michael and his angels fought against the dragon** [Satan]**, and the dragon and his angels fought back. But he was not strong enough, and they lost their place in heaven. The great dragon** [Satan] **was hurled down** [to Earth]—**that ancient serpent called the devil, or Satan, who leads the whole world astray. He was hurled to the earth, and his angels with him...**
>
> **Woe to the earth and the sea because the devil has gone down to you!** [to indwell the Antichrist and begin The Greatest Persecution]. **He is filled with fury because he knows that his time is short..."**
>
> **Then the dragon was enraged ... and went off to wage war against the rest of her offspring** [Christians in the Church]—**those who keep God's commands and hold fast their testimony about Jesus** [during The Greatest Persecution]. (Rev 12:7-9, 12, 17 NIV)

There are a lot of things being described here that will be explained elsewhere. [19] There it will be argued that this passage is describing Satan's incarnation of the Antichrist at the time of the "abomination of desolation" just prior to beginning The Greatest Persecution.

The point that is important to notice here is that, at some point during the Endtimes, the Archangel **Michael** will cast **Satan ... to the earth** where he will begin to persecute **those who keep God's commands and hold fast their testimony about Jesus**, which will be The Greatest Persecution of both Israel and the Church. In other words, the Archangel Michael stops protecting God's people and allows Satan to come to Earth, indwell the Antichrist, proclaim himself to be God in a rebuilt Jewish temple, and begin The Greatest Persecution.

It should not surprise us that the Archangel **Michael** is described as restraining Satan from initiating the **abomination that causes desolation** and that leads to The Greatest Persecution of God's people (Matt 24:15-21).

Earlier in Daniel an Angel tells the Prophet that **Michael, one of the chief princes** had helped him defeat a powerful demonic being named **the prince of the Persian kingdom**, and that later **Michael** would help him defeat another demonic being named the **prince of Greece**. These demonic beings are so powerful that the Angel says **there is no one who stands firmly with me against these forces except Michael your prince** (Dan 10:21 NASB). Perhaps this is because no one else in the angelic realm can (cf. Dan 10:12-13,20-21; 11:1).

Likewise, **Michael** is clearly described in the NT as the spiritual being that is in direct confrontation with Satan. In Jude 1:9 we read that **the archangel Michael ... was disputing with the devil about the body of Moses** (NIV). Likewise, based on Michael's activity in Revelation 12, it is likely that he is the Angel that binds Satan during the Millennium (cf. Rev 20:1-3).

> **And you know what is holding him** [Antichrist/Satan] **back, for he can be revealed only when his time comes. For this lawlessness is already at work secretly, and it will remain secret until the one who is holding it back** [the Archangel Michael] **steps out of the way. Then the man of lawlessness will be revealed.** (2 Thess 2:6-8 NLT)

The biblical evidence from Daniel chapter 12, Jude 1:9, and Revelation 12 all point to the Archangel Michael being "the Restrainer" that Paul predicted would keep the Antichrist from taking **his seat in the temple of God** and **displaying himself as being God** and beginning The Greatest Persecution.

Myth #12 in Pre-tribulationism is that the "Restrainer" of the Antichrist in 2 Thessalonians 2:6-7 is the Holy Spirit, and His removal refers to the "Rapture" of the Church. The truth is that Daniel told us the Archangel Michael would be restraining the powers of evil from starting The Greatest Persecution which will be immediately preceded by Antichrist's Claim to be God that Paul said the "Restrainer" was prohibiting. The Archangel Michael is the best biblical candidate to be the "Restrainer." [20]

D) Myth #13: Revelation 3:10 is promising the Church's Rescue before the "tribulation"

In Revelation 3:10 Jesus says **to the church in Philadelphia**: **"Because you have obeyed my command to persevere, I will protect you from the great time of testing that will come upon the whole world to test those who belong to this world."** (NLT)

Understandably, Pre-tribulationism has been especially interested in a verse that is telling Christians that Christ **will protect** them **from a great time** of suffering in the Endtimes. Osborne comments: "This is one of the more commented verses in Revelation, especially since it is the most important single passage in the book for the dispensational [Pre-tribulational] position." [21] Accordingly, the Pre-tribulationist MacArthur writes of Revelation 3:10:

> Jesus' promise to the church at Philadelphia is more than a promise to that local body of believers and more than a promise to keep them from ordinary testing. That "hour of testing" will "come upon the whole world," and it will test all those "who dwell upon the earth." The Lord promises that the whole church, those who "have kept the word of My perseverance," will be kept from the perils and agonies of the Tribulation (Rev. 3:10). [22]

Thus, for Pre-tribulationism, Revelation 3:10 is a promise that the Church's Rescue will occur before "the Tribulation."

Once again, the fundamental mistake MacArthur and other Pre-tribulationists make is distorting what "the Tribulation" means. As thoroughly discussed elsewhere, both the Greek word used in Christ's Endtimes Teaching (*thlipsis*), and the English word "tribulation" often used to translate it, specifically mean "persecution," not suffering in general, or the wrath of God (cf. ch. 3, sec. E).

But Pre-tribulationism uses the term "tribulation" to refer to the entire period of the Endtimes, including The Beginning of Birth Pains, The Greatest Persecution, and Christ's Wrath. But it is vital to distinguish between the persecution that the Last Generation Church will experience, from Christ's Wrath that the Church will be rescued from. The biblical sequence of Endtime events demonstrated in previous chapters makes this clear.

In Revelation 3:10, Christ is promising to **protect** Christians from something that is going to **come upon the whole world** in the Endtimes. What is it? Pre-tribulationism claims it will be The Beginning of Birth Pains and The Greatest Persecution of the Antichrist. However, there are several clear arguments against this.

First, the previous chapters of *Christ Endtimes Teaching* have clearly demonstrated the biblical sequence of Endtime events. In Matthew 24:29-31 Jesus clearly taught that it will only be **"immediately after the persecution** [*thlipsis*, The Greatest Persecution, cf. vs. 9, 21] **of those days** that **He will send out His angels with a loud trumpet sound, and they will lift up and gather together God's elect people from one end of the sky to the other, from everywhere on Earth."**

Secondly, Pre-tribulationism claims that Jesus is promising the Church will be rescued from The Greatest Persecution in Revelation 3:10. But neither Jesus, nor the Apostles, ever promised that. Paul wrote: **In fact, everyone who wants to live a godly life in Christ Jesus will be persecuted** (2 Tim 3:12 NIV).

Pre-tribulationism claims that the Church will be rescued from the Endtime "tribulation" before entering the Kingdom of God. But Paul and Barnabas told early Christians: **"Through many tribulations** [*thlipseōn*] **we must enter the kingdom of God"** (Acts 14:22 NASB).

Pre-tribulationism claims the Church is destined to be rescued from the Endtime "tribulation." But Paul told the Thessalonians:

> **We sent Timothy, our brother and God's coworker in the gospel of Christ, to strengthen and encourage you concerning your faith, so that no one will be shaken by these persecutions** [*thlipsesen*]**. For you yourselves know that we are appointed to this** [i.e. persecution]. (1 Thess 3:2-4 CSB)

Pre-tribulationism claims the Church cannot experience the Antichrist. But Jesus told **God's elect people** (*eklektous*, Matt 24:22) that they would **see standing in the holy place 'the abomination that causes desolation,' spoken of through the prophet Daniel** (Matt 24:15 NIV).

Contrary to Pre-tribulationism, everything Jesus described in His Endtimes Sermon are things the Church is promised to experience before Christ's Return or the Church's Rescue.

Accordingly, instead of promising <u>any</u> of the seven churches in Revelation 2-3 exemption from persecution, He repeatedly promised them the opposite. He promised them **hardships** (2:2-3); **afflictions, suffering, persecution ... even to the point of death** (2:9-10). This included three churches that were "persevering" in their faith, just like the church in Philadelphia (cf. 2:2, 13, 19; 3:8, 10). [23] In fact, Christ had only praise for **the church in Smyrna** and yet promised them **you will suffer persecution** (Rev 2:8, 10).

There is no biblical support for claiming that Revelation 3:10 is promising the Last Generation Church protection from "tribulation," suffering, or persecution. So what was Christ promising to **protect** these Christians **from**?

So again, what was Christ promising to **protect** these Christians **from**? We may be helped in answering that question by considering a suggested translation of Revelation 3:10:

> **"Because you have obeyed my command to persevere, I will protect you from the great time of <u>temptation to sin</u>** [*peirasmou*] **that will come upon the unbelievers in the whole world to <u>tempt</u>** [*peirasai*] **those who belong to this world."**

This suggested translation is based on the NLT. There are two differences. First, the translation of the noun *peirasmou* and its related verb *peirasai* in the Greek text. These Greek words can either mean: 1) an attempt to learn the nature or character of something, <u>test</u>, *trial*; or 2) an attempt to make one do something wrong, <u>temptation</u>, *enticement*. [24] The fact that these words can be translated as the latter is reflected in the marginal note of the NASB which offers the option of "temptation" and "tempt" in Revelation 3:10.

Temptation to sin fits the context of Revelation 3:10 best. Why? Because the Endtime event Christ is speaking of **will come upon the whole world** to afflict **those who belong to this world"** (NLT). The NASB refers to these people as **"those who dwell on the earth."** This phrase is used 10 other times in Revelation and "always refers to unbelievers, the enemies of God" [25] and never includes believers (cf. Rev 6:10; 8:13; 11:10; 12:12; 13:8, 12, 14; 14:6; 17:2, 8). Accordingly, there is a second change in the suggested translation from the NLT. It is accurate to state the event **will come upon the unbelievers in the whole world.**

Therefore, what makes more sense? That God intends to "test" **unbelievers** in the Endtimes to "attempt to learn their nature or character"? Or to punish **unbelievers** in the Endtimes by allowing them to be "tempted" into greater sin and judgment?

God will have no purpose to "test" the character of **unbelievers** in the Endtimes. Revelation teaches they will be completely wicked and unrepentant (cf. Rev 9:20-21; 13:8, 16-17; 16:8-11). In fact, their depravity will be the very reason that God will allow them to be tempted into greater sin and punishment.

Therefore, the suggested translation of Revelation 3:10 is:

"Because you have obeyed my command to persevere, I will protect you from the great time of temptation to sin that will come upon the unbelievers of the whole world to tempt those who belong to this world."

This translation helps us to avoid another possible mistake in interpreting this text. The common translation of **trial** (NIV, ESV) suggests Christ is promising exemption or rescue from suffering in the Endtimes. Obviously, Pre-tribulationism uses this idea to claim Revelation 3:10 is a promise to be exempted from the suffering of The Greatest Persecution. But for the reasons shared above, this is not biblical because the NT promises the Church persecution.

Therefore, it seems that Christ was promising to **protect** these Christians **from the great time of temptation to sin that will come upon the unbelievers of the whole world to tempt those who belong to this world.**

So what is this referring to? It is not referring to the suffering of The Greatest Persecution, [26] but to the **temptation to sin** during The Greatest Persecution. The **great time of temptation to sin that will come upon the unbelievers of the whole world to tempt those who belong to this world** seems to be referring to the temptations of the Antichrist to deceive the whole world into the great sin of worshipping him. This **great time of temptation to sin** in the Endtimes is described elsewhere by Paul when he writes:

The coming of the lawless one [Antichrist] **will be in accordance with how Satan works. He will use all sorts of displays of power through signs and wonders that serve the lie, and all the ways that wickedness deceives those who are perishing.**

They perish because they refused to love the truth and so be saved. For this reason God sends them a powerful delusion so that they will believe the lie and so that all will be condemned who have not believed the truth but have delighted in wickedness. (2 Thess 2:9-12 NIV)

Revelation 13 explains that this **powerful delusion** sent by God will include Antichrist's Resurrection which will successfully tempt the entire pagan world to worship him and accept his **mark** (cf. Rev 13:1-17). It will be impossible for the pagan world to resist the temptation to this great sin, and it will result in their extraordinary and eternal punishment (cf. Rev 14:9-12).

As Paul explained, God's purpose in all this temptation and supernatural deception will be **so that all will be condemned who have not believed the truth but have delighted in wickedness** in the Endtimes.

Through the temptations of the Antichrist, God will be exercising what Paul described in Romans 1. There he describes the unbelieving world as those who **did not think it worthwhile to retain the knowledge of God, so God gave them over to a depraved mind, so that they do what ought not to be done. They have become filled with every kind of wickedness** (vs. 28-29). Therefore, such people are simply "given over" by God to their depravity and deception, all leading to their punishment.

This seems to be the Endtime **temptation** that Jesus was promising to **protect** all Endtime Christians **from**. By the power of the Spirit, every Christian will **obey** Christ's **command to persevere**, will not worship the Antichrist or take his mark, and therefore, will not be condemned with the pagan world. [27]

What Jesus is promising all Christians in His promise to the church in Philadelphia is what He prayed for on Earth. He said, **"My prayer is not that you take them out of the world but that you**

protect them from [*tērēsēs ek*] **the evil one**" (John 17:15 NIV). Notice that the Greek here is identical to the promise in Revelation 3:10 to **protect from** (*tērēsō ek*). It will not be Christ's will to take the Church **out of the world** during the deceptions and temptations the Antichrist will unleash during The Greatest Persecution. Rather, for His glory, all believers in the Last Generation Church will be "overcomers" and resist all temptations of the Antichrist.

Myth #13 in Pre-tribulationism is that Revelation 3:10 is promising the Church will be "raptured" before The Greatest Persecution. The truth is that Jesus clearly taught the Last Generation Church would experience The Greatest Persecution. Therefore, it seems Revelation 3:10 is a promise to **protect** Christians **from the great time of temptation ... that will tempt those who belong to this world** to worship the Antichrist, take his **mark**, and be eternally damned.

---

[1] Erickson points out that Amillennialism has also contributed to the great error of "imminency":

> The Amillennialist believes in the imminence of Christ's second coming. While this term has many different shades of meaning, it does mean, in general, that the Lord could return virtually at any time... Thus with no major events of long duration yet to be fulfilled [according to Amillennialism], the Lord could come at any time.
>
> It should be noted, however, that while this tenet is shared by amillennialists and premillennialists, it does not produce the same mood or tone in the typical amillennialist that it often does in the premillennialist. [The Amillennialist] has noticeably less preoccupation with the details and sequence of the last things and less curiosity about "signs of the times." (*Guide*, 75)

[2] Lahaye & Jenkins, 6.

[3] Hitchcock, *End*, 109. While Pre-tribulationism claims the "rapture" is signless, a Preterist like France is so committed to seeing everything in Matt 24:4-26 as only applying to the destruction of the Jerusalem temple in A.D. 70 that he claims regarding the visible coming of Christ described in vs. 27, 29-30:

> [It] will carry no prior warning. So the disciples' request for a 'sign' for his *parousia* was misguided; unlike the messianic pretenders, with

their offer of 'signs' [cf. v. 24], the Son of Man will give no warning sign of his *parousia* (918).

As a result, he falls into the Pre-tribulational false teaching about the supposed "imminency" of the Rapture.

4 Carson, *Matt*, at ch. 24. Likewise, Piper writes:
> I think the answer to the question, Does the New Testament teach that Jesus may come at any moment? is no. The reason is that the New Testament teaches that there are events yet to happen before he comes... [T]his does not diminish the urgency of the commands to watch and be awake and alert and ready for his coming. In fact, I will argue that we have no warrant to be sure that his coming is ever more than a few years away. (203)

5 Lahaye, 106.

6 Ibid.

7 Knoor, 147.

8 Hitchcock, *End*, 142-3.

9 The NLT unfortunately over-translates when it renders 1 Thess 5:3 as: **When people are saying, "Everything is peaceful and secure," then disaster will fall on them as suddenly as a pregnant woman's labor pains begin.**

On the contrary, the more literal Greek text is reflected in the NASB which says, **they are saying, "Peace and safety!"** Therefore, Paul's meaning is much less clear than the NLT makes it.

10 Carson, *Matt*, 571.

11 *BDAG* #1.

12 Green, at 1 Thess 5:3.

13 Ignoring the biblical context that Christ gave us in His Endtimes Teaching, many scholars suggest the **people** will be **saying, "Peace and safety"** (1 Thess 5:3) because they will be experiencing it. Green writes: "the apostle replies that in a time of political tranquility and social prosperity destruction will come on them suddenly" (at 1 Thess 5:3).

Wanamaker claims people will be essentially saying "everything [is] fine" (180). Morris says, "people [will be] in [a] fancied security" (96). Bruce is not helpful here. Still, for reasons given in this section, these interpretations would seem to be wrong.

14 Wiersbe at 2 Thess 2:1.

15 For an explanation of the suggested translation of Dan 12:1 see ch. 7, sec. C.1 and endnote there.

16 Walvoord agrees with the context of Daniel 12 and writes: "The opening phrase of chapter 12, *and at that time*, makes clear that this passage is talking about the same period of time as the previous context, that is 'the time of the end' (11:40)." (*Dan* 282; see Young, 255; Wallace 191; Hill, loc. 6767 for agreement).

17 *TWOT*, 779; cf. Gen 32:7; Judg 2:15; 10:9.

18 *TWOT*, 673.

19 For more on Rev ch. 12 see appropriate chapter in book #3: *The Greatest Persecution*.

20 As noted, Wiersbe, a Pre-tribulationist, supports the view that the "Restrainer" in 2 Thess 2:6-7 is the Holy Spirit. He writes:

> The restrainer is a person who is today "in the midst," but will one day be "taken out of the midst." Many Bible students identify this restrainer as the Holy Spirit of God. Certainly, He is "in the midst" of God's program today, working through the church to accomplish God's purposes.
>
> When the church is raptured, the Holy Spirit will not be taken out of the world (otherwise nobody could be saved during the tribulation), but He will be taken out of the midst to allow Satan and his forces to go to work. The Holy Spirit will certainly be present on the Earth during the day of the Lord, but He will not be restraining the forces of evil as He is today. (2 Thess 2:1)

Apparently, the idea here is that the Holy Spirit is "in the midst" of the Church and will be removed. But no versions translate it that way, including the more literal NASB. The Greek more likely means, "something taken from the middle" or between, which can certainly refer to Michael being removed from between Satan and God's people.

Accordingly, Green remarks on 2 Thess 2:7:

> The verse in no way indicates that the Holy Spirit or the church will in some way be taken out of the world. This is hardly an adequate foundation for the commonly held teaching that the rapture of the church will happen sometime before the antichrist is revealed!

MacArthur being a Pre-tribulationist is understandably opposed to the view that Michael is the "Restrainer." His reason? MacArthur claims: "Michael does not have the power to restrain Satan (Jude 9)" (*MNTC, Thess*, 277).

Regardless of his interpretation of Jude 1:9, the Archangel is clearly portrayed as having the power to throw Satan out of Heaven in Revelation 12.

Another reason that some reject the claim that the "Restrainer" is the Archangel Michael is that a neuter pronoun (**what** NASB) is used in v. 6. However, neuter pronouns are used elsewhere in the NT to refer to Angels.

In Hebrews we read, **Are not all angels ministering spirits** [*pneumata*, in the neuter gender] **sent to serve those who will inherit salvation?** (1:14 NIV). This is also true in the case of an evil angel or demon (cf. the use of **it** 7 times in Matthew 12:43-45).

Nevertheless, in 2 Thess 2:7 Paul does refer to the "Restrainer" with a masculine pronoun. Therefore, the Archangel Michael can be a thing/being that Paul could refer to with both a neuter and masculine pronoun. Admittedly, the same is true of the Holy Spirit in the NT. Therefore, Walvoord is wrong to state, regarding his view that the "Restrainer" is the Holy Spirit, "this is the only view that adequately explains the change in gender in verses 6-7" (*Thess*, loc. 2096). On the contrary, the Archangel Michael does the same.

Stott quotes Augustine to say regarding Paul's reference to the "Restrainer," "I frankly confess I do not know what he means." Stott himself believes it is referring to government and does not even mention Michael (*BST*, Thess). Stott's view is the most common traditional view (cf. Tertullian, Chrysostom, Bruce, 173, Morris, 131.) However, this ignores the fact that the "Restrainer" is referred to in the masculine sense in v. 7 meaning it is a person or being, not a government.

Others suggest the "Restrainer" is the Gospel, but Green and Wanamaker (250-51) rather clearly refute this view.

Perhaps the most common view among modern scholars is that the "Restrainer" is actually "lawlessness" or ultimately Satan himself (Green, Wanamaker). Wanamaker suggests "the decisive issue" is explaining Paul's reference to the "Restrainer with both a neuter and masculine participles."

Wanamaker's solution? "[T]ake *katechōn* ["restrain"] as meaning "to hold sway," "to rule," or "to prevail" and this refers to "lawlessness" (253). But BDAG reveals Wanamaker's mistake because the meanings he wants to give to *katechōn* do not exist in ancient Greek or the NT. By far the most common meaning was to "restrain" as it is translated in all versions. Other meanings include "to keep in one's possession" (*BDAG* #3) But this does not mean what Wanamaker wants it to mean, such as "to rule."

Unfortunately, none of these scholars even mention the biblical data pointing to the Archangel Michael being the "Restrainer." Nor do they recognize that he is a biblical explanation for "the decisive issue" of Paul using both neuter and masculine Greek to refer to him.

This is definitely a much better solution than distorting the Greek to actually make Paul say the "Restrainer" is supporting the Antichrist, instead of stopping him. Again, the context clearly tells us that is not what Paul meant.

[21] Osborne, 192.

22 MacArthur, *MNTC*, Matt 24. Walvoord, as expected, interprets Rev 3:10 from a Pre-tribulationist view like MacArthur and writes: "The expression seems as strong as possible that the Philadelphian church would be delivered from this period, which is the great tribulation, Daniel's seventieth week (cf. Dan. 9:25–27)" (loc. 1318). Thomas agrees (469ff).

Osborne has a Post-tribulational interpretation of Rev 3:10, claiming it refers to "protection" from Endtime events including "the trumpets" punishments during Christ's Wrath (193-4). For reasons shared in chapter 11, sec. D.2 this is unbiblical.

Mounce seems to at least partially support the view argued in this chapter:

> The hour of trial is that period of testing and tribulation that precedes the establishment of the eternal kingdom. It is mentioned in such passages as Daniel 12:2, Mark 13:19, and 2 Thessalonians 2:1-12. It is the three and a half years of rule by Antichrist in Revelation 13:5-10...
>
> The hour of trial is directed toward the entire non-Christian world, but the believer will be kept from it, not by some previous appearance of Christ to remove the church bodily from the world, but by the spiritual protection he provides against the forces of evil. (103)

23 Pre-tribulationists claim the Philadelphian church is the only one promised protection in the Endtimes. But there is no evidence of this. Why was the Philadelphian church promised protection? Jesus said it was **Because you have obeyed my command to <u>persevere</u>** (3:10). But such praise was not unique to this church. As noted here, Christ praised 3 other churches for the same thing (cf. 2:2, 13, 19; 3:8, 10).

Therefore, why, according to Pre-tribulationism, was the **church in Philadelphia** alone promised protection? First, this is a faulty premise. It is best to understand this promise would be extended to all the churches who were persevering. Why? Because perseverance is the proof of saving faith and real Christians. All Christians are promised protection in the Endtimes.

Rejecting this biblical view, Pre-tribulationism has developed a complicated and obscure view of Church history to support their claim that the Philadelphian church was somehow unique. The theory is that each of the seven local churches Christ spoke to in the first century, actually represent different eras or time periods of the Church throughout history. In other words, this aspect of Pre-tribulationism makes the same mistake as Historicism (cf. ch. 3, sec. B).

Tim Lahaye has presented one of the clearest descriptions of this interpretation of these churches. For example, he claims the church in Thyatira represents the Roman Catholic Church starting about A. D. 600. He further claims that the Sardis church represents the Protestant Reformation starting about the year 1520 (Lahaye, 24).

Using such a scheme, he then concludes that the Philadelphia church began about 1750 A.D. and will continue until the "rapture." Therefore, Revelation 3:10 written to this local church is a promise from God that the universal church on Earth at the time of the "rapture" will experience that promise.

Obviously, there are several problems with this. First, Pre-tribulationism claims to be a defender of interpreting Scripture "in its most natural, normal, customary (i.e., literal or face value) sense" (Van Kampen, 6). But they have abandoned that rule in their effort to make Revelation 3:10 fit their theories (and desires!) on the Endtimes.

Secondly, a common sense and unbiased reading of Revelation 2-3, and a knowledge of various periods of Church history, disprove the theory. These Scriptures do not describe the attributes of specific periods of Church history. Nor can periods of Church history be so clearly defined. For example, the Roman Catholic Church has remained a powerful influence in this world, even since the Protestant Reformation.

Thirdly, there is no indication whatsoever that Jesus intended His words to these local churches to be predictions about the future of the universal Church.

Fourth, the theory only reflects an Evangelical and western view of Church history. Its omission of massive Christian movements in Pentecostalism/Charismaticism, Greek and Russian Orthodoxy, and revivals in Africa, Asia, and South America, make it a very questionable biblical prophecy about Church history. Accordingly, as Osborne concludes: "Even dispensational [Pre-tribulational] scholars like Thomas (see his excellent discussion, 1992:511-15) opt for the view that the letters address historical situations in Asia Minor, not periods of church history" (105).

Finally, Pre-tribulationism forgets that this interpretation of Revelation 2-3 violates its claim that the NT taught from the very beginning that the "rapture" could occur at "any moment." At least according to Lahaye, regardless of what other Scripture taught, the "rapture" could not have occurred at least until 1750. In conclusion, the necessary Pre-tribulation scheme to explain why the church in Philadelphia was given a unique promise of escaping the Greatest Persecution has no truth to it.

[24] *BDAG*. For Rev 3:10 *BDAG* oddly places the noun *peirasmou* under the definition of: "an attempt to make one do something wrong, <u>temptation</u>;" but places the verb *peirasai* under "to endeavor to discover the nature or character of something by <u>testing</u>." First, this is inconsistent. Surely the noun and verb in the same verse have the same general meaning. Secondly, defining the verb here as "testing" ignores the arguments in this section.

[25] Osborne, 193.

26 Admittedly, the *peirazō* word group is used to refer to testing by suffering in Rev 2:10 where we read: **Do not be afraid of what you are about to suffer. I tell you, the devil will put some of you in prison to test [*peirasthēte*] you, and you will suffer persecution for ten days.** Here "testing" refers to suffering at the hands of **the devil**.

Therefore, this same meaning could be applied to Rev 3:10 to suggest it is being used there to refer to suffering as well. But this would not be a reference to The Greatest Persecution as claimed by Pre-tribulationists. The "testing" or "tempting" described in Rev 3:10 is experienced by only unbelievers. The Greatest Persecution will not primarily be a time of suffering for them.

27 See remarks on Post-tribulationism's efforts to make Rev 3:10 fit its view in ch. 11, sec. D.2. For a good discussion of the complicated issues regarding the precise grammar of *tēreō ek* in Rev 3:10 see Thomas (470ff).

As noted above, the decisive factor is the broader context of the teaching of Scripture. It has been argued in this section that Rev 3:10 is a promise to protect Endtime Christians from the temptations of the Antichrist to take his mark during The Greatest Persecution, and which will result in the condemnation of the entire pagan world. Therefore, the meaning of *tēreō ek* in Rev 3:10 would seem to be "protect or preserve while remaining in."

Therefore, it is also suggested that the NLT **protect you from** (cf. CEV) is a helpful translation. Likewise, the GNT has **keep you safe from**. This seems better than the more obscure and common translation of **keep you from** (NIV, NASB, ESV, NRSV, NET, CSB, NCV, KJV, NKJV). Still, contrary to Pre-tribulationism, this author is not aware of any modern English versions of the Bible that translate *tēreō ek* in Rev 3:10 as anything like "rescue you out of."

Chapter 16

The Practical & Spiritual Harm of Popular Teaching on the Endtimes

Contents

A) Popular but false teaching about the Endtimes has left the Church unprepared to glorify God in The Greatest Persecution, resulting in lost eternal rewards

B) The "Thessalonian Panic"

C) The vulnerability of shock caused by not obeying Christ's command to "**Watch!**" for signs of His Return

D) Pre-tribulationism mimics false prophets

E) Amillennialism leaves the Church unprepared for the Endtimes

F) Help to be prepared for the Endtimes

Primary Points

- Because the popular and false views on the Endtimes are painless, they are also useless. One of the most evident dangers of believing and teaching false and popular views on the Endtimes is that it leaves the Church unprepared for The Greatest Persecution.

- All of a Christian's suffering is wasted if they do not **endure persecution patiently**, and courageously, peacefully, and joyfully. Only what is done in God's Spirit of **love, joy, peace** (Gal 5:22) glorifies God and will be rewarded.

- Anxious, discouraged, and confused Christians <u>will not</u> glorify God in the Endtimes. And those who do not correctly understand the Endtimes will be much more likely to fail in these things when the Endtimes begin.

- Believing false teaching on the Endtimes will cost you rewards for all eternity if you are in the Last Generation Church.

- The Thessalonian church was scared out of their mind because they did not understand the biblical sequence of Endtime events. The same will be true for many Christians in the Last Generation Church.

- Why did the Thessalonian Christians have such a lazy attitude toward understanding Paul's teaching on Endtime events? Because the Thessalonian Pastors did not value Paul's teaching on the sequence of Endtime events.
- The popular but false views on the Endtimes discourage Christians from intelligently and diligently watching for signs of Christ's Return. As a result, many in the Church will be unprepared to glorify God when The Beginning of Birth Pains begin.
- Unfortunately, those who teach Pre-tribulationism are like the false prophets in the OT who falsely assured God's people they would not experience the disasters God was warning of through real Prophets.
- The future, physical, and literal interpretation of biblical prophecy is far more important for the well-being of God's people than any of the historical, spiritual, metaphorical, and often questionable and out-of-context meanings Amillennialists want to emphasize.
- Being deceived is the most dangerous thing of all.
- God wants your whole mind to be controlled by His Love, so that your whole heart can be controlled by the **love, joy,** and **peace** of His Spirit, so that your whole life will glorify God.

A) Popular but false teaching about the Endtimes has left the Church unprepared to glorify God in The Greatest Persecution, resulting in lost eternal rewards

A.1) The purpose of Christ's warnings

In the Church today the Endtimes is viewed as a morally neutral theological topic. Therefore, it is claimed there is really no need to persuade Christians of a particular view. For example, John Piper in a recent book on Christ's Second Coming, points out several unbiblical beliefs about Pre-tribulationism. Still, he writes:

> The main aim of this book is not to change the minds of those who hold a pre-tribulational view of the second coming. My main aim is that both of us would love the Lord's appearing, whichever view we hold. [1]

It is true of course that nobody's eternal salvation depends on their view of the Endtimes. But if Dr. Piper really believes Pre-tribulationism is unbiblical, as he argues in his book, then why would he not want to "change the minds of those who hold a pre-tribulational view of the second coming"? More seriously, his view ignores the very real practical, spiritual, and even eternal costs for Christians who would enter the Endtimes with an unbiblical view of this doctrine. Those painful and eternal costs are the topic of this chapter.

It was noted in the first chapter of *Christ's Endtimes Teaching* that all of the popular but false views on the Endtimes have one thing in common: They are relatively painless.

The apathetic view claims it is not even God's will for us to understand what will really happen to the Church in the Endtimes. That enables the Church to ignore the painful realities that Jesus warned us of. Likewise, as will be demonstrated in a moment, Amillennialism also practically ignores the suffering the Church will experience in the Endtimes. And of course, Pre-tribulationism actually promises the Church will not experience the Endtimes at all.

Unfortunately, one of the most evident dangers of believing and teaching these false views on the Endtimes is that it leaves the Church unprepared for The Greatest Persecution. Popular views either diminish the need to understand The Greatest Persecution, or claim the Church will be exempt from it. Therefore, proponents of these views rarely if ever teach anything to prepare the Church for The Greatest Persecution.

Many will respond, "So what. Even if it's true that the Last Generation Church will experience The Greatest Persecution, does it really matter if we understand that ahead of time?"

First of all, it is not necessary to know all the practical ramifications of Biblical truth before we should consider it essential. We need to assume that anything that God's Word teaches for the Church is absolutely critical, even if we may not yet be certain why.

What Pastor in his right mind would stand before God and claim that portions of NT Scripture "don't really matter"? Yet that is the implied message of those who ignore or distort Christ's intended purpose and meaning for His Endtimes Teaching.

Because all the popular views on the Endtimes are rather <u>painless</u>, they are rather <u>useless</u> to prepare the Church to glorify God if the Endtimes begin in our generation. This was explained further in chapter 1 where some of the following points were made.

Many talk as if there will be no consequences if God's people do not understand God's word about the Endtimes. They are wrong. There is always a cost when God's people do not correctly or confidently understand God's Word. This is true of the doctrine of the Endtimes. This is <u>not</u> simply an academic debate. The current confusion and controversy in the Church on this doctrine would greatly hurt Christians if the Endtimes begin any time soon.

All of these rather painless views on the Endtimes ignore the fact that Jesus wanted to warn His Church about the unprecedented catastrophes and persecutions of the Endtimes. Why was Jesus so concerned about warning His Church of these things? To help them be prepared to face them in a God-glorifying way.

Notice in the following text that Jesus said He was warning His followers about the Endtimes in order to protect them:

"Since they persecuted me, naturally they will persecute you... <u>I have told you these things so that you will not stumble in your faith.</u> For you will be expelled from the synagogues, and the time is coming when those who kill you will think they are doing a holy service for God... Yes, <u>I'm telling you these things now, so that when they happen, you will remember my warning.</u> (John 15:20; 16:1-2, 4 [2])

Jesus warned His followers about the challenges of the Endtimes because He believed it would help them **not stumble** in their Christian **faith**. Unfortunately, many today do not believe the Church needs such warnings.

However, if the Endtimes began today, many Christians would be greatly confused, and that confusion would greatly hinder their ability to enter the Endtimes with courage, clarity, and confidence. That is not what God wanted. Which is why Jesus gave us a rather simple, clear, although painful sermon about what the Endtimes will mean for the Church. This was so His people could be spiritually prepared for the Endtimes if they occurred in their lifetime.

But what do popular views of the Endtimes teach us? Either we will not even be here for these things, or the details of the Endtimes don't matter. Saying the details don't matter, means that Christ's warnings don't matter either. Frankly, there seems to be an arrogance in the apathetic view on this doctrine. It seems foolish to believe that Christians will be quickly equipped to respond to the Endtimes in a God-glorifying manner when they have never been taught correctly on this doctrine.

It is often assumed that God's people can be prepared to face the Endtimes in a God-glorifying way even if they don't understand what Christ was warning His Church of. Do you know better than Jesus? He believed the Church needed to know the substance and sequence of Endtime events. Do you? Jesus intentionally and faithfully warned His Church about these things because He knew the Church needs to know more than what many are teaching on this topic.

A.2) The great pain of The Greatest Persecution

Jesus wanted to warn His Church that in the Endtimes, **"there will be the greatest persecution of God's elect people. It will be greater than any persecution since the world began, and it will never be equaled again"** (Matt 24:21). Many teachers in the Church today talk as if it was not important for Christ to give this warning to His followers. But Christ believed the warning was important because He wanted His Church to be as ready as possible to endure the Endtimes in a God-glorifying way.

Part of the problem is that most Christians have had relatively safe and prosperous lives. This is especially true of American Christians. As a result, many of them experience anxiety and depression when faced with relatively minor difficulties. This does not glorify God, and such a spiritually weak response to the much greater suffering of the Endtimes will not either.

In The Greatest Persecution, Christian husbands, wives, teens, and children will experience unimaginable chaos and turmoil because virtually everything in their life will be changed. More than changed, virtually everything and everyone in their life will be lost.

They will lose their homes, jobs, money, freedom, life, and the life of their loved ones. We see a glimpse of what The Greatest Persecution will be like when we read what God has allowed to happen to His people in the past:

> **Others were tortured ... Some were jeered at, and their backs were cut open with whips. Others were chained in prisons. Some died by stoning, some were sawed in half, and others were killed with the sword.**
>
> **Some went about wearing skins of sheep and goats, destitute and oppressed and mistreated... wandering over deserts and mountains, hiding in caves and holes in the ground.** (Heb 11:35-38 NLT)

Does what your Pastor teach on the Endtimes help you and your family be ready to experience <u>that</u> in a God-glorifying way?

Or what about what happened to the Jews who were persecuted by the Antichrist's forerunner, Antiochus Epiphanes, as reliably recorded in the Book of Maccabees. [3] We read:

> Mothers who had allowed their babies to be circumcised were put to death in accordance with the king's decree. Their babies were hung around their necks, and their families and those who had circumcised them were put to death. [4]

> It also came about that seven brothers were arrested along with their mother. King Antiochus was torturing them with whips and the rack to compel them to eat pork against the dictates of the law... After this was done he commanded that [one of the sons'] tongue be cut out, his scalp be sliced away, and his limbs be amputated while his mother and brothers looked on... The mother ... saw her seven sons perish [by similar tortures] in the span of a single day. [5]

Jesus said The Greatest Persecution will be like that. Christians will be ripped apart by wild beasts in the arena like the early Christians in Rome. They will be pulled apart by the rack and burned alive as the Roman Catholics did to Christians during the Inquisition. It will be like what the Nazis did to the Jews in the concentration camps during the Holocaust. Does what your church teach on the Endtimes help you be prepared for such things?

A.3) The great test of The Greatest Persecution

Do you know what will be the <u>most important</u> and challenging task for you if you encounter the Endtimes? <u>Will you glorify God?</u> The Bible says, **Whatever you do, do it all for the glory of God** (1 Cor 10:31 NIV), including suffering in the Endtimes. Accordingly, Revelation tells us one way to do that during The Greatest Persecution:

> **Anyone with ears to hear should listen and understand. Anyone who is destined for prison will be taken to prison. Anyone destined to <u>die</u> by the <u>sword</u> will die by the sword. This means that God's holy people must <u>endure persecution patiently</u> and remain faithful.** (Rev 13:9-10 NLT)

As will be demonstrated elsewhere, all real Christians will **remain faithful** during The Greatest Persecution. [6] None will deny Christ, **receive** Antichrist's **mark** (Rev 13:16), and lose their salvation. But not all Christians will obey and glorify God by **endur**ing **persecution patiently**. Therefore, notice something important. It will <u>not</u> be enough to just **endure** the intense suffering of The Greatest Persecution. Many unbelievers can merely endure suffering.

All of a Christian's suffering is <u>wasted</u> if they do not **endure persecution <u>patiently</u>**, and courageously, peacefully, and joyfully. Only what is done in God's Spirit of **love, joy, peace** (Gal 5:22) glorifies God and will be eternally rewarded. Responding to the suffering of The Greatest Persecution with the sinful nature's fear, selfishness, complaining, and discouragement will <u>not</u> glorify God or be eternally rewarded. [7] The Apostle warned:

> **If anyone builds on this foundation** [of Christ] **using gold, silver, costly stones, wood, hay or straw, their work will be shown for what it is, because the Day** [of evaluation] **will bring it to light. It will be revealed with fire, and the fire will test the quality** [value NLT] **of each person's work. If what has been built survives, the builder will receive a <u>reward</u>. If it is burned up, the builder will <u>suffer loss</u> but yet will be saved.** (1 Cor 3:12-15 NIV)

We see again that the issue here is loss of eternal rewards, not eternal salvation. Still, notice that there will be something much worse than experiencing the intense suffering of the Endtimes. It will be failing to glorify God, wasting that suffering, and losing potential eternal rewards for the suffering, because you did not **endure persecution patiently** in the Spirit's **love, joy,** and **peace**. Merely suffering while being afraid, selfish, and depressed will be like **wood, hay or straw** in terms of eternal value. Only glorifying God with the Spirit's courage, peace, joy, and love will be considered like **gold, silver** and **costly stones** to God.

God's purpose for the Endtimes is to test the faith and character of His people. Those who are not correctly taught on this doctrine will be much more likely to fail those tests. As a result they will lose rewards for all eternity. That is the eternal cost for believing false teachings about the Endtimes and being unprepared for them if they begin in your lifetime. It will affect how you experience eternity.

The Apostle John warned, **Many deceivers ... have gone out into the world... Watch out** that you are not deceived so **that you do not lose what you have worked for, but that you may be rewarded fully** (2 John 1:7-8). Do you see it? Believing false teaching will cause a Christian to **lose** being **rewarded fully** for all eternity. The Great White Throne Evaluation will reveal that those who taught the popular and false views on the Endtimes, will cost their followers for all eternity in lost glory and rewards.

Anxious, discouraged, and confused Christians will not glorify their God in the Endtimes. And those who do not even understand that the Last Generation Church will experience The Greatest Persecution, will be much more likely to fail in courage, faith, and clarity on the truth when the Endtimes begin.

For example, Christians who have not been taught correctly about the Endtimes will be unprepared to obey Christ's command to evangelize. Jesus said that during the Endtimes, **"this gospel of the kingdom will be preached in the whole world as a** (last) **testimony to all nations, and then the end will come"** (Matt 24:14 NIV). Frightened, disillusioned, and confused Christians will not be much of a **testimony**, nor able to exercise the faith and courage that evangelism during The Greatest Persecution will require. When the Endtimes begin, it will be a time for bold witnessing, not for wallowing in fear and confusion.

Many doubt the practical and spiritual cost of being deceived about the Endtimes. But seeking and believing false and painless interpretations of Christ's Endtimes Teaching will cost you and your loved ones in many ways, especially if the Endtimes begin in your lifetime. In fact, the cost will last you for all eternity, as warned above.

Many arrogantly assume today that you can be spiritually prepared to face the Endtimes in a God-glorifying way even if you do not understand what Scripture teaches on this doctrine. But do not follow them. It is easy to assume you can **endure persecution patiently**, including seeing what your loved ones will experience in The Greatest Persecution, with God-glorifying faith. But many Christians are missing something God wanted to give them to help them have a solid faith in the Endtimes.

God knew what you needed to be prepared for the Endtimes. And one of those things was all the prophetic Scriptures He provided to give His people an accurate understanding of the Church's future. But false and popular teaching on the Endtimes has currently stolen this gift of God from the Church. He wanted to tell us the future of the Church, and popular teaching distorts or devalues His message.

Why would we doubt there is a cost when God's people do not correctly understand God's word?

B) The "Thessalonian Panic"

The Thessalonian church illustrates several of the practical dangers of <u>not</u> correctly understanding the biblical sequence of Endtime events.

[Please stop and read 2 Thessalonians 2:1-5]

The Thessalonian **brothers and sisters** were **easily shaken** and **alarmed** by false teachers who claimed **the day of the Lord has already begun** (2 Thess 2:1-2 NLT). **Shaken** translates a Greek word (*saleuthēnai*) used elsewhere to describe the earthquake that occurred at the Philippian jail (cf. Acts 16:26). The full phrase Paul used here literally means to be, "shaken from your mind" [8] (cf. ESV).

As a result, NT scholars describe these Christians as suffering from "acute confusion," [9] and being "shaken loose from their mental moorings." [10] These Christians were also **alarmed** (*throeisthai*) and in a constant state of fright. [11] They were scared out of their mind. [12]

Why did this "Thessalonian Panic" occur? Because these Christians did not understand the biblical sequence of Endtime events. This is why they believed a false teacher's **spiritual vision ... revelation, or letter** that claimed **the day of the Lord has already begun** (v. 2 NLT). Evidently, there was one thing the Thessalonians did understand. They understood that **the day of the Lord** was Christ's Wrath (cf. ch. 14, sec. B).

Therefore, the Thessalonians understood correctly that if **the day of the Lord has already begun**, then they were living on Earth in **the day of God's wrath** (Rom 2:5) when He **will punish the world for its evil, the wicked for their sins** (Isa 13:11).

The Thessalonians also understood that real Christians were promised to be rescued from **the day of the Lord** and **God's wrath**. Paul had clearly told them in his first letter **to wait for ... Jesus, who rescues us from the coming wrath** (1 Thess 1:10).

Therefore, what conclusions were these Christians coming to that made them **shaken** and **alarmed**? It would seem they believed they had somehow missed "the secret, silent rapture" and had been "left behind." (Sound familiar? It is the name of a very popular fiction series supporting Pre-tribulationism). And if they had been "left behind," then perhaps the persecution they were experiencing was the wrath of God. Accordingly, many of them were probably tempted to doubt even their salvation.

Why were the Thessalonians vulnerable to the false teaching that **the day of the Lord has already come** (v. 2)? Precisely because they did not understand the biblical sequence of Endtime events. Many teach today that it is only important to know what will occur in the Endtimes, but not the sequence these events will occur. But the Thessalonians prove otherwise. It was not because they did not understand what was to occur in the Endtimes. Rather, someone had thrown them into confusion because they did not understand the sequence of Endtime events.

This is why the Apostle chose to effectively correct their error by once again teaching them the proper sequence of Endtime events. He simply wrote:

Concerning the coming of our Lord Jesus Christ and our being gathered together to Him [Christ's Return and the Church's Rescue], **we ask you, brothers and sisters ...**

Don't let anyone deceive you in any way, for that day [the day of Christ's Return, the Church's Rescue, and Christ's Wrath] **will not come until the rebellion occurs and the man of lawlessness** [the Antichrist] **is revealed, the man doomed to destruction.** (2 Thess 2:1-3 NIV)

Why didn't the Thessalonians understand this sequence of events? It was not because Paul had failed to teach them this before. He told them in this very passage: **Don't you remember that when I was with you I used to tell you these things?** (2 Thess 2:5 NIV). What were **these things**? The biblical sequence of Endtime events the Apostle taught in this very passage of Scripture. These included: Christ's Return (**the coming of our Lord Jesus Christ**, v. 1), the Church's Rescue (**our being gathered to him**, v. 1), Antichrist's Claim to be God (v. 3), and Christ's Wrath (**the day of the Lord** which they were rightly afraid of, v. 2).

But there is something especially remarkable about Paul's question to the Thessalonians: **Don't you remember that when I was with you, I used to tell you these things?** (2 Thess 2:5). **When** was he **with** the Thessalonian Christians? Acts indicates that Paul was in Thessalonica perhaps for no longer than three weeks! [13] Luke records **Paul went into the synagogue** [there] **and on** [only] **three** [probably successive] **Sabbath days he reasoned with them from the Scriptures** (Acts 17:2 NIV). Rather immediately afterwards, Paul was forced to leave Thessalonica (vs. 5-10).

Therefore, the Thessalonians had only been Christians for, at most, only a few weeks **when** Paul **was with** them. Even so, Paul taught them the proper outline of Endtime events! And he expected them to understand **these things**. That is a rebuke to many in the Church who either do not understand the Endtimes, or do not believe it is important to do so.

Why didn't the Thessalonians sufficiently understand this doctrine? Because their leaders lacked the **noble character** needed to study this topic with diligence, humility, and courage. On the other hand, Scripture records:

> **Now the Berean Jews were of more noble character than those in Thessalonica, for they received the message** [even about the Endtimes] **with great eagerness and examined the Scriptures every day to see if what Paul said was true.** (Acts 17:11 NIV).

If **the message** Paul preached in **Thessalonica** included the biblical sequence of Endtime events, then the same was probably true in Berea. And no doubt, because of their attitude toward biblical truth, the Bereans understood the Endtimes better and would not have been vulnerable to false teaching like the Thessalonians.

Do you see how the Church today reflects the Thessalonian Pastors and Christians? Pastors promoting and teaching the metaphorical and apathetic views of Endtime doctrine do not value the specific and biblical sequence of Endtime events. Therefore, neither do their people. As a result, they do not have a clear and firm understanding of the specific and biblical sequence of Endtime events. Therefore, those being taught the popular and painless views on the Endtimes will be vulnerable to the same Thessalonian deception, confusion, and panic, when the Endtimes begin.

Likewise, do you see how popular Pre-tribulationism would lead to the same? Pre-tribulational Pastors teach the myths that Christ's Return for the Church's Rescue will occur "at any moment," without any events signaling it, and it will be "secret and silent." Remember as well that Pre-tribulationists teach that The Beginning of Birth Pains will be Christ's Wrath. Those believing such a **myth** will also believe they are experiencing Christ's Wrath when the wars, famines, and plagues begin in the Endtimes. Believing such **myths** will certainly make someone vulnerable to believing **the day of the Lord has already begun** (2 Thess 2:2) like the Thessalonians.

Unfortunately, considering the amount of confusion and error on the topic of the Endtimes in the Church today, it is feared that many will experience what the Thessalonians did. As noted in chapter 1, about <u>half</u> of American Evangelical Christians say, "it is impossible to know the circumstances that will precede Jesus' return" (sec. A). This is a result of the popular Endtimes views that do not value the Bible's teaching on "the circumstances that will precede Jesus' return."

This ignorance is also a result of popular Pre-tribulationism teaching **myths** about "the circumstances that will precede Jesus' return." Like the Thessalonians, such people will not be able to recognize or understand the beginning of the Endtimes. And they certainly will not be prepared for it.

Therefore, those who believe these popular views on the Endtimes will suffer the very same doctrinal errors, emotional trauma, and "Thessalonian Panic," if they face the Endtimes. They too will be confused, alarmed, and spiritually weakened at the very time they will desperately need clarity, conviction, faith, courage, and strength.

Especially imagine the disappointment and disillusionment of those who have been taught Pre-tribulationism when they begin to experience The Beginning of Birth Pains and the emergence of the Antichrist. *Webster's* defines "disillusionment" as "being defeated in expectation or hope." And that is precisely how Christians in the Last Generation Church will feel who have been taught and believed they were to be "raptured" before any Endtime events began.

As explained earlier (ch. 14, sec. F), in the teaching of Pre-tribulationism, being "raptured" before the Endtimes begin is the **blessed hope** (Tit 2:13). Those who enter the Endtimes believing this will have their **blessed hope** crushed. And Proverbs warns, **When hope is crushed, the heart is crushed** (13:12 GNT). That is not how you want to enter the unprecedented challenges of the Endtimes.

All of the above will happen mostly because Pastors did not teach the biblical substance and sequence of Endtime events. Instead, they taught Christians that they were to be rescued before the Endtimes began (Pre-tribulationism). Or they were not taught much at all (Pan-tribulationism and Amillennialism).

Notice one more thing that may happen to Pastors who have taught false or shallow and obscure things regarding the Endtimes. When the Endtimes begin, their church's trust and respect for those Pastors may be understandably and severely damaged, if not irreparably destroyed. Disillusionment and doubt about their leaders may sweep over these churches and be very difficult to overcome.

At the very time the Last Generation Church will need confidence in their leaders and teachers, these men may lose their spiritual and doctrinal authority. As a result, at the very time God's sheep will need shepherds, they will be **confused and helpless, like sheep without a shepherd** (Matt 9:36 NLT).

C) The vulnerability of shock & disillusionment caused by not obeying Christ's command to "Watch!" for signs of His Return

In chapter 2 you read:

> [Christ] wants His Church to be watching and ready for [the Endtimes] when it begins... This is why throughout Christ's sermon on the Endtimes He said: **"Be on guard! Be alert!"** ... **"keep watch"** ... **"What I say to you, I say to everyone: 'Watch!'"** (Mark 13:33, 34, 37 NIV). **Watch!** for what?
>
> Current events in our world that would signal the beginning of the Endtimes, and that Christ's Return is near. (sec. B)

Christ commanded His Church to be alertly watching for the biblical signs of His Return in current events (cf. ch. 10, sec. D). The popular but false views on the Endtimes discourage Christians from doing this. Pan-tribulationism claims it is not God's will for us to know the biblical sequence of Endtime events, so those taught by this view do not even know what to be looking for.

Amillennialism's refusal to sufficiently value the future, physical, and literal fulfillment of biblical prophecy has the same numbing effect. "Historicism" claims Endtime events have primarily been fulfilled in the past.

Pre-tribulationism claims there is absolutely nothing that Christians need to be alert for in the Endtimes because the very first event of the Endtimes is the "rapture" that could occur any day.

All such views discourage Christians from obeying Christ's command to **"Watch!"** As noted in chapter 10 (sec. D):

> Obviously, this command is widely ignored in the Church today... popular views on the Endtimes discourage this very thing. It is the popularity of these false teachings on the Endtimes that has led to the statistic that 45% of American

Evangelical Christians claim: "it is impossible to know the circumstances that will precede Jesus' return." Therefore, it is impossible for such Christians to intelligently obey Christ's command to **"Watch!"**

As with all of Christ's commands, there will be consequences for Christians who disobey His command to **"Watch!"** intelligently and diligently for biblical signs of His Return. As noted in chapter 10, "it would seem the clearest sign the Endtimes have begun will be the Antichrist's Resurrection" (sec. D). This is discussed further in the next book, *The Beginning of Birth Pains*. There it is warned that when the Antichrist's Resurrection occurs, mistaught Christians will be freaking out, and be very confused and afraid.

Because of that, the Antichrist will have a great advantage over those believers who were not prepared to face him. Which again, is what all of the painless, popular, but false teachings on the Endtimes lead to. The Antichrist's unique weapon over such Christians will be: Surprise. Shock.

When we are shocked by painful events, we are emotionally **shaken** and **alarmed** like the Thessalonians, and therefore, mentally and spiritually weakened. Shock makes it all the more difficult to exercise faith at a time when it is most necessary.

Peter's admonition will be incredibly important in the Endtimes:

Dear friends, don't be <u>surprised</u> at the fiery trials you are going through, as if something strange were happening to you. Instead, be very glad. (1 Pet 4:12-13 NLT)

When the **fiery trials** of the Endtimes begin, God will expect His people to glorify Him by being **very glad**. But because popular teaching has left many unprepared for these things, they will **be surprised**, shocked, confused, and afraid.

Likewise, Jesus said, even when these devastating Beginning of Birth Pains occur, **"see to it that you are not alarmed. Such things must happen, but the end is still to come"** (Matt 24:6). But much of the Church will disobey Christ and be **alarmed** by The Beginning of Birth Pains because popular and false teaching on the Endtimes will leave them unprepared.

D) Pre-tribulationism mimics false prophets

The previous chapters have made it clear that there is not a shred of biblical evidence for Pre-tribulationism. So why have "36% of Protestant Pastors claimed Pre-tribulationism best reflected their beliefs on the Endtimes"? Why is unbiblical Pre-tribulationism so popular in modern Christian culture? Because it is the most painless view of the Endtimes available.

Pre-tribulationism is based on the very attractive promise that the Church will never experience The Beginning of Birth Pains or The Greatest Persecution. Just that simple and wonderful guarantee gives Pre-tribulationism a great advantage over all other views on the Endtimes. Why? Because as the Apostle warned in 2 Timothy:

> **A time is coming when people will no longer listen to sound and wholesome teaching. They will follow their own desires and will look for teachers who will tell them whatever their itching ears want to hear. They will reject the truth and chase after myths.** (4:3-4 NLT)

This warning was discussed in chapter 1 of *Christ's Endtimes Teaching*. And those who teach or believe Pre-tribulationism are among the foremost examples of what the Apostle predicted. As noted in chapter 1, there is a long history of God's people rejecting His real Prophets and believing false ones. Why? Because God's real Prophets were telling the people difficult truth.

However, the false prophets were teaching **whatever their itching ears want**ed **to hear.** Unfortunately, those who teach Pre-tribulationism have become the false prophets of our day. In fact, how God described false prophets is eerily similar to those who teach Pre-tribulationism:

> **But I** [Jeremiah] **said, "Alas, Sovereign LORD! The prophets keep telling them, 'You will not see the sword or suffer famine** [like those Jesus warned of in The Beginning of Birth Pains and The Greatest Persecution]**. Indeed, I will give you lasting peace in this place.'"**
>
> **Then the LORD said to me, "The prophets are prophesying lies in my name. I have not sent them or appointed them or spoken to them. They are**

> **prophesying to you false visions, divinations, idolatries, and the delusions of their own minds.**
>
> **Therefore this is what the LORD says about the prophets who are prophesying in my name: I did not send them, yet they are saying, 'No sword or famine will touch this land.'**
>
> **Those same prophets will perish by sword and famine. And the people they are prophesying to will be thrown out into the streets of Jerusalem because of the famine and sword. There will be no one to bury them, their wives, their sons and their daughters. I will pour out on them the calamity they deserve.** (Jer 14:13-16 NIV)

Notice that God was <u>not</u> going to protect His people from the painful consequences of accepting false teaching. Christian, your spiritual and even physical well-being depends on how accurately your Pastors teach Scripture. This fact will become especially evident in the Endtimes.

E) Amillennialism leaves the Church unprepared for the Endtimes

Again, in chapter 12 you read:

A recent survey claimed that 50% of Protestant Pastors <u>deny</u> or are <u>unsure</u> that Scripture predicts there will be a physical Antichrist in the future. Instead, some believe the biblical prophecies about the Antichrist simply refer to the spiritual reality of growing evil in the Endtimes. (sec. A.1)

Such an unbiblical belief is the result of the invasion of metaphorical interpretation in the Church. Amillennialism is a foremost promoter of this. And such a view obviously leaves Christians unprepared for a real, literal, and murdering Antichrist.

However, as noted earlier, other Amillennialists do claim there will be a real and literal Antichrist in the future. However, they say so little about it that they too leave Christians unprepared for his Reign (cf. ch. 12, sec. B.1).

For reasons that are unclear and unbiblical, Amillennialism simply refuses to value the future, physical, and literal fulfillment of biblical prophecy. It ignores the fact that almost 600 biblical prophecies that have already been fulfilled in history, were fulfilled in a physical way, as in a person, place, or event. (cf. ch. 12, sec. A.4).

Amillennialism seems to do everything it can to encourage God's people to ignore the reality of coming wars, famines, plagues, the Antichrist, and The Greatest Persecution. As a result it also ignores Christ's clear command to be watching current events for signs of His Return (cf. Mark 13:33-37; ch. 10, sec. D).

For example, the influential Amillennialist Kim Riddlebarger writes of The Beginning of Birth Pains that Christ taught about (cf. Matt 24:3-8):

> These signs are not given to us so that well-intentioned Bible prophecy experts can correlate current events to the immediate coming of Christ... Rather, they were given to comfort [only?] the [1st century] disciples and the church which would soon be born so that even in the difficult and perplexing times which were about to begin, God's people could rest assured that he was in control... They are signs of the certainty of Jesus Christ's second coming. [14]

There is probably some truth to what this author is saying. But why completely ignore the context of Christ's Endtimes Teaching? Contrary to Amillennialists, the disciples did not ask Jesus, "Will God be in control of Endtime events?" Rather, they asked, **"What will be the sign of your coming and of the end of the age?"** (Matt 24:3 NIV). And that is precisely what Jesus gave them. Signs the Church is to watch for (cf. Mark 13:33-37) so we know the timing of Christ's Return, not simply its "certainty" as Riddlebarger claims.

As suggested earlier, Amillennialists are like the Pharisees who **strain out a gnat but swallow a camel** (Matt 23:23-24) because they **have neglected the more important matters of** God's Word on the Endtimes. Instead of carefully teaching on the physical and literal fulfillment of biblical prophecy, they often focus on questionable spiritual applications that have nothing to do with the meaning of the prophecy itself. As a result Amillennialists are guilty of leaving much of the Church unprepared for the Endtimes. For example, in the book above, Riddlebarger makes the following statement:

[The] prediction of the destruction of Jerusalem and the antichrist desecrating the temple presents us with the frightening image of an unprecedented period of persecution of the people of God immediately before the return of the Lord. [15]

That is a very important biblical truth for which Christians need a great deal more explanation. But that's the only such statement Riddlebarger gives in an entire book supposedly dedicated to helping Christians understand important aspects of the Endtimes. Why does this author do this? First because like most Amillennialists, he refuses to value the future, physical, and literal fulfillment of biblical prophecy.

Secondly, like many Amillennialists, he is unsure if the above statement is even true. He writes:

[T]he antichrists (i.e., the beast and man of sin) [will] demand worship for themselves... This is a possibility which awaits final confirmation when the event itself comes upon us. [16]

Really? The Antichrist's "demand" for "worship" in the Endtimes is only "a possibility" that we cannot be certain of until we have "final confirmation"? Contrary to Amillennialism, Revelation chapter 13 teaches this very clearly. But such uncertainty about the biblical specifics of the Endtimes is typical of Amillennialism. This is because it has adopted the apathetic view of Pan-tribulationism that the biblical substance and sequence of Endtimes events is not important.

In another book, Riddlebarger again demonstrates how Amillennialists are like the Pharisees who **strain out a gnat but swallow a camel** (Matt 23:23-24). In a 169 page book on the Antichrist, the author refers to this reality briefly when he writes:

Antichrist will be the supreme persecutor of Christ's church and will exercise his reign of terror through state-sponsored heresy... He will be a persecutor on the order of Pharaoh, Nebuchadnezzar, and Domitian and will commit acts of blasphemy that make the desecrations of Antiochus IV, Titus, and Nero pale by comparison. Therefore, these figures from redemptive history should serve to prepare us to face the future. [17]

That's pretty much all that is said about the reality of the Antichrist in a 169 page book entitled: *The Man of Sin: Uncovering the Truth about the Antichrist*. The rest of the book supports the author's primary point that is stated here:

> Instead of fearing and dreading the Antichrist ... we should be longing for the second coming of Jesus Christ. For Satan and his cronies have already been defeated by the blood and righteousness of Jesus. [18]

The author is wrong in at least two ways. First, he implies that just because someone would emphasize the reality of the Antichrist and encourage the watching of signs for his coming, it would mean they are "fearing and dreading the Antichrist" in a sinful or unbiblical way. Not true. Such people would simply be obeying Christ's repeated command to **"Watch!"** (Mark 13:37) for the Endtime events He taught would be signs of His Return. Including the Rise and Reign of the Antichrist (cf. Matt 24:15).

The author above makes a second mistake that is typical of what Amillennialism wishes to emphasize. It sounds spiritual to say, "Satan and his cronies have already been defeated by the blood and righteousness of Jesus." But this is at best only half the truth.

Christians in the Last Generation Church will also need to <u>do</u> something to be victorious over the Antichrist. As noted above, Revelation warns that during The Greatest Persecution some **will be taken to prison** and others **will die by the sword** (13:10 NLT). What will be required for these Christians to glorify God and have a faith that conquers the fear Satan will want to instill in them in the face of this imprisonment and martyrdom? The text says such persecution **means that God's holy people <u>must</u> endure persecution patiently and remain faithful** (13:10 NLT).

God desires to equip Christians to **endure** Endtime **persecution patiently**. But Amillennialism is failing badly to serve God in this. And it does so by flowery sounding half-truths like "Antichrist has already been defeated by Jesus' blood." No. The Antichrist's will, purpose, and glory will also be defeated when Endtime Christians joyfully and willingly shed their own blood and are executed instead of denying their love for Jesus. But Amillennialism has relatively little to say about that because for reasons that are unclear and unbiblical, it simply refuses to value the future, physical, and literal fulfillment of biblical prophecy.

Again, Riddlebarger is an example of this. As noted above, he is willing to make the brief statement above about the literal future Antichrist. But, throughout the book he attempts to diminish, if not disprove this. For example, he writes:

> When John speaks of the two beasts in Revelation 13, he is speaking of the Roman Empire and its imperial cult [over 2,000 years ago]. The beast from the sea (vv. 1–10) refers to the imperial cult in Rome. The key figure in this is Nero, under whose reign the persecution of Christians began...
>
> The beast from the earth (vv. 11–18) [the False Prophet] refers to the imperial cult and its priests in Asia Minor at the time John was given the series of visions we know as the Book of Revelation (about AD 95)...
>
> Futurist interpretations of the connection between the Antichrist and the beast of Revelation 13 are highly problematic [actually, not at all]. Therefore ... futurism (the idea that Antichrist is revealed at or about the time of ... the seven-year tribulation period) collapses under its own weight. [19]

In typical Amillennial fashion, Riddlebarger claims that the Roman emperor Nero fulfilled the prophecy of the "beast" in Revelation 13. It is asked again, how does such a claim help Christians to prepare for the real and literal Antichrist that is coming? This Amillennial interpretation of this prophecy is not only unhelpful but unbiblical. Contrary to Riddlebarger, and all Amillennialists and Preterists, there is no evidence that the Apostle John thought he was referring to Nero who died about 30 years before the Revelation was written. In this case, Revelation would not be a prophecy of the future.

After stressing the supposed past fulfillment of prophecy regarding the Antichrist, Riddlebarger is at least willing to admit:

> Nero and the events associated with the destruction of the temple may point ahead to another fulfillment at the end of the age. This is especially the case if some of these prophecies have double fulfillments (e.g., the Olivet Discourse—Matt. 24:10–25) and if the beast of Revelation 17 is an eschatological figure who will appear at the time of the end. [20]

Again, after spending the vast majority of the book diminishing the reality of the future Antichrist in the NT, the author is willing to admit that Revelation 13 "<u>may</u> point ahead to another fulfillment at the end of the age." Riddlebarger's lack of confidence does nothing to help the Church be prepared for what Revelation 13 clearly predicts.

The future, physical, and literal interpretation of biblical prophecy is far more important for the well-being of God's people than any of the historical, spiritual, metaphorical, and often questionable and out-of-context meanings Amillennialists want to emphasize.

As a result, Amillennialists are guilty of saying relatively very little to help the Church be prepared for what the Last Generation Church will experience. The shock, confusion, and dismay that the Thessalonian Christians experienced, will also be experienced by those being taught by Amillennial teachers when the Endtimes begin.[21]

F) Help to be prepared for the Endtimes

Some encouraging things about facing the tests of the Endtimes will be shared in subsequent books of the *Endtimes Essentials* series. This will be especially true of Book #4, *The Greatest Persecution*, which will have more to say about the challenges and biblical promises concerning this event. A couple of helpful things can be offered here to help you prepare for the Endtimes if they occur in your lifetime.

The first thing we can do to prepare for the Endtimes if they occur in our lifetime is to have a biblical understanding of this doctrine. Stop believing false teaching that denies, ignores, or diminishes what will happen to Christians and their families in the Endtimes.

One of the reasons the *Endtimes Essentials* materials were developed was to protect you from all the popular but false **myths** (2 Tim 4:4) that are being taught in the Church today about the Endtimes. Admittedly, the conclusions in the *Endtimes Essentials* are a lot more painful than these **myths**. But the Endtimes will be even <u>more</u> painful if you encounter them believing these popular **myths**. Being deceived is the most painful and dangerous thing of all.

Another purpose of the *Endtimes Essentials* is to encourage you to <u>spiritually prepare</u> for the Endtimes. As noted above, God will want you to glorify Him in the Endtimes. What will be required to do that?

Your faith and trust in God's love for you must rule your whole heart. How will you know your whole heart trusts God? Nothing in the *Endtimes Essentials* materials will make you AFRAID.

The author has written some proven studies on effectively being **transformed by the renewing of your mind** (Rom 12:2 NIV). These studies recognize that most Christians logically understand that God loves them. But their constant struggles with anger, anxiety, depression, and lust reveal that hidden and hurting parts of their heart have not fully experienced the truth of God's love for them. Usually these parts are stuck in some past painful experience that imprinted them with lies about themselves and God.

God wants your whole mind to be controlled by His Love, so that your whole heart can be controlled by the **love, joy,** and **peace** of His Spirit, so that your whole life will glorify God. This is true whether or not the Endtimes begin in your lifetime.

The resources in the "*Christian Essentials* Discipleship Studies" section at www.trainingtimothys.com can help you experience the fruits of the Spirit more consistently. Study #4: *FRUIT from the Spirit's Power*, is especially helpful to provide a biblical evaluation of your spiritual health and maturity. It's companion, *FREEEDOM from Satan's Strategies* will provide biblical wisdom on how to **be transformed by the renewing** of those hidden and hurting parts of your heart. As a result, you will be better prepared to glorify God in the Endtimes if you have been chosen to be a part of the Last Generation Church.

---

[1] Piper, 206. Underlining added.

[2] The suggested translation of John 16:1 follows the NLT except where it has **stumble in your faith**. The Greek word here is *skandalisthēte*. It most often means "cause to sin," or "cause offense" (*BDAG* #1 and #2). Therefore, the NASB translates it here as spiritually **stumbling**. This is reflected in the suggested translation.

However, the Greek word at times refers to "falling away" from the faith (cf. NIV, NLT). But this does not fit the context well, as no real Christians can lose their salvation and warning false Christians not to do so would not help them. It is better to understand Christ warned them to help them avoid sin in the Endtimes, not to avoid losing their salvation.

3 The *New World Encyclopedia* states:
> 1 Maccabees is a deuterocanonical book written by a Jewish author and included in the Catholic and Eastern Orthodox canons of the Bible. Protestants and Jews regard it as generally reliable historically, but not a part of holy scripture.
> https://www.newworldencyclopedia.org/entry/1_Maccabees

4 1 Macc 1:60-61.

5 2 Macc 7. One writer remarks on the historical reliability of 2 Maccabees: "By the 1930s, historians generally came to the conclusion that the historical documents present in 2 Maccabees - while seemingly out of chronological order - were likely legitimate" (cf. Lester Grabbe, *A History of the Jews and Judaism in the Second Temple Period: The Maccabean Revolt, Hasmonaean Rule, and Herod the Great (174–4 BCE)* (T&T Clark, 2020), Vol. 95, pp. 80–84).

On the reliability of the story of the seven sons, Professor Daniel McClellan writes:
> The story of a parent and seven sons facing death for their fidelity to God's laws is not unique to 2 Maccabees. Five texts share the plotline of 2 Macc 7... It is likely that an oral tradition was in circulation from which these five narratives drew their information.
> https://scholarsarchive.byu.edu/cgi/viewcontent.cgi?article=1137&context=studiaantiqua

6 For more on the perseverance of a real Christian's salvation see appropriate chapter of the "Promises" section of *Endtimes Essentials* book #4: *The Greatest Persecution*.

7 Unfortunately, many Christians do not even know what living consistently in the power of God's Spirit really means. For more on this see Pastor Kurt's study: *FRUIT from the Spirit's Power* available online in the "Christian Essentials Discipleship Studies" section of his website at www.trainingtimothys.com.

8 *LGEINT*.

9 Greene.

10 MacArthur, *MNTC,* Thess.

11 Ibid.

12 Accordingly, the NIV **unsettled** does not sufficiently convey the meaning here.

13 For more on whether or not Paul was in Thessalonica for 3 weeks see *Additional Studies on the Endtimes* (*ASE*), ch. 6.

[14] Riddlebarger, 164. Underlining added.

[15] Ibid. 172.

[16] Ibid. 170.

[17] Riddlebarger, *Antichrist,* 106-7.

[18] Ibid., 113.

[19] Ibid., 109-110.

[20] Ibid., 110.

[21] Piper provides another example of the unbiblical and unhelpful approach of Amillennialism to the doctrine of the Endtimes. Sam Storms, an influential Pentecostal seminary professor has written perhaps the most detailed defense of Amillennialism in recent history. Unfortunately, the lack of certainty he portrays about Endtime events illustrates the worst kind of Pan-tribulationism that fails to honor Christ and help His Church. Piper writes, "Sam Storms makes a case that Matt. 24:4-31 refers 'immediately and primarily' to the events leading up to AD 70. But then he [Storms] concludes like this:

> In conclusion, my argument that Matthew 24:4-31 refers immediately and primarily to the events leading up to and including the destruction of Jerusalem in 70 does not necessarily exclude the possibility that the end of the age is, at least indirectly, also in view.
>
> It may well be that future events associated with the second advent of Christ at the end of the age are prefigured by the destruction of the temple and the city in 70…
>
> In other words, the events of 70 may well portray in a localized way what will happen globally at or in some way associated with the second advent… Therefore, my opinion is that the pattern of events that transpired in the period 33-70, leading up to and including the destruction of Jerusalem and its temple, may function as a local, microcosmic foreshadowing of the global, macrocosmic events associated with the parousia and the end of history.
>
> The period 33-70 conceivably, then, provides in its principles (though not necessarily in all particularities), a template against which we are to interpret the period 70–parousia. (Sam Storms, *Kingdom Come: The Amillennial Alternative* [Mentor, 2013], 279; underlining added)

Piper responds:

> You can hear in the words "not necessarily exclude the possibility" and "it may well be" and "may well portray" and "may function" and "conceivably" an uncertainty that does not provide much guidance for how to see in Jesus's words what may yet be future. Practically, how are we to apply Storms' words, "[These first-century events] may

function as a local, micro-cosmic foreshadowing of the global, macrocosmic events"? If we are left only with the <u>possibility</u> that Jesus intended his words to illuminate the end time, are we to think that they do or don't?

The difference between my view and Storms' view is twofold. One, he only sees a <u>possibility</u> that Matt. 24:4-31 foreshadows events at the very end of the age, whereas I think there is good evidence that both Matthew and Paul understood Jesus's teaching as <u>definitely</u> having the final end in view.

And while Storms might allow that first-century events are the main earthquake, so to speak, in Matt. 24:4-31, with possible aftershocks at the very end of history, I think the events surrounding the second coming are the earthquake in Matt. 24:4-31, and the events of the first century are warning tremors.

The basis for this is mainly the observation that Paul and Jesus conceptualize the second coming in the same way, as shown from their shared language; and Paul makes clear that this language and conceptualization, drawn largely from Matt. 24:4-35, refers to the very end, not only to AD 70. (191, underlining added)

Appendices

Appendix A
Detailed Table of Contents

> *Endtimes Essentials*
> Book #1
> # Christ's Endtimes Teaching
> *The Biblical Sequence of Endtime Events*

Part I
Introduction to Understanding the Endtimes
The most complex & shocking topic in Scripture

1: Understanding the Endtimes   *Enduring this doctrine to be approved*   p. 1
  A) Christ's clarity on the Endtimes
  B) Popular approaches that hinder our understanding of Christ's Endtimes Sermon   *Being afraid, academic, and apathetic*
    B.1) Being afraid of the doctrine of the Endtimes
    B.2) Being academic about the doctrine of the Endtimes
    B.3) Being apathetic about the doctrine of the Endtimes
    B.4) Being unprepared for the Endtimes
  C) Being approved on the doctrine of the Endtimes   *2 Tim 2:15*

2: Introduction to the Endtimes   *Their purpose & pain*   p. 23
  A) The purpose & pain of the Endtimes
  B) The importance of understanding the Endtimes
  C) The 7 Primary Endtime Events
  D) A preview of *Christ's Endtimes Teaching*

3: Introduction to Christ's Endtimes Sermon   *The clearest, most important passage of Scripture on the Second Coming*   p. 35
  A) The battle over Christ's Endtimes Teaching

B) Expect Christ's Endtimes Teaching to be fulfilled in the future

C) Start with Christ's Endtimes Teaching, not the OT

D) Understand <u>who</u> Christ's Endtimes Teaching is meant for *The meaning of* eklektous

E) Understand <u>what</u> Christ's Endtimes Teaching is warning of *The meaning of* thlipsis

Part II
Christ's Endtimes Teaching
The biblical sequence of Endtime events

4: The Sequence of Endtime Events According to Jesus Christ *Matthew 24* p. 61

A) Section 1: Jesus' overview of Endtimes events (vs. 4-14)

B) Section 2: The Antichrist's Claim to be God resulting in the Greatest Persecution of the Church (vs. 15-28)

C) Section 3: Christ's Return & the Church's Rescue: (vs. 29-31)

   C.1) Christ's Return will occur immediately after the completion of The Greatest Persecution & will be visible to the entire world (vs. 29-30)

   C.2) The Church's Rescue ("rapture") will occur at the time of Christ's Visible Return (v. 31)

   C.3) Christ's Wrath comes after the Antichrist's Wrath (vs. 37-41)

D) A summary of the sequence of Endtime events in Christ's Endtimes Teaching

   Table: Endtime Events According to Christ's Endtimes Teaching

   Graphic: Endtime Events According to Jesus

5: The Sequence of Endtime Events According to the Apostle Paul: *1 & 2 Thessalonians* p. 81

A) Paul confirms what Jesus taught about the timing of Christ's Return & the Church's Rescue *1 Thess 4:13-17*

B) Paul confirms that the Church's Rescue does not occur until Christ's Return: *2 Thess 1:6-7*

C) The Church's Rescue will not come until after the Antichrist's Claim to be God: *2 Thess 2:1-4*

   C.1) The Church's Rescue occurs simultaneously with Christ's Return

   C.2) The Church's Rescue will not occur until *after* the Antichrist's Claim to be God

   C.3) Christ's Return and the Church's Rescue ("rapture") cannot happen "at any moment."

D) A summary of the sequence of Endtime events in 2 Thessalonians

Table & Graphics on Endtime Events According to Jesus & the Apostle Paul
- E) Paul's correction of popular errors regarding the Endtimes
  - E.1) Christ's Return and the Church's Rescue will be visible to the whole world
  - E.2) The Church's Rescue occurs after The Greatest Persecution
  - E.3) Several events must occur before Christ's Return and the Church's Rescue
  - E.4) The biblical sequence of Endtime events is clear
  - E.5) Endtime prophecies will be fulfilled in a literal way, as in a physical event, person, or place

6: The Sequence of Endtime Events According to Revelation 6-7   p. 98

- A) The Revelation of Jesus Christ is for the Church
- B) The Beginning of Birth Pains, Christ's Return & the Church's Rescue in Revelation 6-7
  - B.1) The Birth Pains, Greatest Persecution, & Christ's Return & Wrath in Revelation 6
  - B.2) The Church's Rescue in Revelation 7
  - B.3) Comparing the sequence of Endtime events in Matthew 24 & Revelation 6-7
    - Table: Sequence of Endtime events in Matthew 24 & Revelation 6-7
    - Graphic: The Endtimes According to Revelation 6-7

7: The Sequence of Endtime Events According to the Prophet Daniel   p. 112

- A) Endtime Events According to Daniel 7
  - A.1) Daniel 7 is for the Church
  - A.2) The Beginning of Birth Pains in Daniel 7
  - A.3) Antichrist's Claim to be God in Daniel 7
  - A.4) The Greatest Persecution in Daniel 7
  - A.5) Christ's visible Return will stop The Greatest Persecution because it will include the Church's Rescue
- B) Endtime Events According to Daniel 9
  - B.1) Daniel 9 is for the Church
  - B.2) The Beginning of Birth Pains in Daniel 9
  - B.3) Understanding Daniel's Last Seven Years
- C) Endtime Events According to Daniel 12
  - C.1) Daniel 12 is for the Church
  - C.2) The Greatest Persecution & the Church's Rescue in Daniel 12
- D) A summary of the sequence of Endtime events in Daniel
  - Table: The sequence of Endtime events according to Daniel
  - Graphics: The Endtimes According to Daniel

8: Conclusions on Christ's Endtimes Teaching *The Pre-wrath Rescue position* p. 128

- A) Summarizing the biblical substance and sequence of Endtime events in support of the Pre-wrath Rescue Position
  - A.1) 7 Primary Endtime Events in their biblical order
    - Table: 7 Primary Endtime Events According to Scripture
  - A.2) The biblical Pre-Wrath Rescue position
    - Graphic: The Pre-Wrath Rescue Position
- B) 6 biblical beliefs of the Pre-wrath Rescue position
  - B.1) The biblical details of the sequence of Endtime events are important.
  - B.2) The Church's Rescue occurs <u>after</u> the Antichrist's Claim to be God. Therefore, the Last Generation Church will suffer the Antichrist's Wrath in The Greatest Persecution.
  - B.3) Christ's Return for the Church's Rescue will be visible to the whole world.
  - B.4) The Church's Rescue will occur simultaneously with Christ's visible Return.
  - B.5) Christ's Return & the Church's Rescue will be preceded by multiple signs
  - B.6) The Greatest Persecution is not Christ's Wrath, but the Antichrist's Wrath
- C) The Church's historical testimony supporting the Pre-Wrath Rescue Position

9: The Nature of Christ's Return & the Church's Rescue p. 145

- A) There will be two appearances of Christ during His Second Coming
  - Table: Contrasting Christ's Two Appearances During His 2nd Coming
  - Graphic: Christ's Two Appearances in His Second Coming
- B) The Last Generation Church will know when Christ is coming: *Understanding Matt 24:32-51*
  - B.1) Illustrating the need for the Church to know when Christ is coming (Matt 24:50-51)
  - B.2) How will we know Christ's Return and the Church's Rescue are near? (Matt 24:32-35)
  - B.3) Until Endtime events occur, no one can know the timing of Christ's Return (v. 36)
  - B.4) When Endtime events occur, Christians will know Christ's Return is near (vs. 37-42)
  - B.5) Christ's Return will come like "a thief in the night" for unbelievers, not Christians (v. 43)
  - B.6) Unbelievers will be completely surprised by Christ's Return, but <u>not</u> Christians (vs. 44-51)

10: Commands in Christ's Endtimes Teaching   p. 171
- A) "Watch out that no one misleads you" (Matt 24:4)
- B) "Guard yourself against fear" (Matt 24:6)
- C) "Always be ready for action" (Luke 12:35)
- D) "Watch!" (Mark 13:5)
- E) Wait (Matt 25:1-13)
- F) Work (Matt 25:16; cf. vs. 14-46)

Part III
Biblically Evaluating Endtime Views

[Note: This section is considered supplemental and not essential to understanding the material in *Christ's Endtimes Teaching*. However, it will be especially helpful to those who have been taught the popular Pre-tribulation view of the Endtimes.]

11: A Biblical Evaluation of Various Views on the Endtimes   p. 184
- A) Pan-tribulationism denies any view
- B) Pre-millennialism is biblical but often misused
- C) Post-millennialism is attractive but unbiblical
- D) Post-tribulationism rightly corrects Pre-tribulationism, but has several biblical problems
    - D.1) Theological problems in Post-tribulationism
    - D.2) Exegetical problems with Post-tribulationism

12: A Biblical Evaluation of Amillennialism & Preterism   p. 198
- A) A biblical evaluation of Amillennialism
    - A.1) The perspectives and problems in Amillennialism
    - A.2) How are we to interpret the meaning and fulfillment of biblical prophecy? *"Spiritualized" versus physical meaning*
    - A.3) Interpret the meaning and fulfillment of a biblical prophecy in a literal way when there is no biblical or reasonable basis to do otherwise
    - A.4) Expect a biblical prophecy to be fulfilled in a physical way by a person, place, or event when there is no biblical or reasonable basis to do otherwise
    - A.5) Metaphorical interpretations of biblical prophecy make it more difficult to be certain God is keeping His promises
    - A.6) Amillennialism's unbiblical interpretation of Revelation 20:1-3
- B) A biblical evaluation of Preterism
    - B.1) Understanding "the end of the age" & refuting Preterism   *Matt 24:3*

B.2) Understanding "this generation" & refuting Preterism *Matt 24:33-34*

   B.3) Preterism ignores the fact that many biblical prophecies have more than one fulfillment *Isa 7:14-16; Rev 1:1-3*

13: A Biblical Evaluation of Pre-tribulationism p. 234

   A) Introduction to Pre-tribulationism

   B) 8 Pre-tribulation myths already addressed

   B.1) Myth #1: The events described in Christ's Endtimes Teaching apply only to Israel and therefore, nothing in His sermon applies to the Church

   B.2) Myth #2: The Church will never encounter the Antichrist or experience The Greatest Persecution

   B.3) Myth #3: Christ will come in a "secret & silent rapture"

   B.4) Myth #4: The Church is not mentioned in Revelation chapters 4-17 as being on Earth

   B.5) Myth #5: Christ's Return for the Church and His visible Coming are described as two different events in Scripture, separated by 7 years

   B.6) Myth #6: Christ's Return and the Church's Rescue described in Christ's Endtimes Teaching is merely a gathering of Jews at the Battle of Armageddon.

   B.7) Myth #7: God's Endtimes plan for Israel and the Church are completely separate and do not overlap in any way

   B.8) Myth #8: A literal interpretation of prophetic Scripture leads to Pre-tribulationism

14: When Does Christ's Wrath Begin? *The Cosmic Signs* p. 258

   A) Myth #9: The "tribulation" is Christ's Wrath which we are promised rescue from

      Graphic: The Biblical Pre-wrath Rapture Position vs. the Unbiblical Pre-tribulation view

   B) Defining Christ's Wrath

   C) Christ's Wrath is not the persecution of Christians

   D) The Cosmic Signs mark the beginning of Christ's Wrath

   E) The Seals of Preparation prepare the world for Christ's Wrath

   F) What is the "blessed hope"? (Tit 2:13)

15: Refuting More Myths in Pre-tribulationism *Imminency, the Restrainer, & Rev 3:10* p. 279

   A) Myth #10: The Rapture will happen at any moment, without any warning signs

   B) Myth #11: Unbelievers will be experiencing "peace and safety" before the Church's Rescue

   C) Myth #12: The "Restrainer" of the Antichrist is the Holy Spirit, and His removal refers to the "Rapture" of the Church (2 Thess 2:6-7)

   D) Myth #13: Revelation 3:10 is promising the Church's Rescue before the "tribulation"

16: The Practical & Spiritual Harm of Popular Teaching on the Endtimes   p. 303

A) Popular but false teaching about the Endtimes has left the Church unprepared to glorify God in The Greatest Persecution, resulting in lost eternal rewards

    A.1) The purpose of Christ's warnings

    A.2) The unimaginable pain of The Greatest Persecution

    A.3) The monumental test of The Greatest Persecution

B) The "Thessalonian Panic"

C) The vulnerability of shock caused by not obeying Christ's command to "**Watch!**" for signs of His Return

D) Pre-tribulationism mimics false prophets

E) Amillennialism leaves the Church unprepared for the Endtimes

F) Help to be prepared for the Endtimes

Appendix B
Glossary for the *Endtimes Essentials*

10-Nation Endtime Coalition

The ten kings/nations who unite with the Antichrist to destroy Endtime Babylon (cf. Rev 17:16-18). They form the base of world-wide power for Antichrist's Beast Empire (cf. Rev 17:12-14; Dan 2:41-44; 7:7, 23-25).

Antichrist' Beast Empire

The final Beast Empire that will uniquely rule the entire world (cf. Dan 7:23). It will be initially formed by an alliance between the Resurrected Antichrist and the 10-nation Endtime Coalition.

Antichrist's Claim to be God

Antichrist's "abomination of desolation" when he enters and desecrates a rebuilt Jewish temple and proclaims himself to be God. (cf. Dan 9:27; Matt 24:15; 2 Thess 2:3-4).

Antichrist's Religious Covenant

A 7-year "covenant" with **many** unbelievers throughout the world to begin a religion worshipping the Antichrist (cf. Dan 9:27). It will promote peace in the world and allow Israel to rebuild its Temple in Jerusalem. He will violate this Covenant in Israel at its midpoint and commit His Claim to be God in the Temple.

Antichrist's Resurrection

At the beginning of The Beginning of Birth Pains, the Antichrist will emerge as the first and foremost of the False Christs Jesus predicted (cf. Matt 24:4-5). This will be the cause of Antichrist's quick rise to worldwide adoration (cf. Rev 6:1-2; 13:3-4; 12, 14; 17:8, 11; 2 Thess 2:9-12). Antichrist's Resurrection will also probably be the the clearest certain sign that the Endtimes have begun.

Battle of Armageddon

A final battle between Christ and the Resurrected Antichrist and his armies (cf. Rev 16:12, 14; 19:19-20; Ezek chs. 38-39). Christ's defeat and destruction of His enemies here finishes Christ's Wrath and ushers in Christ's Reign for the Millennium

Beginning of Birth Pains

Catastrophic wars, famines, and plagues that enable the Antichrist's rise to worldwide worship and power (cf. Matt 24:4-8; Rev 6:1-8). The people living on one fourth of the Earth will be killed (cf. Rev 6:8). It will include the destruction of the economic and military power of Endtime Babylon leaving the Remaining World to be ruled by Antichrist (cf. Rev 17:15-18).

Christ's 1,000-year Reign

The literal 1,000 year Millennium with Christ ruling on the Earth (cf. Rev 20:1-9 and numerous OT prophecies). Its purposes include rewarding **those who had been beheaded** (Rev 20:4) during The Greatest Persecution, and to begin to fulfill God's promises to Israel.

Christ's Endtimes Teaching

Matthew 24-25 (cf. Mark 13:1-37; Luke 21:5-36), the "Olivet Discourse. The clearest teaching in all of Scripture on the substance and sequence of Endtime events.

Christ's Return

Christ's first visible appearance during His Second Coming. It will be visible to everyone on Earth and will immediately result in the Church's Rescue ("rapture") before Christ's Endtimes Wrath. (cf. Matt 24:29-31; 1 Thess 4:15-17; 2 Thess 1:6-10; 2:1-4).

Christ's Wrath

God's punishment on unbelievers after the Church's Rescue (cf. Matt 24:29-31, 37-41; Rev 6:12-17). This is part of the prophesied "Day of the Lord" and consists of the Trumpet and Bowl Punishments (cf. Rev chs. 8-9, 15-16). It is completed with the Battle of Armageddon.

Church's Rescue ("rapture")

The "rapture" in which all Christians still living in the Remaining World will be lifted off the Earth by Angels to meet Christ at His Return (cf. Matt 24:29-31; 1 Thess 4:15-17). It occurs at the end of the Greatest Persecution (Satan's/Antichrist's wrath against God's people) and immediately before Christ's Wrath against unbelievers.

Daniel's Last Seven Years

Known as "Daniel's 70th Week." It is a period of exactly 7 Jewish years (of 360 days each). It begins with Antichrist's Religious Covenant and ends with Christ's Return (Dan 9:27). Its purpose in Israel is to finish God's plan for their sin, rebellion, and punishment (Dan 9:25). It will also be the last seven years of the Church Age (Rev 13:5-7).

Endtime Babylon

The economic super-power in the world when the Endtimes begin (cf. Rev chs. 17-18). It is a nation, centered in a city, that once served God but is now a spiritual Prostitute promoting the idolatrous religion of Money in the World.

Because the Antichrist will desire all of the world's worship, he will completely destroy Endtime Babylon. **The ten horns** [10-nation Endtime Coalition] **... and the beast** [Antichrist] **will hate the Prostitute** [Endtime Babylon] **and these will permanently remove all people from her and strip her naked and they will completely devour her body and will completely burn her up with fire... in one hour** (Rev 17:16; 18:10, 17, 19 [1]).

Greatest Persecution (Antichrist's Wrath)

Antichrist's Reign & Wrath with the murdering of Jews and Christians (cf. Matt 24:15-29; Rev 6:9-11; 13:5-10; Dan 7:21-25). This aspect of Antichrist's Reign occurs after the Antichrist's Claim to be God in the "abomination of desolation" and lasts exactly 1,260 days, ending with Christ's Return (cf. 2 Thess 2:8; Rev 12:7-17)

Great White Throne Evaluation

When every human who has ever lived is personally brought before Christ's throne to be evaluated for punishment or reward (cf. Matt 25:31-46; 2 Cor 5:10; Rev 20:11-15). This will occur at the beginning of Eternity.

Last Generation Church

The Christians (**elect**) living on the Earth during the Endtimes (cf. Matt 24:15-29). They will experience The Beginning of Birth Pains and The Greatest Persecution. Many of them will be martyred (cf. Rev 6:9-11). Some of them will be among those who are rescued ("raptured") from Christ's Wrath and **come out of the great tribulation** (Rev 7:13-14).

Rising Antichrist

The **little horn** (Dan 7:8; cf. 8:9) that represents the emerging Antichrist as the leader of a relatively minor country, probably somewhere in the vicinity of Russia (**Magog**; cf. Ezek 38:1-2). However, he will be famous and admired world-wide because when he is killed and resurrected he will be recognized and worshipped by the entire pagan world.

Resurrected Antichrist

This will be the Rising Antichrist **who** will be **fatally wounded and then** come **back to life** (Rev 13:14 NLT; cf. 13:3) to become the Resurrected Antichrist. **The whole world** will be **filled with wonder and follow the** Resurrected Antichrist (Rev 13:3 NIV).

Wrathful Antichrist

After the Resurrected Antichrist commits "the abomination of desolation" in a Jerusalem temple and Claims to be God, he will be the Reigning Antichrist. His authority with transition from world-wide worship and admiration to absolute obedience. This will include the killing of God's elect people.

Seal Preparations

The false Christ's, wars, famines, and plagues that prepare the Remaining World for Antichrist's Rise and Reign. They are the first four of the "seals" broken on a scroll that release "riders on horses of destruction." They result in one fourth of the Earth being killed (cf. Matt 24:4-8; Rev 6:1-8)

Trumpet & Bowl Punishments

Christ's Wrath on the Remaining World after the Church's Rescue during "the day of the Lord" (cf. Rev chs. 8-9, 15-16). Their culmination is the Battle of Armageddon.

---

[1] For an explanation of the suggested translation of Rev 17:16 see *Endtime Babylon*, ch. 1, sec. A.

Appendix C
The Endtimes According to Jesus, Paul, & Daniel

Endtime Events According to Jesus

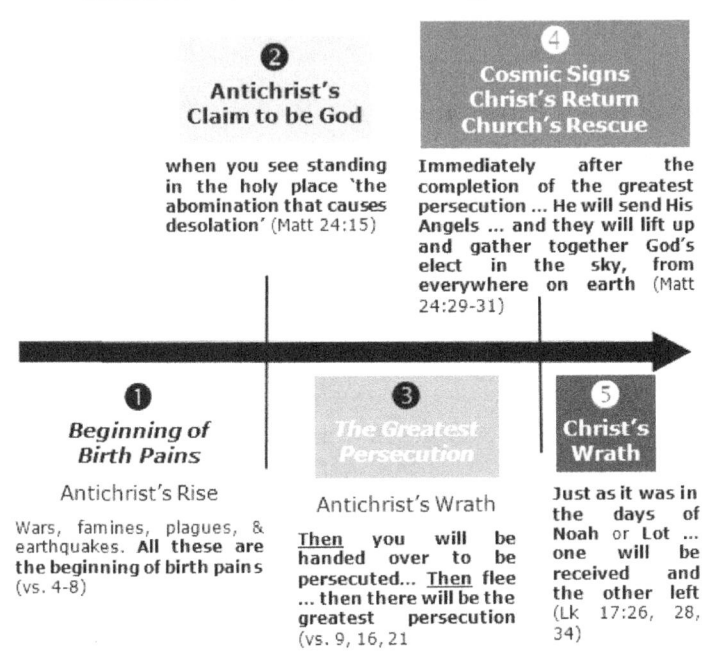

② Antichrist's Claim to be God

when you see standing in the holy place 'the abomination that causes desolation' (Matt 24:15)

④ Cosmic Signs / Christ's Return / Church's Rescue

Immediately after the completion of the greatest persecution ... He will send His Angels ... and they will lift up and gather together God's elect in the sky, from everywhere on earth (Matt 24:29-31)

① Beginning of Birth Pains

Antichrist's Rise

Wars, famines, plagues, & earthquakes. **All these are the beginning of birth pains** (vs. 4-8)

③ The Greatest Persecution

Antichrist's Wrath

<u>Then</u> you will be handed over to be persecuted... <u>Then</u> flee ... then there will be the greatest persecution (vs. 9, 16, 21)

⑤ Christ's Wrath

Just as it was in the days of Noah or Lot ... one will be received and the other left (Lk 17:26, 28, 34)

Endtime Events According to the Apostle Paul

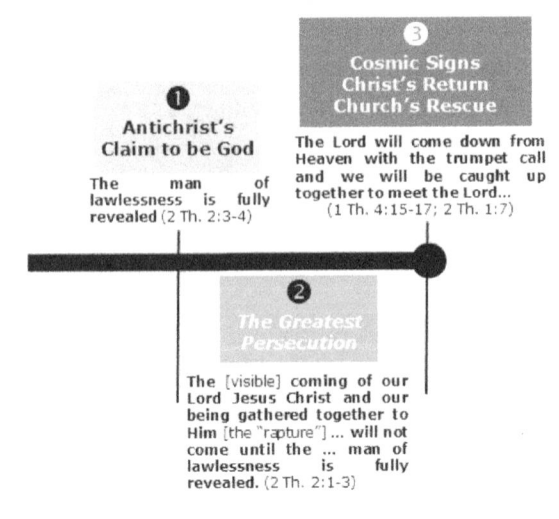

① Antichrist's Claim to be God

The man of lawlessness is fully revealed (2 Th. 2:3-4)

③ Cosmic Signs / Christ's Return / Church's Rescue

The Lord will come down from Heaven with the trumpet call and we will be caught up together to meet the Lord... (1 Th. 4:15-17; 2 Th. 1:7)

② The Greatest Persecution

The [visible] coming of our Lord Jesus Christ and our being gathered together to Him [the "rapture"] ... will not come until the ... man of lawlessness is fully revealed. (2 Th. 2:1-3)

343

Endtime Events According to Jesus in Rev 6-7

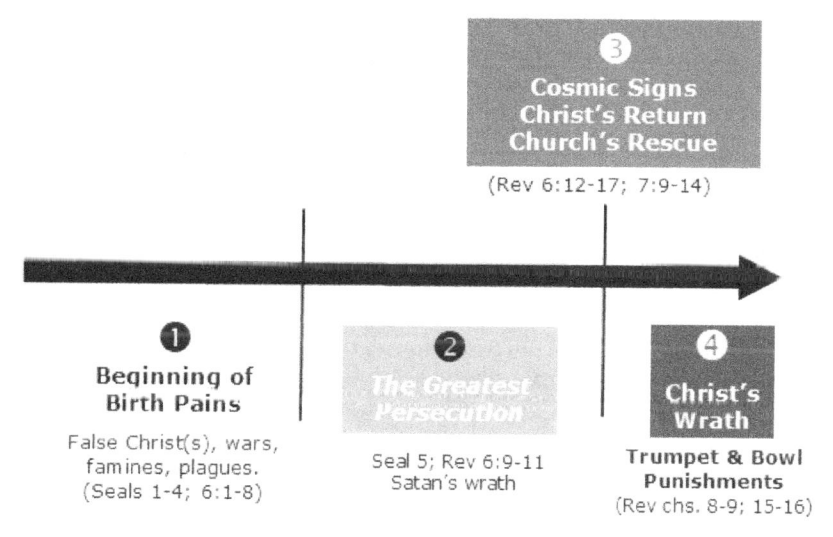

③ Cosmic Signs / Christ's Return / Church's Rescue
(Rev 6:12-17; 7:9-14)

① Beginning of Birth Pains
False Christ(s), wars, famines, plagues.
(Seals 1-4; 6:1-8)

② The Greatest Persecution
Seal 5; Rev 6:9-11
Satan's wrath

④ Christ's Wrath
Trumpet & Bowl Punishments
(Rev chs. 8-9; 15-16)

Seal Preparations for Christ's Wrath

Endtime Events According to Daniel

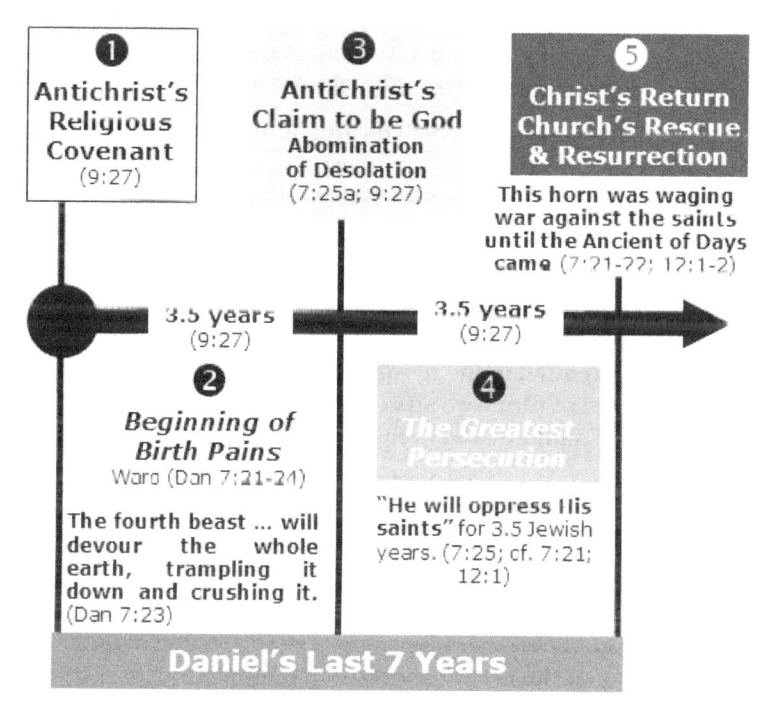

① Antichrist's Religious Covenant (9:27)

③ Antichrist's Claim to be God / Abomination of Desolation (7:25a; 9:27)

⑤ Christ's Return / Church's Rescue & Resurrection
This horn was waging war against the saints until the Ancient of Days came (7:21-22; 12:1-2)

3.5 years (9:27) | 3.5 years (9:27)

② Beginning of Birth Pains
War (Dan 7:21-24)

The fourth beast ... will devour the whole earth, trampling it down and crushing it. (Dan 7:23)

④ The Greatest Persecution
"He will oppress His saints" for 3.5 Jewish years. (7:25; cf. 7:21; 12:1)

Daniel's Last 7 Years

Appendix D
Christ's Endtimes Teaching

Summary of *Endtimes Essentials* book #1: *Christ's Endtimes Teaching (CET)*

The big idea: The Church's Rescue occurs <u>after</u> The Greatest Persecution at Christ's visible Return, but before Christ's Wrath.

Key texts:

Matt 24:1-31- the most important <u>teaching</u> on the Endtimes.

Key Greek words: (*CET* ch. 3, secs. D, E)

Eklektous = **God's elect people**, always refers to the Church in the NT (Matt 24:22, 29, 31)

Thlipsis = **persecution**, the context of Matt 24 (vs. 9, 21, 29). Other versions make Jesus err in v. 21.

(Matt 24:29-31) **"Immediately after the completion of the greatest persecution [*thlipsin*], then 'the sun will be darkened, and the moon will not give its light; the stars will fall from the sky and the heavenly bodies will be shaken.'** [Cosmic Signs]... **And then all the peoples of the Earth will mourn when they see the Son of Man coming on the clouds of Heaven,** [Christ's visible Return] **with power and great glory** [to begin Christ's Wrath]. **He will send His Angels with a loud trumpet sound, and they will lift up and gather together God's elect people** [*eklektous*- always the Church in the NT] **in the sky, from everywhere on Earth** [Church's Rescue "rapture"].

(2 Thess 2:1, 3-4 NIV) **Concerning the coming of our Lord Jesus Christ and our being gathered to him** [the Church's Rescue] **... Don't let anyone deceive you in any way, for that day will not come until the rebellion occurs and the man of lawlessness** [the Antichrist] **is revealed ... in God's temple, proclaiming himself to be God.**

(Rev 6:12-13, 16-17 NIV) **He opened the sixth seal... The sun turned black ... the whole moon turned blood red, and the stars in the sky fell to earth** [Cosmic Signs]**... They called to the mountains and the rocks, "Fall on us and hide us from the face of him who sits on the throne and from the wrath of the Lamb!** [Christ's Wrath] **For the great day of their wrath has come.**

(Rev 7:9, 14 NIV) **After this I looked, and there before me was a great multitude that no one could count, from every nation, tribe, people and language, standing before the throne and before the Lamb** [the Church]. **They were wearing white robes... Then one of the elders asked me, "These in white robes —who are they, and where did they come from?" I answered, "Sir, you know." And he said, "These are they who have come out** [Church's Rescue] **of the great persecution** [*thlipseōs*]**.**

7 Primary Endtime Events

#	Endtime Event	Description
1	The Beginning of Birth Pains	False Christ(s), wars, famines, plagues, and earthquakes. (cf. Matt 24:4-8; Luke 21:11; Rev 6:1-8; Dan 8:24-25)
2	Antichrist's Claim to be God	The "abomination of desolation" when the Antichrist enters a rebuilt Jewish temple and proclaims himself to be God. (cf. Matt 24:15; 2 Thess 2:4; Rev 13:5-6; Dan 7:24-25; 9:27)
3	The Greatest Persecution	Antichrist's wrath against God's people. (cf. Matt 24:9, 16-21; Rev 6:9-11; 12:7-17; 13:7-10; Dan 7:21, 25; 12:1, 7)
4	The Cosmic Signs	The sun, moon, and stars signaling Christ's Return. (cf. Matt 24:29; Rev 6:12-13; Joel 2:30-31)
5	Christ's Return	His visible, glorious appearing. (cf. Matt 24:30; Rev 6:14-16; 2 Thess 1:6-7; Dan 7:13-14; Tit 2:13)
6	The Church's Rescue	Lifting up both living and dead Christians (cf. Matt 24:31; 1 Thess 4:13-18; 2 Thess 2:1; Rev 7:9-14; Dan 12:2).
7	Christ's Wrath	Wrath against His enemies. (cf. Matt 24:37-41; Rev 6:17; 1 Th 1:6-7)

The Biblical Pre-wrath Rescue Position
Confirmed by Christ's Endtimes Teaching, Revelation, Paul & Daniel
(*CET* chs. 3-8)

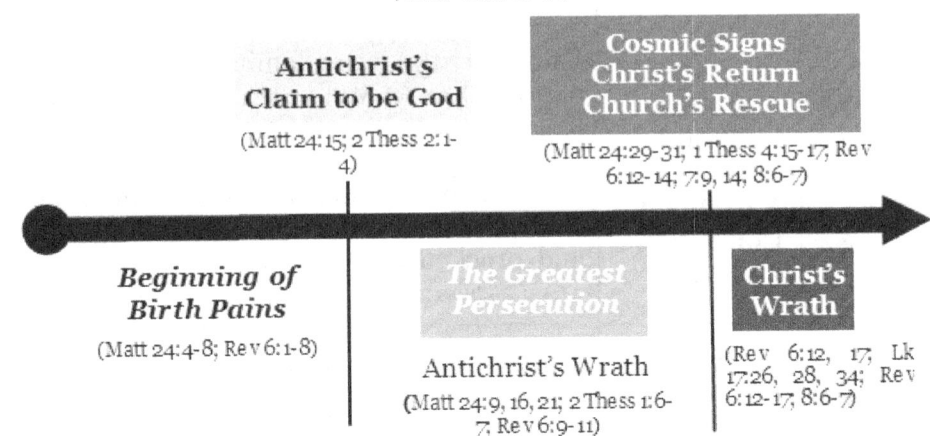

Antichrist's Claim to be God
(Matt 24:15; 2 Thess 2:1-4)

Cosmic Signs Christ's Return Church's Rescue
(Matt 24:29-31; 1 Thess 4:15-17; Rev 6:12-14; 7:9, 14; 8:6-7)

Beginning of Birth Pains
(Matt 24:4-8; Rev 6:1-8)

The Greatest Persecution

Christ's Wrath
(Rev 6:12, 17; Lk 17:26, 28, 34; Rev 6:12-17; 8:6-7)

Antichrist's Wrath
(Matt 24:9, 16, 21; 2 Thess 1:6-7; Rev 6:9-11)

Christ's Two Appearances in His Second Coming
(*CET* ch. 9, sec. A)

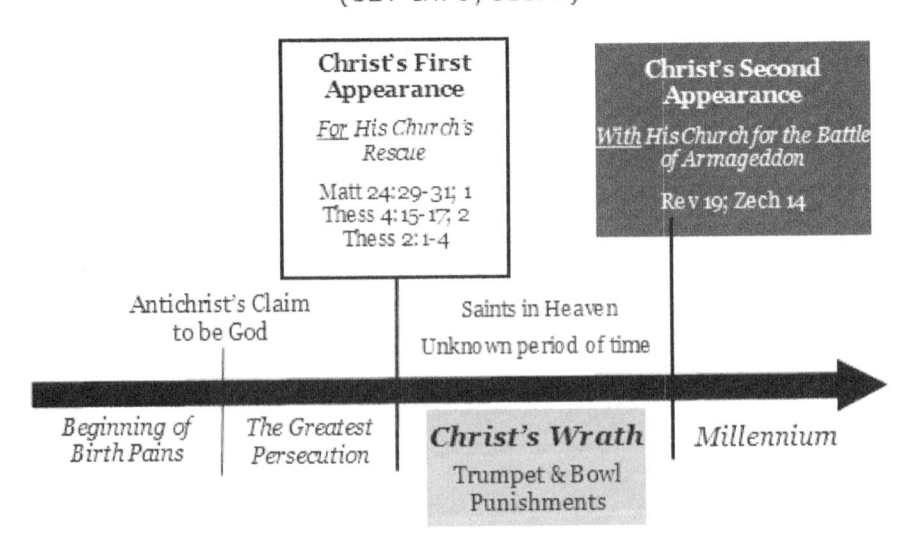

Christ's First Appearance
For His Church's Rescue
Matt 24:29-31; 1 Thess 4:15-17; 2 Thess 2:1-4

Christ's Second Appearance
With His Church for the Battle of Armageddon
Rev 19; Zech 14

Antichrist's Claim to be God

Saints in Heaven
Unknown period of time

Beginning of Birth Pains | *The Greatest Persecution* | **Christ's Wrath** Trumpet & Bowl Punishments | *Millennium*

7 Popular <u>Myths</u> about the Endtimes (*CET* chs. 11-16)

#1: The details of the Endtimes don't matter (Pan-tribulationism). <u>BUT</u> this dishonors Christ because He intentionally shared a specific sequence of Endtime events.

#2: Biblical prophecy will be fulfilled in merely spiritual realities (Amillennialism). <u>BUT</u> almost 600 prophecies have already been <u>fulfilled</u> and <u>every single one of them</u> was fulfilled in a physical way by a person, place, or thing. God has not changed how He will fulfill biblical prophecy.

#3: Christ's Endtimes Teaching is <u>not</u> for the Church (Pre-Tribulationism). <u>BUT</u> Christ addressed His sermon to **the elect** (*eklektos*) 3 times, which refers to the Church in the NT.

#4: The Church will never encounter the Antichrist or experience The Greatest Persecution (Pre-Tribulationism). <u>BUT</u> Jesus promised **the elect** will.

#5: Christ will come in a "secret & silent rapture" (Pre-Tribulationism). <u>BUT</u> no Scriptures teach this…anywhere.

#6: The "Rapture" will happen at any moment, without any warning signs (Pre-Tribulationism). <u>BUT</u> Jesus taught many things will happen before His Return & the Church's Rescue.

#7: The "tribulation" is Christ's Wrath which we are promised rescue from (Pre-Tribulationism). <u>BUT</u> "tribulation" (*thlipsis*) means "persecution" which we are promised, and this should never be labeled as God's Wrath.

Made in the USA
Monee, IL
07 November 2023